STRANGER IN THE EARTH

Thomas Sugrue's association with Edgar Cayce began when Sugrue was a college student profoundly interested in philosophical and spiritual matters. Hugh Lynn Cayce, a classmate and close friend, invited him to spend a holiday with the Edgar Cayce family. There he watched medical readings, spent long hours talking with Cayce about the implications of the great psychic's work, and received a Life Reading that identified his previous incarnations as all having been involved with religious teaching, writing and study. This record of Sugrue's association with Cayce is *"brilliantly written, stimulating, sensitive."* —Kirkus

STRANGER IN THE EARTH

THE STORY OF A SEARCH

By Thomas Sugrue

PAPERBACK LIBRARY

New York

PAPERBACK LIBRARY EDITION

First Printing: February, 1971

This Paperback Library Edition is published by arrangement with Holt, Rinehart & Winston, Inc.

Paperback Library is a division of Coronet Communications, Inc. Its trademark, consisting of the words "Paperback Library" accompanied by an open book, is registered in the United States Patent Office. *Coronet Communications, Inc., 315 Park Avenue South, New York, N.Y. 10010.*

For my girls:

Mary and Patsy

I am a stranger in the earth:
hide not thy commandments from me,

PSALM 119, VERSE 19

ONE

MISS ICEBERG was late. It was after nine o'clock. The March sun had wriggled through the dirty pane of the window and was half way across the room, examining the blue paint on the walls, exposing the dust on the baseboard. I sat on the edge of the bed, leaning on my crutches, watching it. In winter the sun touches only the brightest of surfaces, leaving slatterns undetected. But by March, with the promise of the equinox, it stoops and looks closely at rugs and furniture. The housekeepers of the hospital were shamed before my eyes.

In the quiet of the room my wrist watch made a small, frantic sound. It seemed excited, frightened. Was it speeding up, going faster, in an effort to save me from the ordeal ahead? If enough time passed before the nurse appeared it would be too late to begin the treatment. The watch was quivering. The small hairs on my wrist shook to its vibrations. The sunlight, moving slowly, inspecting carefully every inch of the room, seemed unaware of the need for hurry. It reached the watch, crept over the edge of its case, and stared at its face. It was twelve minutes after nine.

Was it too early to hope? My heart quickened a little. The watch raced on. I remembered the nervous pacing of a doctor when I asked him about the treatment.

"Is it as rough as they say?"

"It is definitely uncomfortable; extremely so. Unfortunately we can give you nothing to help the situation. Any aid of that sort would act as a depressant on the heart, and you must have the free and uninhibited use of your heart."

He smiled wanly.

"You should be proud that you are in such good shape. Lungs, heart—everything vital must be in excellent condition before a patient is allowed to take this treatment. You passed with flying colors."

7

"Thank you. I am glad to hear that. The treatment is always efficacious, isn't it? There isn't any chance that it won't help me, is there?"

He looked at his own watch, a handsome instrument of yellow gold that clung to a heavy chain and bulged the cloth when it lay in his vest pocket.

"Artificial fever therapy," he said, "has been found to be helpful in eighty per cent of the cases in which it is used."

Eighty per cent. Could I depend on it? I was almost entirely a compound of minorities, of contradictions: son of a Connecticut Irish Catholic Wilsonian Democrat, educated in Virginia at a university founded by the Presbytery, trained on a Republican newspaper, hired to hymn the nation's great by a popular magazine, enamored of the mystical way. The twenty per cent was almost bound to include me. But I would not believe it. I had never before been seriously ill. The twenty per cent in this case was a minority from which I was excused. The doctor was not worried about it; he was concerned with the discomfort I would bear. He was a gentleman; he disliked putting me to torture.

Fifteen minutes after nine. I could definitely hope now that Miss Iceberg would not come. The telephone would ring and someone would tell me that the treatment had been postponed. Something had happened—the hot box was out of order, the nurse had not reported for duty, the doctor had been called away. I could go back to bed and read again about Saint Teresa of Avila scolding Jesus: "If that is the way you treat your friends it is no wonder you have so few of them." I could browse through *Ulysses*, peregrinating with Stephen Dedalus and Leopold Bloom, lover of the internal organs of animals. Fitz was in town. He might come by and read something to me, perhaps *Antony and Cleopatra*. The nurses would run and hide when they heard his voice, booming like winter surf on the coast of Maine. Later, when Mary came, I might induce her to help me sneak out for dinner at Jack Bleeck's. The doctor might come in and explain that he had decided on a new treatment, something less uncomfortable, and with a smaller margin for error.

At twenty minutes past nine Miss Iceberg walked into the room, pushing a wheelchair. The sound of my wrist watch faded. Hope retreated to the center of my stomach and lay there, gnawing at itself. The sunlight jumped on the wheelchair and ran over it on a thousand little feet, looking for dirt and chipped paint.

8

"I can walk down," I said. I was not an invalid yet. They could hold the twenty per cent for a while. I had a four to one chance.

"You will ride in the wheelchair," Miss Iceberg said quietly.

She was prepared for her day's work. Every pattern of feminine charm, however minute, had been erased, not only from her body but from her being. Her face wore no cosmetics; it also wore no expression. Her hair has hauled back and trussed at the cerebellum. The pores on her neck were open, staring at the room. The uniform covering her body brushed the light off sharply. In the whiteness of the spirit all things are one. Only in darkness is there form and differentiation, only in shadow do the atoms make mischief, congregating in postures that titillate the mind. How would she look in a black lace negligee?

I slid off the high bed and sat in the chair. In defiance of her I took my crutches with me, resting their ends on the footboard. People who saw me would know that I could walk if I were free of this white, formless captor.

But what about the black habits of nuns, of penitents, of priests? A reminder of the flesh, a symbol of the mortification they endured while the limitations of the body persisted? White would be presumptuous on them. For the nurse it was practical.

"Watch your elbows, please," she said.

We rolled through the narrow doorway and went down the hall to the elevator. In the open square where the office force worked lights were blazing, clerks were answering telephones and tapping typewriters. I looked away from them. They were healthy, normal people, not worried about percentages.

We stopped at the elevator and Miss Iceberg moved to my side. A rinsed, bony hand shot a finger at the call button. Last night did she put perfume behind her ears and throw snares of chemistry and magnetism at a man? She gave forth no sense of a body or a personality now. Something without individuality, without humanity, something fashioned in a lecture room and finished in a sterilizer, had taken their place. Would is react to conversation?

"How do I get back up? Will you carry me in your arms?"

"You will return on a stretcher," she said.

I refused to shudder. The pain didn't matter; the humiliation didn't matter. It was the exile that tore at my mind. No one would treat me as an equal, as an adult. Whoever was near me when I spoke leaned forward anxiously, gazed solemnly over my head, and answered in carefully selected words of one or two syllables. Explanations were reduced to primary states of complication. Information of the most trivial nature was kept from me. My attempts at levity with the doctors caused them to look grave and subdued; when I teased the nurses they went cold with fright. Above all things they feared a patient who might go mad while their backs were turned, or while they were giving him a bath. If I asked why the window was open wide I was told that fresh air was good for me. If I asked for the result of a blood test they brought me orange juice and the evening paper, straightened the bedclothes, and asked what else they could do for me.

"Comfort me with apples," I said one day. They left without a word. Later the head nurse came in and talked to me for a long time about the need for faith and a steady hand in times of crisis.

"I am glad to know that you appreciate Mr. Roosevelt," I said.

"I have always been a Republican," she said coldly. "The Democratic party is a rabble."

We were silent then, and after a moment she left and did not return.

It made me think of a time long ago, when the World War of 1914-1918 was being fought. In Salem Grammar School we gathered each Friday afternoon to hear thrilling speeches and stirring poems about courage, freedom, and soldiers brave and true. I was in sixth grade—red-haired, freckle-faced, in homemade knickers. I enjoyed thoroughly the programs; I sang lustily the songs: *Keep the Home Fires Burning, Till We Meet Again, Over There, Tipperary,* and sometimes the Civil War anthems—*Tenting Tonight* and *Battle Hymn of the Republic.* One day there was a pause in the performance. A girl in the seventh grade was shaking her head vehemently, refusing to speak her piece. I looked away from her; I could not bear to watch another person's embarrassment. Then suddenly my teacher was leaning over me, the lilac odor of her sachet was weighting the air I breathed, and she was saying:

"Take this paper and go up on the stage. Read what is written on it. Remember to speak clearly and to look up often."

I took the paper and walked up on the stage. I looked at the audience and smiled. Some of the girls in the front row

10

smiled back at me. I looked at the paper in my hand and began to read from it:

THE DRUMMER BOY AND THE FLAG

Once there was a boy who longed to be a soldier, but he was too young. So he ran away with the troops that were leaving his town and became their drummer boy. . . .

The story was fascinating. The drummer boy went through many battles. In one of them he was wounded. In another he kept the flag of his regiment from touching the ground by seizing it as its bearer fell forward, dead. I read on with mounting enthusiasm. When I finished there was hearty applause. I bowed, left the stage, and returned to my seat. My teacher patted me on the arm. "You did very well," she said.

But one of the eighth grade pupils told me later that the principal of the school said to someone, "Yes, he read well; but since it was so short a piece I think he might have learned it by heart and given it from memory." Thenceforth I never was able to face an audience or a person in authority without seeing the calm, unfettered arrogance of my school principal settled upon the audience or the person which was to judge me, and before my case was heard or a word was spoken, I accepted defeat. The flag was still aloft, but the drummer boy was in retreat.

The elevator car arrived and Miss Iceberg wheeled me into it. Two women moved out of our way. One was middle-aged, fleshy, ugly in her face and hands. She stood in a corner and stared at me with the merciless curiosity of the unmannerly. I didn't mind her eyes; they were faded and incapable of perceiving much. It was her nose which irritated me. It pointed at me. On its bridge spectacles were balanced, and suddenly I felt that a bird was looking at me.

The women got off at the ground floor. We went to the basement. It had a closed, uneasy atmosphere. All cellars are like tombs, dug into the earth, with a great weight poised overhead. Sound has nowhere to go when the walls are reached; it returns to its source, clamoring to be taken in. Nothing can drain off the dampness, the insulation, the clammy quiet of a cellar.

We rolled along the corridor to the physiotherapy room, the sound of our passing knocked back at us by the concrete

11

of the tunnel. We stopped by the scales and waited for the head nurse. She bounded up to me, a little Norwegian with yellow hair that ran from her head as if frightened by a storm. She was smiling, amiable, and she judged me correctly at once.

"You are able to use your crutches? Good. Then you can step on the scales and we will see how much you weigh."

Proudly I slipped the crutches under my arms and stepped from the wheelchair. Miss Yellowhead adjusted the counter-weights.

"One hundred and forty-two. What is your normal weight?"

"About a hundred and fifty."

"Good. You have lost only eight pounds. You will lose a few in the treatment, but afterward you will gain them back quickly if you eat well. Now, can you walk to the treatment room? It is the last one, at the end."

I swung along by her side, purposely stepping freely, throwing weight on my legs. There was nothing really wrong with me—just knock out the bugs that were sapping my strength and I would be well. The difficulty lay in the fact that the germs were either undiscoverable or unidentifiable. My blood was scattered in laboratories from the Battery to the Bronx, but all that resulted was a vague muttering about "mixed strep."

"Here we are; this is your new office," Miss Yellowhead said.

It was a narrow cell, a slim section of the large room, fenced off by thin partitions. It contained nothing but a table and chair for the nurse, and the cabinet. The cabinet looked like a cheap coffin, a poorly made receptacle of wood large enough to hold a body. The top was more curved than the lid of a casket, and at one end there was a hole big enough to admit a man's neck. Beyond this a shelf jutted out to hold the patient's head. The cabinet rested on a long table. Behind it was a short wave diathermy machine.

Miss Yellowhead lifted the lid and showed me the interior. The inside of the cover was studded with electric light bulbs, all aglow. These provided part of the heat. The remainder came from the diathermy machine. The entire cabinet was an attachment fashioned and fitted to the electrical instrument. I would lie on a set of slats and another set would descend on me when the lid was closed, hovering so close that I would not be able to turn on my side. The external heat of the light bulbs and the internal heat from the diathermy machine would combine to raise my body temperature, thus destroying the germs.

The theory was simple. When certain germs invade the body the system fights against them by means of temperature, accelerating the normal heat until the invaders are destroyed by it. This happens in pneumonia, influenza, etc. Other germs do not bring about such a reaction. Either the body does not recognize them as enemies or it has other methods of defense—methods which often do not work. Since fever is a general agent of battle, killing all germs at one temperature or another, why not induce fever artificially in the body and thus kill germs which refuse to succumb to other agents? It would be necessary only to ascertain at what temperature a germ was vulnerable. By inducing this temperature in the body the germ could be destroyed.

"You have had the typhoid treatment already?" Miss Yellowhead said, looking at my chart.

"Yes. I was given the maximum dose several times. There was not much reaction—one degree of temperature."

"What a pity. You will not have that trouble with the cabinet. But it is so uncomfortable."

She looked at me with genuine sympathy.

"But you will not have to worry for a long time about catching typhoid fever."

"No, I am free to die of other causes."

"Can you lift yourself up to the cabinet?"

I pushed on the crutches and wiggled myself to a sitting position at the edge of the slats. Miss Yellowhead draped me with a towel, took my robe and gown, and put my crutches in a corner.

"Now, if you will lie down on your back," she said, "we can begin."

I swung around, put my neck in the curve cut out for it, and watched her lower the lid. At the last instant, and without looking, she snatched the towel. The lid fell shut. Miss Yellowhead looked at her watch and at the electric clock that stared down at us from the far wall. I wished the clock were somewhere else, out of my sight. Its hands were paused at 9:31.

"How long must I stay here?" I asked.

"Until three o'clock."

"How high will my temperature be allowed to go?"

"To 107 degrees."

"That will kill everything but me, won't it?"

Miss Yellowhead smiled. She was almost human, except for the bright white armor of the uniform. Under it was the same neuter machine that occupied all nurses while on duty.

"Yes, your little bugs will all be killed."

"Is it true that the body expires at a temperature of 108?"

"Oh, that is the rule, but there is no danger here. There is a whole degree between 107 and 108. We will keep close watch on you. There will be a nurse here with you all the time."

"The one who brought me down?"

"Yes. She has gone upstairs to return the wheelchair."

Miss Iceberg. She would sit in the impregnable aloofness of her Arctic personality while I, beside her, soared to within a degree of expiration. From time to time she would take my temperature, to make certain that I did not slip away and elude my punishment. Naked in a cabinet, with sixty lights shining upon me, I would lie beside her while we watched the clock. What foolish fellow said that love is a matter of propinquity?

Miss Iceberg returned, followed by a doctor. He talked to me as if I were a child, though usually he made an effort to regard me as an adult. He looked at his watch, looked at the clock, said he would see me in the evening when I had returned to my room, and went out. Miss Yellowhead went with him. I heard their footsteps on the concrete, receding quickly, leaving me alone with the clock and Miss Iceberg.

My arms were inside the cabinet. I had known that this would be so and was prepared for it. I would not be able to scratch my nose, or my chin, or my ears. Therefore I must not itch in any of these places. Now, watching Miss Iceberg poke a pencil into her hair, the first temptation arose. My head itched at a spot corresponding to the point at which the pencil hit her hair. I pulled my mind into a point, aimed it at the spot, and burned out the itch. It took a little time, and while it was happening Miss Iceberg went out of the room. She returned with a tray laden with carafes, glasses, and thermos jugs.

"What do I get to drink?" I asked. "Plain water?"

"No," she said. "Plain water and salt water."

"The change will be nice," I said.

She explained solemnly.

"You will lose a great deal of salt through perspiration. It must be replaced."

She sat down at the table and bent over a chart, making entries. I watched her while my mind drowsed. For an instant I saw a prognathic, flat-nosed creature, hair streaming over her shoulders, forehead low and slanting, eyes blank with incomprehension. But only for a moment: Miss Yellowhead's figures were hard to read; Miss Iceberg was puzzled. Quickly she compared, reflected, decided. The vision of her ancestor faded. She was again the modern phase of female evolution, poised on the brink of objectivity, testing her wings for the flight to reason.

Would she make it soon, and successfully? Her brow was now a lovely thing, high and squared to fit the expanding brain. Her chin had not receded too far; her jaw was firm. Her nose still had little form, though it was lifted from her face, and had a line and a point. Her hair was tied up on her head. All of her was gathered to attention while she contemplated the chart. For the time being her quarry of the ages was reduced to this—a set of figures, a jar of water, and a pile of salt.

Her detachment seemed no effort. Was the change so easily made, so quickly effected? Man was made with his freedom from the world half won. All of his sexual organs could be placed in a teacup. Woman from the curled ends of her hair to the painted nails of her toes was a mechanism of reproduction, an engine of ecstasy, a mimic of the earth. What man could dismiss as an appetite she must consider as a vocation. What consumed him in a few of his moments concerned her through most of her days. Could she dismiss it so lightly; could she set it aside without fear that it would reach out and envelop her in a moment when her guard was relaxed?

In America anything is possible, a fat man who had become rich once told me. He said it because he, a person without talent or energy, drilled a hole in the ground and found oil at its bottom. He had not expected wealth; he had not deserved it. He was, in fact, uncomfortable with it, for it possessed him. Nature had put the oil there, squeezing it from decayed and buried vegetation through millions of years. Other men had given it value, inventing the internal combustion engine and popularizing its use in the automobile. Now the fat man, acted upon by these separate movements in the flight of time, was saddled with money and bridled with responsibility. "Anything can happen in America," he said, and he looked around with what I thought was a worried, almost haunted look, as if he expected another catastrophe to strike him at any moment.

America is a force quite separate from her people. The fat man knew it; he had felt its touch. Miss Iceberg did not know it, but she too had felt its touch. Its mark was on her body, for a proof. "In five hundred years," an Irish writer said, "all you Americans will look like Indians." It showed first in the women. They were more plastic, more adaptable. Already the typical American beauty, the magazine cover girl, had a high forehead and high cheekbones, with eyes widely spaced. In some of the old New England families it was evident in the men. I had often as a boy been puzzled by the fact that all the Yale football captains, in the traditional photograph which showed them seated on the Yale fence, looked alike. They had high foreheads and high cheekbones, with eyes set well apart; their noses were straight and well-shaped; their chins were firm and cleanly cut. Miss Iceberg, though traces of her Scottish ancestors still showed in her face, was molded in the image of the evolving American girl. The Scottish touches, developed to the point of caricature in her faraway cousins, were in her softened and blended into the dominant pattern—a radiant, bleached, and Anglicized Pocahontas.

She was taller than her mother; on this I would wager my ration of fresh water for the day. Almost all children of immigrants were taller than their parents. It was because of diet, the learned finders of causes said. But diet was the force itself; it was America translated into spinach, sweet corn, gooseberries, sea grapes, soybeans, Virginia apples, Texas lettuce, Colorado beets, Idaho potatoes, Florida and California oranges, Kansas wheat, Connecticut strawberries. How often had I seen immigrants fresh from the Slavic lands—men and women who looked as if they had been pounded down with mallets—and watched their sons grow taller than the corn? They were given freedom as well as food, turned loose on the playgrounds instead of in the wheatfields, given a football instead of a hoe. In my town, where once the honor of the school was defended by Leary, Neary, Keating, O'Connor, Patterson, Kenny, and Sullivan, now the line from tackle to tackle was held by Kazemekas, Hermonat, Staugaitas, Lyskiewicz, and Marcelonis, with Butkus and Karaban in the backfield. One generation had not smoothed from their faces the signs and symbols of their race, but it had begun the work, and the fire that blazed in their beings and shone forth from

16

their eyes and their countenance was melting the suffering of a thousand years, so that the hands of freedom and hope could shape it into softer lines.

They were spread across the land now, working and building and begetting—Klimaszewski, Strusinski, Sosnowski, Slomezenski, Kwasnieski, Kalinoski, Sawicki, Rybinski, Usokiewicz. And their wives were Sheas, Scullys, Nardellos, Dalys, Bradleys, Schultzes, LeBlancs, and McKees. Their children would be strong and beautiful, and their sons would more resemble a Yale football captain than a Marshal Pilsudski or an Ignace Paderewski.

But if America was aflame in the spirit of her men, in the souls of her women there was holocaust. In the span of my own memory American girls had stripped themselves of their garments, so that now they were more scantily clad when on the street than formerly they had been while in bed. They had taken to painting their faces completely and for all occasions, so that only by her runover heels and her look of uncertainty was a streetwalker more conspicuous than a virgin. A foolish law prohibiting the sale and manufacture of alcoholic beverages, now happily repealed, had been the means of letting her into saloons, where now she stood side by side with men, stridently voicing her opinions, occasionally buying the bartender a drink, sometimes crying into her beer. The Prohibition law, designed to bring her husband home safely past the peril of the saloon, had instead precipitated her into the bar, so that now both faced the dangers of drink, and together conquered them or were conquered by them.

She had taken to smoking cigarettes on a wholesale, frightening scale. Her butts, stained a bloody red by her painted mouth, were in ashtrays and gutters from Kennebunkport to Key West and Nogales. She was still the madonna, her rouged and lacquered face pensive above the nursing child, warm ashes dropping on her bare breast; but the shadow of a plan, the stirring of an ambition, was in her psyche. Already she had somewhat abandoned her traditional technique of retreat and conquer. At times she assumed the offensive, became the suitor. The suddenness of her attack, and the novelty of it, often brought success.

Gradually she was becoming more economically secure. She had a vote, a place in business, and freedom from irritating conventions of pseudo-morality. She had also the insurance of chivalry, the device which had protected her when

17

she had no personal weapons. Insinuated into the American worship of success, chivalry was more powerful than ever. Freed from the need to actually protect his woman, man now glorified her, laboring long and with cunning to win for her the equipage of a queen. She was freed of drudgery, drenched with luxury, relieved of frequent childbearing. Her health was improved; she lived longer. Her husband, the trust funds set up, the insurance paid, died of coronary thrombosis at forty-nine. The wealth of the nation fell into her hands. A national holiday was declared in her honor. There was nothing which could not be hers; she had only to desire it.

Her temptation was great. All men adored her, and her morals were her own to make. Divorce was easy; her husband took the blame as well as the expense. It was part of the gentleman's code, the constitution of chivalry. Why not, then, reach out and take it all, seize mastery from man, run the country in fact as well as in fancy?

Somewhere I had read that an alarming number of girl babies had appeared in the country, that the land was being inundated with small females. Was it an invasion? Were the armies of Eve descending on America, moving in through the breach made by the heroines of the Flapper Age? It would be an easy conquest. The men would succumb without a struggle. Their acquiescence to monogamy was purely formal; women had invented it and had thrust it upon them; if women now repealed it, so much the better. The new polygamy would be without burden of any kind for the husband. His wives would support themselves, maintain separate homes, and contribute to his support. He would live alone, as a bachelor, having dates with his various mates at their convenience. Could a more idyllic existence for a man be imagined? And it would be the woman's own choice! In such a society, he would have time to write poetry, sail a sloop, and read philosophy.

Miss Iceberg lifted her head and stared at me, her eyes hazy with disinterest. I turned my gaze to the clock. Its hands had moved to indicate twenty minutes of ten. They seemed like a drooping, disdainful moustache on the face of a cynical, contented pedagogue.

"Ah, Professor," I said—to myself, of course, since I did not want to disturb Miss Iceberg—"fancy meeting you here."

"Not at all," the clock said—also in my head, since it was equally thoughtful of Miss Iceberg—"this is a temple of science. It is you who are out of place, with your romantic

18

improvisations. May I remind you that you take unprecedented liberties with the facts we give you about our research?"

"You may," I replied, "and you do. I acknowledge you as the high priest of our century. Science is the religion of our time—the only thing in which all men have faith. In the Dark Ages the church sold Indulgences; pious frauds wandered through Europe placing fake relics on broken bones and running sores. In this age of enlightenment science sells us vitamins, and causes transubstantiation in spinach through the mystical mantra of calories. I have seen hardened newspapermen who would not believe a drowning bishop if he told them he was wet, report enthusiastically and without skepticism the most fantastic dreams of an obscure professor of chemistry. I salute you, Professor. Long may you live!"

"There is reason for the people's faith in science," the clock said coldly. "There was no reason for the faith of the Dark Ages."

"Faith is the mother of reason," I said, showing some irritation. "She spawns syllogisms to support her. When I discovered that speculation in metaphysics was denied me—'You aren't allowed to think about such things,' said the frightened old women of my church—I turned to science for a field in which to exercise my imagination. Its theology is so young, I thought, it will change constantly, and speculation will be tolerated, even welcomed. But I found that you and your fellow priests seek out heresies and condemn them as ruthlessly as did the early church. So I think what I please in both cases, as did Aquinas and Bacon, as do the Jesuits and the physicists. And the end of all thinking is a mysticism beyond the grasp of any man, without limits or dimensions, without beginning or end. It can no more be postulated than sunlight can be imprisoned. No conjecture is more wrong or more right than another. It is only more useful or less useful for the moment. The goal is truth, but it is too far away for anyone to plot a path straight to it. We approach it in circles, and the best to which our minds can achieve is the ability to perceive whether the circles are narrowing or widening. That is the limit of all knowledge."

"I have no time to waste on a man who cannot keep his temper," the clock said. "What resemblance is there between a modern American girl and an Indian squaw?"

It was a very satisfactory Professor, a perfect companion. I could get along without Miss Iceberg.

"None whatever," I said. "It is the American man who resembles the squaw. His wife looks like a Pequot warrior."

"Saloon philosophy," said the Professor. "You invent nonsense to prove nonsense."

"Have you observed closely the genus business executive, hurrying to catch a commuters' train, slightly bent at the shoulders, carrying in one hand a briefcase, in the other a purchase made for his wife during the lunch hour? You don't think he resembles an Indian squaw?"

"Not at all. He is the most potent force in the world today. His wife merely reflects at first hand the good things he has done for our civilization. She is well groomed, well dressed, and immaculately turned out, because modern science has relieved her of the drudgery of housework, emancipated her from an unhealthy excess of clothing, provided her with tailored raiment at a reasonable cost, and lavished upon her good foods and beauty aids which help her to make the very best of whatever natural equipment she possesses. She is poised and gracious in this new world because she is sure of herself. She is no longer dominated, no longer treated as an inferior being. In short, she is emancipated."

"In shorts she is indeed emancipated," I said. The Professor glared.

"You," he said, "are an escapist. The situation you have predicted with such calamitous detail is patently something which you yourself greatly desire."

"That is true," I said. "By partially disrobing and presenting themselves in clothes and cosmetics which point out their best planes and curves, the American women present a temptation en masse. One block away every woman in town looks like the latest model of Venus. If styles were static it would be easy enough for the men to become adjusted to this ocular aphrodisiac. But fashions shift with such rapidity that the retina is constantly being enticed by something new. First the women showed us their legs, an inch at a time, until there was nothing left to show. Now bosoms are back in style."

"Are they showing those an inch at a time?" said the Professor, perking up a little.

"The disclosure is circular," I explained. "The circumference is gradually narrowed, but there is always a circle of some sort."

He lost interest.

"Once it was perfume," he said—did he sigh a little, or was it the minute hand of his moustache, lifting itself a little closer to ten o'clock?—"perfume and long, shining hair. Now it is legs and breasts: gams and bizocks, I believe you call them. Well, what is the difference, and what difference does it make? The sight of all these splendid, emancipated women makes it more difficult for you to settle to the notion of living with one of them. That has always been man's trouble; there is nothing new about it. Monogamy for man is difficult. It is a discipline. But it is a discipline he needs."

"From a mystical standpoint he needs it very much," I said, "though why you endorse the system I cannot imagine, unless it is true that science is only a more subtle form of religion. But it is not the difficulty of settling down with one woman which disturbs men—that is only a matter of discovering the one woman who most nearly resembles all the other women who have seemed attractive, a process which is described as 'falling in love,' and which I will discuss with you at some later time, when you are less inclined to defend sentimental indulgence on the grounds of morality. It is the settling down which is disturbing."

"Oh, men have become used to that, and it is the best thing for them. Now they seek adventure in business and science, without leaving their offices and laboratories. They contribute to civilized living, and they support happy and thriving families."

"That is true for those who are businessmen and scientists. Have you noticed how few seek adventure in the arts—in painting, in sculpture, in music, in literature in its pure form? Very few who have real talent, and many of these are women supported by well-to-do husbands. There is a point here which is easily recognizable. The reward of modern adventure is money. If that seems a desirable end then life is exciting and entirely satisfactory."

"The monasteries are still open," the Professor said coldly.

"Let me finish. I wish to point out that settling down with an American girl is increasingly an economic adventure. She expects, in her home, an electric icebox, a vacuum cleaner, an oil-heating system, a radio, a phonograph, a telephone. She wants at least a part-time maid. The laundry is to be sent out. When a baby arrives she will patronize the diaper service. If she does the cooking the meals will be simple. Almost everything is packaged, canned, or frozen, and the time needed to fashion elaborate meals can better be expended on something else—a game of bridge, a lecture, or a cocktail party. The family is small (it is too expensive to have a large one) so the icebox cannot be kept full of snacks and tidbits. Dinner guests are few, hospitality is sparse, and friends do not feel free to drop in whenever they are in the neighborhood. Family life, once a full, rich stream, is cut down to a trickle. Neighborhood life, that once was informal and enjoyable, is narrowed, regimented, and enormously complicated.

"Settling down for the man is becoming increasingly a process of social sterilization—perhaps I should say that in the fashionable American group of today the husband is his wife's eunuch, socially speaking. That is something he has submitted to willingly, of course, but this empty kind of life is becoming more and more expensive for him. It takes little more than a year now to convert a luxury into a necessity, by the standards of modern advertising. Some men, I agree, enjoy this drive for money. Others do not. They are unwilling drones. They would like to be free to pursue creative work, and to live by their efforts at creation. A new automobile every year and two weeks in January at Miami Beach are not goals which set them on fire."

"They should become farmers," the Professor said. "They can create spinach."

"Does it not seem incongruous to you," I said, "that a long-legged, well-built, athletic young woman should require 3,000 pounds of complicated machinery in order to traverse two blocks to the neighborhood store and bring home an armful of groceries?"

"Why shouldn't she use the family car?" he replied. "It is better that an automobile be run occasionally. What good does it do to let it sit in the garage?"

"It might do the woman some good. Walking is said to be excellent for the health. However, I have nothing against American automobiles, even when they are used to haul groceries. They are made to last for a number of years, however. Why change them once a year, just to be stylish?"

"Proceed," said the Professor. "You were going to explain why you wish to escape."

"It would be pleasant to find release from the burden of running a race which I am not interested in winning. I would like to build a yawl and sail it around the world, taking at least thirty years for the trip. So I conjured up a world in which woman replaces man, while science does the work formerly performed by the woman—particularly in the home."

The Professor snorted. "A world in which you would live as a glamorous courtesan, I suppose," he said.

"I hadn't thought of it, but it's a good idea. I had fancied myself as a bum, a man desirous of being freed from the earth, but without the courage to undertake the necessary measures. I thought an invasion of female souls might accomplish the task for me. A few men can father an entire generation, relieved of the harness of monogamy. That would free most of the male souls and they might perhaps be sent to other worlds. But I don't believe it. Freedom from this or any other world must be won by the soul itself. I foster no notions of riding to heaven on the tail of a saint, or a kite of prayers, or on the wind of a woman's revolution."

"I didn't think you did," said the Professor quietly. He lifted the end of his moustache to twelve minutes before ten and looked away from me. I was dismissed.

A little to the Professor's right one of the cellar windows showed me a few squares of sidewalk. Feet continually passed by, but no well-shaped ankles appeared among them. Sunlight worked its way through the dirty panes, seeming hesitant about entering the room. A little of it got as far as the floor, then paused. I wished it would come and bathe my face, as it had on a morning four years before—four years to a day, in fact. It had caressed me then on the streets of Haifa, and for once I had opened myself to it. How long and how lovely had been that day! Remembering it was a benediction.

TWO

EARLY in the morning, before the day was dry, I stood in front of the Grand Nassur Hotel, waiting for the automobile which was to take me to Jerusalem. The sun was drinking thirstily from the streets and fields. The pavement on which I stood turned dry while I watched it. The bartender came out and ran the shutter up on his open-air saloon. In the racks beyond the tables I could see the month-old London newspapers I had read the night before. I turned my eyes to the road at my right and followed it upward with my gaze until it trickled from sight. Beyond it, at the horizon, the top of Mount Carmel had just been lighted by the dawn. Should I ride up there and stand where Elijah stood, looking out at the Mediterranean, looking down on the plains of Sharon? There was a Carmelite monastery on the mount. One of the monks would be my guide. I could imagine the conversation.

"It is good to see you at so early an hour, my son. There is still time to attend Mass, if you wish. Are you a Catholic, my son?"

"Yes, Father, and I am interested in the legends of the mount. The Essenes have a particular fascination for me. It is obvious that preparations were made for the coming of Christ, and that He was trained for His mission by very wise counselors."

"But there was no need for that, my son. He was the only begotten of the Father; He was God."

"I understand, Father, but He rehearsed the dilemma of man. He submitted to obedience under His parents; He experienced the dark night of the soul during His forty days in the desert; He was tempted in Gethsemane. He must have been trained. There would have been no point in His entrance into the earth by way of a woman's womb were it His intention to manifest perfection from the beginning. He could have come as did Melchizedek. He could have delivered the Sermon on the Mount as His Father delivered the Ten Commandments."

"These are large questions, my son. They have been debated by wise men through many centuries. Holy Mother Church has decided—"

"Holy Mother Church has decided not to tell all she knows. Forgive me, Father, but I think it is a mistake. At the time when most of these questions were decided by the church there were only two classes of people, the literate priests and scholars, and the illiterate masses. The number of people capable of discussing such matters was extremely limited. It was important that they agree among themselves, if only in a half-hearted, compromise fashion, so that the complex structure of the Christian metaphysic could be reduced to a set of simple statements of dogma capable of being learned and recited by the least common denominator of public intelligence. So they agreed, though what they thought privately is another matter.

"Probably you have never been present, Father, at a conference of radio or motion picture executives, where the discussion centered on the problem of translating a mature play or story into a radio drama or cinema aimed at the mind of the American twelve-year-old."

"Perhaps you would like to go to Confession, my son. There is much on your mind. The sacraments have been found very efficacious in such cases. They renew faith, and that is what we all need. These matters are too much for us."

"I am confessing now, Father. I am worried—not about the church, for if it hasn't sense enough to save itself then it doesn't deserve to survive. I am worried about Christianity, about the doctrine and the example of Christ, and the people of the world who would embrace and cherish it if it were given to them in its purity and truth. If they were privileged to see it clearly, they would believe."

"We must pray, my son, that they receive the gift of faith."

"Prayer needs assistance, in these days. There is now a large body of literate laymen and laywomen in the world. The least of them is as capable of discussing the metaphysic of the faith as were the men who decided it. They should be allowed to do so. They should be encouraged to do so. Modern science confuses them, though actually it has produced the key to the mystery and supplied the evidence they need for a resurgence of faith. They should know this; they should be taught it—"

"My son, in our universities, in our schools—"

"There should be a library and a lecture room attached to each church. There should be a scholar attached to each rectory. Laymen should be encouraged to become scholars and teachers as well as listeners and devotees. There should be debates on these matters among the laymen—not with the idea of arriving at any decision, but only to stimulate interest, to set people searching, to reconcile faith and reason, to understand modern science and integrate it with religion. Christianity should be a living faith with all of us. Theology should be tabletalk in every home, now more so than at any time, when the laboratory is proving it to be true."

"Holy Mother Church knows best, my son."

"Does she know that she is no longer moving forward, that

she is losing ground, and that she will continue to retrogress until she decides to release to her faithful something more substantial than the Holy Catechism? Does she know what a harvest is to be reaped by the promulgation of a technique of mysticism for laymen of the Western world? Does she know what effect a single volume of metaphysics aimed at the intelligence of a college senior would produce?"

"There are such books, my son, many of them."

"Forgive me, Father. I mean a book which is readable, well-written, not mined with snide remarks about the dissenting Protestant sects, not backed up in its reason only by the smug assurance that Rome can do no wrong."

"We have made mistakes, son. There have been times when we erred. But in time the mistakes were corrected."

"There is one which was not corrected, Father. You and I are here on this earth, along with the rest of humanity, because of one common sin. It is symbolized for us in the fall of Lucifer. It leads the heptad of deadly divergences. It is the most subtle of our enemies. It is, in fact, ourselves—our ego, binding us here with pride. What else keeps the church from making peace with the dissenters but pride?"

"You do not understand, my son. The whole position of the church rests on this point. She cannot give in."

"There is no need for her to give in. There is no need for anyone to give in. Protestant sects differ more in the types of people they embrace than in the theologies they avow. The Reformation followed the Renaissance, the dawn of the individual. The rise of printing gave impetus to the natural facts of mental and emotional difference among personalities. The pitiable state of error into which the church had fallen through the temptation of her spiritual and temporal power over people was the beginning. It supplied the cause. But when the first schisms were effected the breach was widened and the schisms made multiple by the natural differences that had developed among people.

"When in the Middle Ages women had no choice of costume they wore identical habits and thought little of it. Now that a variety of styles is available no woman wants to wear a dress or a hat which is like a dress or a hat she has seen on another woman. That is an extreme, but it demonstrates the change which has taken place in five hundred years. The opportunity for a man to develop his mind and exercise his aesthetic tastes resulted in the differentiation of that man from all other men. At first this differentiation was only visible in isolated individuals, such men as led the various revolting groups in their break from the church.

"There is a theory, Father, that the church is all-wise. Why did she not then, when the defections were young, move with wisdom and cunning? Why did she not then invite the theologians of the schisms to meet with her theologians, and there at the conference table set forth this thesis: that the stream of Christianity had reached a place where the narrow gorge through which it had raced opened on a broad, flat plain, and that here it was obvious that any attempt to confine it in a single channel would fail. Divergence would take place; multiple streams would break from the main flow and meander over the plain. Some of them might become larger than the mother stream. Yet since all had come from the same source, and eventually in their journey to the sea would be joined together again, why not now make a bond of friendship and understanding that would give each the comfort of knowing, as it scoured a way through meadow grass and daisies, that it was not alone, and not singly and with improper direction cutting a way to the sea?

"If such a meeting had been held, and a body of broad and basic principles agreed to by the men present—principles involving man's identity, heritage, and destiny, and his hope in the supreme example set by Jesus Christ—Protestantism and Catholicism could have marched on side by side, and by this time, had they met regularly in council, and had they clung to the determination to settle all disputes by friendly arbitration, none of the Christian denominations would be as far removed from each other as are some of the theological groups within the Catholic Church itself.

"For the differences, though they are made to seem theological, are not. They are variations in personality, in the aesthetic senses, in race, in emotional pattern. Some people prefer austerity in their religion. Some prefer incense and plaster statues of saints. If Christ was all things to all men, why cannot His church be likewise? If there existed a friendliness among the hierarchies, an understanding of their common purpose and a means of cooperating to bring it about, bigotry would disappear among the peoples themselves, for they believe they are reflecting tremendous decisions of truth made by higher minds.

"Religion, good Father, is a personal thing. Each man has Christ within him—that is axiomatic, if he is of God and has a soul, for Christ is the manifestation of God in the earth—and each man must find Him in his own way, cutting a path through the labyrinths of his heart and mind, until he reaches the ultimate temple of his soul, where the Master awaits him. Externals can only assist him; they cannot lead the way. In the beginning Christianity was a broad technique for the use of the average person, something he could practice in private as well as in public. Then it became a massive organization, and its services a demonstration of political and communal solidarity rather than an affirmation of the example of Christ and the determination to imitate Him. The way of imitation was gradually closed to the layman. Christ was taken from him as an example and set over him as a God. The command He Himself gave—'Be perfect as is your Father in heaven'—was compromised. 'No one can be perfect,' the faithful were told.

"But that is a long and dreary story. The belief that he cannot be successful in the life of the spirit is one reason why the layman has turned his efforts to material success. Christ is too far away, and there is no middle victory for which to wage a battle. The externals remain, but they are suspect; their validity is questioned; their worth seems doubtful.

"All that could have been avoided by one wise move, one stroke of genius when the schisms were forming. It is better to let a young man see the world on his own terms; he will return home and settle down the sooner. How wonderful it would be if all the Christian churches were at peace, and were friendly and cooperative, depending for their membership on the natural differences in people. The liturgy would have been given many forms—simplified, translated—but it would not have been swept away entirely, as it has been in most of the sects. Individual chapels for meditation would have replaced the confessional in some cases, but a form of self-examination, of penance administered by the conscience, would have remained, and with it a communion revered as a privilege rather than exploited as a commodity.

"There would be a unity among Christian peoples which does not exist today—and which may never exist. And that council of all the churches, attended by laymen as well as clergy, would be powerful enough to stop wars and make temporal rulers settle their disputes by discussion and arbitration.

"In America a large flaw in the oneness of the people, and in their happiness together, would not exist. Differences in material wealth, in ancestry, in race, are there no barrier to a man. But often his religion is, though it is no longer considered of importance in his life or in the life of the nation. It is only a relic of the past, a slight stigma, and when the church fails completely the stigma will vanish.

"It could have been otherwise. Christianity could have been every man's badge of honor. Instead it is like the campaign button of a defeated Presidential candidate. Of course, so long as he is not dead, the man may presumably be chosen to run again by his party, and his second effort may be successful."

"Ah, yes, my son. We must keep up hope. Our hope and our faith sustain us. Holy Mother Church in the end will triumph over her enemies."

"If the church is a true reflection of Christ, yes. In that case she has but one enemy. You understand, Father, the symbology of the cross: man's will athwart the law of God. The surrender of the ego through free will—not my will, but Thine, O Lord, be done—is the consummation of the mystical union. Is not the church often too concerned with maintaining its identity in the world, and too little occupied with losing its identity in God? She was set up as a way of access, as a transforming agent, able at once to understand those who came to her from the world for solace and those who bent to her from heaven to give assistance. Many have come to her from the world, but they are kept in the outer chamber. The key to the door of the inner chamber is not given to them.

"It may be lost. Do you possess it, Father?"

"My son, I am but an humble priest."

"I hope so, Father, though humility seldom knows itself at sight. But let us consider something while we are waiting for the Mass to begin.

"The evolution of the soul proceeds from unconsciousness to self-consciousness to superconsciousness. In the beginning each soul was a part of the spirit of God, undifferentiated. With the gift of self-consciousness it became differentiated, individual. But it was not instantly severed from the mother spirit, any more than the human embryo is separated from the mother immediately after conception. It awakened gradually to awareness of itself—probably all souls were created simultaneously, as an integral part of the story of the cosmos.

"Self-consciousness was a slow process. The ego leaned heavily on the spirit, as the human personality leans on race, heredity, and environment. When complete self-consciousness

29

was established, a period of independence began. It now became the task of the soul to proceed by its own genius to the state of super-consciousness, wherein it was to recognize anew the identity in which it previously partook, while retaining its awareness of itself and the memory of its experiences.

"Generally speaking, humanity is at present in that dangerous middle state of complete self-consciousness. It is every soul's destiny to eventually reach the superconscious state, but it can be lost for a long time, wandering in darkness, doing harm to itself and others.

"That is why the church dwells in this middle state. That is why pride, which leads to a wrong turn, is the first of the Seven Deadly Sins. This is the critical state of the journey; this is, in multiplicity and ramification, the dark night of the soul.

"There are many here who still are nourished by the unconscious, who cling to the mother spirit—aborigines, primitive tribes. There are souls here who are close to the superconscious—saints and near saints. But largely the earth is peopled with souls who need the thread which will lead them through the labyrinth of ego that stretches from the source to the goal, from the self-conscious to the superconscious. That thread is morality, and it is the church's mission to point out its existence, its whereabouts, and its power.

"Those who have difficulty in seeing it, who are inclined to let it slip from their grasp even when their hands are placed upon it, can be aided by faith. Later, when they have followed it for a long time and the end is not yet in view, they will ask a question—how do we know it will lead us from the wilderness?

"There are tremendous numbers of such souls in the Western world just now, and for them the question is not being answered. True, they continue to hold the thread, but the reasons they are able themselves to conjure up—that it is gentlemanly, that it is necessary for communal prosperity and national integrity—will in the end prove inadequate. They only circumvent the question; they do not answer it.

"The church contends that it answers the questions. Perhaps it does; I am sure its answer is adequate for the faithful. But the skeptic is unimpressed. The church still proselytes admirably among the poor and the simple, building orphanages and dispatching missionaires. It is even successful with intellectuals who are on the edge of the superconscious, who suddenly sense by their own psyche that they are almost out of the wilderness. But the skill and the cunning, the art and the genius, to move the great inert middle mass, is lost. It was argument, dialectic, the democracy of theology, which once kept this mass moving along. Without this the people are unconvinced and uninspired. They have camped with the thread in sight, its thin line disappearing into the thickets ahead, and they have set about to make themselves comfortable and abandon the journey.

"Yet in making themselves comfortable, in examining the ground and putting to use its natural advantages, they have uncovered unmistakable evidence that the journey will succeed if it is resumed. But they do not recognize this evidence, largely because they are intent on putting it to other purposes, and have forgotten, temporarily, the journey. They call the evidence scientific truth. The church should have the ability to show them that it is also spiritual truth. It does not. If it could somehow acquire the ability, and use it, the great inert mass might begin moving forward again, so that those in the vanguard would be emerging from the wilderness and those in the rear would be leaving fresh tracks for those just entering. If the mass does not move it will have no leaders calling back encouragement, and those just entering the labyrinth will collide with those already there. That is now happening, and with evil results—race riots, for one thing.

"Father, can you realize what would happen if this mass in even one spot, such as America, moved?"

"America! Ah, my son, what a country! Tell me; is it true that everyone in America is rich? Are the women all beautiful? Do the bishops eat off gold plate? Does even the poorest parish priest have a limousine at his command? I have heard these things, my son. Are they true?"

"I will tell you, Father, but first you must answer my questions. Is this the place where the Essenes taught? Was Mary one of twelve maidens prepared as vessels for the coming of the Messiah? Was the approximate time ascertained by astrology, clairvoyance, and through visions? Was Mary's also a virgin birth? Was she third in line at the temple procession when the priests perceived clairvoyantly that she had been indicated as the chosen vessel?"

"My son"—and this would no doubt be recorded in heaven as the supreme understatement of a virtuous life—"you seem confused."

31

No, I would not go up to Mount Carmel. All my life I had kept silent about these things when conversing with the faithful and those bound by vows. Now was no time to speak. Yet I could not go up to that place of the sacred groves and the miracles of Elijah, that sanctuary of the Essenes, and remain silent while its mysteries were hushed about me. Long ago a pope, fretful at a controversy between the Carmelite monks, who held to the legends of their mystical lineage, and the new school of ink-bemused scholars, who attacked the legends as fables, ordered both sides to desist from the discussion until he rendered a verdict. None was ever handed down, and the subject matter of the argument has remained taboo for both sides. Thus link by link, now a little, then a little, the chain of historical mysticism was broken and the fragments buried, so that now the church was made to appear as if it had emerged, fullblown and vested for a solemn high Mass, from the Last Supper.

Yet it would not bother me a whit, I thought as I stood looking at the mount, were it not for the souls that were thereby turned from the path, thinking they had come to a false sign. The church would be as stubborn about admitting this as was Barnabas when Paul set forth to teach the Gentiles, so why bring it out on this morning air to trouble a monk before his breakfast?

It was time, anyhow, for the passion of it to die in me. The sunlight had crept to the place where I stood and had crawled up my legs to my belly. Wherever it touched the strength ran out of me and the loneliness of exile poured in. I would not have a heart for helping or for hurting until night had come again.

There are some who brighten in the sunlight and go forth in it to perform prodigious feats. There are others who live in the shadows, fugitives from the bright angel who sustains them, too feeble to face his countenance and carry on the business of life. I was one of these, marked for it from birth. When the doctor slapped my bottom the town clock was striking six and the long May afternoon was nearly done. At six o'clock on any evening thereafter I was ready to face the world, but by then most of the other warriors were returning from the battle. When day came and the sun struck down again at the earth a great and fathomless despair took hold of me, and I wanted with all the heaped up longing of humanity's bitter history to be out of my ragged robe of flesh and away, far away, from the cluttered, grubby, uncomfortable and impractical planet which held her inhabitants with so soiled a hand. The sight of men and women expending their bodies in physical labor in order that those bodies might continue to live and thus labor more—the dead eating the dead in order to remain dead—drenched me in a hopelessness that steamed and burned as the day wore on and the heat from the sun increased. The rational soul, immersed in the irrational body, was confused and dumb while the labors of the flesh went on. Only at night, when the tasks were finished, was it free to emerge from its cell and speak, to contemplate with sorrow the days of its captivity, and to sing a little in joy that another of them was done.

"Your car is here, sir. This is your driver."

The bartender had come from the cafe and was standing beside me. He nodded toward a black sedan of American make that had pulled up to the curb; he smiled at the young man who stepped from the driver's seat. The lad was a Moslem; on his head he wore a red fez. He was clothed in a blue business suit, and although he could not have been more than twenty-five his middle protruded like the abdomen of an aging American businessman. His face was set in the most complete expression of happiness and satisfaction I have ever seen on a human being who has been weaned. He was proud of all that pertained to him that morning—the car, the clothes he wore, and the job he was to perform, which was to carry me in his conveyance to Nazareth, Cana, Tiberias, and Jerusalem. His name, he said, was Ahmed. Without being asked he put my bags into the car. I told him I would sit in front. I did not want to be alone in the back seat with the sunlight coming in at me from the desert and the legions of my thoughts of Him marhing through my mind.

This was the land in which He lived, wherein He wandered and taught, converting some, antagonizing others. Here He performed His miracles; here He gave Himself up and was crucified. Over the roads I was to travel His disciples walked when they set out from Jerusalem to conquer the world. I would pass their shadows on my way, as I returned to the source of the miracles, the Transfiguration, and the Ascension, with a question gnawing at my mind and heart—why had the disciples failed? I had no intention of asking them, ghostly and canonized as they were, exiled from their homeland, enshrined in foreign temples, worshiped by alien hordes. Nor would I ask their descendants and local representatives. I intended to ask Him.

Ahmed was pleased to have me sit beside him. He explained that the car was new, that he alone was privileged to drive it, and that it was filled with power. The speedometer, I noticed, registered kilometres instead of miles. Wrapped around the radiator cap was a string of blue beads, the Moslem protection against the Evil Eye. At home a young man with a new car might tie a racoon's tail to the radiator cap, but the motive would be decorative. Did Ahmed believe in the power of his beads, or was it a matter of tradition and custom, like the tipping of a gentleman's hat when a lady of his acquaintance passes?

We were an odd pair, I thought, Ahmed and I—he with a fez and a protection against the Evil Eye; I with a gold key dangling from my watch chain, engraved with Greek letters; smoking, both of us, American cigarettes, and riding in an American car at sixty kilometres an hour toward Nazareth; belonging, both of us, to religions which acknowledged Jesus, but which had warred on each other for centuries. My religion called Ahmed an infidel; Ahmed's religion regarded with amusement and Oriental patience the monumental arrogance of Christian theology. Yet we sat, side by side, peaceably discussing automobiles and cigarettes, while we sped over ground on which our ancestors fought bloody and historic battles. The speed of our passing seemed symbolic. Tolerance and transportation had progressed.

The founder of Ahmed's religion was a reformer, a man who smashed the idols in the courtyard of the Caaba and pronounced the truth of one God. Always it had seemed to me that the legend of the manner in which Mohammed established the validity of his mission composed the most romantic passage in the story of religion. He had received the first verses of the Koran, he said, from God Himself. Certain gentlemen of Mecca expressed doubt of this statement, and proposed a test. It was known, they said, that Mohammed possessed no poetic gift. He was a businessman, a wealthy trader. But poetry was the supreme art of his country; there were poets in Mecca greater than any in the world. If in their judgment the verses of the Koran recited by Mohammed were surpassing in beauty and excellence, so that no poet of the land could match or excel them, then admittedly they were of divine origin and Mohammed was a qualified prophet. So Mohammed recited his verses to the critics, and they were agreed that in all the broad lands of Arabia and Persia no poet lived who could compose such transcendent lines. As for the notion that Mohammed himself had written them, that was ridiculous. He had received them from God. He was a prophet; his word was law. The Moslem religion was begun.

Mohammed looked askance at Christianity. It had, he thought, fallen on evil days. He believed in the Christian God and in Christ, but he felt that a reform was needed. He proposed it. The church, mired in heresy and schism, turned him down.

That was a mistake comparable to the Reformation. Mohammed took up arms, and now Ahmed and I belonged to different religions. He was allowed more than one wife, but was forbidden the use of alcohol. I was confined to one wife, but was allowed all the whiskey I needed to endure such a state. Both of us were largely deprived of the legacy of Jesus—the inspiration of His example, interpreted in faith and with reason; integrated, explained, and woven into our nights and days, as a mystery to ponder, a hope to cherish, and a great enfolding presence in which to find expansion for the mind and employment for the heart.

"How long will it take us to reach Nazareth?" I asked.

"We will be there for lunch," he said. "I have arranged for you to eat at the hotel."

We were moving swiftly on the hard, smooth road. It seemed a point of honor with Ahmed not to let the needle of the speedometer drop below sixty. I didn't mind; there was nothing to look at; on all sides and as far as the horizon there was unrelieved desert, the plain of Esdraelon, a great field of sand.

It was a young country, geologically. Only 25,000 years ago mountains were thrown up along the coast and a part of the Mediterranean Sea was cut off. Slowly the water disappeared, and a land of sand, limestone, and red clay came into being. Now only the Dead Sea remained of the great salt inland sea. Once the lake of Galilee was salt, but fresh water streams, washing it, finally carried the salt away, down to the Dead Sea, by way of the Jordan River. There it remained; the Dead Sea had no outlet.

It was a poor country, barren and tawdry. Why had it been chosen as a stage for some of the world's greatest adventures, and for the most significant drama of all time? Perhaps because it was so lately born, and not bound by the vibrations of evolution, the untold generations of lizards and crocodiles, of megatheria and brontosauri.

I smiled at the infantilism of my thoughts—presuming to

35

reach a reason hung high in the rafters of heaven—and rubbed my cheek to hide the grin from Ahmed. Humor is so gregarious a pleasure that to indulge in it privately while in the presence of another seems rude.

Properly, at that moment, I should have been meditating on Nazareth, the home of Jesus. If in this pilgrimage I was to find solace and wisdom, the search should begin now, as the realization of every Christian's dream approached me. But I could only wonder whether Nazareth really was the town in which Jesus lived. The Old Testament does not mention the place. It was four centuries after Christ before El-Nazur was identified as the village mentioned in the Gospels as Nazareth. Was it? Could it be that Jesus was being identified as a Nazarite, one of those dedicated to God, and that Nazareth meant only a place where Nazarites dwelt? They were a well-known sect, zealous and holy, but they did not live in communities. Or did they? How did I know? Jesus was an Essene. That seemed to be true. His mother was one; so was Joseph. Carpentry was one of the trades followed by the men of the sect—they were allowed to work only at constructive, helpful labors. They wore garments made in a single piece. But did they live at Nazareth? Was there such a town as Nazareth in the time of Christ?

The same question had to be leveled at Cana, where the first miracle was performed. When Nazareth was discovered a search was made for Cana. Two possibilities were considered: Kefr Kenna, about four miles north northeast of Nazareth on the road to Tiberias; and Khirbet Kana, about nine miles north of Nazareth. Khirbet Kana was a deserted site, a ruin. Kefr Kenna was a town of about a thousand people. It was chosen.

"Will we stop at Cana?" I said to Ahmed.

He looked at me and smiled. Without his fez he would have been exactly like a Syrian boy I knew at home.

"Wouldn't you like to see the jar which held the water that was changed into wine?" he asked. "They will show it to you."

"Let's stop anyhow," I said. "I don't want to miss anything, even the fakes."

He nodded. He understood. We were united in skepticism. Under the ease of his nature and the pleasant form of his smile I sensed the same broad, good-natured contempt for this religion of mine which existed in the countries where it held sway as a faith. Why I clung to it myself I did not

36

know. I had been told that I was a heretic, a renegade, a fanatic, a heathen. No one but a Jesuit, one lady had said bitterly, would consider that I was still a Catholic.

It would be easy to let go, to join the drifting herds who wandered through the fenceless fields of unbelief, putting off the problems of eternity for the very sensible reason that nothing but foolishness had been offered for their solution. However grand and lofty was the opening revelation of a religion, eventually little men with small minds insisted on reducing it to the level of their personal understanding. The details of creation were flung out through the cosmos, beyond the understanding of the highest archangel, but theology trapped them in a catechism. The sin of every metaphysician was his inability to say he didn't know; to invent an answer was human, to admit ignorance, divine. So every great single truth eventually was surrounded and shut away from sight by half-truths, quarter-truths, theories, guesses, and approximations. Each generation in its unfoldment desired to sit before the single truth and, contemplating its sublimity, speculate on the details. Some students wandered away never to return, when they found that such speculation was denied them. Others busied themselves with digging in the dirt, just for something to do.

Far back on the film of my memory was an evening when I talked with a devotee of the theological closed shop. As the spring night brought forth from me speculation on the nature of God and His handiwork the voice of the devotee rang out in sharp, clipped sentences: "You can't believe that. It's a heresy. It was condemned by Pius I in the second century.

"You are not allowed to believe that. It is a doctrine of Origen condemned by Saint Pontian in the synod held at Rome in the third century.

"You cannot have that opinion. It was held by Jovinian and condemned by Saint Siricius.

"All of those things were settled long ago. You are not allowed to discuss them."

It was a soft, lovely night, and his voice was harsh. From somewhere the scent of apple blossoms came toward us. The perfume stopped my anger, so that I only said, politely, "Go and tell the priests to tell the bishop to tell the College of Cardinals to tell the Pope that I have reopened them."

It would be easy to go from the church, but to do that would end what hope I had for myself and the world. Somehow I could not believe that the cause was lost. If He said

37

so; if He demonstrated by His absence from the temples which advertised His habitation that the scheme of marching together was abandoned, then I too would strike out toward the hills by myself. At least I would be moving; the journey would be started. Now I only waited, as it seemed I had always waited, for the army to stop idling and begin the march. Stripped to its essence Christianity had but one message beyond the revelations of other religions: we shall go together, it said, and we shall help each other. That was His offer, and He went before us to show the way. He promised to meet us. He left us a guide. But still the multitude did not move, the army did not march. Only a few went forth to meet Him, and each of these went alone.

Continually I was concerned with the army that was at rest. Only with the greatest unwillingness, I knew, and under direct compulsion, would I ever go forward without it. My destiny was bound up with it; I was enlisted in its ranks. But how I wished it would lift its guns, shoulder arms, and set forth. If only the commanders would agree on strategy, so the companies could unite and go forward. Here, idle and discontented, we gave our energy to digging more latrines, furbishing our weapons, extending and improving our barracks, and getting into mischief.

Mischief! The word exploded my thoughts. Palestine and Ahmed and the road to Nazareth disappeared. The roof fell in. A shower of objects struck me from all sides: glasses full of whiskey and soda, tinkling with cubes of ice; bottles popping their corks and pouring wine into thin-stemmed goblets; men and women talking, laughing, gesticulating, drinking, dancing, playing cards, singing in barroom harmony—all these drifted up and past and through me, until I shook them off and stared fixedly at the clock. It was twenty minutes past ten. Miss Iceberg was looking at my chart.

"What's the matter?" the Professor asked. "Is your conscience bothering you?"

"Yes," I said. "It's a special kind of conscience and it bothers me only under one circumstance. None of those memories would have returned to plague me except that when the particular recreational activity took place I had not done my work. That is, I had completed the tasks of my job, but I had not done that extra few hours of study or composition which represent my special assignment—the search, the quest, call it what you will; it is something that I must do or suffer in my conscience.

"It has nothing to do with material or professional success. Often I have finished a piece of writing and gone out to enjoy myself, only to be miserable all of the evening. On other occasions, after completing an assignment, I have expended the remainder of my mental energy reading a volume of philosophy or metaphysics and making notes, or composing a sonnet, or forcing my way through a hundred pages of Gibbon."

The Professor dropped his moustache a little and pursed his lips.

"That sounds like tithing—giving a percentage of your labor to the cause of the Lord, or in this case to something you variously identify as knowledge, art, or wisdom. Did you then seek the same recreation which on other occasions gave you no pleasure?"

"Yes, I sought the same recreation, and found relaxation and happiness in it. But whereas when my conscience bothered me I was uneasy, talking too much and boring my companions—jabbering to keep my thoughts at bay, I suppose; when I had paid my tithe I was quiet and at peace, and no person, however repetitious or vain or confused or superficial, was to me either dull or irritating."

"I suspect you are a mystic," said the Professor with sorrow. It was as if he had discovered that I had tuberculosis, or an occupational disease of some sort that would force me to give up my work and live on charity.

"Why don't you leave the rest of us and go somewhere to develop this talent—if that is the right word?" he asked. "Your arthritis, or neuritis, or whatever it is, may be no more than the conflict of your real self with an uncongenial world."

"I am not a mystic," I said. "I am not even much of a sinner. We have been over that ground before. I am concerned with what seems to be the failure of Christianity. It may be only an apparent failure; in truth we all may be marching on toward the goal. It is obvious that since religion got out of politics, politics has become religious."

"Religious? You mean the New Deal?"

"No, though the New Deal is a temporary phase of it. I mean democracy. Do you remember what I said about the emergence of individuality as the real cause of the Reformation?"

"You were talking to a monk on Mount Carmel when you said it, but never mind; I heard you."

"Well, this development of the individual brought about the individual's participation in government as well as in religion, and as he read Scripture and discussed politics the two became allied in his consciousness, so that one became a reflection of the other. Applying the practical view of politics to religion he ceased to look for immediate perfection in man, and became more tolerant in his judgment of other men's morals as well as of their theology. Applying the humanitarianism of the New Testament to politics he became more insistent on the right of every man to freedom, security, and opportunity. In the end this will result in a fair chance at earthly happiness for all men, which is wholly desirable.

"But religion, which formerly busied itself with these virtues of the modern state, is needed less and less. Religion stripped herself of her real mission in order to fill in during an emergency—working for charity, justice, and fair wages, when these were no concern of the state. It is now her duty to resume her mission. But she has not done so."

The Professor nodded. "At last I see what you mean, though it seems to me it is all abecedarian. The church was indeed a pioneer. Now Christianity is part of the basic philosophy of our civilization. It is our political chatter, where once it was an innovation, a special message carried only by the disciples of Jesus. Therefore the church, which for a time was a large factor in Western life, and which once held temporal power, can now return to the specialized function it performed in pagan times, the preparation of groups of mystics for the life of contemplation and virtue which seems to please their curious minds. Well, that is reasonable, and it seems to have happened. This country is full of small groups of metaphysicians and esotericists."

"Indeed it is," I said, "and they are all busy and successful; their members are active and enthusiastic. But would they have sprung up if the orthodox sects had offered the same opportunity for intellectual exercise? I confess I do not believe a soul can fly to the Father on faith alone. There must be an expansion of consciousness, and mind is the only instrument we have for building that expanded consciousness. After a certain time, as the saints testify, the movement of expansion takes on a life of its own, and proceeds without effort."

"Well, I think your heresy, or stumbling block, or whatever it is which has brought you to this lamentable state of disintegration, is in that belief of yours. Whatever platform of metaphysics a man constructs to raise himself to the level at which it is possible for him to fly, is jerry-built, is it not, and one type of architecture will do as well as another, so long as an edifice is raised on which he can climb upward—good works, devotion, mental exercises, charity—is one superior to the others?"

"Perhaps not. It is only that these platforms are not being built, and that is what seems to me a state of danger for humanity. People are using the lumber to lay out fancy patterns on the ground. How each one builds his tower—what plan he employs or what hours he chooses to work—does not matter. But the urge to build such a structure must come from somewhere, and it is not enough that isolated instances of deprivation and tragedy so stir certain individuals from time to time. There should be a mass recognition of the need to build, and there should exist the means for beginning the structure—plans general enough for everyone and flexible enough for individual adaptation. That mass recognition can only come in these years by an appeal to the mind, a reasonable set of syllogisms acceptable alike to science and religion. The people believe in science. If science proposes that God be recognized, and states that the need for reaching Him is as pressing as the need for vitamins, then the renascence of the spiritual life will be accomplished. Science can make those statements, based on its present knowledge. The wave theory, relativity, quantum physics—these provide the way."

The Professor regarded me solemnly. "Let us recapitulate," he said:

"You are a person beset by a strong fear for the spiritual well-being of man. This fear is partly for yourself, of course, but not wholly so, since you refuse to seek by yourself what you believe to be the path of salvation. You have in some way identified yourself with all of mankind. It may be a subtle form of masochism or a Judas complex, or a reflection of the Adamic archetype. These are technical terms. In Christianity it is recognized in the symbol of Original Sin, and baptism is performed as a means of removing the inhibition.

"However, since the feeling you have that only a spiritual revival will save the world proceeds from this fear, it is obvious that you have conjured this up as a cure for your own state of disquiet. You would have the whole of humanity removed from its normal destiny and put to a task it has no desire to accomplish—you would turn workmen from their labors and put them on their knees, there to chant a perpetual Ave. For themselves? No. For you; to assuage the troubles in your soul. It is a Gargantuan excretion of selfishness, I would say, a colossal expansion of Puritanism, a Blue Law on a cosmic scale. Let humanity now and henceforth be dedicated to sainthood, in order that you, riding on the tailboard of its effort, may be carried to heaven. I repeat—why don't you let humanity alone and seek heaven by yourself?"

He was looking at me severely and I turned away from his gaze. Miss Iceberg glanced up and found me looking at her.

"It is time for me to take your temperature," she said. "Would you like me to wipe off your face first?"

"Yes, and may I have a glass of water?"

She ministered to me with the precision and warmth of a machine. When she was finished I looked back at the clock. It was twenty minutes before eleven. The Professor had pursed his mouth and was tugging absently at his chin.

"I have been considering your case with the idea of helping you," he said. "I think we can assume that your physical troubles in part at least reflect the discord in your spirit. You have not made a happy adjustment to life. If you had been otherwise situated, you might have been more successful. Had you become a teacher, for instance—surrounded by the theoretical environment of books and the freshness and idealism of youth—this troubling of the waters might not have come to pass. But you chose a cynical profession, one inhabited in these times largely by skeptics. The clash was constant and heavy, and the necessity was upon you to be passive in your resistance. There was a violent and positive reaction within you in potentiality, and the repression of this brought about the physical result which now besets you.

"There were times when you tried to play the part of a skeptic yourself—attempts full of vigor, fire, and assertion, but with no conviction. They also caused damage. In the end these efforts became a pattern—a set of external actions which completely belied your internal beliefs. You probably welcomed, subconsciously, the germs which invaded you."

"Knowing that this was ahead of me?" I said. I was already uncomfortable. My temperature was up and I was perspiring steadily from all parts and places. The irritation of the flesh that comes with fever was growing. I wanted to turn and twist, but I had to lie still.

"At any rate," the Professor went on, "since medicine is being applied to the body, why not apply medicine to the mind and heart? When the germs have been extinguished by the fever you will be well in the region where effects are visible. But what about the region of causes? If it is true that some of your trouble originates in an internal dissension—and this seems to be so—why not set about to remove that dissension and bring about mental and spiritual peace, so that the healing of the body, when it is accomplished, will be backed up by a healing of the mind?"

"I would give up what little comfort is left to me in this hellish contraption if that could be accomplished," I said.

"Perhaps it can. Time will pass slowly for you while you are incarcerated. You already know that from watching my face. There will be other treatments after this. Each one will seem longer than the preceding one. You will need some form of diversion. I propose that you set yourself the problem of psychoanalyzing yourself. You are in a position physically which approximates the old-fashioned version of hell. Why not face the problem of judgment in your mind? Start at the beginning of your memory and let it unravel. It may be that you will discover the block, the inhibition, the neurosis. It is there somewhere. If you can discover it, face it, and come to peace with it, you will have done as much or more for yourself than the doctors and the cabinet."

He lifted his moustache and regarded me solemnly, waiting for an answer. It was fifteen minutes before eleven. I had four and a quarter hours to go, and my temperature had not nearly risen to the appointed 107 degrees. It would be a long wait until three o'clock. Each new moment seemed to stretch and grow greater than its predecessor. I looked at Miss Iceberg. She was mixing me a drink of salt water. Her countenance was serene, her coiffure unruffled. She was not going to thaw. I looked at the window. Feet were still passing by, the heavy, thick-ankled feet of stout women going to market. I could see the ends of their shopping bags swinging in short arcs at the top of the panes. All the pretty ankles were tucked under desks, or hidden behind counters, or snuggled in bed waiting for dusk and the sound of music. I listened for sounds in the cellar room. There were none. No one was allowed to visit me here. I was alone and must remain alone, except for Miss Iceberg and the Professor—alone and naked in a coffin made of pine, with sixty lights shining on me and a woman in white mixing me a drink of salt water.

"All right," I said to the Professor, "I will do it."

THREE

FROM THE BEGINNING there were two of us, I and the one who was behind me, who saw into the shadows, and who was closer to the place from which we had come. Always we were aware of each other, and from the instant when I knew myself to be here I knew also that he was with me, and I was never lonely or afraid. He had no actual part in me; he did not eat, or sleep, or become tired; but he knew everything that I did, he saw all that was done to me, and he considered it from the standpoint of our common plight. We were prisoners, both of us, and we wished to escape, though we did not know how it was to be done. He was constantly concerned with this problem, for he had freedom to consider it without interruption. He was not forced to learn things at school, or to rehearse manners at home, or to run errands. They did not, in fact, know that he was there, with me, though for a while I believed that they did know. I once heard a visitor say to my mother, "What is his middle name?" "Joseph," my mother said. So I thought he was Joseph, and I called him that. Later I found that they were not aware of him. But I let him keep the name, for I did not know what else to call him. Besides, the term Joseph served no other purpose in my life. I asked my mother what it meant and she said, "Nothing. Everybody has a middle name."

That was the kind of logic I observed in all grownups. Why did they get married? Because they wanted to have a home. Couldn't they have a home without getting married? No, they could not. Why did the men go downtown to work? To make money. Couldn't they stay home and make money in the cellar, or in the back yard? No, they could not. If God wanted people to eat things that were good for them why didn't He give the things a good taste? He did give them a good taste; I didn't appreciate it.

These grownups, these other human beings in the world, I regarded without the slightest affection. They were not alive in the same way that I was alive, obviously. They were a different kind of thing, like horses, or dogs, or trees. Cats walked by without paying me any attention, intent on stalking a bird or a field mouse. People passed me by in the same way, going to town or coming from it. In my own home they talked to each other as if I were not present. They did not care about the things which interested me, and I was not concerned with what they discussed—whether this man or that man or another man should be elected. Why not elect all of them and cut off their heads?

The men carried fires around with them in little bowls, and sucked the smoke into their mouths. The women had big things for feeding babies, things that stuck out and almost hid their faces when I looked up at them from the ground. They were always sitting in chairs instead of running and jumping, and I had never seen one of them slide down a bannister. Most of them were ugly.

They made me understand from the beginning that I must do as they said. This was for my own good, so that I would grow up and be as they were. The horror of this destiny is probably what drove me into the acute mental suffering which forms the first moment of life I can recall, the initial scene on the film that unfolds when darkness and longing take me back to the beginnings of a journey which seems never to have progressed in the right direction.

We were lying in the grass, Joseph and I, and we knew everything that was going on around us. A bird was muttering in the small cherry tree. Our mother was working at the sewing machine. The grass was dusty; it needed a shower of rain to wash it off. The wind was rustling things in the garden, snapping the tips of the young cornstalks. A dog had knocked the cover off the garbage pail. A woman had walked down the street, a heavy woman wearing new shoes. The sound of her came up the driveway and entered the grass.

Joseph said, "Be quiet. Something is wrong," and we were still. All around us the world was busy. What was it doing? What *was* the world? What purpose did it have? We were in it, caught somehow in a thing called a body. If we wanted to go down to the corner of the street we could think about it and see it, and see ourselves there, but we would not actually be there until we took our body with us, something that was difficult, troublesome, and which took time.

The body served no useful purpose except to keep us in the world. It was, in fact, a nuisance. It prevented us from being where we wanted to be. It picked up dirt and had to be bathed. It had to eat food—gross and ugly things with sour and sickening tastes. Terrible stuff came out of it because of the food. It had to sleep every night, and it had to stay where it was told to stay.

All this was because of the world, and it would get worse. It would be necessary later to go to school, and, after that, to work. Grownups did not play. They had rough skin, they gave out harsh odors, and they looked sad. We were to become one of them.

"I think we are in the wrong place," Joseph said. We had tried to hear the earth talking, and the grass. We had listened to the wind, and tried to see the flowers growing. There was an almost to it; we almost heard what the wind and the grass and the earth were saying, but it was not quite clear, not quite in our language. We had almost seen the flowers growing, but not quite; they did not move while we watched. We were sent out of doors to be in the sunshine; it was good for us, they said. But it made our body sick at the stomach and it drove Joseph entirely away. I had to go to a shady spot and bury my face in the cool grass before he would come back.

We loved the shade. In the sun there was turmoil and our body burned and freckled; we could not think. In the shade there was quiet; life was growing, but it was not racing, it was not being popped into another form like kernels of corn. Our body that swelled with food and excrement, that sweated vile poisons, that itched and hurt, that became tired and irritable—this was held in narcosis by the sweet, green grass, and when its lungs were filled with earth-scented air Joseph and I could think, and contemplate the sky.

Always we saw it as a sea of cool, soft water, in which we swam with the ease and speed of thought. Over all of the world we went, and away from it, never to return. Where we had come from we did not know, but to that place we returned. It had magic and music and angels who laughed.

"I remember that much from your dreams," Joseph would say. He never had any dreams himself because he didn't

46

sleep. He stayed awake and watched my dreams. Whenever I woke up there he would be, and he would know what had awakened me and what I had been dreaming.

"Try to remember more," I would say, "so we will know just what it is like."

"I wish we could go there now," he would answer, and we would become aware again of our body. It was a cumbersome thing, and would become more so as it grew larger. Even now it hindered us in our desires. It would not let us get close enough to a blade of grass, or to the inside of a buttercup. Its eyes crossed and its vision blurred when the object was brought close enough for real inspection. When it drew a deep breath—at our command—and sucked mightily at the perfume of a flower, the fragrance disappeared, lost in the effort. We could place a cheek or a nose against the earth, but we could not get into it, past the surface and down to the caves where things began to grow and the elves and fairies lived. We could run dirt through fingers, but already the skin covering the fingers was becoming tough, losing its sensitivity.

When our body did not stop us, people did. In order to know the taste of a thing it is necessary to hold it for a long time in the body's mouth. People would not let us do this. They told us to swallow. In order to really find out about water it was necessary to let it flow over the body for a long time. People would not let us do this. They chased us away from faucets.

More than anything we wanted water, great seas and oceans of it, surrounding us always. We wanted it to wash over us, to bathe us, to float us away. We made the valley a lake, we turned the streets into rivers. When it rained we knew what was happening. The place from which we had come was nearby and a little of it was spilling over.

"Do you think they will ever take us back?" I would ask.

"I don't know," Joseph would answer. "I don't know why we had to leave."

The rain would stop, and we would be alone again. Children would come from the houses and run to the gutters to make dams and sail paper boats. We liked to stand and let the torrent run over the feet and legs of our body. When it was ended we walked back to the garden, to see the drops still sitting on the leaves of the tomato plants, still running down the bean poles, still shining from the high tops of the sunflowers.

In winter the snow brought loveliness that stayed. Even when a crust had formed over the fall I could break through it and bring up a handful of flakes as fresh and fluffy as when first they fell. The patterns were broken, of course, but this was bound to happen; the best way to see the beauty of the flakes was to catch them as they fell, on the back of a fuzzy mitten. They rested lightly on the small Angora hairs and there was no heat to melt them. None was ever like another; you could catch them all day and never find two alike.

Said Saint Thomas Aquinas, "Is it easy to understand how natural bodies devoid of knowledge are moved and act for the sake of an end. For they tend to an end as directed thereto by an intelligent substance, in the same way as an arrow, directed by the archer, tends to the mark. . . . Therefore it is also clear that every work of nature is the work of an intelligent substance. . . ."

It was the intelligence that intrigued us, the mind which had worked out this infinite display of patterns. It was our introduction to the problem of diversity. Years later, when we had studied the Jesuit Kircher's arrangement of fifty objects in a manner to produce combinations whose number contained sixty-nine digits, and when we had considered the variety of different thoughts produced in a lifetime by the average brain—each one dependent on all previous thoughts, yet different from any of them—we understood how infinite variety, far from being impossible, was inevitable. But the snow in those young years seemed magical; the matchlessness of its form and the tenderness of its touch were as ravishing as the first kiss of sleep. "Forms which are in matter originated in forms that are immaterial," observed Boethius.

There are persons who say they have found in snowflakes the designs of chairs, tables, utensils, and automobiles. Well, where does an inventor's mind go for inspiration? There is no place it can go except to the repository of all intelligence, where the idea of a chair is bound to be, with all its ramifications and diversifications. If the inventor decides to use the idea, so much the better for mankind, which is tired of standing. But there is no reason to be surprised if, sitting in a chair, a snowflake falls in your lap containing a duplicate of the chair's design. If man has made anything by himself it is his wretchedness, not his glory, and it may be the plan of this wretchedness which is rained on the world when, now and then, in places about the world, black snow falls.

But snow is the particular benediction of those who love the abstract, the mathematicians and metaphysicians, who are more concerned with the cause than the effect, more enamored of the pattern than the product which is fashioned from its dimensions. When the muscular, warm, ambitious materializations wither and die in the autumn, a time comes when the speculative, the inferential, the inductive, may walk abroad in safety and with profit. When the snow falls these eyes of reason are rewarded as is the botanist when spring whips through the meadows. The first forms of thought, delicate idioplasms, are handed to them by the billion, a fresh assortment of ideas from which to choose next season's styles for earth. Nor do they quickly go away; they remain, beckoning the mind—glistening in the sun, turning blue in the twilight, striking sparks at night from the runners of sleds.

We were sure, Joseph and I, that snowflakes came from the stars. There was an affinity between them, in color and in shape, and all winter the bright white angels were closer and sparkled more brightly. They shot some kind of magic at the earth, we believed, and when it got here it exploded and filled the air with snow. The frost that covered the window panes also was part of their work. The stars were drawing pictures of the gardens and fields they were going to fill the next summer. When summer came we looked for the designs wherever we went, on farms and in forests and meadows. Sometimes we found them.

"The end of any intellectual substance," said Saint Thomas, "even the lowest, is to understand God." Joseph and I did our best. We knew that God existed outside of the world into which He had, for an as yet undiscovered reason, pushed us. That He was in the world Himself we did not know. We had been told otherwise; everyone said He was in heaven. His handiwork was obvious—the stars, the snowflakes, the grass, the rain, the drifting clouds that importuned us to follow them. We knew that we belonged to Him; that relationship we understood better than those who told us about it. He wasn't at all the way they described Him. But why He had made the world and why He wanted people to live in it we did not know.

The answer that was given to this question was the most absurd we had heard. It was the keystone in the arch of mistrust, disillusion, and embitterment that little by little we built. God made the world, we were told, so that people could live on it and be happy. We were incredulous, Joseph and I.

"Be quiet," he said. "You can see how wrong it is. Do not believe it."

Be happy in the world? How was that possible? With a body that could not fly, and which got dirty and had to be fed; with no angels or fairies or little people for friends; with no water except what came through pipes; with all but a little of the land shut away—how could a person be happy? Grownups were not happy; they had to work, and that was hard.

The world was here when we came. By careful questioning I discovered that it was here when the first man came, whose name was Adam. He, in fact, was made especially to live in the world.

"So you see," Joseph said, "it isn't true that the world was made so that people could live in it and be happy. It was made first, and then people *had* to live in it."

"I wonder what will happen when we die," I said. "Shall I ask?"

"Yes," he said. "Just say, 'What will happen when I die?' "

So I did. They told me that I would go to heaven and that my body would stay here and be buried.

"There," Joseph said, "that proves it. If we were supposed to live in the world and be happy we would stay here, not go back to heaven."

"We would be happy, too, if we were meant to be," I said. "We would be able to fly like the birds, and go anywhere we chose. We would not have to eat, and there would be more water. We could swim in it and play in it all day long."

One day my mother said, "I am going to church. Would you like to go with me?" I said yes, I would like to go, so she dressed me in a white sailor suit and took me by the hand. We walked down the long hill into the valley, and through the section devoted to business. As we came to the village green I saw what I knew to be a church. When we reached the entrance to it I turned aside to go in. My mother pulled me back.

"Not that one," she said. "That is not our church."

Then I saw, on the other side of the green, another

church, larger and more beautiful than the one I had tried to enter. It had spacious grounds and a tall, lovely steeple. Eagerly I walked on, and when we came to its entrance I turned aside to go in. Again my mother pulled me back.

"That is not our church either," she said. "Ours is farther up the street."

There were no more steeples in sight, but I walked on. After a while the street dipped into a hollow. There in the shadow was a church, quiet, dark, and ugly. We entered it, and sat in a pew. Terrible sights were painted on the windows. My mother disappeared into a black box that was nailed against the wall. It looked like a coffin. Would she come out again? There were a few other people, mostly women, moving around in the half-darkness, as if they were in the presence of the dead. Suddenly two things swept by me—they were black and faceless and flowed like elementals. Terror seized me. I was about to cry out when Joseph loosed the fingers of fear and put them away from me.

"They are nuns," he said. "You have seen them before."

In a few minutes my mother came out and we left the church. On our way home she tried to explain why we could not enter the other churches. We did not belong to them; some people belonged to one church, some to another. Then the churches did not belong to God? Well, they were dedicated to God, which meant that people used them as places in which to pray to God. Didn't they pray at home? Yes, but they liked to go to church also. Could I join the pretty church on the green? No, because I was born a Catholic and so I would have to remain one. Even after I grew up? Yes, I could not be a Congregationalist.

It was a bad explanation, naturally, since there is no good explanation for the stubborn pride and muddleheaded viciousness which in the first place set up the conditions that bred schism and in the second place maintained and fostered them among both orthodox and dissenting; the conditions of distrust, intolerance, and bigotry which nurtured the rebellion and refused to acknowledge the victory it had won.

As we passed the pretty church organ music came from it.

"How nice it would be to go in there and think about God while the music plays," Joseph said. But we never saw the inside of that church, through all the years in which we lived in the town, though many times Joseph and I crept near to it when the organ was being played and listened to

51

the music. The organist was a jolly, friendly man, and we could tell that he was very much like us from the way he played—soft and lonely music from the faraway part of the heart that is lost and cannot find its way out to the light and the air. Bonaventure said that wisdom is experimental knowledge of God, a gift of the spirit which emerges when "the soul tastes divine sweetness." Listening to the music of the organ as it came from the Congregational church, our body huddled against a tree or a granite step, pretending we were there for some other purpose, fearful of being discovered by a Catholic or chased by a Protestant, we tasted divine wisdom, Joseph and I, and knowledge rose a little in our thoughts, enough to give battle to the despair and hopelessness that seemed always about to engulf us. God was not quite as bound and ordered and circumscribed as people said. He did not entirely govern His actions, His likes and dislikes, according to the opinion of His creatures. It was God Who was everywhere, and Who judged, not His creatures. It was possible, in fact, that His creatures were quite wrong. It might be all right for me to join the church of the beautiful music.

I needed that knowledge. Joseph was away from me more often and for longer periods as I grew older, for he could not bear the tasks I was put to and the torment of being with people. He wanted to be with me in separation from all others, and to contemplate only our problem and how we might solve it. He was not with me, therefore, when a shock came which drew up from the ends of my being what life was there, and held it in a grip so painful that the tears which sprang to my eyes seared and stung the lashes.

I had been going to church each Sunday, watching the Mass and listening to the priest when he stood in the pulpit and talked. I liked what he read from the story of Jesus, and I believed what he said when the book was laid aside and he explained the gospel. It was comforting, despite my worry about the difference in churches. Jesus had come from heaven. He knew the way. He explained it. He said He would meet us. "In my Father's house are many mansions: if it were not so I would have told you. I go to prepare a place for you. And if I go and prepare a place for you, I will come again, and receive you unto myself; and where I am, there ye may be also. And whither I go ye know, and the way ye know. . . . If ye love me, keep my commandment." What was the commandment? To love God and to love people. Jesus told about it in the Sermon on the Mount, and when He ended He said, "Be ye therefore perfect, even as your Father which is in heaven is perfect."

I believed this, all of it, and I believed that everyone else did, and that all people loved God and were trying to keep His commandments and be perfect. Then one day as I listened absently to the conversation of a group of adults I realized that this was not so. They did not believe what Jesus said, or what the priest said, or what they themselves said when they spoke with me. They only pretended to believe it.

They spoke of honesty, truthfulness, honor, decency, charity, friendship; yet they expressed admiration for a man who made a lot of money by sharp dealing. They laughed over his methods; it amused them that he had "put one over" on somebody else. "You've got to keep your wits about you if you want to get ahead," they said with little, knowing smiles. I was stunned, stricken; and I remembered suddenly many things which proved that what I now had heard was so.

They had read me stories in which the heroes practiced trickery to get what they wanted—Jack and the Beanstalk, Puss in Boots, and a long succession of thieving, lying rabbits. The idea was to get ahead—which meant, so far as I could gather, doing precisely what Jesus said not to do. Virtue was all right for me, apparently, but not for them. They never said, "If only I could be good, be perfect, feel the presence of the Lord." They said, "If only I had money, a big house, and one of those new automobiles."

They did not love their neighbors; they liked some, they disliked others. They did not love God; they feared Him. They were not meek, they were not humble, they did not turn the other cheek. They went to church on Sunday and they spoke in pious tones of the priests and of the Mass. But their conversations, their books, their magazines and newspapers, their actions and their opinions reflected a path of conduct entirely separated from that which Jesus had asked them to follow.

Even when they said they loved me they meant it only temporarily. Ten minutes later I might be a bad boy, thoroughly disliked. Such vacillations struck me like blows from a hammer, a hammer that hit me in every place at once. If I were good, then I must always be good. If I were bad, then I must always be bad. I was prepared to be either, for it was a judgment entirely in their hands. Since it was not based on Jesus I could not anticipate it; thus I never knew from one minute to the next which I was. Much of it was predicated on their own convenience and comfort, and I learned to stifle many simple and reasonable requests rather than be told that people were too busy to grant them. Much of it had to do with believing the lies they told me, too. Neither God nor the Bogey Man would have carried out the weird punishments they predicted, and I knew it, just as I knew that the foods which they told me tasted good had vile and terrifying effects on my taste buds.

These people sat about me in the pews in church and heard the words of Jesus. He told them not to worship Him, but to imitate Him; to cleanse themselves of Pride, Covetousness, Lust, Anger, Gluttony, Envy, and Sloth. But they turned the insolent crudeness of their faces upward and seemed not to hear. They were joined in one great and vacuous countenance of pretended piety. They were fooling God. They had shut Him up in this place and He could only see them when they came to visit Him. That was what they thought. I could see it on their faces.

There are people in the world who compare themselves to God, measuring the difference with prayer, and laboring with humility to make the gulf less vast. But they are so few that the mark of them is not known, and generally they are thought to be foolish. Humanity in the mass is divided into two types: people who compare themselves to others and people who compare others to themselves. The former are the ambitious, the envious, and the poor. The latter are the proud, the smug, and the rich. I did not know this in those early days. I had not come upon the notion that the world is an end in itself. Nor had I encountered Saint Denis, who saved Jesus for decent Christians by plotting the mystical way of the church. It would have helped me to know that in his opinion symbols give a very incomplete idea of God. These symbols were the things which bothered me: the aspects of divine personality, God's anger and sorrow, His ornaments and whims. The grownups seemed so sure of them, so familiar with them, yet so indifferent to them in all but their admonitions to me.

There are but two things which man really knows of himself—that he exists, and that outside of himself there is another existence. So say the philosophers, who thereafter write volumes telling what, beyond this, is obvious, safe to assume, easy to deduce, possible to predicate, and reasonable to conclude. But there is something else which every man knows from the instant in which he becomes aware of himself and that which is not himself. He knows his identity, his relationship to that which is beyond him, his reaction to it. He knows, to put it colloquially, how he feels about things. Later this feeling will be called his personality, his character, his genius. It will, to those who know him, be himself; it is what will come to people's minds when they think of him. They will consider it as something which has developed since birth, as an emerging mixture of heredity, environment, training, and will. But it was there all the time, coexistent from birth with the knowledge of his presence here and his awareness of the world and its other inhabitants.

It was this identity, in fact, which became aware of the other two aspects of awareness. They happened to it. Everything thereafter, also, happens to it, but does not change it, for the interplay between the world and the new citizen is external to it. Only the results of the interplay affect it, only the spiritual reverberations cause it to react. For this identity, though primarily an awareness, is in essence a state of expectation, and it does not change throughout life except to register disappointment or joy at the fate of its hopes on the playing field of time and space. It receives all the acts, thoughts, and emotions of the personality over which it watches, but it does nothing to influence them. It is still, and it waits, and it knows for what it waits, for it is the spirit.

It was this identity, this underlying sea of spirit bearing Joseph and me and our body upon it, which was not injured or shocked at what I discovered about people. It seemed to expect such facts. It was this identity which moved and shuddered with ecstasy at the sounds of the organ music, so that our body trembled and desired to weep.

We were learning things, Joseph and I, but this strong thing which held us where we were thrust into the world, and from which came our certainty that we lived and moved, remained the same. It has not changed in all the years, except to be sorrowful when we were wasteful with our days and nights, to shudder like a bride at the sight of beauty, or to seep up through our body and fill it with the wonder of a higher world when now and then after the pencil was laid aside something of loveliness was seen lying on the page.

The house in which we lived was on a slope that looked down at a valley and up at a hill that ran north to the Berkshires. In the valley lay a town that called itself Naugatuck. It was part of a state called Connecticut. Both names were meaningless and made ugly sounds in the throat when spoken. There were factories where the men worked. There were houses, kept by the women. There were children. There were schools, churches, banks, stores, offices. There was a village green and a Town Hall with a clock in its tower. None of it meant anything, so far as Joseph and I could fathom.

The women seemed to dominate all that happened. They talked a great deal, shouted at the children, and grew fat. Most of the time they wore house dresses—ugly, ample prints. Their hands were red and coarse. They wore no cosmetics. They used no perfume. They were constantly darting about their houses, muttering and sweeping. What a man could want with one of them was incomprehensible to us.

There were times when they dressed differently, in skirts and shirtwaists, with hair piled up and a faint scent about them. They then went to church or "out" for the evening. Some of the younger, unmarried women, seemed pretty in such clothes, but they always walked toward town, and that did not interest us. If they had gone toward the hills we might have wanted to go with them. In the hills in the night there might be magic, elves, and even God, walking softly through the forest. It would be nice to be there with a pretty woman, whose hands were white and whose hair had the odor of flowers and rain.

There was nothing which either Joseph or I could discern about the relationship between husband and wife. Christian marriage had an outward look of frustration and desuetude. It was as spiritless as the tired horse of the Sicilian huckster who came to our street to sell vegetables to the sniffing, tasting, garrulous housewives. I never saw a husband near a wife except when the two were walking on the street together. There had been a wedding for each couple, I was told. I did not know that this wedding, supposedly symbolic of the union of two souls joined in a mutual hegira toward the ancient destiny of man—in theory a merging of the separate egos that God might labor through the selfless mixture to bring about His purposes—was now but a legalization for mating, a signal in public that a maiden in private was content to be ravished; a rite strewn with liturgy and performed in a church; the shattering of Hymen to the music of the Mass; the final degradation of Isis, the Virgin of the World, and her daughter, the Mother of God.

The men seemed inconsequential to the scheme of life. They went regularly to the factories and returned from them; they sat on the porches and smoked their pipes; they weeded the gardens and mowed the lawns; they said little, and when their wives called they went to them.

But one day on the main street of the town Joseph and I saw a man who seemed different from the others. He walked with a stride that was long and quick, and his head was high and free at the shoulders. An inner happiness had pulled the corners of his mouth into a permanent smile. He hummed to himself, and he swung a light cane. Perhaps it was a blackthorn stick, for he was Irish. He had bright red hair and his name was Father Higgins. He was one of the priests of our church.

We liked him, Joseph and I. He seemed the sort of man who knew where he was and what he was doing. We wanted to ask him about God and Jeus, and we rehearsed how we would begin the questioning, if some day he should stop when he spoke to us—or to me, rather, for like everyone else he did not know that Joseph was present. But he never stopped. He turned his marvelous head that seemed to hover over his spare body and the smile widened as he spoke: "Hello, little Red!" (My hair was almost as bright as his.) Then he passed on. That was all, but when he had gone there was a glow of joy within us; the sea of our spirit had risen, and we were happy, Joseph and I.

It was not until he was to leave our church and go to another one, in a distant part of the state, that we discovered the truth about him. My mother and another woman were talking over the news of his transfer. They were sorry to see him go and they were worried about his welfare.

"Who will look after him over there, where he will be the only priest?" my mother said.

"Perhaps he will get a good housekeeper," the other woman said.

"Someone ought to go over there and tell her about him," my mother said. "What will she do if he comes home on a cold night without his overcoat? She ought to keep the worst-looking coat in town in reserve, because that's all he will ever wear. Anything better he will give to the first bum he meets."

"And his shoes," the other woman said. "Can you imagine a man stopping on the street and exchanging his good shoes for an old pair worn by a bum? He's done that often."

"How will the housekeeper get enough money from him to buy food?" my mother said. "He will give it all to the poor."

The other woman sighed. "He's too good for the good of himself," she said. "I've never seen such a priest. He's like the Lord Himself, with his love for the poor. I hope someone looks after him over there."

As we listened to them a feeling of incomparable peace came over us. There was one man in the world who followed the path of Jesus. He gave his money to the poor, and when that was gone he took off his clothes and gave them also. In him the expectation of our identity seemed realized. Joseph and I were both swallowed up in a great wave of affirmation that rolled up from under us. It was like the flood surging up to the Ark. Instantly there was a yearning that seemed strong enough to lift our body—a yearning to go with Father Higgins to the faraway church he was to serve, and there to help him succor the poor, following in the way of Jesus. That was the way to heaven.

Yet I knew that I could not stir from the place in which I had been set. Nor could Joseph. I was too small, and, far from being able to help others, I had myself to be helped, a circumstance which gave me pain and which caused Joseph to disappear from the scene entirely. But the knowledge that such a man lived, and that such a way of life was open, kept warm and hopeful the dreams we now devised, and filled the hour before sleep that was our sanctuary with plans that were sure and certain of success. There was a way back to the place from which we had come. We had discovered it. We would, when the opportunity came, seek to follow it. Meanwhile there was the knowledge of it, and of a man who followed it; and there was, coming suddenly upon us now and then, the benediction of the music from the church nearby the green.

The organist seemed sometimes to be playing for himself, to be filling the loneliness of his exile with memories of the land beyond our life. One melody that he returned to again and again I recognized years later when I heard the drowning melancholy of Tchaikovsky's *Pathetique* symphony. Years later, too, I met the wife of the organist. She was a widow then, and she told me of the man who had been her husband. He was enmeshed in music, she said, enchanted by its magic and convinced that it came to man from the stars, which are watchmen set out in the depths and the night of the soul. He played for the consolation of his spirit, and he played best when the church was empty of people and the door was flung open to let in the listening light of day. It was then that I heard him.

He died, and Father Higgins died. "I knew that was going to happen when he went over there," my mother said. "Pneumonia. I'll bet he gave his overcoat away during that last cold spell. I wonder if he got enough to eat? Probably not."

I was sorry for my own sake that Father Higgins was dead, but for his sake I was glad. He was home again, gone from the stink of sweat and the pressure of food in the belly. Perhaps another like him would come along, and this time I would not be afraid to speak, and we would be friends, he and Joseph and I.

But no one like him ever appeared, and in time the hope of it faded. There was no ally to join our cause in all the world, it seemed. "They must be dead," said Joseph. "We are here by ourselves. You will have to grow up, and then perhaps we will find out what it is you must do. I think it is a sad thing, but I am not sure. I only feel it."

It was a feeling I shared completely. Everything that was not beautiful pressed against me; I could feel it at my temples and against my bowels. As I walked in the streets ugly houses struck out with rays that hunted through me, until everything was in hiding but the agony and shame of their sin against form and grace and aspiration.

The sound of women shouting in anger poured me full of revulsion; the shock pressed every part of me against the broken tar blocks of the street and the blistered paint of the houses. My consciousness of being caught and imprisoned was expanded to the limits of pain, and for Joseph and the spirit that held us up I was bitterly sad.

The grownups were sending me now to the children's Mass, in the basement of the church. It was a dark, low-ceilinged, ominous place, without ornament. The Mass was read quickly, the sermon was brief and condescending. Then the children assembled in groups for Sunday School. The little room in which my class met was bare and almost without illumination. The lessons were simplifications of the gigantic symbolism of the biblical characters from Adam the Arche-type to Jesus the Fulfillment. The stories were presented as being literally true. Their emotional aspects were stressed. The nuns spoke joyously of any devotion or sacrifice which occurred in the narrative. They smiled; their eyes became bright; they closed the Bible history and held it close. The girl students imitated this rapture; they knew all the char-acters and their sacrificial idosyncrasies. The boys were apa-thetic. They stared at the floor, jiggled the marbles in their pockets, and looked unhappy. There was no priest to teach them, to speak of Joseph and Joshua and Samson, to inflame them with the legend of the Grail and the saga of the Cru-sades. The holy men were busy with the Masses upstairs, or were in the rectory eating breakfast.

The oppression which swept over me during this class be-came finally too great to bear. Not only did Joseph and I reject all that we heard; we spat it out. We were filled with a sickness and a loathing for the whole interminable farrago, for the vomitously sentimental adoration of everyone in the the New Testament but Judas and Pilate, for the gross and cowardly fear of God's prettiest displeasures, for the eleva-tion of the warm and human figure of Jesus to an unap-proachable throne at the apex of an icy cosmos. There came a day when the misery of it flooded through our body, and we could not make the body enter the room.

"I will be sick if you make me go in there," it said to us.

I hesitated. Never before had I failed to perform what I had been told to do.

"Let's go outside," Joseph said. "I've had enough, too."

Still I hesitated. Then slowly, as if it were being melted by a warm sun, the feeling of duty slipped away. Strong and sweet with the certainty of goodness the sea of spirit rose in its place. The need to enter the room receded. The need to ever go near it again disappeared. All three of us—the body, Joseph, and I—were lifted and carried out of the damp dungeon of the basement by the power we knew to be our salvation and our grace. We stood outside in the sunlight. We walked down the street, past the Congregational church, where the organ was playing. Squirrels were running across the lawns of the green. Cardinals and red-winged blackbirds flashed through the spaces between the trees. People looked at me with something like tolerance and approval. I could hear in every part of my body the sounds of the morning, and I could smell the virtue and faith of the day. I wanted to say something that rushed up in me from the remnants of my conscience, from the vestiges of the disciplines I had been taught. But I did not dare move my lips for fear people would think I was talking to myself.

"Dear God," I said in my head, "I cannot go there any more. I will find You in some other way."

I was sure that He had Himself directed me away from the spot, but that feeling came, I knew, from the spirit beyond Joseph and me which provided all my dissensions from the dicta of the grownups. And lest it some day prove to be not of the Lord but of Lucifer, I hedged. When that was done I went forward in my joy, making new music in my mind when the sounds of the organ no longer reached me.

There was a strange reaction to my desertion from Sunday School. Nothing happened. No one in my family mentioned it; in the years that followed it was never brought up. None of the other students said anything to me about it. The nun, if she missed me, said nothing to anyone. In that town where the slightest deviation from an intolerable norm was invariably discovered and punished by the lashings of a hundred tongues, my revolt from the catechism and the blood-drenched crucifix went unnoticed and unscorned.

I have never known an adult lay Christian, either Protestant or Catholic, who remembered more than an unrelated phrase or two of his catechism. Twenty years after it was taught me I read the advanced catechism again. I was immersed then in the study of such men as Plotinus, Erigena, Augustine, Aquinas. Still the definitions in the catechism made no sense: the symbology was not clear, the functional terms were obscure, the prose was abominable, and the magnificent logic of man's immersion in the variations of God in order to discover the heart of his Creator was lost in a fuzzy fusing of the damnation complex with a highly sentimental attachment for Jesus. Each generation has its own language, and there may have been a time when people derived enlightenment and inspiration from the text of the catechism. It meant nothing to me, and it seems to have meant little or nothing to most of my contemporaries who at one time or another learned it by rote. I know now what would have inspired me, what would have meant God to me—a lecture on astronomy, or a talk by a physicist versed in the world of the atom. I would have slept at the church door, waiting for him to arrive.

61

But he, like Father Higgins' successor, did not come. I went to church upstairs now, and I attended the late Mass, which was sung, with all the candles lighted and the choir answering the priest. Sometimes there was Benediction, and then the incense, joining the music, brought almost a vision of God. But it was more the product of my feeling that it should happen than any genuine immersion in the psychic stream. That occurred only when I was alone, usually in the time just before sleep. Recapitulation of the day's events was ended; planning for tomorrow was finished. Sleep was only a little way off, moving swiftly over the fields. The emptiness which lay between us had to be filled, or the nausea of life in the world would engulf me. So I pressed hard against my mind and blotted all the pictures from it. Soon music came in their place, music from voices and instruments unnumbered, yet soft and single as an insect's hum. At first it seemed to pour down upon me from heaven; then it came from all about me and from underneath; and it was the trembling of multitudinous strings—strings that held the sun in place and kept the earth moving through its ellipse. "From harmony to heavenly harmony this universal frame began," wrote Dryden, and long before him Pythagoras told his pupils that music, astronomy, and arithmetic were the laws which held the cosmos in its course. It must have been that music I heard in the moments before sleep carried me mercifully from the prison of my senses and lifted up the mind of me—the part which I shared with Joseph—into the faraway spheres where consciousness is multiple and the force of life is swift and subtle in its flight.

When they gave me a violin and I took lessons it was pleasant to stand with the instrument under my chin and play whatever notes came into my head. The great symphonies I heard at night did not come back to me, but other melodies took their place, lonesome and somber voices that seemed like the weeping of a faraway mind. They made me melancholy. The life in me turned inward, reversing its field of motion, like a hurricane rising from a warm and fretful sea to turn against the clock and go off keening through the world, its center quiet as a dead man's heart. The center of me was still squeezing itself together to be far away from the earth. My fingers grew numb, until I could not feel them touch against the strings. Finally I ceased playing and remained without moving; to have twitched an eyelash or wiggled a finger would have brought agony.

The withdrawal of the flood that normally held me pressed against the air let the atmosphere sit heavily upon me. I could not stir; my gaze could not wander. Yet in front of me passed all the forms of living things, and gradually I was farther from them. They became awkward, impractical, hopelessly confused, as I saw them from a greater distance. They were like ants, finally: small, busy, futile. They did not make music, like the wind and the rain and heaven itself; they did not grow blossoms, like the flowers, or turn golden in the autumn, like the leaves of trees. They did not flow through the land, like water, or stand on mountains like the cedars and firs. They did not fly like birds or race like deer. They covered themselves in darkness and dust, shutting their bodies from the light with rough and suffocating clothes. They moved slowly, stumbling on high steps. They stayed away from the hills and the forests; they hid from the rain; they submitted to constant slavery for money that was used to buy ugly things—sharp, shiny pins; pieces of grotesque and uncomfortable furniture; silk dresses that could not be touched by small, dirty hands. And the tragedy which pushed downward on me with the heaviness of lead was that I was to be as they were. The hopelessness of avoiding it was almost too much to bear. My mind turned as numb as my body, and even Joseph paused in his swift prowling.

My melancholy seemed to free him from his chains. With the body quiet and almost without existence, while I filled up with nothingness and misery, Joseph came forth to examine the walls of our prison, to inspect its jailers, and to rage against the impossibility of escape. He pressed his hands against the hills that hemmed in the valley; he leaped up and snatched at the clouds; he buried his face in the dirt and wept. He even looked down on me with suspicion, for I had given in a little to the world.

I had learned to love the taste of a blackberry, crushed and broken in my mouth; I had come to like the perfume of the morning, the taste of sourgrass, the sight of snow turned blue in the twilight. I had fallen before the loveliness of autumn; I yearned to catch the odor of burning leaves, put it in an incense pot, and have it served at Mass. My taste buds filled with lust when my teeth bit into an apple, and I was more than a friend to early plums when they blushed and yearned to be ravished.

In January when the white drifts piled up I stood on the front porch and leaped into them head first, pretending they were water. In spring and summer and autumn, and even in winter when the roads and paths were open, I haunted the hills. There the white birches grew, and the young streams chattered like women. Violets could be found early, and forget-me-nots. In summer there were blackberries, huckleberries, blueberries, and wild strawberries. In autumn there were apples, and the trees had colors like the sounds of music. In winter there was snow, with its lace and chiaroscuro, its lightness and its touch that turned so instantly from coldness to the warm desire that was its ruin. All these I let into my heart, saying to Joseph, "They are our friends." But although he agreed with me he looked restlessly for other things, for elves and fairies and leprechauns, for those who could speak and tell of themselves. "They will know," he said. "They will be able to tell us why we are here and what we are to do and how we can get out." It thrilled me to hear this, and my body shuddered at the last words—get out—and I helped Joseph look for the little people, and for the tall lady fairy he always expected to see tiptoeing past the farthest tree.

We never saw her, or anyone who was not as draped with flesh as were we. But Joseph never gave up hope, and he tried to sustain me in his faith. I wanted to believe, and I tried; Joseph said it was necessary to believe, and he chided me for not looking always, wherever we were, for "our friends."

"They are somewhere, and they will help us," he would say, and then he would fret for them, especially when the world was pressing against us and I was plunged in melancholy, my violin held under my chin.

"I will help you look," I would say, "as soon as I can move."

"No you won't," he would answer. "Your mother will come in and smile at you and run her fingers through your hair and say, 'Guess what I have in the oven?' and you will sniff and say, 'Apple pie,' and forget about me and about our friends."

Then he would give himself up to despair, while I began to rouse and to realize that there truly was an apple pie in the oven, and that Joseph, for all his preoccupation with other things, had smelled it first.

FOUR

THE PROFESSOR looked away politely while Miss Iceberg took my temperature. I was as wet now as it was possible for me to get, and the combined pressure of a set position and a rising fever had forced me into the only physical act of compensation possible. I rolled my head from side to side on the wooden slab that held it.

"You shouldn't do that," Miss Iceberg said. "You'll tire yourself out."

Anything I could have said in answer would have branded me a maniac. I stopped rolling my head and fixed her with what I conceived to be a gentle gaze, though my eyes must have glittered with heat.

"Would you like me to talk instead?" I asked. "I can recite poetry."

She paled slightly, but her hand remained steady.

"You should not talk either," she said. "You must try not to excite yourself. Those are the doctor's orders."

She was beginning to come apart herself, though the outward signs as yet were few—some hairs straggling down her neck, a spot of sweat on her upper lip, a slow retreating of the freshness from her uniform. Inside of her food was moving through her intestines, giving up its useful content, inching along toward the bowels. While my pores gasped and spat, hers breathed easily, soiling her skin without haste.

"Could you talk to me?" I said. "It would save me the labor of thinking. It would be restful, and I might learn something."

She bent over the chart, not bothering to answer. My head, of its own volition, began moving again, rolling from side to side. The fever was mounting toward its goal.

"Let the woman be," the Professor said irritably. "We have things to discuss. If she were a man you would pay

65

no attention—such a mind and personality would not interest you. But because there are lumps of fat in odd places on her body, more water in her blood than there is in yours, and a charge of negative something or other in her that titillates certain positive antennae in your aura, you waste precious time gazing at her curious shape, inventing fatuous remarks and hoping like the fool you are that the negative charge will reach out and envelop you."

"How many times have I said that to myself!" I answered. "How many times have I turned resolutely away, only to waste twice as much time later on. Each man seems to have his quota set, and he fills it sooner or later."

"Oh, it's more a nuisance than a curse," the Professor said. "Actually there is nothing else in the world that will really soothe a man's nerves. Without female companionship he becomes either useless or dangerous, unless he has embraced the spiritual life—that seems to provide a negative, or female charge in itself, that keeps the balance.

"But have you considered this aspect of the positive-negative arrangement in marriage? Probably not, since you are still too young to experience it. I was reminded of it when you mentioned the apathy that seemed to exist between the married people of your town.

"That apathy is common to most marriages, and it results, I think, from a partial neutralization of the separate charges. So far as the physical appetites are concerned they remain constant; regularly they are drained off and by natural processes they build back again. But the masters of these appetites—the emotions, tastes, weaknesses, and eccentricities of the participating personalities, they do not rise and fall and return fresh and eager for each new experience. They play against each other constantly, at a higher, less material rate of vibration. Actually, they have no fleshly center, no particular anatomical organs through which they express themselves. Yet when they are engaged in mock combat as a preliminary to the more violent sexual encounter, they seem a part of the basic physical pattern, a reflection of it, and therefore as reliable as the pattern itself.

"But the personality actually is part of another pattern, and is concerned mainly with another problem. Thus the courtship, which is a long preliminary to the mystical consummation, is not a true indication of the condition that will prevail in the marriage. Then the personalities will, while living in conditions of intimacy, pursue their main objectives. The role of assistant to Eros will be dropped, except as the drama is by common consent renewed."

Why is he bothering with this elementary background, I thought? Who does not know it? It has been the basis of comedy since Adam complained that the second apple didn't taste like the first. Man's positive charge is equally attracted to all women; woman's negative charge is attracted equally to all men. The negative in man, the positive in woman, causes the interplay of personality. The woman in man chooses his wife for him; the man in woman chooses her husband for her.

"This brings about the ordinary disillusion of marriage," the Professor went on. "The participating personalities find themselves, when pursuing their separate objectives, not related in the harmony which marked the interplay of courtship. It is popular in this country to suppose that the woman yearns for the overtures of intercourse to continue indefinitely. Elsewhere it is legendary that the man, tired of jousting with an opponent whose every move he knows in advance, looks for fresh opposition. It is not the outcome he wishes to change, since after a certain point that is without thought or plan, and therefore invariable. It is the preliminary duel of personalities he wishes to vary by the delight of a new antagonist.

"It is not an illusion, this difference of tension and joy between the play of familiar and unfamiliar personalities. While the familiar personalities pursue their separate objectives, remaining in the everyday intimacy of marriage, some of the negative charge of the female rubs off on the male. They become somewhat neutralized with regard to each other, and if the rubbing is constant and aggravated, there is repulsion one from another."

"Science at last agrees that familiarity breeds contempt," I said. "What you mean is that in sex the approach can be varied infinitely, but the angle is always the same. Remove the infinite variation of approach by stabilizing the participants and there is nothing left but the angle. The music is gone. Dancing is awkward and self-conscious."

"Precisely, except that there is more indifference than contempt, more neutralization than repulsion. The men and women of your town were all eager for the thrill of dalliance, yet they had lost the power to play with each other. They

67

did not know that the power was lost; each believed it purposely was suppressed by the other personality involved, and that therefore within himself or herself it was frustrated, left not only without an opponent but without the possibility of one, since divorce was unthinkable. So each blamed the other and dreamed foolish and impossible dreams of courtship with princes and princesses, actors and actresses, soldiers and dancing girls."

He sighed.

"It is precisely at that point, according to metaphysics," I said, "that the higher purpose of marriage begins. The preliminary phase is purposely abrasive. It is a discipline, a novitiate. If the participants have a single and understanding view of the spiritual, if they properly grasp the destiny of their souls and the implications of their abundant sexual power, they will derive a freshening of the positive and negative forces of their personalities and will substitute for the preliminary play of their personalities a combined dalliance with their mutual destiny, which is also the destiny of mankind."

"Very pretty," said the Professor. "What does it mean, celibacy?"

"A preparation for the time when celibacy will be forced upon them," I said, "first by the retreat of their physical powers, then by the retreat of the physical shell itself. Actually, spiritual understanding on the part of a husband and wife intensifies and expands the meaning and the pleasure of the sexual act. It gives it an end beyond itself, it imparts a symbology that translates for them—imperfectly at first, but with increasing depth and clarity—the possibilities which lie beyond the present pattern, in the less dense spheres of existence, where the driving force of sex is completely identified with mind, and where the soul which holds them both spans all creation."

"In which case," said the Professor, "sex is no longer sex, but the force of life itself. Sex in the earth is only the medium through which the life force is channeled. The overabundance of it in man is what drives him forward in evolution. If he mated in season, as does the rest of nature, he would still be living in trees." He sighed again. "So little of the surplus is used to good purpose; there are a few geniuses, saints, and servants of humanity. So much time and money is expended devising means of using up the surplus in harmless but entertaining ways. Here indeed is one point on which you convince me. Sex is the weapon of our liberation, yet we employ it to enslave ourselves. Our art, our literature, our work, our play—they are one long aphrodisiac, self-devised, self-administered, drearily unsatisfactory."

He sighed again. "Yet I cannot believe that your theory of the spiritual purposes of life, though it agrees with the moral nature of evolution, is anything but a convenient and high-sounding dream."

"You are on dangerous ground," I said. "No one has been able to prove that dream life is any less real than waking life. It lacks sensory perception, but it has expanded consciousness and is free of time. Have you read Dunne's *An Experiment in Time?* He kept a record of his dreams for twenty-five years. He found many of them to be prophetic, or clairvoyant. But the remarkable thing is that they showed an equal concern with the past, the present, and the future. Time as we know it seemed not to concern them at all."

"Highly unscientific," said the Professor, "recording his own dreams."

"Nonsense," I said. "Who else would submit to such an experiment? But let me tell you this, though it is evidence only for some of the superficial qualities of dreams, all of them long ago proved.

"The magazine for which I write recently sponsored a contest to discover how common is the experience of the unusual and prophetic in dreams. Hundreds of accounts were submitted. I examined all of them. Each, I discovered, fell into one of three categories, and these categories applied to the past, the present, and the future.

"The first category, applying to the past, was filled with dreams in which lost objects were seen in the places where they had been dropped, hidden, or stowed away. When the dreamer awakened and went to the spot the article was there."

"Naturally," said the Professor. "When it wasn't there the dream was forgotten. Only the successful ones were reported to you. However, I grant that the unconscious can help the conscious in matters of memory. The location of the misplaced articles was only forgotten; it was not unknown."

"Good enough. There is no need to argue the point. The second category, concerned with the present, was filled with testimony of this sort: the dreamer saw clearly either death or great danger approaching a friend or loved one, usually when the person endangered was separated physically from the dreamer by a considerable distance in space."

"And the danger was real or the death actual," said the Professor. "Moreover, the time proved to be right—the dream and the danger or death occurred at the same hour. That is telepathy; it seems to happen naturally between people who are emotionally attached, or who are deeply sympathetic. Go on."

"The third category, having to do with the future, contained dreams in which coming events were revealed to the dreamer—trivial, tragic, important, joyous, but always personal events. They were very much of the type gathered by Dunne."

The Professor was thoughtful, ticking softly while he gazed at Miss Iceberg. For a moment I thought he was watching the rise and fall of her bosom, a movement which for the first hours had been hidden from us by the stiff, fresh set of her uniform. Slowly, steadily, the cloth had softened and molded itself to the flesh, until now the two moved together. Miss Iceberg was beginning to look like a woman.

But the Professor was thinking of something different and farther away—my welfare, and how it might be stimulated and made more real.

"Let us be practical for a little while," he said. "There is a science of dreams. It is new and doubtless imperfect, but it has helped many people. The original theory of Freud has been altered by modern psychoanalysts. The statement that all our troubles stem from sex is probably right in the sense that the sex force is also the life force. All our troubles spring from the fact that we are alive, and our aliveness is directly related to the sex force, of which the feelings and activities we ascribe to the world are but a part. Freud mistook the part for the whole."

The vision of a play on words streaked through my mind, accompanied by the picture of a poolroom, the sound of the cue ball sharply striking its object, and the noise of men's laughter, quick on the upswing. I fought back the pun and listened.

"Do you recall," said the Professor, "any dreams which might be helpful to us? Was the childhood you have described to me troubled by any recurrent dream? Or have you, in maturity, been bothered by any dream about your childhood?"

There was no way out of it. We were going to talk of dreams in the scientific manner; dreams of frustration, dreams of pain and fright, dreams of hushed desires. The Professor was a modernist; for him knowledge of the subject began with Freud, *circa* 1909. Of what use would it be to remind him of Hippocrates, who said, "In dreams are seen the nutriments which are good for the body"; or to tell him of Aristotle, Galen, Aretaeus, Cicero, Avicenna, Ficino, Janitsch, Kerner, Puysegur, Schopenhauer, DuPrel, and others who had found what Hippocrates said to be true and set down evidence for it?

DuPrel had written: "When in the year 1831 the professional Commission, which had been engaged in its investigation since its appointment several years before, caused its Report, confirming all the substantial phenomena attributed to somnambulism, to be read in the Medical Academy of Paris, the deep silence of the assembly betrayed the disturbance of their minds. Then, when as usual it was proposed that this report should be printed, the Academician, Castel, rose and protested against the printing of it, *because if the facts were true, half of our physiological science would be destroyed.*"

DuPrel also wrote, at the conclusion of his essay, "Dream a Physician": "There are sceptics who do not indeed deny the facts of somnambulism; but disparage their value because they are of a morbid nature . . . but they are only morbid in regard to the exciting cause and for the Person of the external consciousness, not at all in regard to their transcendental content; and this scruple cannot better be removed than by the proof that dream is a physician, that the transcendental Person is the physician of the empirical Person . . . our normal self-consciousness does not exhaust its object, our Self—it comprehends only one of the two Persons of our Subject. Man is a monistic double-being—monistic as Subject, dualistic as Person. The contention of monists and dualists is thus resolved by comprisal of alternatives."

And further on in *The Philosophy of Mysticism* DuPrel wrote: "We are not temporally and spatially divided from that beyond, are not first transposed there by death, but are already rooted therein, and what divided us therefrom is merely the subjective barrier of the threshold of sensibility. This threshold thus limits consciousness and therewith self-consciousness . . . were our five senses to be suddenly taken away, and senses of entirely different kind given to us, though standing on the same spot we should believe ourselves inhabitants of another star."

The vision flooded out before me—blinding streams of involution, cunning and intricate labyrinths of differentiation, then the sickening lurch of the soul thrown into consciousness of itself, alone and unguided, creeping through the wonders of creation, working its way toward a home at first remembered certainly and seeming near, then half-forgotten, set in a faraway place beyond attainment, and finally dismissed as a folk tale, a myth, a legend, the compensation of a frustrated desire.

Now the Professor waited for my answer.

"No," I said. "There were dreams in my childhood, but none of them plagued me, none was a frequent visitor. I never had nightmares, I slept alone. No one was overfond of me; no one neglected or persecuted me. I have no bitter memories."

"Except those which concern the church," he interjected.

"They have been absorbed into a larger problem; they affect everyone, not me in particular. Religion in our civilization is in a state of transition; apparently it is moribund, but actually this is a condition of passivity, or negation, which is necessary before the heavy charge of fresh, positive life can be received. I am concerned that this state of passivity, or negation, will cause the church through habit and pride to refuse entrance to the power which will come to quicken it, like an old maid who, too long trained in virtue, turns away a prospective lover without emotion or consideration, through an automatic impulse."

The Professor nodded. "If we continue to state our predicament we may arrive at a definition of it which will suggest a solution.

"Now it is also true that you believe this quickening power is already here, and that it is being rejected—that a fusion of theology and modern science would clarify both subjects in the mind of the average man and energize him with an enthusiasm which would result in a new Age of Faith."

"That is so," I said. "It involves many things which seem difficult, especially to lazy, complacent men. Men with great minds would have to consecrate themselves to the task of synthesis and fusion, and the church would have to embark on a program of enlightened teaching, aimed particularly at adults and conducted in the classroom, not promulgated from the pulpit. Thus would theology, philosophy, and metaphysics rise from their graves and once more walk abroad with common men."

"Hallelujah!" the Professor cried. "Science through modern physics has made the universe mystical. Matter is no longer real, no longer material; it is electricity, waves, energy, vibration. Form and solidity are patterns of wave length and vibratory rate. Eddington says that spirit is the sea and the waves are matter. It is kismet, it is victory, it is Q.E.D., eh?"

"Excellent metaphysics," I said coldly.

"Of course, theology is ninety per cent speculation and ten per cent inspiration—call it revelation, if you like," he went on. "In my opinion one is only an intensification of the other. Also, theology has been ravished now and then by both expedience and politics. Science is exact. Your students will find that the two disagree in many details. But if they are true men, and they recognize that basically the two studies rest on identical truths, they will resolve the differences. That is your hope, isn't it?"

"It is; and my worry is that no one is about this business. I fear that the new and quickening power, refused and frustrated, eventually will explode and destroy the church in order to make way for itself, in which case it will feel impelled to deny a great deal that is good in the church in order to point up the final evil which brought about its destruction."

"The old case of throwing out the baby with the bath," the Professor said. "But why is it that you do not have dreams of anxiety in connection with this concern of yours? Is there no recurrent dream whose events might suggest such a fear?"

"None that I recall. But before we consider the possibility further let us consider what we mean by dreams and symbols. There are all kinds of dreams and all kinds of symbols. There are symbologies common to all men; there is a symbology peculiar to each individual. Apparently we dream whenever

73

we are not awake; we observe ourselves falling into it as we go to sleep; we are conscious of being lifted out of it as we come awake. But what is dreaming, and what does it mean? I would like to go into this matter, if you have time."

"I *am* time," said the Professor. "I am the reflection of eternity, the mortal ghost of God."

"Then let us begin with what is common to both of us —our Creator, Who is called God. And for this discussion let us dispense with opinion and argument, confining ourselves wherever possible to accepted ideas and undisputed evidence."

The Professor chuckled. "I wonder how far we will get, talking of God and not arguing. Proceed."

"There is first the Godhead, the realm of spirit which is unknowable and which cannot be comprehended in any way. In the Jewish Cabala it is called Ain Soph. In other religions it is the Essence, the Absolute, the Unmanifested, etc. It represents a line of demarcation beyond which man's imagination admits it cannot go. From this Essence came, in some fashion, God. This is also an intellectual convenience, a limitation for the support of reason, like the zero in mathematics. It is a paradox, obviously, since it provides a starting point for a Being Who is considered eternal.

"The Cabala represents Ain Soph as a circle and God as the center, He being the Individuality into which the divine Essence withdrew in order to manifest itself. This provides for God in both His aspects, as an Individual and as a Creator. He is Himself as unknowable as the essence of which He is an expression. We are still marking off limits, drawing a chessboard on which our reason and intellect can move. For as Aquinas says, it is by our reason and intellect that we understand God.

"The Creator's first need was an Agent. Therefore He created the Word, the Image, the Son, the Archetypal Man, the Pleroma, the first Adam, the Atman, the Christ, Osiris, Balder, Dionysius, Oannes, Zoroaster, the Demiurge, the Grand Man of the Zohar—the multipilicity of titles alone indicates how common is this idea in religion. It is the first form of divinity on which the reason and intellect can get a grip. See how it is seized upon by the philosophers—

"Says Thomas Aquinas: 'Now *word* is taken strictly in God, as signifying the concept of the intellect.' Hence Augus-

74

tine says: 'Whoever can understand the word, not only before it is sounded, but also before thought has clothed it with imaginary sound, can already see some likeness of that Word of Whom it is said: In the beginning was the Word.

" 'Word expresses relation to creatures. For God, by knowing Himself, knows every creature. Now the word conceived in the mind is representative of everything that is actually understood. Hence there are in ourselves different words for the different things which we understand. But because God, by one act, understands Himself and all things, His one only Word is expressive not only of the Father, but of all creatures.'

"Says John Scotus Erigena, the Irishman who lived at the court of Charles the Bald and passed his time teaching and writing theology under the sponsorship of Charlemagne's son: 'These Ideas (i.e. the eternal archetypes of things), which are the first causes of individual existences, are contained in the Divine Wisdom or the Divine Word, the only-begotten Son of the Father. Under the influence of the Holy Ghost (or the fostering divine love) they unfold their effects, which are the created objects, or the external world.'

"Says Plotinus, the intellectual father of Augustine: 'Particular souls, by reason of what they have in common, can only be understood as derived from a General Soul which is their cause, but is not identical with all or any of them . . . containing as identical with its own nature the eternal ideas of all the forms, general and particular, that become explicit in the things of time and space.'

"Says the Zohar, one of the books of the Cabala: 'The Spiritual Man is both the import and the highest degree of creation . . . as soon as the Man was created, everything was complete . . . for everything is comprised in the Man. He unites in himself all the forms.'

"Says a writer on Hinduism and Buddhism: 'It is taught (in the Upanishads) that the Atman created the universe and then entered into it as soul. . . . It is the Atman who alone exists and creates the universe.'

"Says a modern theologian, Dean Inge: 'In reference to the world, Christ is the Agent in creation.' He also says, 'Christ is the ideal, representative man, the archetype of the race, as Adam is the concrete, imperfect copy of the arche-type.' "

"Enough!" cried the Professor. "I am instructed; I am taught; I am convinced. Proceed."

"The Archetypal Man spans creation, bringing about form and substance by limiting Himself. This happens first on the celestial plane, then on the spiritual plane, then on the mental plane, and finally on the emotional and physical planes.

"We can comprehend this with a fair amount of clarity if we recall that of this macrocosm we are the microcosm, a reflection in miniature. Our life force is the Essence; our individuality, which is both we and that from which we proceed, corresponds to God. Our intellect is the agent of our individuality, spanning creation as we comprehend it, expressing itself in form and substance by limiting itself, by concentrating on the manifestation of ideas.

"Finally, it is immersed in less mental, more concrete forms of thought. It is imprisoned in them and sacrificed for them. Its task is to raise these lower forms to a higher state, thus aiding in evolution while also developing and bringing to completion an image or reflection or portion of the Archetypal Man, distinguished thereafter by the memory of its separate journey through creation. Plotinus says, 'When he (the Soul) shall have crossed over as the image to its Archetype, then he will have reached his journey's end.' Meister Eckhart says, 'Between the Soul and the only-begotten Son there is no distinction; for what the Son reveals to us is just this, that we are the same Son.'

"Thus we have involution and evolution. The descent of spirit into matter is the sacrifice of the Archetypal Man. He involves himself in the limitations He has brought about in creation. He 'sheds His blood' by taking upon Himself the task of human consciousness—an image of Himself given a free will, placed in the uttermost reaches of creation, and allowed to roam. When incarnation takes place the process of involution is completed and the process of evolution begins. Here the blood of Christ—His image imprisoned in consciousness and gradually discovered there—takes away all sin, and another soul is exalted to union with Christ and companionship with God."

The Professor nodded. "I see, I see," he said. "You wish to establish the geography of the mind, so that we can ascertain where dreams might come from, or where, if you wish to put it that way, they are. We are constantly running into that obstruction of place when there actually is no place, or time when there actually is no time."

"That puts you out of existence," I said.

He waved a hand. "My archetype remains. Now in this matter of the continuity of the mind, what are we to consider? Archetypes are well known and have an honorable history—they are the ideas in the spiritual world from which the forms and patterns in the material world proceed. They have come down from Plato to Dr. Jung, the psychoanalyst, with hardly a dissenting voice. The subconscious mind should be a reflection of an archetype. There should be racial memories, also. But excuse me; I have taken over your task. Proceed."

"If we were created by God, or by Him through His Agent," I said, "then we are contained in Him, and our consciousness reaches back to Him, just as it goes forward to Him in the matter of the soul's destiny. Since it was at the foundation of the world that the soul began its journey as an individual, saying goodbye to its participation in omniscience, it is the record of this journey which is won back as the mists clear and the image of the Archetypal Man emerges, to draw us on and enlarge our understanding."

The Professor regarded me. My head was tossing back and forth on the wooden slab. Miss Iceberg, after her most recent quest in search of my temperature, had reduced the voltage on the diathermy machine. That meant that I was past 106 degrees, coasting toward the goal of 107. It was almost noon.

"Are we not voyaging somewhat afar in search of what may be found close at home?" the Professor asked. "Dreams are the habitat of mystical experience, and for those who believe in the survival of consciousness they provide an indication of what that state is apt to be like. But to study the dreams of an average person it is not necessary to suppose we are dealing with a stream of consciousness which stretches back through eternity to the First Cause."

"I believe that it is necessary to thus suppose," I said. "In fact, sir, unless all philosophy, all theology, and all revelation are to be judged as false, it is obligatory. You have yourself written stories; at least you have invented tales and told them

77

to your children. Those tales had heroes and villains—Jimmy Cottontail and Harry Fox, for instance."

"Heavens, no!" said the Professor. "My stories were all about a little dog named Frowsy."

"Then consider Frowsy," I said. "At first he was mostly you. His personality had to be guided by you in its every move. There was little more to begin with than a name and the mental picture of a dog. Little by little, as you invented adventures for him, Frowsy began to have a life of his own. Before long he was leading a completely separate existence, so that what he did was as much a surprise to you as it was to the children. Then he began to infect your own personality. Little by little you became Frowsy."

The Professor looked sheepish. "Oh, come," he said. "Let us not descend to explaining God by supposing that He does things as we do. Perhaps it is true that we are the microcosm and He the macrocosm—or, as you will perhaps insist, His Agent is the macrocosm. The parallels are apt and ready: our body is like the material cosmos, our minds are like the Agent of creation, our life force is from the sea of spirit which is God. But who made these comparisons? Man. I have not heard God speak a word."

"He is a personal experience for everyone," I admitted. "Until you have gone back in your own mind far enough to see, trailing toward infinity, the fiery trail of yourself, you will not believe the testimony of any who have made the journey. That is what it means to be without faith.

"To have too much faith is also detrimental; there is then no urge to seek proof of what is believed."

I was silent, looking at Miss Iceberg, who was crumpling under the heat that came from my coffin and yielding to the impact of the Professor's steady movements.

"Oh, go ahead," he said. "I realize it is all speculation. Even the most basic knowledge is conditional."

"That is because we are in a conditioned environment," I said. "For evidence let me present some scientific facts. Consider our knowledge from the standpoint of size, or physical magnitude. When physicists began to study the world of the atom—which is, in size, as our world is to the universe—they found that the normal laws of measurement, motion, etc., no longer worked. In the atomic world different laws were in power. When astronomers studied the other extreme of size they found the same condition. In the outward reaches of space, where the stars are like pollen in the wind, other laws, strange and incomprehensible, are enthroned.

"The knowledge we have found, then, is only true for our environment, for this peculiar condition, sensorily perceived, poised midway in size between the satellites of the atom and the archangels of God.

"The microscope and the telescope, reaching downward and upward into these worlds—though the most powerful microscope has yet to see an atom—discovered for us this limitation of our knowledge. Likewise sleep, which frees consciousness from the sensory environment, reaches into spheres beyond our own, where other laws are in force, and where the reason of our world seems unreason.

"The logic of dreams has been discovered and dismissed as nonsense as often in history as wise men have occurred and been followed by fools. The list of those who have pointed out that in sleep the mind is enlarged and freed from time reads like a roll of the world's great men. Yet even today, when the great mass of earthbound mentalities has been offered a theory of dream logic suited to the limits of its imagination, with the line of continuity drawn sharply at birth, it disbelieves.

"Every philosopher expounds his conclusion; every theologian treasures his certainty; every metaphysician sets forth his syllogism; every man selects his opinion."

"And is entitled to do so," said the Professor. "He doesn't know anything about God but he knows what he likes."

He laughed, and I joined him. Miss Iceberg looked at me and quickly rose, gripping the handle of the water pitcher. We watched her while she poured me a drink.

"Tell me," I said to her. "Are you a monist or a dualist, a Thomist or a Scotist, a Spencerian or a Kantian? Are Plato's writings a revelation of the Pyramid Initiation? Was Apollinaris right? Did the Essenes hide something from Josephus, or did Josephus hide something from his readers? Is the *Pistis Sophia* a revelation or just metaphysical symbology? Why is Plotinus so difficult to translate? Did the Atlanteans discover the secret of atomic power and destroy their continent by its misuse? Did John write his gospel or dictate it to his grandson? Do you consider the phallicism of baseball a coincidence or the reflection of a subarchetype?"

She put down the water pitcher and left the room. I heard her walking through the basement, calling for Miss Yellowhead. The Professor and I laughed again. Then he looked at me with friendly, thoughtful eyes.

"How persistently we labor at the secret of our identity," he said. "Yet so long as each is a different spark of consciousness, illumination must be personal and there can be no single light for all. That will only come as we grow together, as our separate sparks become a single fire."

He sighed and dropped his arms a little. I thought he looked wistful, even sad.

"Perhaps we should ask Joseph," he said, forcing a smile. "He ought to know. Come, Joseph, tell us the answer. What is the sleep mind?"

Down the corridor I heard Miss Iceberg returning. Someone was with her. She was fetching Miss Yellowhead.

"Joseph is not here," I said to the Professor. "That is what is wrong with me. He is gone away."

FIVE

THERE must have been a time when I learned to read, tracing letters in a child's book, but I do not recall it. I remember standing once by my desk in the second grade room, holding a book and staring at a word which I could not pronounce. "Try it," said the teacher. I said nothing. I was afraid to say what was in my mind; I knew it was wrong. "You will stand there until you pronounce it," the teacher said. She was redheaded and Irish, with a small nose and freckles.

The word was "hour" and I did not know what to do with the *h*. But I knew the meaning of the word, and the meaning pressed against me heavily as I stood, squeezing my fingers against the book, gazing at the *h*. All around me quiet moved like a tide, lapping at the edges of my consciousness, moving up the beaches of my mind. I heard the clock on the wall ticking, and from outside came the sound of sparrows chattering and the noise of young leaves rustling in the spring wind. Suddenly in a panic Joseph was pulling at me to go out into the quickening, seed-laden air, to leave our body standing at the desk, dumb, untended, and alone. Joseph never came to school except to take me away from it. He hated the system of education which was bound to teach me, so he said, nothing but the technique of being a slave. After education came work, as everyone knew. What good was a thing which resulted in evil?

The presence of Joseph nearly made me ill. The struggle between what he wanted me to do and what I was being forced to do took place in the middle of my stomach. There was only one way to end it. Forcing my lips open I spoke.

"Whore," I said.

"Sit down!" the teacher said.

She struck her book shut and her face turned red. The children giggled, though they did not know any more than I did what was wrong. I had mispronounced the word "hour," that was all.

"You are dismissed for the remainder of the afternoon," the teacher said, and outside the school I was a hero. That was New England in 1913.

There must have been books before and after that, books that were read to me, books that I deciphered myself, conjuring with words and phrases. I do not remember them. In the attic there were stacks of magazines; on rainy days I learned from them of the world beyond the hills that bound our valley, the world of jungles and cattle ranges, deserts and walled cities, tree-dwellers of the African forests, Aztec ruins and Tibetan lamaseries, British colonies, French winemakers, Dutch tea plantations. There were books, too; once I fell asleep with my head on Stanley's *Heroes of the Dark Continent,* opened to the picture of Victoria Falls. My mother came and gently removed it, putting a pillow in its place.

But in my memory the oldest page whose words I still can read is a sheet of the *Naugatuck Daily News,* and the scene surrounding it is as fresh today as when first it passed before me on the skein of time and space. I was sitting in the kitchen of our home, in the rocking chair which my mother used when she nursed the babies, and which my father used when he smoked his pipe. Supper was finished. My mother

81

and my sister were doing the dishes. I could hear them behind me, the sôft even steps of my sister, the sound of a piece of silver dropping in the drawer, the slosh of water. The electric light had been turned on. Outside night had gathered. It was June.

I had read a story which said that P. H. Daly, a local grocer, was slightly injured when his horse, frightened by an automobile, reared and ran away. Below it was a headline which said, "Sun Breaks Speed Laws. Goes 180 Miles a Second, Scientist Says." I read the story. It was the report of a lecture on astronomy, delivered by a visiting college professor. In my memory his name and the name of his school are blurred. What he said is not.

The earth revolves around the sun and rotates on its axis, he had informed his audience, and it also moves with the sun around the center of gravity of the Milky Way, the particular galaxy of which it and its satellites are a part—a very small part, since there are approximately a hundred million suns in the galaxy. All of them are moving in a spiral path around the center of gravity, those toward the center proceeding more rapidly, those at the edge ambling at reduced speed. Our sun, about a third of the way from the center, travels at 180 miles a second. The entire journey of all the suns around the center of their universe is completed in two hundred million years. That is the length of a Milky Way year.

But the Milky Way is only one spiral nebula, one universe, one galaxy. There are hundreds of thousands more of them, perhaps millions, breaking out from some unknown center toward a horizon no man can calculate. The earth is a minor planet of a small sun in a single universe, a planet traveling 580,000,000 miles a year at the rate of a thousand miles a minute. Its sun has a surface temperature of between five and seven thousand degrees centigrade. There are hotter stars, and bigger ones. Betelegeuse has a diameter three hundred times that of this minor sun. There are dark stars, dead and buried in the cold night of eternity. There are stars not yet born, forming in the cosmic womb from the primitive matter of creation. In such a plan time is not a system of measurement; it is a canvas on which creation paints the story of life.

I came to the last paragraph of the report. When the lecture was finished refreshments were served. Mrs. Mortimer Quirke was in charge of arrangements. That was all. I looked up and saw my mother moving through the rooms. My sister was playing the piano. I heard the kitchen clock ticking; five minutes had gone by. But that was in a time which no longer had any connection with me. In my personal world aeons had passed. I had revolved around the center of a universe, struck a large star, and been hurled into the stream of a new and greater galaxy.

Everything was quiet. The gleam of the electric light bulb grew feeble; the chairs, the table, the stove looked battered and discouraged; my mother's step on the stair was slow; the notes of the piano fell dead where they were struck. There was almost nothing of me in the room, and what was there was suffocating; Joseph had almost pulled me from my body. I got up from the chair and walked quietly to the screen door. On the porch I leaped from the top step, cleared the pavement, and landed on the lawn. Then I ran down the lane by the garden to the back fence. There was a tall pole there which anchored the clothesline. I stood on top of the fence and hugged it, looking upward to the sky.

There it was—creation, a great shout of God crying through the darkness—streams of stars pouring out through space like water from the hills flooding meadows in spring. That was where we belonged, Joseph and I; that was the place from which we had come. But how? By what accident? And why? I asked Joseph but he did not know. He was as gagged and bound by the body as was I, though he apparently was less attached to it, and it seemed at that moment that if the body were not between us, holding us apart, he could lift me up to the stars and the roaring winds of space. I understood, or I seemed to understand as I hugged the pole and braced my feet on the fence, that Joseph lay on the other side of my body, around the corner from my senses, and that while it was my task to learn the earth it was his duty to remember heaven. If only I could reach him, or he could reach me! I was part of him, but shut away, locked up in a thing which had only fingers and eyes and ears for senses, while he had the wind and the clouds and lightning by which to know things, and heaven for a home.

There could only be one way to know that heaven. I would have to be in it, become it, dwell all over it at once, as I did with a song when I played it on my violin. Joseph had once been in heaven, and I had been with him—or had I? Was I something ancient, a wanderer of the skies fallen here like a meteor, imprisoned for having lost my direction, or for a sin? Or was I something new, a finger put out by an investigating spirit, poking around in the dirt, looking for worms.

I didn't know, and I cared to know all that I was, all that was Joseph, and all that was the body between us; for now I knew that the body did not hold us both, trapping us together, but kept us apart, separating one from the other. I was on the side toward the earth, Joseph was on the side toward heaven, where lived the spirit which held us both, and which had fashioned the flesh between. Sometimes Joseph came to the window of my cell and whispered to me, pleading with me to go away with him. Sometimes I went to the window to look for him and found he was not there. Sometimes he came in great excitement to reach through the bars and try forcibly to pull me out. But he could not. The cell was strong and tightly sealed. It would take all the power of heaven to set me free, and since it was the power of heaven which had put me in it I could not expect to be liberated.

There came upon me then so great a melancholy that tears like rain raced down my cheeks. With a hard fist I wiped my eyes to keep the stars in view. I did not know their names or their magnitudes or their constellations, but they were the dearest friends I had and I wanted them as my body wanted breath. I wanted to leap free from the pole and the fence and the body which clung to them and spin upward in ecstasy, growing wider as I came nearer the stars, so that when they were close the arms of my being would hold them and they would flame and blaze inside of me. For this I tried to weep myself away.

But in the end the tears stopped and I still was there, standing on the fence with my arms around the pole; and the stars that streamed through space like thought, seething and spitting worlds from their lips, were all so far away that every one seemed cold and still. Was God so far from me as that?

I got down from the fence and walked back past the garden, where peas and beans and corn were growing in the night and where, because my father liked his garden, peanuts and sweet potatoes were busy in the ground and sunflowers were sprouting from it. I went to the flower garden and stood by the roses, waiting for my eyes to heal their redness. At the foot of the rose bushes strawberries grew and were ripe. I fumbled in the dark, picked a few, and put them in my mouth. The wild, stinging taste, sucked from the ground and mixed in the sun, gave me comfort. At least a few things in the world were good.

"Everything in the world is good," said Joiseph, and suddenly I was aware of him, still near me, still lyric and singing. "Why are you happy?" I said. "There is nothing to look forward to but a miserable long life, hard work, sickness, old age, and in the end no teeth and probably nothing to eat."

"I am happy because we are closer together, now that you have discovered the stars, and whenever we want to be together we need only look at them. You have been seeking a church. There it is—the sky. Watch it at night, and you will be lifted up to God, and I will be lifted up with you."

"I thought you were already there," I said, reaching for more strawberries.

"I cannot return until I take you with me," he said. "Every time you raise your eyes to heaven it will help."

"Why can't you show me the way and we'll go now?" I said.

"Because we cannot go back the way we came," he said. "There is another way, through the earth. You can smell it in the rain. You can taste it in strawberries. Your job is to find it and lead us to it."

I went to the cherry tree and sat down on the bench. So that was it. I had been turned away from the heaven and told to find my way back by another road. The tears returned, but gently. There was no use now in tiring myself with anger or desire. The journey would be long and I would need my strength. A little cry would be enough, a funeral for my innocence. When it was finished I felt better. I went back and picked some more strawberries. I looked up at the stars again. It was good to know where I was and what I was here to do. How I was to do it I did not know, but neither, apparently, did anyone else. At least I had Joseph to help me. He remembered what heaven was like, and when I found anything on earth which resembled it he would tell me. He would tremble with joy and seize me in his arms, just as he trembled with fear and tried to carry me away when things that were wrong came near. I could trust him. I could trust the stars. I could trust the taste of strawberries.

There my memory closes the night, with a strawberry in my mouth and a mixture of wonder and desolation in myself. I knew at last who I was and what business I was about, and it filled me with joy to know it and to see it in the heavens. I had come from God. He knew me. I had seen Him once. That was the soul of me. But my heart lagged to feel how far my home was now from the place where He stood, flinging constellations through the sky.

After that there are many pages I can read, pages of books which lie open on the dark shiny surface of a corner table in the local public library, the farthest table from the Old Man. The Old Man always sat at the table nearest the door, and he never did anything except read the *Waterbury Republican* and glare at anyone under twenty-one who entered the reading room. He wore spectacles, and behind them his eyes were like whips. The doors of the library were very heavy; they gave reluctantly; it was impossible to slip in without being noticed. As the aperture widened the Old Man's gaze came up from the newspaper and fastened on whoever was forcing the entrance. If it was an adult he went back to his reading. If it was a child he turned his stare into a long sword that pricked a thousand wounds in the youngster as he crossed the floor to the shelves. At the stacks the Old Man's eyes turned his victim over to the librarians, all females and all gentle, and returned to the editorials attacking Wilson. When a child entered the reading room the Old Man turned in his chair and watched until the little wretch had chosen his book and was seated. Then he turned back to his table, looking up now and then to make sure the child had not moved. I thought he was the head librarian. Years later I found out he was the janitor.

The day after I discovered the stars I went to the library and entered the reading room. I had wanted to go in there for a long time but the Old Man had scared me away. This time my determination and his scrutiny struck a compromise. I went straight to the farthest table from him, reached blindly to the shelf above, took down the first book my hand touched and sat down. I opened it without looking at the title and began to read. It was the first volume of an encyclopedia and I was in the middle of the life of Anaxagoras, who brought reason to Athens and set fire to the Western mind.

I read on through Anaximander, who taught the obliquity of the ecliptic, Anaximines of Lampsacus, who was a favorite of Alexander the Great; Anaximines of Miletus, who was an associate of Anaximander; Anazarbus, an ancient Cilician city; Anbar, a ruined town on the left bank of the Euphrates; Ancachs, a department of central Peru; Ancaens, son of Zeus, who experienced the original slip between cup and lip; Ancestor-worship; Anchises, by whom Aphrodite had Aeneas; Anchor, Anchorite, Anchovy, ancient regime, ancient light, ancillary, and Charles Ancillon, a distinguished French Protestant whose great grandson Johann Peter Friedrich Ancillon became a reactionary Prussian statesman and the faithful collaborator of Metternich. Using the reason bequeathed to them by Anaxagoras these two devised, in 1834, the Vienna Final Act, setting Europe back to feudalism.

When closing time came I put away the book and walked out of the library quickly. I went home by a roundabout way, afraid of meeting someone who would insist on talking to me. I wanted to be alone. I had found a path. It started off in a hundred different directions and parts of it were overgrown and had been abandoned for thousands of years, but it was a path, and a path is made by a great many people taking the same journey. That was all I needed to know. What I wanted to do was not strange or forbidden or unknown.

I went to the reading room again the next day, and after that I went as often as I could. I read about the Greeks and about Griselda, who was patient; I read about Genghis Khan the warrior and Gemini the Twins; I read about the Essenes, who might have been friends of Christ, and about Essence, which in metaphysics is something nobody understands but everybody discusses. I read about the Mamelukes who stripped the Great Pyramid of its alabaster, and about mammals, who suckle their young. I read about bifocals and bismuth, caraway seeds and carrion, hedonism and Heliopolis, Lesbia and Lesbos and Leviticus. I read about Zarathustra and Zeus and Zoroaster. I read about the Popes, the poles, pomegranates, Polyphemus, port wine, prostitutes, Passover, Plato, the praying mantis, Porphyry, Plotinus, Punch, polyandry, Pegasus, and the Passion. And of course I read about the stars and the unfenced prairies of the cosmos, for that was why I had come.

I understood almost nothing of what I read but that did not matter. Knowledge existed, inquiry was permitted, and speculation was, though at times dangerous, the privilege of every person. For me this was a revelation second only to my discovery of the stars. I had found the mind of man, created in the image of the Word. For Joseph it was another victory, and one in which he seemed to anticipate me. As I turned the pages he picked out subjects and urged me to examine them. Often he seemed to know what was coming in the text; sometimes he kept me looking for a thing which was not there—I would read to the end and the anticipation he felt would not be satisfied. What he expected I could never decipher, except that it was concerned with our mutual hope of coming upon the truth of life and death and creation. What was circulated for truth in our environment we did not accept. We had as yet no way of disproving it, but we were certain that ninety per cent of it was nonsense.

What we did come upon in our reading was the great modern superstition that all which has gone before is mistaken and imperfect, whereas all that obtains now, whether an idea or a mechanical device, is ultimate. There was generous use in all the textual matter we examined of such phrases as "he mistakenly held," "it was thought in that time," "opinion at the time was tolerant of," "the first crude efforts to put the theory in action," etc. Apparently nobody had been right about anything up until the moment the encyclopedia was written.

It was obvious without reading any books that the machines made by man were increasing in beauty, efficiency, and strength every day. Was it logical to accept the parallel belief that man's understanding of truth was increasing in depth, reverence, and humility? We thought not. We had discovered in the encyclopedia volumes ideas which had been set forth by Lao-Tse, Buddha, Pythagoras, Socrates, Saint Augustine, Moses Maimonides, Arius, Athanasius, Martin Luther, John Calvin, Duns Scotus, Thomas Aquinas—and we had heard our teachers in school and our priests in church dispensing modern knowledge and wisdom. We longed for the days of the Peripatetics, the Scholars, the Sophists, and the heretics. The only revolutionary things we had seen were short skirts and bobbed hair, an automobile which jumped thirty feet at the County Fair, and a moving picture containing a highly advertised underwater kiss. While it was being performed at the local theater Joseph got up and left me.

During the autumn days which followed that first summer I was afraid to turn on the light at my table in the library when it grew dark. I was afraid the Old Man would come over and scold me. When it was no longer possible to read

I went outside and walked home, kicking the leaves in the gutters, picking late apples from overburdened trees. One day as I was about to give up and close the book I was reading the light at my table went on. One of the librarians had come to get a volume from the shelves just in front of me and had pulled the chain switch. She smiled at me and said, "You shouldn't read without light. Turn it on whenever you need it." "Thank you," I said, and after that I did turn it on when the room grew dark, not even looking at the Old Man to see whether he was watching.

The knowledge I gathered from the encyclopedia volumes was scattered all over me and popped out on my mind like freckles. It had no pattern and it proved nothing to me except the existence of itself. But that was enough to draw me into the first real unity of being I had known. Around the fact of knowledge with its implications of free inquiry and unlimited horizons Joseph and I gathered so close that our body was filled with us and existed only to serve our purpose, turning pages with its fingers and scanning lines with its eyes. Even after leaving the library the unity remained, until the streets, the people, and the light shining from my home broke it up. Then I abandoned it with reluctance and care, making a list in my mind of things to be recalled and contemplated when I was in bed and once more alone.

I had errands to do sometimes, things to buy at the stores for my mother. Often I did not remember them until, well on my way home, I saw a bundle under someone's arm or sighted the grocery wagon going up the street. Then I had to run back, make my purchases, and race all the way home lest I be late for supper. Once I had my foot inside the door when I remembered an important errand. Softly I stepped back and closed the door. I would now have to run all the way to town and back again, and even then I would be a little late. In the street I made a decision. I lifted my right foot and with the heel of its shoe kicked my left shin bone. Then, with tears clouding my eyes, I ran toward town. Whenever the pain diminished I leaped into the air and gave my shin bone another kick. After that I adopted the device for all lapses of memory, sometimes varying the punishment by punching myself, biting my tongue, or pulling my hair. It worked. I had no love for physical pain and in a few months my daydreaming was under control, though one afternoon in geometry class it almost betrayed me.

Through the misfortune of alphabetical seating I was assigned to a place directly beside the teacher's desk. I could have reached out and touched her, and she could not avoid seeing me, at least from the corner of her eye, unless she turned her back completely on the class. Even when she did this none of the pupils moved or made a face. Miss Hopkins had been teaching mathematics for fifty years—she had instructed the grandparents of some of my classmates—and what you did behind her back you might as well do to her face. She saw it either way.

It was a drowsy time of day when the class met. Sunlight poured in through the windows and when the football players went to the board to tackle Euclid I was inclined to become sleepy. There was nothing to do but sit up and look straight ahead, though since I was inclined to squint in strong light I found it safe to turn my head slightly and close my eyes. At first when I fell asleep my head tried to topple and that snapped me awake. After a while I established some kind of control which kept my neck straight while I enjoyed a state of consciousness which wandered back and forth between daydreams and sleep.

Once I was meditating on a reference I had found in the library, an offhand remark about the esoteric meaning of the Pythagorean theorem. I was thinking how shocked Miss Hopkins would be if I asked her to explain what religious significance Pythagoras attached to the fact that the square on the hypotenuse of a right triangle is equal to the sum of the squares of the other two sides, when I went fast asleep.

I awoke suddenly and with a feeling of danger. The room was still. Miss Hopkins was staring at me, a small, tolerant smile of triumph on her firm little mouth. I knew what had happened. She had watched me fall asleep and then had asked me a question. It had taken weeks to catch me, but she had succeeded. I hadn't the slightest notion what she had said. Yet while I stared at her, smiling my acknowledgment of defeat while I reached hopelessly back through my mind for a fragment of help, I heard her voice say, in my memory, "Why would it be impossible to have railroads in heaven?" Could that be the question? It was odd, but it was typical of Miss Hopkins. She liked to thrust home the truths of mathematics by startling examples. I waited for the question to dissolve in my mind, for doubt to assail it, for other silly questions to crowd around it. None of these things happened, so breathing deeply to give me strength I said, "Because parallel lines meet at infinity and since heaven is infinite railroad tracks would be impractical. They would meet each other constantly and trains could not run on them without colliding."

For several long seconds Miss Hopkins said nothing. Then her smile increased, her eyes laughed, and softly she said, "I could have sworn you were asleep."

I did not confess the truth. I was busy examining what had happened in my mind. The trick of listening to memory was familiar to me. The mind stepped aside as far as possible; concentration relaxed but held a light rein on the question, and before long the answer appeared, always suddenly and always with clarity and impact. But in these cases the fact remembered was one I knew. Now I had remembered something I did not know. Or did I? It must have entered me while I was asleep and not had time to get firmly settled, so that it was still in sight when I woke up.

Something like that happened every time I woke up, but in reverse fashion. There was a dream fleeing down the corridors of my brain, and I watched it out of sight. Sometimes I tried to follow it, sometimes I tried to haul it back. I was never very successful. The dream was happening in a different world. Bodies did not have the same consistency nor thought the same patterns in that world, and when I came close the dreams dissolved and slipped away. At night I watched them reappear as I went to sleep. Now they moved in against the world I held, and as the two environments met I tried to leap from one to the other. I was unsuccessful. I fell asleep and remembered nothing. Sometimes I tried bringing myself awake, snapping backward as I fell toward sleep, hoping to observe the dream as it lay there waiting. But when I was awake I was awake; there was no dream nearby to watch.

Now another phenomenon had exhibited itself, the entrance into me while I slept of sounds from the world which my mind had left. Did this always happen? I had a sudden belief that it did, for there was constant evidence that the dream world, always close by, leaked into the waking world whenever the mind was not alert or when it voluntarily stood aside. How often had I lain in bed, trying to summon the courage to get up, only to relax and close my eyes in defeat. Each time I did this I found myself, after a few minutes, getting up from bed with ease and alacrity, but without any act of volition on my part or any knowledge of when the movement was to take place.

The same thing happened when I had to get up from a comfortable chair, or when I had to perform a disagreeable errand. For a little while I gave up conscious thinking; I stepped aside from myself. Immediately I was aware of a roaring torrent of thought sweeping through the spaces of my mind. What was happening around me in the physical world was a minor contribution to the stream, a country creek flowing into a broad river. It was something from this main flow which eventually picked me up and pushed me on my way, slapping my concentration back into place just as I was beginning to single out patterns of action in the mass of people, places, moods, postures, aspects, attitudes, fashions, and movements that were passing, it seemed, just in back of me, and in back of the world.

That wild and seemingly disordered torrent did things to me at other times. If I walked along, thoughtless, it threw thoughts into my head, thoughts which had little sense and ordinarily no connection with me or my interests. Often my lips opened and spoke a word significant of the thought, to my embarrassment and consternation. When there was a personal meaning it was always a startling one. A moment of embarrassment, long past in time, would leap at me with ten times its original force of confusion and shame, so that my face burned and I moaned in anguish. A fact I had tortured myself to remember for days would be tossed in the lap of my memory suddenly, inexplicably, without a preceding or a following thought. Suddenly and inexplicably, too, there would be given to me a revelation concerning something I had read in the library or something I had learned in school, a revelation of its function in life and its place in the pattern of man.

These gifts puzzled me more than the others, for I could not find the matter of these revelations listed anywhere as valid interpretations of the ideas they concerned, or even as ancient and discarded interpretations. Where had they come from? Me? Joseph? I could hardly believe that either of us was responsible, for where would we obtain such information? True, the revelations were based on the theory that man's destiny is to become wise and discover God, and this was the theory which Joseph and I believed, whereas for several hundred years it had been the fashion in Western civilization to consider a comfortable enhancement on earth as man's destiny and greatness of material wealth the supreme demonstration of his species. Therefore we could have formed the revelations in our prayers and meditations. But we hadn't. I knew we hadn't. Somewhere they had been set forth and believed, and some day we would find them, under a stone or in a tomb or on the map of death.

I seemed to myself in those closing days of puberty to be an increasingly complex and an increasingly integrating being, spreading steadily over the continent of my mind while the center from which I observed these advances and where I marshaled knowledge against the enemies of wonder and doubt, grew more certain of its strength and more confident of its logistics. At least the edges had been conquered from the wilderness of my identity, and there was a lifetime in which to cut and snipe at the rest.

When my eyes grew tired from reading at the library desk I raised their gaze to the soaring stacks of quiet books and sucked in the happiness they promised, shivering in the half-joyful, half-frightened apprehension which an ectasy long off in time visits on the bodies it has chosen to ravish. On that day I would be wise and discover God. He would be standing in a temple in the center of myself. By that time I would not be the same self, however. I would be expanded to the ultimate horizons of the stars. The long silent lines on the bookshelves seemed to promise it. They were armies at my command, and I was a captain set in the center of a small clearing in a vast and unknown land. In it lay creation and Creator, the two intermingled yet withdrawn from each other—the eyes of the Lord with their lids half shut.

All this lay beyond me now. There was I and there was Joseph, and between us, holding me in the earth and anchoring Joseph nearby, was the body. Before me, facing the body, was the world. Beneath all of this, holding it, was the hand of spirit, the Essence about which there was no agreement among men except that it could not be defined.

When I walked from the library the world confronted me, and it struck me with sharp jabs as I went along the streets. I had a feeling that it began where the path leading to the library met the sidewalk. Those who entered the path were in the world of the mind. Those on the street were in the world of flesh. It was a world I disliked and did not want to deal with, but it was a world I could not ignore without finding myself in Middletown, in the asylum on the hill. I lived in it, I was part of it, and in whatever destiny it had I shared. The only destiny I could perceive for it was a continuation of constant and difficult labor, the fruits of which were a poor and graceless living.

In all the books and encylopedia articles I had read the assumption was inherent that at this moment in history man was at the apex of his development. He had begun as a simple nomad, picking fruit and berries, following the sun, living in the open. Gradually he had become a hunter, a farmer, an artisan, and finally a slave. That was the end of him; that was his status now. He was chained to the factory which employed him, the business he owned, or the profession he embraced. For his service he received a living, precisely what his ancestors picked from the trees and bushes. It was a more complex and elaborate living, but it demanded more work.

That, in fact, was the destiny I observed and which worried me, the destiny of more and more work for a better and more ostentatious living. There was a rich man who lived in a mansion at one end of Church Street. There was a poor man who lived in a tenement at the other end of the same street. Both the rich man and the poor man worked very hard, the rich man to get a bigger mansion, the poor man to get a flat with another bedroom for the three younger children. The rich man had built the library; the poor man was privileged to visit it and borrow books from it. Yet I never saw either of them at the stacks. I saw the poor man drinking beer in a saloon, gasping his relief that the working day was done. I saw the rich man riding in his limousine, a frown on his face. Neither seemed happy, both were busy, and both were making a living.

There was something beyond a living, something called happiness, but it was to be achieved by making a better living. This would provide a larger house with fresher paint and more lawn to mow, more rooms to clean, more beds to make, and more electric lights to turn on and off. There would be a telephone, an automobile, and a cottage at Lake Quassapog, on the other side from the rich man's summer mansion. But there would still be no more time for reading, for talking, for thinking. There would still be no culture such as the Athenians had, no meetings of the townspeople, with discussions and perorations. There would still be no festivals of the drama, no crowning of poets.

The factories would remain and more poor people would come to take the place of those who moved from the tenements to cottages on the hills. The shabby wooden business buildings would stay, as would the odor of vulcanized rubber and the industrial system which kept all mature and responsible people laboring each day from a hearty New England breakfast to a spare New England supper. They wanted to get ahead, to make good, to succeed. With whom and for whom? Surely not with God, and surely not with themselves, for the long hours of labor, whatever material goods they might secure, could only keep an inner world static. They must want to make good for others, for their families, and for pride's sake. Much of the town was ugly, and those who were poor had to live in this ugliness. They wanted to be freed from it, to dwell where there were lawns and trees, to dress well, to eat well. After that they wanted jobs which did not soil their hands, and after that they wanted power. Was there any way to escape this pattern?

The necessity for doing something about it, for either following it or escaping from it, was not far off for me. People stopped being children and went to work at a startlingly early age. Already I had lost two of my best friends. The law stated that when a child was fourteen he could, with his parents' consent, leave school and take employment. My friends had taken advantage of the statute; one of them spent his fourteenth birthday in the factory, the other finished his term in seventh grade before going to work. What frightened me was that both of them *wanted* to leave school. They disliked books. They disliked study. They wanted to make money. In winter they went to the factory before daylight and came out after dark. They put on long pants, smoked cigarettes on the street and, so they said, kept pipes in their homes.

They were the extreme, but wherever schooling stopped and work began the pattern was repeated. Grown men came from college and went to work as doctors, as lawyers, as merchants, and, for all I knew, as thieves. At a certain point education ceased and work began. From there on existence consisted largely of making a living and being a success. The remainder was a matter for Henry McCarthy, the only man in town who wore a silk hat. Sooner or later Henry would put on his hat and go to your house. The family rode in the first car; the pallbearers were friends who worked nights or who were too ancient for anything more difficult than sitting up at a wake and carrying a coffin filled with a friend. Henry's silk hat didn't frighten me, but it was a warning. It was waiting. Nothing could stop me from growing up, going to work, and, eventually, dying. I was no different from anyone else. The same size plot would take care of me in the cemetery, the same silk hat would be reverently removed at my grave.

Except in the matter of work I did not want to be different. I liked people, all of them, without distinction and without degree. As I grew toward them from childhood I observed that they were kindly, given to thoughtful deeds, and quietly, bravely unhappy. The instant I perceived that they were not content I loved them all. They were, I realized, my brothers in the truest sense. They were exiled, lonely, confused, and filled with trouble.

In two ways they were different from me. They were resigned to a goal of material success and they accepted heaven as an advanced state of earthly comfort to be acquired by regular attendance at Mass and reception of the sacraments. I didn't believe these things but nobody knew I didn't. I had no idea how I was going to circumvent the business of making a living or the finality and authority of sacramental salvation, but I was going to make a fight for it.

Meanwhile I had to study the phenomenon of becoming a person. It was apt to happen to me any minute, snatching me off my bicycle and transforming me into a man, something in long pants striding up Church Street to keep a date at the town green. It was difficult to imagine but I did my best. I studied all the grownups I saw, looking for what I was to become. Particularly I studied them at dances and at wakes, two places where, I found, they most revealed their inner selves.

There were always wakes in the neighborhood, especially during the pneumonia months, and I was now playing my violin occasionally for country dances. At the wakes I watched and listened; at the dances I watched while I played. I learned a great deal, but nothing that helped me in my personal problem, nothing except that each man is an island universe in the cosmos of God's mind, with stars forming, planets breaking off, and a personal movement in counterpoint to creation. Like an astronomer I charted the movements within each universe, trying to fathom the plan or break through to the central agony behind the peripheral storms.

People are quiet at a wake. The women sit with the body, the men gather in the kitchen. The drunks, who wander in occasionally, try to whisper their condolences and be sorrowful. When they get in the kitchen and tell stories they are apt to forget, and no drunk can control his laughter. It shakes him apart. There are long silences in both rooms, then conversations in undertones. When there are a lot of people the talk is broken up into dozens of little discussions, and the sound in each room becomes a drone, the men striking a lower note than the women. When I first went to wakes a bowl of clay pipes was set on the kitchen table, with packages of tobacco and boxes of cigars nearby. Later there were only packages of cigarettes. At some of the early wakes I attended oil lamps were used for illumination and the long New England kitchens were filled with shadows.

The men sat in little chairs provided by the undertaker. I watched them as they crossed or uncrossed their legs, folded their arms, filled clay pipes and sucked in smoke that broke out then from the edges of their mouths. They had bent shoulders, rough hands, and a stunned look in their eyes, as if a stranger had attacked them without reason and was continuing to belabor them. They seemed uncomfortable in their clothes, aware of their mission, and resigned to it as they were resigned to everything in the pattern of their lives. I watched them for a long time before I realized the most important thing about them. They were gentle. It was a trait I had hitherto associated with women, who made capital of it along with their physical weakness. But the men I saw at wakes, the middle-aged, gray-haired men, were continuously gentle. Gentleness was a part of them, and when at midnight they knelt beside their chairs for the rosary they were reverent. Looking through the door I could see the women struggling downward to their knees, each assuming as she did so a solemn, pious look. The men did not have to change their expressions. They looked like holy friars, with melancholy shining from their eyes and suffering cut into their faces with a cunning tool.

I was glad to be with them and glad to know that I would be a man. They were lean-faced and thin-nosed, and the muscles they had used for thirty years in their daily work had twisted their bodies out of shape. They prayed in strong, low voices, each one looking as if he had been through a special hell. The same thing would happen to me, but if I attained the peace and gentleness they possessed the suffering would not matter. It was the work they did which I dreaded, the suffocating monotony of fifty years of days in a factory, making rubber boots for lumbermen a thousand miles away. Against that I would fight, but not against the gentleness and peace which the men themselves had won. I was proud to pray with them for one of their number who had finished his last boot and put away his cutting knife for good.

I hoped it was for good. Each time I knelt at a coffin and watched a body while I prayed for its soul I had one question in my mind: "Where are you?" I looked around the edges of the face for flickers of light or movements that would betray a departing spirit. There were none. All the marks of life and all the implications of personality were gone. I knew there was a theory that it takes the soul three days to withdraw from the body, and I had read that this was the origin of the three-day interval between death and burial, with blessed candles at the head and feet of the corpse and friends to pray lest the Devil interfere and try to steal the soul. Each time I watched for a sign and each time I saw nothing. I got to my feet, turned to the chief mourner, and said what I had been taught to say: "I'm sorry for your trouble." I did not add any comments on the appearance of the corpse, as some of the old folks did.

Once I heard a lady say, "Doesn't he look wonderful? You wouldn't think there was a thing the matter with him." There probably wasn't anything the matter with him except that he had abandoned his body and gone to a different environment. Into a deeper, darker, more solid environment? Was the earth a step on a stairway leading downward to a density and an insensibility greater than that of human flesh? Or was it a step on a stairway leading upward to a freedom that exhilarated the spirit and expanded the mind? Or was it a purgatory in itself, from which the psyche emerged cleansed and wakened? I didn't know, nor did any of the mourners know who sat with the dead man while his soul leaked away and his flesh rotted. All they knew was that some day it would happen to them, and they sat quietly in this knowledge, talking to each other about little things that were not concerned with death.

The dances were like wakes possessed by demons, and I was the demon who engineered the possession. A lot of normal young people sat around talking in small groups. Then I raised my bow, tapped my foot, and swung into *Margie, Sleepy Time Gal,* or *Avalon.* Immediately the groups broke up, each boy took a girl, and the floor was covered with possessed people. No matter who the dancers were they no longer resembled themselves. Their faces changed; their eyes threw out a dreamy, schizophrenic look. Their bodies assumed strange, distorted positions. Were they really possessed, I wondered, or were they merely trying to say, "This is what I really am. See my nobility, see my beauty, see my gracefulness?" Or were they pretending to be something they knew they weren't, playing house with each other in a grownup, romantic way? How the girls posed, gently restraining their fatal allure; how the boys protected them, grim and faithful for a verse and three choruses. So much of that I could endure and no more. Then we had a square dance.

The old folks came from the refreshment room then and whirled each other around in a free and easy way that gave the relationship between man and woman a homely touch, like a kitchen joke or a parlor giggle. It was a relief from the dagger in the heart, sailboat in the moonlight mood which constantly demanded waltzes. But either way dancing was pretending, a stylized love play condoned as a community art. The couples looked as if they had been teleported from half a hundred parlors and porches and frozen in the attitude in which they were found. As soon as the music stopped they broke from each other and stood politely apart, waiting for the signal which would legalize the resumption of their brace. Every dance was an overture to a monstrous concupiscence that somehow was never let loose, and which, so far as I knew, existed only in theory. I had heard of it, that was all. When the dance was over I put my violin in its case and went home. The dancers left the hall. Often I overheard them say they had a good time.

Next day I would see many of them going to and coming from their work. Passing by the factories I could hear the machines, smell the rubber, and feel the heat. The importance of a good time was not difficult to understand. There were few enough good times once you were a laborer. Even the jail seemed better than the factory. It was cooler and it had no odor. Sometimes I listened at its windows to the drunks in the cells. They seemed no more than ordinarily unhappy. I felt very close to them, separated only by my silence about all I thought and felt.

I was not afraid of work. I carried special delivery letters and packages on my bicycle, collected tickets at one of the moving picture theaters, and fiddled for anyone who would pay a price. It was the tossing away of life when manhood was reached which appalled me, the voluntary submission to a slavery more barbarous than that from which the Negroes had been freed. On the town green stood a memorial to the local men who had fought in the Civil War. On its side were carved the names of battles—Chancellorsville, Cold Harbor, Manassas, Petersburg, Malvern Hill, the Wilderness, New-market, Gettysburg. At the top was a statue of a Union soldier. Each day he watched thousands of men and women go into the factories in the morning and come out of them at night. They made a moderate living except when the factories closed, which happened often during the summer. There were no pensions; there was no accident insurance. The best you could hope for was good health and a fairly early death.

But all you had to do to escape it was walk over the hills that surrounded the valley and go into the world to seek wisdom and God. Why did they stay and submit?

SIX

IT WAS noon, and the Professor, his hands folded, looked piously at my rolling head. Miss Iceberg sat quietly at her table, flicking a look at me now and then. The outline of her bosom at last was clear; the starch in her uniform had given in to nature.

"Not much," the Professor said, looking at her. "You should see some of my girl students."

100

"In my condition," I said, "the brain becomes subject to odd fancies. I wish they were full of cold beer."

"There was a girl from Tennessee," the Professor said. "She sat in the front row at my lectures for four years. Then she took a postgraduate course and I had her in seminar. Melons. Lovely white melons. I had to learn my lectures and deliver them by rote. Couldn't trust myself to extemporize from notes."

"Why did she want all that education? Was she eccentric?"

"She was fascinated by history, poor thing; daffy about the past while with every moment of the present those incomparable masterpieces were growing older and heading toward an inevitable sag. At least she"—nodding toward Miss Iceberg—"will be spared that."

Miss Iceberg looked up and found me staring at her chest.

"Would you like some more orange juice?" she asked quickly. Miss Yellowhead had given her a quart of it as a bribe, to be used when I was uncooperative.

"Yes," I said. She gave me a full glass. When I had finished drinking I gazed earnestly into her eyes and sighed.

"It must be difficult to be a beautiful and attractive woman and at the same time retain the cool professional detachment which nursing requires," I said.

She wiped my face, giving my forehead an extra lick.

"You shouldn't talk," she said. "Really you shouldn't. I know it's difficult but it's half over now. At three o'clock you'll be finished. The morning hours are the worst. It is more irritating at the lower temperatures—102 is the most trying. You won't mind it so much from now on."

She went back to her table.

"No soap," the Professor said.

"She has to keep her job."

"There was a girl once in my class who had a peculiar habit," he said. "She sat in the front row too, but I didn't notice her at first because she was flat-chested. Then I observed that during each lecture she crossed her right leg over her left, loosened the right shoe, and let it dangle from her big toe. Day after day it swung back and forth before me like a pendulum. I began to have curious feelings about the girl. I dreamed of her shoe swinging back and forth. I imagined her bosom was large and full. Finally I mentioned the situation to one of my friends, a psychiatrist. He told

101

me something which I did not know and which, I confess, astonished me. Next to her breasts a woman's big toe is the most sensitive part of her secondary sexual equipment."

"But why did the shoe-wagging affect you? Did you realize subconsciously that she was waving a rather important piece of sexual apparatus at you?"

"I don't know. Figure it out for yourself." He yawned and dropped an arm to one minute past twelve. "I always get this way at noon and midnight. It's the way I'm forced to look, like an old prude hiding behind my hands from the facts of life. Piety begets passion, but not for the Lord."

An incredibly old pair of feet, almost staggering, went by the window. The shoes were poor, the trousers were frayed. I looked back at the Professor and found him wistful again.

"I had not remembered that puberty is so lonely and so desperate a time," he said, "watching the playtime of life slip away before life itself is well begun. I suppose all boys feel it, even the most insensitive. Girls don't because they are not as free in puberty, and because the only thing that concerns them in life lies beyond puberty.

"Is there anything as free in all the world as a boy of twelve or thirteen? He is big enough to roam the neighborhood and the town, he has a bicycle and a fielder's glove and a jackknife with eight blades; he fishes and swims and hunts and has a dog who is more faithful to him than any human will ever be. He plays baseball, football, basketball, tennis, hockey, and dozens of games he makes up with other boys so he can be continually running, jumping, punching, wrestling, and climbing over fences. He steals apples, smokes cornsilk cigarettes, studies the batting averages of the major league baseball stars, and when he is completely exhausted plays cards and checkers and chess and mumblety-peg, and picks fleas from his dog.

"His father admires him and his mother and sisters adore him. The pantry is full of things he loves and remnants are put in the icebox in case he might want them. He is cared for, loved, and is loose in a world of wonders with energy that has no end and a body still small enough to relax in a pear tree or wriggle under a fence. His appetites are large and all of them are satisfied. Then one day he looks down and sees the shadow of a man at his heels, and he is himself the man."

102

"You are talking about your own memories, I know, but you might be describing mine."

"All boys are alike, and exceptions prove the rule. You stood for hours in the warm sun as I did, throwing a baseball to another boy who threw it back to you. The impact of the ball against your glove, the rhythmic swing which ended with the ball going from the left to the right hand and being thrown with a lazy follow-through motion—these make a memory that is like wine for both of us, and for millions of others. That is what we seek when we go to a baseball game now, or listen on the radio to the World Series; and that, thank heaven, is what we get—an immersion in that memory, a return to boyhood.

"I think the basis of woman's eternal envy of man is puberty. Then he lives in the Golden Age of man, and the sight of his freedom haunts her."

He looked pityingly at Miss Iceberg, as if for an instant he not only understood but forgave her. Then he turned again to me.

"But you were a very sad boy despite all that. I was not. I found a library, I worried about knowledge, and I did not want to grow up. But the library was my father's and he helped me understand knowledge. I was never worried about God, or about the slavery of labor. My father was a professor before me and happy in his work. I had an example of a way of life that is pleasant and rewarding, a means of freedom for the body from physical labor and an emancipation of the mind from tedium. I determined to follow the example.

"I cannot help wondering whether such an environment might not have changed your childhood, particularly those long, somber moods. But I think not. I suspect you were born to melancholy, though you seem well able to laugh now."

"I think when I learned to laugh," I said, "that I saved the structure of my existence, at least for a while."

Miss Iceberg looked at her watch, picked up the thermometer, and came toward my coffin. Mechanically she lifted the lid, her eyes on the wall. Our fingers met, fumbled, and I took the thermometer. She shut the lid.

"Does it matter now?" I said. "Haven't we reached Nirvana?"

She stared at me gravely.

"I must not let your temperature go too high," she said.

103

The Professor cleared his throat.

"May I suggest," he said, "that your sense of humor saved you for a joke? At the moment you are probably the most brightly lighted person in the city. You are lying stark naked within half a foot of a rather pretty girl whose sole interest in you is centered in a thin column of mercury which—"

"There is no need to explain the joke," I said.

"Three minutes," said Miss Iceberg. She lifted the lid and I handed her the thermometer. She examined it closely.

"Am I all right?" I asked.

"Yes," she said, not looking at me. "You are doing nicely."

"Oh, come along," the Professor said. "What happened next?"

SEVEN

I WAS SITTING one May afternoon on the green, watching the Town Clock across the street and thinking of the thousands who would be in the factories for another hour while I sat on a bench in the shade of rustling maples, hearing birds and smelling the fresh, cool lawns. Behind me the fountain babbled. Before me women promenaded, pushing prams. The Old Man at the library would be missing me, but even books could not hold me in on such a day. Yet even the beauty of the day could not keep me from searching, as I increasingly did, for stratagems and plans which would help me to escape from the pattern that seemed my fate. "Over the hills!" Joseph said. "Over the hills!" I knew he was right, but I wanted to know why.

When I fell back through my body and leaned against Joseph we were as we had always been. There was no change in our perception of ourselves, only a widening of the horizons which bounded our problem, only a knowledge in greater detail of what lay about us. Books and the stars were new dimensions for our thoughts, but that which we were remained unaltered, an awareness set in a world that was dressed with flowers, anchored with trees, and scourged by a tumbleweed called man. These were the two great certainties, that we three—I and Joseph and our body— existed, and that the world also existed. Of the two I was more sure of the reality of my tripartite self. It existed and it was changeless. Music and wonder and prayer welled up in it like fountains, melancholy searched it, pride gave it pain, and sleep was its mother and its friend. Time passed beyond it, washing against the body that was its rim, leaving the heart untouched. It fed on knowledge and longed for adventure. Its substance was love, its home was heaven. What it was doing on earth it only faintly discerned.

Its conception of the world was partial and confused. What grew in the ground had a soft hazy being, as if its spirit had not yet crystallized the pattern and given it a will of its own. The earth with its undissolved rocks was a reservoir of material, nourishing the forms already created while waiting to be formed itself. Human beings were crystallized patterns with personalities and free wills. They moved, grubbed in the dirt, and pondered their dilemma, their problem of body and spirit. They baked mud, grew wheat, built wheels and levers, and from themselves plucked song and affection. They were slightly luminous beings, with a soft fringe of light about their faces when they smiled and spoke. A few of them went off to quiet places and put down their thoughts in books. The rest said nothing. Sometimes they paused and were quiet, as if listening for a sound beyond the wind. That was all. They did not know where they were going any more than they knew whence they had come. They were the moving world, living on the still and quiet world which sprang from life itself.

Was life the tumbling, roaring stream of thought and symbol which lay just behind the trinity of myself? Did it lie behind all men and behind all forms, pushing them into existence with an idea for a guide and a pattern for a mold? Was the mind of man a watchdog for his form, and were its thoughts taken from the stream of life, to be applied to the problems externalized by the world? If so then there was another stream of life, another river of existence in which order and harmony prevailed and where there was peace and a cessation from the roaring turmoil of building, shaping, breaking, and reshaping. Was that where man was going?

It was where he wanted to go, whether it existed or only was raised up by his passion for relief. The heaven he talked about was a place of rest and nothingness. Did he want such a destiny because the force which had formed him and which sustained him now was so wild and vigorous and chaotic, or because he remembered the quiet arms of God?

It was indeed a seething, jumbled, restless mass that lay behind life, but the mind of man was an escape from it, a release from its excitement and infinite activity. My mind, which composed the awareness labeled I, could look at it from a distance, and could become almost completely oblivious of it (except for observations at the edges of my concentration) by looking at the world and engaging in conversation with other people. That escape, that objectivity, meant something. It was a chance to accomplish something. But what?

Sitting on the green that afternoon I was further from a solution than ever. The burgeoning earth, the whispering leaves of the maples, the slowly moving perambulators, all sucked me toward the stream that drowns will and consciousness, mixing them with whatever flow is passing, tossing them up on the bank a little farther on in time. Drowsily I heard, coming into the mixture of distant and nearby sounds, into the melody of babbling fountain water and rustling leaves, the rhythmic clock of a woman walking on high heels. She was coming through the green on one of the concrete walks which led from the high school past the fountain and the statue to Church Street. Lazily I turned to look.

She was a girl I knew by sight, a young thing new to the town and very pretty. I had seen her playing tennis, and I had passed her by in school, where she wore a middy blouse and low-heeled sport shoes. I had never seen her as she appeared now. She was transformed.

Above high-heeled slippers her legs were sheathed in silk stockings. Beyond the legs a short skirt rippled so that her thighs were outlined and endowed with a slow, undulating motion which made the tips of her shoes seem like the ends of whips, flicking the pavement as if it were the hide of a horse. She wore a shirtwaist of translucent material, and

106

under it a slip. Beneath the slip her breasts moved in rhythm with her hips and toes, but in an offbeat, and with a compensating side action which gave the impression that they were rolling, like a boat in a gentle sea. Her face was serene, her hair was curled and piled on her head, her arms swung in time to her body. In her left hand she held a handkerchief.

I must have watched her for several seconds before anything happened. Then a warm, intolerably vigorous feeling moved through my blood and filled every portion of me. I felt it running down my legs and pounding through my neck into my head. A thick, sticky taste filled my mouth. My sight blurred. I felt tipped to one side, off balance inside myself. A searing heat and tumbling weakness filled my belly and crept out from it. Had I been standing I would have had to sit down. Without knowing I was present the girl passed by. I watched her until she was out of sight.

So this was it. Lust: "animal desire for sexual indulgence; sensuous appetite regarded as sinful"; from the old English by way of the Teutonic tongue. I had looked it up many times, wondering when it would happen to me. Once its past tense had been list. "The wind bloweth where it listeth," Jesus said to Nicodemus, and that is what he meant. The wind does not blow where it wants to, but where lust impels it: "and thou hearest the sound thereof, but canst not tell whence it cometh, and whither it goeth; so is everyone that is born of the Spirit."

When it was gone from me Joseph was by my side and a thousand things were clear to us: the little houses standing neatly on the hills, the tired and pensive men who came every evening from the factories and went back to them every morning; the patience, the quiet, the acceptance they all showed by the pattern of their living and working and dying. They blew where they listed, and marriage gave them something to blow against, a tree that swayed and bent and received them. Everyone was like everyone else in this, and I was no different, nor ever had been. Nor could I hope to be. There was no escape.

It had nothing to do with love, of that I was certain. Love was a means of caring for everything. Lust was a streak of the life force, reaching out through me toward a rare and beautiful creature who seemed like a priestess prepared to receive the gods, a sudden and presentable sacrifice appearing on the altar of spring. The girl combined at the moment

107

I sighted her everything I had ever admired in a woman. I wanted her. Love had nothing to do with it. Love was for God and the things which God had made, music and flowers and nebulae, forests and mountains and rain. I could love the souls of women, as I loved the souls of men, en masse, but I did not love this girl. I lusted after her. I wanted her body.

In the days and months which followed that afternoon I tried to take the feeling apart and discover a way of controlling it. I thought of women in reference to the charts in physiology books, pictures which stripped them to their muscles, nerves, and inner organs. I thought of them at the functions and habits which remind each of us, daily, that we are animals and scavengers, keeping ourselves alive by devouring the life of other things, rotting where we sit or as we walk, washing death away from us with every exhaled breath. I considered them as a surgeon might, dissecting their bodies into arms and legs and organs which, in their isolation, I could heartily loathe. None of it was of the slightest use. Lust came when it pleased, and if a woman were not present it assembled one. It seemed, in fact, unrelated to woman in its origin, just as food is unrelated to the growth of a man's appetite. Once the appetite is accumulated only food can satisfy it, but until that time food can lie about in the form of an apple or a pear or a steak in perfect safety.

But when a man becomes hungry, I considered, he can usually get something to eat. It was not that way with lust. Lust was turned away from every door; it had more curses than Job had sores, and more power, apparently, than all the angels which the church could muster and all the obstacles which custom could devise. "It will never kill you, like hunger," said Joseph, "but it will drive you to this—" and he turned my eyes to the factories, the cottages on the hills, and the trickle of perambulators and sauntering wives. And on that first afternoon that is the way I felt about it. I saw the snare and the bait, and the inevitable springing of the trap. "It bloweth where it listeth," and "man does not live by bread alone." I did not think of it as sin, but as power; if I did not control and employ and adapt it, it would control and adapt me. The spirit seemed a long way off, unless lust was a lash of its tail, striking humanity and driving it on to procreation, companionship, and whatever destiny waited beyond the hills of evolution.

Lust knocked Joseph back and away from me when it struck, and by the time it had mounted all the parapets of flesh there was little left of me either. I was immersed in the flame, and with it I reached for the thing I desired to consume. When it died away I was weak and the flesh was pleasantly drowsy and numb. It was then that Joseph returned, with a tremendous burst of strength, so vigorous and alert that I wondered whether there was not a clue in the nature of lust to the power we dreamed of finding, the power which would melt away our body and bring us together. Lust had a force and identity all its own, a force and identity not connected with women, morality, or love. Yet all three of these were vitally concerned with the activity of its force and the nature of its identity. Women received the force, morality controlled it, and love transformed the nature of its identity into a reflection of the transformer. What seemed odd to me was that lust came so early in a man's life, struck so often, and chose such incongruous times and places for its visitations.

Or was it? What environment was more suitable for the torch of reproduction than a forest in the spring or a lake in August moonlight? A woman had to be materialized if the flame was to be fed, but that for a while was of minor importance. It was well for a young man to know the spontaneity and unpredictability of the force that more than any other was to shape his life. It was wise to watch it rise, creep up the beaches of his being, flood them, and ebb away. Particularly was it helpful to listen in the afterward to the sounds about him, which had not changed their tempo or intensity; to look at the moon or the quiet firs, and to know that had he for the occasion materialized a woman she would still be lying in his arms. Most of all it was instructive for him to realize that if he were a woman he would have materialized a man.

That seemed an easy fact to retain but it wasn't, in New England. In that land it was openly preached that woman, through an edict of divine providence, was created free from sexual desire and submitted to the lust of man only because of her good nature, her need for a home, and her sense of duty toward God, who wanted her to perpetuate the race. Eve had made a mistake but she had been deceived. The

109

point was that Adam should have explained the error to her and refused to partake of the apple. But did he do that? Not Adam, the pig! He took a bite, and he took it of his own free will, without any serpent to persuade him. And he liked it. Eve didn't. She realized that the flesh was too coarse for her; she had sensibilities; she was a lady. But Adam was a brute. He liked the apple and he has been liking it ever since; and Eve, because of this degenerate taste, has had to suffer. So went the story. Old maids swore by it; married women suffered its truth silently; maidens went about with soft eyes and quaking hearts, waiting to be attacked.

Thus I became, while still in short pants, a sinister male. I had been going to parties for as long as I remembered. The first I recall were noisy, loaded with food, and during them children were allowed to carry on in a manner which made me wonder whether the mothers in attendance were not intent on returning their offspring to the state of chaos whence they had come. This was the slugging and scream- ing stage, and I disliked it. The girls made every instant hideous with their howling and the boys went around with their eyes glazed and their jaws hanging loose, looking like the Neanderthal Man or a degenerate of the Cro-Magnon period.

Suddenly a great reticence overtook both boys and girls; kissing games were introduced—Postoffice and Spin the Bottle. This was puberty, a brief reproduction of the friendly age of concubinage, when chemistry had learned manners but was under no obligation to theology. It was not directly unpleasant except for the element of surprise. You never knew what girl, during the interim between gatherings, had come to like you. When Postoffice began you found out; she sent for you again and again, and since she might be the homeliest child on the street that was something to endure. Still, a kiss in the dark was the same whether the girl was pretty or ugly so far as I was concerned. It was a push on the mouth, not hard enough to bruise. What mattered was whether the girl wanted the kiss. If she did I wasn't worried and tried to do a good job. If she didn't, or I thought she didn't, I excused her in a hurry.

I only sent for girls who had sent for me. That was out of character for a boy but it was the only way I could act. Anyone in the world could be my friend, but he had to make the decision. That to me was a sensible procedure. So far as I was concerned all people were likable and most of them were lovable. How they felt about me was another matter, something I could not predict. If they liked me they would do something about it and we would become friends; if they disliked me they would ignore me and no harm would be done. So far as girls were concerned I could only hope that one of the pretty ones would like me. The pretty ones seemed more aggressive and more sure of themselves than the plain and homely females, so perhaps I would be fortunate.

Suddenly the kissing games stopped. Parties were conducted on a new system—romance. A boy invited a girl to a party or a girl invited a boy. There were dances, polite conversation, and games which exercised the brain and the reflexes. Couples wandered off into quiet places. One of the mothers read fortunes in tea leaves. There were refreshments, politely eaten; then the couples left together, the boy escorting the girl to her home. This was romance, and most of us found it a little embarrassing. The change had come too quickly.

I was invited to one of these parties by a girl whom I liked well enough and whom I would have invited to the Postoffice providing she had previously invited me. Of my own volition, however, I would not have laid either tender or violent hands on her. She was just a nice girl who sometimes asked me to help her with a problem in mathematics. The party was held on a winter night, clear and bitterly cold. In such weather it is not only necessary in Connecticut to wear gloves, but to keep your hands in your pockets. I did this and the girl put an arm through mine and a hand in my pocket. At a certain point in the road she deliberately lurched and staggered against a bend in the fence, so that I was pulled against her. "Oh," she said, "now look where you've got me!" I knew she wanted me to kiss her so I did. I had to take my hands from my pockets and put my arms around her to pretend that she was being forced. Her lips were cold and so I'm sure were mine. Between us was a mass of clothing several inches thick—her coat, mine, and the various garments each was wearing underneath. My hands grew stiff. I became aware of the night around me and the stars staring down. If this was what ruined Lancelot he was a foolish man.

When I left her at her home I ran most of the way to town to get myself warm. I slowed down as I reached the

Catholic church, and that night I gave my religion a really bitter thought for not providing me with a career that would take me from labor and romance and dullness, a vocation that would harness my mind and my lust to the pitifully small chariot which continually tried to carry all of humanity to heaven. The church was a dark, forbidding place, and in it no one had ever spoken to me a kind or helpful word. Priests had threatened me with purgatory, nuns had seized me by the shirt, and once the janitor had said to me, "Get the hell out! Can't you see I'm cleaning up? They aren't hearing confessions today." From the pulpit lust was damned and forbidden and money was requested. It was declared unequivocally that Jesus Christ dwelt in the altar. This was something he did not do for the Protestants, whom Catholics were not obliged to love and whom they were urged not to marry.

There were no books in the church; there was no library or room where a man could go to think and to pray by himself. There were tall, suffocating confessionals, that was all. If a man had done a good thing there was no place for him to come and tell the Lord about it. The church was only for sinners, the confessional was a dark place where dark things were told:

"Bless me Father for I have sinned. I disobeyed my parents six times; I got into two fights; I swore a dozen times; I lied four times (I am lying now, because so far as I know I have not lied or knowingly disobeyed my parents and I fought because a couple of parochial school kids jumped me, and it's either swear once in a while or get called a sissy and have to slug somebody. But I have to make this up for you because my mother said it was time for me to go to confession. What I really want to tell you is that I seriously doubt that the Roman Catholic Church is the legal and only operating representative of Christ on earth. It seems to me that Christ is every man's Elder Brother, as accessible to a Protestant or a Hindu as he is to a Catholic. As a matter of fact Father I know that is so, though I cannot prove it. But some day I will. Now nail me to the church door and banish my soul to hell, and be sent there yourself for the sin of pride. See you in hell, sir!); I also had improper thoughts but I did not submit to them. That is all, Father."

"Very well. Try to do better next time, especially about fighting and swearing. God does not like boys who fight and

112

swear. Say seven Our Fathers and seven Hail Marys for penance. Now recite the Act of Contrition."

"Oh, my God, I am heartily sorry for having offended Thee. (Who are you, God? I want to know.) I detest all my sins (whatever they may be; this man doesn't know any more than I do) because I dread the loss of heaven and the pains of hell (if there is any hell which I have not already endured I shall be happy to skip it); but most of all because they offend Thee my God (Who are You?) Who art all good and deserving of all my love (You are good and You are love so how can You deserve it or need it? I need it, God. I need You. Where are You? Who are You?)."

I had my own church, an imaginary one, on the green. Behind the fountain lay a graceful spread of lawn, with a grove of maples for its crown. There in my mind I built a structure such as the town had never seen. It was a church in the New England style, but very large, with great skylights and enormous windows, so that all day it was flooded with sunshine. From its sides two buildings extended as wings; they also had skylights and great windows. One of them was a library, the other contained a series of rooms where people went to consult with priests and priestesses about the nature of God and the destiny of man.

In the rear of the main building there was another extension, a semicircular building with a greenhouse for its fringe, a greenhouse with a tall ceiling and faraway sides, so that on the coldest day in winter it seemed like a summer garden, with fountains babbling, birds sniping at the hush, and flowers always blooming.

In this building the priests and priestesses studied, meditated, and talked among themselves. Here all the new knowledge of the world was received and analyzed and fitted into the old knowledge, so that there was never a contradiction, never a loose end. Each priest, when he entered this place, said to himself: "Everything that I know may be wrong; all that I seek may be undiscoverable. Nevertheless I shall have faith in goodness and labor for wisdom. In each man I meet I shall look for that which I worship in my Creator, and when I have found it I shall love him for it. What is left of him I shall take also to my heart, and pray that it be healed. I am a corpuscle in the body of God; I shall endeavor to perform the function for which I was created, and I shall

113

endeavor to know all else that was created and He Who made it."

His life was devoted not only to study and to meditation but to physical labor, ministering to the ill and to the afflicted, and consulting with anyone who came to ask questions of truth or to seek counsel and guidance. The priests and priestesses had built the church and they maintained it; their barracks were in the basement, that of the priests under one wing, that of the priestesses under the other wing. If a priest and priestess fell in love they were married, given the blessing of the church, and sent into the world as servants of the poor, the helpless, and the uninstructed.

The priests and priestesses did their own washing, cooking, and cleaning. In summer the hills surrounding the town glistened with the harvest of their fields, and in the kitchen under the church great stores of food were cooked and preserved for the winter. At the top of one of the hills the church had a farm. It was run by a priest and priestess who had married, and it supplied the church with meat and dairy products and with the wool from which they spun their garments.

Priests and priestesses dressed alike, in a white robe of woolen cloth gathered at the waist with a leather belt. In summer they changed to cotton; in winter they wore dark blue capes when they went out of doors. The priestesses lined their capes with scarlet, the priests used a lining of light blue. On their feet both priests and priestesses wore sandals made from the hides of animals killed at the farm.

If a woman of the town fell ill a priestess went to nurse her. If a man of the town was arrested, a priest went to represent him in court. Those who were drunken or homeless or afraid came to the church and were succored. Its doors were never shut, its lights were never dimmed. Over the door was engraved the 19th verse of the 119th Psalm: "I am a stranger in the earth: hide not thy commandments from me."

Any man could enter the church and ask for a priest or a priestess and speak with him or with her of the things that troubled him. In a small, quiet room, with light streaming from a skylight and books on the table, he sat and talked, telling what lay in his heart:

"I know not who I am, nor whence I came, nor what I am here to perform. This is a dark place, full of fears and

114

shouting. The land gives me sustenance and they who are my fellows take it from me. I hear there is a God, locked up in a thousand churches. I am told there is a devil, loose in the fields and in the streets. I am condemned because my body takes heat and seeks to warm with it the womb of a woman. What is my sin and who shall punish it? Am I a name in a book or a tree without roots or a thought which God has cast out to the land of rejection, where things which come imperfect from the mold are scattered and left to decay?"

The priest or priestess then said: "We read shadows which are made by the passing of light. What seems true is only the reflection of truth, thrown from a hundred thousand suns, flickering briefly on the dark wall of our world. What we know is what the mind knows and what the heart feels. The mind is an edge of another mind, from which it is cut off. It is shut up, sealed out, and blinded. It can only listen as the mind from which it is cut off goes by, and try to remember what that mind is like. The heart is an edge of another heart, from which it is cut off. It is shut up, sealed out, and blinded. It can only listen as it beats to the beat of the heart from which it is cut off, and try to recall the rhythm and the music from which that faraway ecstasy is made. You are a mind and a heart cut off. This is what we know about you.

"The great mind is the mind of God, to which your mind must return, and the great heart is the heart of God, to which your heart must return. Then your thoughts will know the thoughts of all creation, and your heart will beat with the heart of God.

"But now you are alone, sent on a long adventure, to help God bring creation to its flower. You are His agent, bearing His love. Your heart hears faintly His song. Make yourself a part of that song, that those who have lost the tune may find it. Consider not whether you are fed or clothed or housed, but only whether you love and pray and serve. When you work, think of God. When you rest, let Him hold you. When you reach out, touch His hand, and then put your arm around a friend."

After that the priest or priestess spoke to the man about his specific problems, reading from books, explaining such wisdom as existed on the subject, and advising what seemed the right thing to do from a spiritual viewpoint. Then if the man was comforted he would say to himself the 7th verse of the 116th Psalm: "Return unto thy rest, O my soul; for the Lord hath dealt bountifully with thee." He could go then into the church and pray, if he liked, or go to the library and read something suggested by his counselor, or go out of the church and to wherever he pleased. When he chose he could return with a new question, or with the same one if it still troubled him.

On Sunday a priest or priestess celebrated Mass. When the Host was elevated the congregation chanted the 116th Psalm: "I love the Lord, because he hath heard my voice and my supplications. Because he hath inclined his ear unto me, therefore will I call upon him as long as I live. . . . I will take the cup of salvation, and call upon the name of the Lord. I will pay my vows unto the Lord now in the presence of all his people . . . in the courts of the Lord's house, in the midst of thee, O Jerusalem. Praise ye the Lord."

Those who wished to receive communion did so, but not at this Mass. Each communicant passed the night somewhere in the church, praying, meditating, reading. An hour before dawn those who felt ready gathered at the altar and knelt before it. As the sun rose a priest who had also spent the night in preparation came and celebrated Mass, giving communion to those who awaited him.

That was my church for the poor, the disconsolate, the unfortunate, the too warm of heart, the untidy, the lecherous, the drunken, the skeptical, the abandoned, the witless, and all who were filled with a fever to know God and to feel the grasp of His hand. There seemed no place in the other churches for any of these, so I did not consider that I was setting up a schism. My church was for the untended, the unwanted, and the disbarred.

Its lights glowed more brightly than ever as I passed the green on that night during which, despite zero weather, I had become a ruthless lover. I longed to walk across the snowpacked lawns and enter it, there to be relieved of the pattern of life whose threads were now gathering around me with cunning and sureness. Habit took my feet instead along the streets, guided me home, undressed me in the dark, and tucked me in. Next morning when I awoke a six-inch salting of snow covered the foot of my bed. Habit ceased temporarily and it took the power of will to get me from under the covers and stand me, naked, in the middle of the room. Only the kitchen was warm, with oatmeal and coffee waiting on the back of the stove, the coffee clear because my father had put eggshells in it. I was never late for school, but that morning I was half an hour early. I ran all the way.

The day was a trickle of melancholy, but I remember it largely because of the one which followed it. It leaped up like a wild thing and tore the robe off my sorrow. The night sky which I had long used for illumination in my mind gave suddenly way to day, and I saw for the first time clearly by the light of the sun.

It happened in science class, where I sat without anticipation while Miss Lowell called the roll. I was staring at a window, hardly seeing what was beyond it, when she finished, stood up, and turned to the blackboard. On it she had sketched a diagram, and now she began to explain it, walking back and forth slowly, her white shirtwaist throwing off the light, her brown skirt blending with the desks and the walls. Whenever she revealed a new scientific fact to us an ethereal smile lifted up her young, oval face, and she seemed transported. On this morning she was enraptured.

She had explained to us, she said, the molecule, the smallest particle of matter. She had shown us how each bit of matter is made up of countless molecules, since one of them measures in diameter only $\dfrac{1}{125,000,000}$ of an inch. Very well.

This morning she wished to explain the molecule itself. The explanation was not in the textbook we were using but she wished us to have it, so that we would know what the new scientific discoveries were based on when we read about them. Science was moving very rapidly and a great many interesting and surprising facts could be anticipated in the next few years. Very well.

The molecule was not the smallest particle of matter. It was the smallest unit used in constructing specific substances. Actually the molecule was made up of atoms, and it was the atom which was the smallest particle of matter. It was not, however, matter as we popularly suppose matter to be, something solid and tangible. It was electricity, positive and negative electricity, nothing more. There was, therefore, no such thing as matter. Everything was electricity, either posi-

117

tive or negative, in patterns of atoms and in quantities of molecules. Very well.

Moreover everything was not, as we supposed, in a position of rest except when operated upon by some force external to itself. Everything was in motion. Everything was in motion, everything was electricity, and nobody knew what electricity was. Very well.

She went on talking. She explained her diagram of the atom, a crude thing which by modern belief would be considered highly inaccurate. She explained the electron and the nucleus. She described the orbit of the electron revolving around the nucleus like a planet circling its sun. She described the different kinds of atoms, each the basis of a separate element, the elements in turn composing all the forms of matter which exist, including man. She continued her beatific smile. She said, "Very well."

I sat quite still; inside I had been struck and exploded. Everything that I knew was running away from a blazing place in the center of me. Already I was forming plans. In the public library I had seen one of the attendants put a new set of science books on a shelf in the reading room. I knew the exact spot. I had examined the volumes casually. They were tall, with red binding. The library would be open at three o'clock that afternoon.

At three o'clock I was in the reading room. Even the Old Man had not come yet to take his place and read his newspaper. I found the volumes I wanted: *The Outline of Science,* by J. Arthur Thomson, G. P. Putnam's Sons, 1922. Under "Foundations of the Universe" I read:

"Every atom of matter, of whatever kind throughout the whole universe is built up of electrons in conjunction with a nucleus. From the smallest atom of all—the atom of hydrogen—which consists of one electron, rotating round a positively charged nucleus, to a heavy complicated atom, such as the atom of gold, constituted of many electrons and a complex nucleus, we have only to do with positive and negative units of electricity. All matter, therefore, is nothing but a manifestation of electricity. The atoms of matter . . . combine and form electricity. Atoms and molecules are the bricks out of which nature has built up everything; ourselves, the earth, the stars, the whole universe."

The page seemed to glow as I read the words printed on

it. The room glowed. I glowed. The way was discovered. The road was found and it was open.

"There exists the theory that the particles of positive and negative electricity, which make up the atoms of matter, are points or centers of disturbances of some kind in a universal ether, and that all the various forms of energy are, in some fundamental way, aspects of the same primary entity which constitutes matter itself."

I sat back and rubbed the words against the cheek of my heart. "In some fundamental way" . . . in the way of God, of course. "The same primary entity" . . . the stream that lay behind me, the river of heaven's mind, the Mississippi of creation.

"Einstein's theory shows us that there is something in the nature of an ultimate entity in the universe, but it is impossible to say anything very intelligible about it. But a certain aspect of this entity has been picked out by the mind as being what we all call matter. The mind, having done this, also partitions out a space and time in which the matter exists. It is not too much to say that the whole material universe has, in this sense, been created by the mind itself."

That was it: from the infinitely great to the infinitely small life whirled out of nothingness, flashed through mind as a form, a pattern, a face and a force, then trickled back to the quiet pool whence it had come. Pouring forth it broke into atoms, and these mind fashioned into molecules, piling them into suns and mixing them into the multitudinous forms which flickered wherever a world turned cool and green.

We were not, then, Joseph and I and our body, hardened in a mold and set in a distant land of exile, aeons of light years from heaven. We were drifting lazily through a great stream of thought, a group of atoms and molecules held in pattern by the idea of ourself, and made real by the force of life. We were a small portion of the whole mind, set off by itself to explore the consciousness of creation as a personal adventure. Every other person was like us, a group of atoms and molecules held in pattern by the idea of himself, a small portion of the whole mind, set off by itself to explore the consciousness of creation as a personal adventure.

I repeated the fact to myself again and again, until it was like a psalm, singing through me as if I were the reed of a flute. I stared at the page, then at the shelves and walls of the library, imagining that I saw them vibrating with the life

119

of their atoms, streaming and twinkling as did the stars, each book and piece of wood a universe in itself.

What I remember most from that afternoon is the lassitude which came over me, the fragrance of rest which drifted into the nostrils of my soul. For the first time in my memory I was relaxed and content. A dull pain which seemed always to have pressed against the back of my head, tensing my spine and pulling at my temples, was gone. I had found the other door to the room in which I had been shut, the door which opened outward on the place I was to go. I had only to examine the room carefully, remember the details, and wait.

When I left the library that afternoon I walked like a bridegroom approaching his bride. I stopped to pet a cat. I talked to a cross-eyed boy without looking away. I carried an old lady's bundles. At the top of the hill I met one of my friends and patted him on the shoulder as if he had done a splendid thing. He smiled and said, "What do you know, kid?" "Not a thing," I said. "Not a thing."

After that the world was a place of peace for me, and I dreaded nothing in it. I worked in one of the rubber factories, hauling bales of scrap to the acid pits; I worked in a woolen mill, running the mechanical mules that take wool from the carding machines and spin it into thread on bobbins; I worked in a bank, counting pennies from kiddy banks, clipping coupons, checking insurance policies, and writing advertisements about thrift. I spent hours playing baseball, football, basketball, tennis. I learned to dance, tied my shoelaces at the bottom, and carried a handkerchief from a different girl in each pocket. I existed on an endless wave of unperturbed exuberance. At my church on the green the new wisdom was given to all who came for counsel. The priest or priestess said:

"You are passing from eternity to eternity by way of time and space. All that will remain of you when the journey is finished is what you have experienced, what you have learned, and what you have observed. Therefore experience, learn, and observe with goodness and love, so that in you God will have a messenger who returns in joy and who brings with him wisdom. You will therefore help God to experience Himself, you will further His plan for creation, and you will reside more closely in the nature of His existence. You are

120

not away from Him, you are within Him. Look around you and discover His countenance."

One day I stood by my desk in high school, reading a few pages of the next day's history lesson so I would not have to take the book home. Classes had been dismissed; the building was almost empty. Suddenly I had the feeling that I was being watched, that someone was standing behind me. I looked around and saw the Girl.

I knew her slightly. She was a Junior. I was a Senior. I had danced with her a few times. Now she seemed unhappy; there was melancholy in her look. She wore a middy blouse and a plaid skirt. Her hair was bobbed and curled. Her eyes were the color of the morning sea in summer. She was a Swede from Swede Hill.

"There's going to be a party and the girls are asking the boys," she said. "I wondered if you would like to go with me."

I said yes very quickly. I had never been able to watch any person's embarrassment without suffering intensely, and to cause it myself was unbearable.

For one transforming instant her eyes flashed like sunlight on a nest of waves, and her mouth broke open like a flame striking a haystack. Then she was gone, fleeing up the corridor.

That was how she became the Girl. We went to parties and dances and movies together. We skated and sledded in winter, canoed and swam in summer. She was a mass of energy with a smile on top, a collection of laughter not quite recovered from being a tomboy. I liked to be with her for the way she leaned over a fence, the way she rubbed snow on my face and kissed me while it melted, the way she could be quiet, staring at what lay around her with the reverence of a nun. She seemed like a boy, the boy I had ceased being myself; I had a sudden wild notion one day that she was Joseph. Was this how a man came to love a woman—by finding in her a part of himself? Was that what it meant to love someone more than yourself?

One winter night we walked home slowly from a dance. She played along the way, throwing snowballs, pushing me into drifts. When we finally reached her home she put her arms quickly around my neck, kissed me, and whispered in my ear:

"I can't have any more dates with you. My family won't allow it. I've got to go out with Swedish boys. They don't want Irish boys to come up here any more. Please don't be angry with me."

She vanished as she had vanished on that first day, leaving me with only the warmth of her tears on my cheek. She was gone before I realized they were there. After a while, when my heart could pump blood enough to give movement to my body, I walked home.

Swede Hill and Kelly Hill, the Irish section, lay at opposite ends of the town, with the valley containing the business section between. Late at night the Irish boys, coming from dates on Swede Hill, passed the Swedish boys, coming from dates on Kelly Hill. All of them were aware, at least vaguely, that some day they would return to their respective hills and marry their own kind. All of them, that is, except me. The strength of my desire for the Girl, together with its deceptive innocence, had trapped me in a simple delusion. I had mistaken the aura of my own tolerance for a reflection of the tolerance of others.

From the top of my hill I could see the town almost in its entirety—the Town Clock, the church steeples, the smokestacks of the factories, the roofs of the schools, the ribbons of streets, the geographical patterns which determined the other patterns, ethnic and economic. That night I stood and watched it all. Rays from a moon that had just risen painted the snow. There was a ghostly, impermanent air about every object, as if its reality depended on a dream already dwindling in the brain of the night which was its host. Suddenly and to my astonishment I laughed.

I could see before me, stiff and quiet, all the little ideas which had come here from the Old World and settled down side by side without mingling or exchanging more than a diffident, "How do you do?" There were the hills, Swede and Kelly and Cracker. Cracker Hill was where the Yankees lived. There was Little Italy, across the river, and there was Union City, where the Poles, Lithuanians, Hungarians, and Russians were gathered. There were the Catholic churches (one for the Poles, two for the Irish), the Episcopal church, the Congregational and Methodist and Lutheran and Baptist churches, the Polish National church, and the meeting houses of various smaller denominations, with spires as yet not tall enough to glisten at night and be seen from my hill. I could discern also, shining on the high terraces of the hills, the great houses of those who had come early and gathered much.

All of them together, races and faiths and classes and denominations, seemed like things which had crawled from the sea to live on land, crustaceans and bivalves and eels, each with the aptitudes and appendages it had developed for existence at its peculiar level in water. Now all were at a single level and immersed in air. Change, they knew, was imperative; so they studied the crab, the well-to-do native who had come before them and successfully made the transition. Since it would benefit them not at all to become like each other they remained carefully apart, crustacean and mollusk and eel, each with his eyes on the crab. The crab in turn, mildly curious and a little resentful, studied them, considering their possibilities as food. Leaning against a tree and watching them all as they slept, each one alone in the fortress he had piled up on the sand, their fences seemed so fragile and their hopes so foolish that I laughed. Already the crab was obsolete, succeeded by a speedier, less encumbered version of himself; yet the crustacean and the mollusk and the eel kept on in their striving to emulate him, guarding meanwhile their identities as crustacean, mollusk, and eel, lest a bivalve begin to crawl or a crustacean show a tendency to coil.

I had seen all this before—egos ripped from their roots, straining for a new identity, clinging in bigotry and intolerance to the traits by which they had known themselves as a people in their previous environment, fearful lest these be taken from them before others were fashioned to take their place. Why on that night, alone and injured in heart, I stopped to laugh at them I do not know, except that as I gave up my being to laughter I seemed to be joining in the judgment of God. For if America has an essence it is the essence of change. America in her spirit is a compulsion to change, a divine lust to alter, to reshape, to mix, to experiment, to build and raze, to invent and make obsolete, to transmute, transform, melt and remold, and always to mingle and sculpt and finally pound out something new under the sun. The Micks and Polacks and Hunkies and Swedes, the Catholics and Episcopalians and Lutherans and Congregationalists, were only ingredients. They could no more keep from becoming one people with one identity than they could

123

keep the rain which fell on the hills from eventually finding its way to the sea. But they would try. They had come to America to find freedom. They did not realize that freedom is like the kingdom of heaven; to find it a people first must lose itself.

There was another reason why I laughed that night, for I might have regarded these facts without humor; I might have embraced them in melancholy. I laughed because I had a friend.

He was deaf in one ear, weighed a hundred and fourteen pounds, had fought through the World War as a combat man by the time he was twenty-one, and had a nose so often broken that its retention of form was a miracle of surgery. He worked in one of the rubber factories, lived with his widowed mother and a large family of brothers and sisters, and at seven o'clock each evening stepped out of his house dressed and ready for the work which was his life.

He was the most gifted comedian I have ever encountered; he could mimic what life had done to him and join in the laughter. He was not a paid performer; he never appeared on Broadway nor even attempted such eminence; he played with amateur groups, with minstrel shows, and for wounded and disabled veterans in hospitals and sanatoria. He never turned down a request; he played in every town and city in Connecticut, in villages, at crossroad inns, and in barns. He sang songs, delivered monologues, and told ambling, zany stories accompanied by facial expressions which projected in caricature each actor in the tale. He could walk across a stage and convulse an audience; the lift of his leg, the hesitation of his foot, were achievements in artistry. He never spent a night at home, yet he never spent a night seeking his own pleasure. If he did not attend a rehearsal or give a performance he went to see professional actors perform, to observe and study their work. From twenty minutes after seven in the morning until five o'clock in the evening he worked at a bench in a factory; from seven o'clock at night until midnight or one o'clock the next morning he was an artist, giving himself to the world. He had to live that way; he would have perished otherwise.

I went often with him to the towns where he played. He did not need an automobile, though eventually he bought one to save time and his aging legs. Almost everyone in Connecticut knew him; he had only to stand on a corner in any town and within a few minutes a car would stop and pick him up. In his pocket he carried a small ocarina, the only piece of worldly goods he treasured and the only possession he did not at one time or another give away. He bought it in Paris and learned to play it during barrages on the Western Front. It had a tone as sweet as a reed flute, and he played it like the harp of his soul. Late at night while we waited on South Main Street in Waterbury for a ride to Naugatuck, five miles away, he would sit on a curb or lean against a post and play the little ocarina—old war songs, Stephen Foster melodies, and a ballad he liked which began, "Ten thousand years seems a long, long time to wait for a dream to come true."

"That's for my angel," he would say. "She's waiting for me on the other side of purgatory. I hope she's worth it."

Then he would offer himself to eternity for judgment, demanding all sorts of concessions because he knew the right people, had touched the hem of a bishop's robe, and could recite the names of seventeen virgins, all living on the same street. As prosecutor I charged him with the most heinous of violations. He declared his innocence and placed the guilt on various members of the clergy, certain judges, and several maiden school-teachers. The accused were brought before me for examination, the schoolteachers being stripped lest any evidence remain hidden. In the end my judgment was always the same—all souls were sent to heaven except his, mine, and those of the most beautiful women. Hell was reserved for us.

Occasionally we tried the Pope, the occasion being a Bull in which His Holiness ordered Irish whiskey substituted for sacramental wine in the Mass. This was obviously an attempt to destroy the Irish race, for as soon as the decree was published every able-bodied Mick in the world enrolled at a monastery. The high point of the trial came when the prosecutor, lifting his nose, cocking an eye, and pointing a finger, said: "Are you or are you not an Eyetalyun?" There was no escape from this and the defendant was found guilty.

Sometimes we sang, not loudly, the songs of Stephen Foster and Thomas Moore, the mock ballads of American outhouse days, and Negro spirituals. He sang a tenor that held harmony close but never violated her, while I grasped the tune by the throat. Sometimes he fell asleep against my shoulder.

He knew the location of every speakeasy in Connecticut; his sense of urban geography never failed to amaze me. In the middle of a block of business establishments, factories, or even residences, he would turn into an alley, cross a yard, skirt a fence, slip into a hallway, and rap the prescribed number of times on a door. Always it was flung open violently when he was recognized; the reception was vociferous and genuinely warm. The owner, the bartender, the owner's wife and daughter, all made him a personal guest. They asked the usual question with genuine joy: "What'll it be, hooch or the good stuff?" The good stuff was in a bottle, the hooch was in a pitcher. Generally speaking the good stuff was anything not manufactured on the premises. Hooch was made in the kitchen sink.

"I'll take a shot of the good stuff," he always said, "and give my pal here some birch beer."

They would look at me a little shyly then, and the owner's wife, who was almost always fat and pleasant, would pour a glass of the black, tantalizing nonalcoholic drink peculiar to New England.

"You take care of him good, eh, Kid?" she would say. They called him the Minstrel Kid, but mostly it was kid. They hung on his words, kept his glass filled, and after a while asked him for a song. He never refused. Then we said good night and went into the hallway, around the fence, across the yard, through the alley, and back to the street.

It could happen anywhere. There had never been as many saloons as there were speakeasies. Some were Irish, and in these the bartenders served home brew and sang ballads. Some were Italian, and in these the owner served homemade wine and sang opera. Some were Slavic, and in these there was whiskey to drink and a melancholy quiet. The Kid was at home in all of them, and in all of them he was loved.

The love he gave in turn was unconditioned and non-specific in its object. He had no sweethearts; he needed none. At home there was "The Mother," as he called her. The rest of the world was an audience which needed cheering up. At parties he settled in the kitchen, talking to the old folks. The only time I saw him evince enmity for a person was one night in a Polack speakeasy when a drunk made remarks about the fact that I was drinking milk. The Kid went for him, though the lout was twice his size.

There was a night I shall always remember, when we rode into Waterbury on a streetcar after attending the rehearsal of a minstrel show in Waterville, a suburban town. The Kid fell asleep, his head on my shoulder. At Exchange Place, in the center of the city, we had to get off. The streetcar went no farther. The Kid refused to rouse. The motorman, who knew him, gave me an understanding smile.

"The Kid is ten years behind in his sleep, poor lad," he said. "Why don't you give him a lift? I've got to move on to the barn."

It was easy. I put him over my shoulder and stepped out. I had only to walk across Exchange Place to South Main Street. There we would soon catch a ride. But Exchange Place at midnight is as brightly illuminated as Times Square in New York; I had to pass a newsstand and an all night restaurant where the local sports gathered and the taxicabs rested. In the middle of the stretch I saw a policeman strolling toward me. I avoided his gaze but I knew he was watching me. Then, after I had passed him, he shouted.

"Hi, Kid! How are you?"

"Hi, Jerry," the Kid called, "I'm fine. Just taking a nap."

Just before I got to South Main Street I passed a restaurant which specialized in hot dogs smothered in onions and chili. We often stopped there to take on food for the final five miles.

"Whoa!" said the Kid. "Let me down."

I put him on his feet and he led me into the restaurant. Fifteen minutes later, completely revived, he was standing on South Main Street playing his ocarina.

He taught me so much that listing it is impossible; yet all of it reduces to a single truth. I had recognized before this time the corollary of the Crucifixion, that as Christ involved His blood in the destiny of creation, so the blood of every man is likewise involved in creation, and his life is a sacrifice and a redemption. The Kid gave me an example of it; his life was a sacrifice and a redemption. Before he was twelve he knew that the arms of his soul were nailed to a tree, and thereafter he squinted at the sun and laughed. He agreed with God. It was funny. Standing in the darkness listening to him play the little sweet potato I could lean against the spirit that held me projected into life and smile. The Kid had taken care of me good. I knew part of the thing I was meant to do.

The rest of it I learned from the Woman. I met her one freezing night as I walked toward home. The headlights of an automobile turned from the road, played over me, and ran along the embankment to a small white cottage. There the car had turned in, but at the driveway it paused, then stopped. As I came along my path was blocked. The Woman called to me from her place behind the wheel: "My car is stuck. Will you help me get it started?"

I knew who she was, though I had never spoken to her, and she knew who I was. Things are like that in a town which has grown to be a little larger than small but is still a great deal less than big. She lived in the white cottage with her mother, a widow. Her father, a businessman, had left them little else. The Woman was about twenty-four, which seemed to me a considerable age. She had been at college two or three years; now she held a local secretarial position. As I took her place in the driver's seat I remembered the figures in her father's estate. I worked in a bank now that high school was finished, and such things clung to the rafters of my brain. The incidents in his passing were routine. He went quickly, leaving little goods and money; his daughter returned from college to take a job and to care for her mother. She had a few casual beaux; none of them was serious. New England was full of such women, many of them attractive, most of them educated. No one thought it strange that they did not marry and were not pursued.

The motor turned over when I stepped on the starter. "Now why couldn't I have done that?" she said. I drove the car into the garage and helped shut the doors. Then she said, "Won't you come in and have some coffee with me? It's a bitter night." She stepped a little closer than was necessary when she spoke and as I received the question I also received her perfume. It had the quick, fresh thrust of a garden made slowly wet by dew. "Thank you," I said. "I will."

The living room had a fireplace. She stirred the drowsy heap of coals that filled it, put some wood on the little flames, and sat me in an easy chair while she went to the kitchen. Flanking the fireplace and reaching halfway around the room were bookcases. I inspected them; they held dozens of volumes of poetry. I selected an anthology and returned to the fire. When she came from the kitchen with the coffee tray and saw what I was reading she smiled.

"I understand you write poetry," she said. "I'm going to serve a little brandy with our coffee. It's from father's cellar —prewar and pre-me, according to the label: twenty-five years old."

"No," I said. "I don't write poetry. I write verse. There is a great difference. Being able to write verse is like having an ear for music; you can remember tunes and write popular

128

songs. Writing poetry is like composing a symphony or an opera."

"Come and sit on the floor. We can watch the fire better. Could you begin writing verse and learn to be a poet?"

"I think not. Poetry begins early. Sometimes it's all over by the time a man is grown up. Besides, nobody cares about poetry any more. A poet nowadays is a comic figure. The hero in our time is a millionaire."

"In our town, you mean. It isn't like that everywhere. Poetry is still loved, and poets are still appreciated, but not in this idyllic valley. Will you read to me—anything at all— something you like?"

As I turned the pages I thought: if there is a place where poetry is loved and poets appreciated, why was I not born there, instead of here where a knack for rhyming is considered in the same category as a sixth finger, an albino child, or a talent for keeping bees? But it didn't matter much. What I scribbled on the backs of deposit slips in the bank was so far from poetry that I was better off in an environment where it was not inspected critically. How infinitely beyond me were the soaring lines of Francis Thompson, who died in the year of my birth!

> *I fled Him, down the nights and down the days;*
> *I fled Him, down the arches of the years;*
> *I fled Him, down the labyrinthine ways*
> *Of my own mind; and in the mist of tears*
> *I hid from Him, and under running laughter.*

I read on while she watched the fire and listened. When the coffee was finished she set the tray aside and brought brandy inhalants. It was I who set these aside. I placed them on the floor, close enough to the fire so the light played on them. When I turned back she had not moved. She was watching the flames. Slowly I bent and kissed the top of her head, at the place where her hair was parted. I moved as if performing in a play I had rehearsed a thousand times. Each detail of the scene was anciently familiar, even the pattern of the fire.

Slowly she turned her head and stared at me, first with a questioning in her eyes, then with a dazed look as the intelligence in her gaze broke into fragments and swam, suddenly and frantically, in a vast lake of longing. Her head moved up toward me as if lifted by water. I watched her arm as it circled my neck, graceful as a serpent in the sun. Then her mouth struck mine with the impact of snowflakes. A flicker of stimulants ran into my nerves, half like pain, half like a pleasure I seemed to have known but could not remember, could not identify. It was warm like sleep and dry like a shock from electricity. I expected it to stop, like the momentary phenomenon of joy from an unexpected and exciting figure in music or poetry. But it didn't, and with a sudden rush of good sense I surrendered to it, only releasing myself now and then for the delight of repeating the sequence. I had never before, I realized, been kissed. What happened previously was physical proximity without spiritual connection. The switch had never been open, the current had never flowed.

After a while she moved a little and put her face by my cheek. Then she whispered, "Why don't you get out of town and find a job using words instead of figures? Then you'll lose that haunted look and be happy. Even a bird with one note must sing it. If he doesn't he droops and dies."

"Do I look haunted?" I was watching the fire through the maze of her hair, seeing the inhalants reflect and distort the flames. I should have set them a few inches closer to the shadows. The effect would have been better.

"Yes, you look as if you are haunted by two and two, by the fact that the result of them is always the same. That's why I wanted to kiss you. I've wanted to do it for a long time. Do you mind? I stalled the motor when I saw you coming."

"No, I don't mind. I'm glad."

"You accept things too easily. You should beat me a little."

She kissed me again, her mouth as soft as my thoughts of God. Little by little the nature of the pleasure which hummed in me found a parallel in my memory. It was like the spurt of happiness which shook me when, after long and concentrated labor on a set of verses, I read them over and realized that so far as my ability went they represented a good and a finished effort. But this was a constant, subdued, accumulating throb that raised my existence to a higher beat.

She moved again and said, "I wanted to take that haunted look away from you for a little while. But even if I do, it will return. Two and two will always make four so long as you use figures. But with words the answer can be five or

130

seven or eight or even three. You'd like that. You need uncertainty, so you can make guesses."

"How do you know that?" It was probably true, and she had made the diagnosis look ridiculously easy. How could I defend myself for not having known it myself? It had never occurred to me that what talent I had for matching words might be trained to make a living for me. My need for escape had dissolved in the maze of molecular patterns which now for the eye of my mind represented reality. The remnant of my discontent was held in abeyance by the knowledge of sacrifice as the reason for all of life's extension into matter. Now it burst forth in an orgy of strength, dragging with it its cross, eager to plant the emblem on a farther and higher hill.

"I know it because it isn't true that a woman wants a man. She wants to be a man, and the man she loves is the man she wants to be. The man I want to be is a poet who thrives on uncertainty, who makes a sword of words and cuts down anything that bars his passage, who makes his own patterns in life and fulfills one allegiance—to himself."

The flames seemed to mount as she talked. I threw her head back and kissed her, softly for the beauty of it, then hard to tell her that I would pour myself into her and make her what she wanted to be. Her arm tightened around my neck and the subdued beat of pleasure broke suddenly into a pounding tide of the sea in which both of us were anchored, and in which, through a common recession, each could find surcease from will and mind and purpose. I felt the rush of a wild, intensified flood from the sleep world, and I watched with wonder as it poured over and in and through me, knowing it also was engulfing her. It was the world of senselessness from which sense had come, and into which now all our senses were dipping for renewal, for furbishing and consecration and delight. Watching myself I drifted in worldlessness, a small light plunged into a great darkness, making little shadows on the earth, shadows that moved and believed themselves alive, that mixed and postured and pretended, making images and figures, until each looked on the other as proof of its own existence, and the hurrying patterns of the flames ran away from me as I moved, believing me to be alive and real.

I set the inhalants into the darkness, and the fire gave itself to us for cover.

EIGHT

"NEW ENGLAND!" said the Professor. "What a mixture of meaning wells up from that name. What a breed it has nurtured, and what a foundation it has given America! I doubt that we shall be able either to live up to it or to live it down."

He looked past me, his gaze dissolving as he turned inward to his memory and to the memory he had appropriated from history.

"If you will allow me to masquerade for a while as a disengaged observer," he said, "I may be able to shed some understanding on the environment which so puzzled you as a boy, though you have long ago, I am sure, fathomed the basic reason for your discontent in this particular matter."

"In a way I have," I said, "but the complete, well-adjusted person should get along in any environment—at least so we are told by both phychologists and saints. Frankly I think the mark of an integrated personality is a certain amount of discontent, this being an imperfect world. But in either case I have refused, as a safeguard against rationalizing my failures, any whisperings of my mind against New England as a birthplace and as a home."

"Sound procedure," said the Professor. "Let us consider New England, then, from an academic and objectively enlightening viewpoint."

"Go ahead. Shall I ask Miss Iceberg to loosen her shoe and swing it on her big toe?"

"Unnecessary. It is one o'clock. The crisis is past. Womanhood is safe until midnight.

"Now then. Let us consider first the fact that New England is the only part of our country which developed a theology. In New England alone there has been an adaptation of Christianity which might be considered native. There were several stages, or 'enlightenments.' Jonathan Edwards

132

led the first, Horace Bushnell formulated the last, which was called the New Theology. Both were Congregational ministers, one in the eighteenth century, the other in the nineteenth.

"Edwards defended Calvinism, particularly predestination, fighting against Arminian theology, which arose in the Netherlands as an attempt to ease man's damnation by emphasizing his freedom of choice. Edwards would have none of this, but he did soften and personalize Calvinism and he started a trend toward modification which his followers continued. You will excuse the dullness of these facts; they are pedantic but important.

"Horace Bushnell, who lived in Hartford, the capital of your state, went to Yale and died in 1876. He transformed the entire New England theology—which by his time was formal, dated, and uninspiring—into a living doctrine of the spirit and mind. He emphasized personal experience, injected a mystical note, and insisted that theology be brought abreast of science, since there could be no disparity between the truth revealed by God in His various manifestations. Creation was continuous, he said, and God was continuously involved in it, with Christ as the central figure or architect.

"It was, you see, a liberalizing and a modernizing movement. It was also a native movement. It was typically American. It implied the idea of humanity as an army marching through creation toward God, not the older notion of a group of exiles wrapped in rags of sin, warming themselves at little fires of lust while waiting to be redeemed."

"Excuse me," I said. "I wish to point out that the older notion, as you express it, is really the younger. Hindu theology specifically indicates humanity as a collective adventure in the plan of Vishnu. It was Christianity which devised the more narrow and time-bound notion of the earth as a Siberia of the soul."

"Well, put it in as a footnote. My students don't know such things and I am therefore not bothered with interruptions. The point is that New England can be said to be more typically American than any other part of the country, since it alone has adapted its religion to the natural genius of our democracy and to our unique adventure in human destiny.

"As a matter of fact this developing theology greatly influenced the Revolution. It had been preached for a hundred and forty years, with a growing emphasis on the natural rights of man, before the Declaration of Independence. The phrase about men being born free and equal is a direct reflection of it. It is a theological truth, not a scientific one.

"Therefore it can be said that New England developed and nurtured the philosophy which was exalted into the political creed of the United States, the metaphysic of American democracy.

"It was natural that this should happen, for though all the religions which came to the New World brought with them their theologies and rituals intact, this New England sect was a hunted one and came here for refuge. It was a young, independent organization, and a democratic one. The Reverend Thomas Hooker, who founded Hartford, issued there in 1639 the first written constitution in history, the Fundamental Orders by which the first colony in your state was governed. It antedated the Constitution which now governs us by one hundred and fifty years."

"Hartford was a theocracy," I said. "I suppose the interplay of church and state had a tendency to stimulate changes."

"Precisely, though the democratic nature of the government was the key to this. Remember that Protestantism implies and in some cases declares the priesthood of the congregation; every man is a minister. If you consider this in relation to Puritanism in New England you perceive that a great deal of the external piety and solemnity was due to the impact of this idea on the average man. He became self-conscious of his role and overplayed his part. A little of that persists today, but largely and happily it has passed, and with it the gloomy, narrow theology which inspired it.

"When all men are priests then for a while all men are priestly, but after not too long a time it is the other way round, and all priests are human. But there is a little of the priestly left, and it is this which gives the New England church its strength.

"There is, of course, no New England church as such. I am speaking of the two branches of Calvinism which came to the Massachusetts Bay Colony, the Presbyterian-Puritan and the Independent-Congregational. These were the parent strains; they gave New England its character, and that character shaped America. An overwhelming number of our leaders came from New England; a majority of them still do. It is an incredibly strong strain, tenacious, vigorous, ingenious, doggedly moral, and persistently godly. It has its

134

accretions and absurdities, but it seems naturally adapted to the task of conquering, organizing, and controlling a wild, lush, vast and incomparably rich land. Theologically it required individualism and positive virtue, and those are the qualities which made America, a new and tremendously exhilarating individualism and a great surge of positive virtue. Call it what you like, romantic humanitarianism, idealistic democracy, it is America and it is the most successful experiment in human destiny conducted during the history of man."

"So far as man remembers."

"So far as man remembers. That spoils the sentence; makes it anticlimactic. But it makes you happy so tack it on.

"Now consider the kind of individual who led this movement. Take the man who founded Hartford, the first permanent settlement in your state. Once in England when this Reverend Thomas Hooker, because of his religious views, was hiding from officers of the Crown, he took refuge with his friend the Reverend Samuel Stone. At the time Reverend Stone was smoking a pipe. Reverend Hooker remonstrated with him, and launched into a sermon on the evils of tobacco. Midway he was interrupted by the pursuing officers, who pounded on the door. Reverend Hooker slipped into a hiding place and Reverend Stone, still smoking his pipe, opened the door and assured the officers that he had no visitors. The officers left, whereupon Reverend Hooker came forth from his hiding place and took up his lecture against tobacco at the point where he had been forced to stop.

"It was he who led a congregation to Massachusetts and later to Hartford. It was under his direction that the Fundamental Orders were composed and issued."

"Suppose he were to return today," I said, "and find that Hartford is the center of a rich tobacco-growing district and the home town of two of our leading ecdysiasts, or stripteasers. Would he be happy?"

"He would, indeed, for it is the nature of individualism to foster change and adaptation. We have become a nation of smokers and a country of sparsely clad women. Likewise Horace Bushnell, who as the leading Congregational minister of Hartford inherited Thomas Hooker's mantle, liberalized and modernized the theology governing Hooker's descendants. That Hartford should raise tobacco and women who are expert in disrobing is therefore not incongruous."

135

"Of course not—any more than it is incongruous for Hartford, being a community founded by a man afraid neither of the King's officers nor the New World wilderness, to gain fame by urging men never to take a chance, to be always insured."

"And so much for facetiousness," the Professor said. "The point is that you were born and raised thirty miles from Hartford, in the center of a state known as 'the land of steady habits.'

"But you were not born into the people of that land, or into their church. You were born to an alien group and an ancient church which had come to the land to serve that group, not to seek refuge for itself. Yet by being born in the land you partook of its archetype, the pattern of its evolving race form. Moreover your own people, the Irish, had for four hundred years been persecuted and subverted by the same government which forced the Pilgrim colonists to New England. You felt strongly the urges of individualism and positive virtue. Yet the head of your church had condemned both of these urges theologically, and in doing so had referred to them as 'Americanism.'

"That was in 1899, in an apostolic letter by Pope Leo XIII. It was entitled *Testem Benevolentiae*, and in it His Holiness spoke of the system which stresses natural virtues rather than the teachings of dogma, and which inclines to individual inspiration and positive virtue as opposed to appointed external guidance and passive, or negative virtue. He was speaking of the system with regard to its appearance in his own church, of course, but he was definite in condemning it and in referring to it as 'Americanism.'

"My guess is that when, a generation later, you reacted intuitively against what seemed a dark and uninspiring church, you were feeling the inharmony of that church with its surroundings. The Congregational church, which attracted you, was in harmony with everything about it. It was, in fact, the architect of that harmony. The other churches had come to serve alien groups in what was necessarily an alien way. The priests in your church were Irish, were they not?"

"Yes, and many of them were natives of Ireland, where the priest is a dictator over his flock. Some of them found it hard to give up this power in America, but there was no way to enforce it, since it was theirs only by consent of the people. I have heard many tales of the strong-arm methods used by priests in Ireland. These methods seemed to me very

136

much like those employed by the early Puritans. Probably they were a remnant of the same period, coming late to this country."

"Perhaps. And now you begin to see the nest of paradoxes into which you were precipitated. In Protestantism, and particularly in New England Protestantism, the minister is the servant of the people, appointed by them and subject to their authority. In the Irish wing of your church the people are the servants of the priests, given into their care by a bishop and subject to their authority. In New England in the generation of your parents this was still largely so, though the people had begun to feel the freedom of their new home and to assert it somewhat."

"That is true. But the authority now is only held in abeyance. It has not been replaced by freedom of the congregation to choose its own priests; nor is that apt ever to happen."

"There is a difference, of course," the Professor said, "between a priest and a minister, a great difference. A priest is dedicated to the mystical life and so, by way of the Mass and the sacraments of Penance and Holy Eucharist, is his congregation."

"He is in direct descent from the priests of the mystery religions and the communicants of his church are modern initiates," I said.

"Precisely. But in the mystery religions and in early Christianity voluntary membership was tremendously significant. In other religions memberships was by birth or geography or social strata. A neophyte of the Christian or Mithriac mysteries, on the other hand, was so by an act of his own will, and by the acceptance of his application on the part of the priests to whom he applied. He was serious in his intention to escape the wheel of life by ascending through the various realms of spirit to the throne of the Lord, in paradise.

"Now let me ask you a few questions. Are you a voluntary member of the Catholic Church?"

"No, I was born into it. It has been pointed out to me on many occasions that if I leave it I shall suffer intense and terrible damnation, because I was born into the truth and if I reject it my sin is monstrous, whereas the Protestants, born into rejection, are forgiven."

"The voluntary Catholics, then, are the converts. Tell me, what have you observed about them?"

"Great Christian zeal, intellectual curiosity, and a slight stain from the minds of those who proselytized them."

"What have you noticed about the others, the involuntary Catholics?"

"Apathy for the Christian ideal, group consciousness, and a casual acceptance of salvation as something guaranteed by membership in the church, not a state of blessedness to be won by personal effort. A reasonable traffic with the sacraments is considered by them to be wise, but as long as a priest can reach him before he dies a Catholic need not worry overmuch. That is not precisely what he is told but that is precisely what he thinks."

"Precisely. You will forgive my repetition of the word, I hope. It is a key utterance with me, a means by which I switch the current of talk back to myself. I tried once to get along without it, for I am aware that such eccentricities are observed by students and used for a quite opposite purpose, as a means of identifying the fossilization process which inevitably begins in a teacher and which eventually fits him for obsolescence and retirement. But I could not do without it. Unless I said 'Precisely' after a student answered a question I could not proceed with my lecture. My thought processes froze and I was unable to articulate the simplest comment. So I thought, well, I must go on and be a dinosaur, and one day it will make little difference whether I am extinct or merely dead. So today I am known to my students as 'Precisely,' though of course I am not supposed to know it. Our conversation was normal, you perceive, until I began this lecture on New England theology and asked you certain questions. Ah, well, let us proceed.

"The point I wished to make about Catholicism as you encountered it is this. The church came here to serve an immigrant class which was not only poor but which was often discriminated against to the point of persecution. The older quarrel between Protestantism and Catholicism took from this a new identification, and Catholics mingled with their religious feelings the feelings of their particular group. Was this not so in your boyhood?"

"Very much so. It was common legend that Protestants kept Catholics from political appointments, from better positions in the factories, from honors in school. The Protestants didn't want us to 'get ahead.' So far as I could observe this was utterly absurd. If a dumb Irish kid could not pass his work in school God pity his teacher if she were a Protestant. It was her fault.

"I realize now that with the Irish this was caused by more than the local situation, which was pleasant and, I believe, commendably fair. Behind it lay all the years since Red Hugh O'Neil was beaten at Kinsale—four centuries of British domination in Ireland. The Irish were so accustomed to British ownership, British discrimination, that their reaction to anyone of English blood was a conditioned reflex. When in New England they found Yankees, whom they identified as English, in possession of the land and wealth, they were prepared to magnify the slightest discrimination into a monstrous persecution. In this matter I don't think the Congregationalists had much of a chance. If they preferred their own company to that of the Irish they were snobbish and discriminatory; any overtures they might make were apt to be misinterpreted as condescension.

"But I did not know this until I was well into puberty. My father was born in Connecticut. My mother came from Ireland when she was three years old. It was from other people that I heard, eventually, that the Protestants 'didn't want us.' Before that I had been only poignantly aware of the religious difference, and what I inferred from this was that the Catholics looked with pity on their misguided theological cousins. The attitude of envy, irritation, and fear came as a surprise to me, particularly as I found it in my contemporaries, in Irish boys and girls of my own age."

"They had absorbed it from their parents and were using it to prepare for their own defeat, to bolster their own sense of inferiority," the Professor said. "Had you noticed anything similar in Protestant boys and girls?"

"None whatever, until the episode on Swede Hill. I had played with Protestant children always and had liked them. When I heard of these same children making nasty remarks about the Irish or about Catholics I suspected that they had been goaded into it, for those who informed me of the canards were the militant Catholics, the pugnacious Irish. Such remarks were never made to me."

"Precisely. And now, to complete our evidence, tell me what caused this attitude to fester and to break out. What was the main point of irritation? Was it theological or economic?"

"It was economic. The Irish were infected with the desire to 'make good.' Each wanted to personify the American

139

success story. Everything was fine so long as success consisted of making the high school football team. Few of the Yankees could match the Irish in sports. It was when the contest moved beyond this, to the arena of economic struggle, where the Yankees had all the strength, that paranoia broke out among the Irish. Suddenly they were an oppressed and suffering people, identifying themselves with their church and their race while they sought with longing and ardor for fulfillment of the great American dream—money."

"Precisely. Now let us draw the threads together and look at the pattern. You found yourself an Irish-Catholic in a New England town, in a land permeated by the spirit of Americanism, which as a theology was declared anathema by your church. You were committed by the fact of your Catholicism to theological dogma, passive virtue, and counsel from others in matters of the spirit. You were also committed to an attitude of disapproval toward those who were the builders and holders of the land, who were now its native people and whose church reflected the history and the spirit of the adventure of colonization in New England.

"Yet your people, the Irish, had come to America to partake of that adventure, and they were partaking of it, nobly. Far from reflecting the attitude to which their church by its theology committed them, they disliked the Protestants only because they envied them their economic success. They wanted to outdo the Yankees at 'making good.' They had more than a normal immigrant's desire for this; they had four hundred years of frustration to sublimate in their drive for wealth and power. They were not intent for a moment on the mystical union symbolized in the Mass. Every one of them wanted a mansion and a million dollars."

I closed my eyes and saw it in a thousand memories—the awareness of the Irish in their new, strange world, where the laws were for, not against them; where they could save money and buy land, and become whatsoever each pleased to become. The freedom confused them; it was a force they were accustomed to sing about, to yearn for, to plot to accomplish, but not to use. Instinctively they looked for enemies, for superiors and inferiors. They were uneasy in a society which had achieved the ambition they themselves had handed down through generations as an ideal, but whose fulfillment had become for most of them a myth. Here the ambition was realized and it was up to them as individuals to take advantage of it. It was no longer the hope of an army or a government or a movement; it was not a cause in which a person could lose himself in a particular way. Now that he had the freedom, what was he going to do with it?

There was a question which always was asked in America: "What are you going to be?" You had to answer it, and the answer was not that you were going to be Irish or Catholic or Yankee or Protestant or even American. You were already that. You had to be something else, and no boy or girl wanted to say in answer, "Oh, nothing." When you might be President how could you content yourself with nothing? The Irish, like the rest of the New Englanders, determined to be something, but in that first generation they hesitated, looking for the shadows of those who would oppose them. They looked too for a cause greater than themselves; the habit of personal ambition was not yet in them. They were trained in sacrifice. They needed a cause; a man could not be idealistic about making something for himself, whether it was money or reputation or fame.

It was a strong urge, this yearning for a cause. When as a boy I heard my mother sing the old songs of Ireland while she rocked in her chair in the kitchen and nursed my brother, a quick and violent urge to be about some battle, to deal smashing blows of liberation, came over me and set me to dreaming of enemies I might fight and slay for Ireland, "the most distressful country that ever I have seen; they're hangin' men and women for the wearin' of the green." My mother sang the old song like a hymn, and when I heard her I wanted to fight and die for Erin and to hear struck once again in Tara's halls the harp of ancient days.

But it did not last, this pattern of race and sacrifice. The immigrants found a cause in their children; they trained and educated them for the American dream; theirs would be the thrust for glory; they would adapt the freedom and greatness of the country to their personal adventures. So these children were raised in an aura of hope and ambition; they were guarded from suffering and they endured only such persecution as they imagined was visited upon them. The limitless opportunities of America were theirs; they needed only energy, intelligence, talent, ingenuity, and a knowledge of what particular things they wanted to accomplish, a vision of the persons they wanted to be.

It was then that some of them began to hang back, to recall and reform and reanimate the pattern of Irish racism, the archetype of a hunted, condemned, persecuted hero

141

whose only fault is his virtue, his shining superiority of mind and talent over those who from envy and fear cast him out. It was a perversion of the original pattern and it sucked in evil. It was ready for what came to seek it out—fascism, bigotry, anti-Semitism, isolationism, power politics, and all the creeping forms of organization which labor by the power of unity to deliver individuals from the responsibility of personal effort. This was the obverse side of the coin of sacrifice, the other end of idealism, a cause in the hire of Lucifer's theologians.

Both generations went every week to Mass. I saw them there, the old folks sitting in the center aisle, following the Mass with reverence, running rosaries through their strong hands; the young folks on the side aisles, nervous and bored, gauging the speed at which the priest was proceeding, giving the responses more quickly than the old folks but without a shred of piety. On the altar the priest raised the chalice, bowed before the Host, whispered the supplication, *"Agnus Dei qui tollis peccata mundi, miserere nobis."* Did the Lord well up in every heart and did the souls of the congregation yearn for union with the Master in Whose image they were cast?

"It was a pattern of contradictions, of paradoxes, of false syllogisms," the Professor went on, "and you were expected to accept it without question. You received neither enlightenment nor explanation, either at home or in your school. You were well instructed in science. Did anyone lecture to you on the history of Christian sectarianism?"

"Not a word was spoken," I said. "Freedom of religion meant keeping quiet about it."

"Precisely. In America the bitter persecution and savage inquisitions which stained Christianity with shame after the Reformation all ceased. This was a wonderful and a blessed thing, and if peaceable arbitration and an intermingling of theologies and congregations did not follow soon it is not to be set against the sects as a great sin. The warriors were weary from the battle; they were content to rest in their tents, leaving the inevitable and exhausting negotiations of peace until later—in this case until generations free from the memory and hurt of hating were raised up. Meanwhile the armies were quiet, the guns were stacked, and the former enemies went quietly about their several ways, civil to each other in meeting but not inviting intimacy. Their children would do that. You did it."

142

"I and others did it. A few even carried their inclinations through to matrimony. Those who did, so far as I know, found happiness. Those who were tempted to and did not found frustration and, in the end, no solace whatever."

"They did not find solace in their religion?"

"They were not the type for that. If in the limited environment in which she exists a Catholic girl does not find a Catholic husband, she does not automatically become possessed of a religious vocation or a leaning toward celibacy. I know Catholic girls who dutifully rejected non-Catholic suitors in their youth only to go to the brink of middle age without another opportunity. Then in hunger and despair of heart they married non-Catholics anyhow. During all those lonely years the church was not able to fill their need; the fundamental, simple desire of a woman for a mate was stronger than the call of the mystical way."

"Precisely. And now let me pull the final thread through, so that the pattern will be complete and clear. The point of the needle strikes there, on the mystical way.

"Is there a mystical way in your church for the average person? Is it reasonable to assume that the Mass and the sacraments and the celibate priests present a highway which will take all the members of the church to the same heaven inhabited by the saints, with perhaps a brief stopover in purgatory?

"Please do not consider this theologically; I mean only to apply history's lesson that all things have decay in their nature."

I felt weary at the need to turn my mind to a subject which had ripped at my heart since I could remember.

"With your permission," the Professor said politely, "I will proceed. We know there was a mystical way for all in the early days of the church, when Christianity was a new and tremendously exciting mystery religion, a cult with a God Who had come in the flesh to found it. His return to earth was believed to be imminent; the wheel of life which had bound man for so many ages was to be broken. Christianity was an emotional and intellectual experience beyond parallel. But as time went on it became less ecstatic and more ritualistic, less inspirational and more dogmatic. The imminence of Christ's return became gradually the immanence of His presence, and it was felt only by the saints and by holy men who applied themselves to the path of union, or yoga, as had their brothers in the East for unnumbered centuries.

"But this was the way of all religions. Even with political power Christianity would not be unique unless it could maintain its atmosphere of immediacy, its aura of realization, its sense of the closeness, almost the contemporaneity, of the kingdom of Christ. This was accomplished when Saint Augustine put a watch on the wrist of creation.

"He threw away the timelessness of the East, the wheel of cosmic nights and days, aeons and ages, civilizations and lives, which had always obtained in religion. He refused to accept the teaching that worlds, ages, civilizations, are but patterns which endlessly repeat themselves in the history of God's thought. He declared each man to be unique, each day a fresh page in creation, each life span a wheel of existence in iself. Every moment was worth living, every thought important, every act decisive. Christ, if not imminent, was nearby, always within the reach of prayer and waiting at death for those who on earth had served him.

"On that basis life was worth living for every man. From the cradle to the grave was not a stretch of karma to endure, not a turn of the wheel on which the soul is bound, but a shining highway leading to the Lord. Man could be up and doing and on his way to heaven.

"It was a new conception of man and of time, and from it stemmed a new experiment in human activity. Augustine has been called the first modern man, the first person to perceive the psychological nature of time, the first philosopher to release God from it and to bind man so tightly with it that he is frantic to be freed.

"He cannot be freed, of course, but he can stretch his bonds, and this is what he does. He extends every moment by filling it with activity. That is modern man in the West. That is how he developed and expressed his individuality, conquered the world, explored the universe—"

"And discovered facts which now give him the uneasy feeling that perhaps Augustine was wrong."

"Nonsense. The man was sublimely right, and because of if we have modern Western civilization. But in achieving this victory it is obvious that we have all become more concerned with stretching the bonds of time than in freeing ourselves from them. We compare our stretching muscles to those of other people, and when in the Mass your priest elevates the Host which symbolizes the way to freedom, those who watch it are really concerned with their dexterity within the bonds. And down through the centuries the church itself

144

has at times shown a lamentable tendency toward this athletic exhibitionism, this childish delight in worldly power.

"This is the final paradox, and the one that hurt you most, though it was a ridiculous concentration of all the paradoxes into a single incident that brought you to the point of release, the objective view from which your mind saw things at their spiritual levels. Laughter, as Hilaire Belloc pointed out, comes from the soul, which is amused at the false values humanity has placed on possessions.

"But you had to be shown this view, you had to be taught how to laugh in this particular way. Your friend did that for you. He was a humorist, a clown by nature. Art is supposed to hold a mirror up to life; humor holds a mirror up to man, and the clown, looking in the glass, is aghast at the donkey ears and idiot grin he sees. But he cannot help reproducing them; he cannot help becoming the mirror himself. Your friend held the mirror up for you. He taught you how to laugh. Do you remember how he did it?"

"Yes. The first thing he did was to laugh at me, and when I looked at myself, sure enough, there was a laughable object—a young man in wide-bottomed trousers on his way to a dance where he hoped to meet a girl to whom he could write poetry."

"Humor works on all levels, in all conditions and situations where mind is apt to consider its labor finished, its journey ended. In America it accepted a multiple task. As the settlers and immigrants adapted themselves to their new environment they tended to regard that adaptation as a complete process of Americanization. As fast as the old crystallizations were broken up new ones formed. That was natural. Man is inclined to regard every step forward as his last, and to consider those who walk farther as impractical and foolish people. Yet life never ceases in its movement, evolution never pauses. There is never an instant when everything which man believes and knows is not changing, and when he attempts to rest, to pause, to swim against the flow, he breaks the surface with ripples of laughter.

"America is a vast experiment in the spirit of man. The end of it is far away. Change is constant and imperative. An American must be made, and nothing must mar the gestation; all that man has been must be recapitulated in the new individual, but his development must not stop at a point already realized in evolution; he must go beyond all that has been

145

reached or his form will be that of a monster and his birth will be a tragedy for the world. Is it any wonder that both laughter and the gods hover near the womb?"

He examined me suspiciously, ticking and half closing one eye.

"I have been observing in you a tendency to put the burden of articulation on me," he said. "You have made a profession of questioning and listening, like a gossip at a church fair. No doubt you are accomplished in the trick of inducing people to talk about themselves. But our project demands that you do the talking and that the subject be yourself."

"I have told you everything," I said.

"You have given me an outline with a few selected details."

"I have given you the core, the heart—things I never before put into words. The accumulations, the accretions, the refinements, are unimportant. I came out of the waters of adolescence as wet as any other boy with the things that happen to youngsters in America. Even the details seldom differ in these experiences: a friend's name, the color of a girl's hair—these may change; the rest is the same. It is the impact of these experiences on the consciousness and the spirit of the boy that is singular."

"Quite singular, in your case, and quite undesirable, I would say. Not that I blame you entirely; your environment was, as I have pointed out, mined with paradoxes. Still, you seemed always to be unnaturally preoccupied with what you believed to be the spiritual life. It would have been more normal for you to forget the conflict or religious sectarianism that was presented to you. In that case you would have had, I believe, an average and uneventful childhood."

"No one forgets that religious conflict. It is not faced, that is all. For better or for worse I dragged it into the open in my mind and I have kept it there. I have dreamed and I still dream of striking a blow to bring it to an end, to restore peace and unity to the only good chance men have had to achieve their destiny together and in not too long a time. I have dreamed of shattering the misunderstanding, of tearing up the minutiae of differentiation, of beating out a single foundation—"

Miss Iceberg jumped up and came to me quickly. She bathed my head and gave me water and orange juice to drink.

"Your well is deep and I am thirsty," I said.

146

"Less than an hour to go now," she said. "Soon you'll be upstairs and in your own room again."

"To her great relief," the Professor said. "By the way, what became of the Woman? She seemed well on the way to being an influence of some sort."

"She was a very good influence; because of her I left town. I went to Washington and Lee University, in Lexington, Virginia."

The Professor showed surprise.

"There are only two formalized societies in America," he said. "You went from one to the other, from New England to Virginia. Why?"

"That fact did not occur to me," I said. "I wanted a small school with a good academic reputation, far enough from Connecticut so I would encounter a new people and experience a new environment, but close enough so that I could go home for Christmas, a time when no man should be alone. It had to be a nonsectarian school and it had to possess a department of journalism. At the time only Washington and Lee fulfilled these conditions."

"I see. But tell me about the Woman. You did not leave for the university immediately. You saw her again?"

"Yes, I saw her again. She had a beauty that grew on me. Only water and flame are always graceful, and she was like a mixture of both. When she raised a wine glass to her mouth and emptied it I saw more harmony and form than I had ever before witnessed in humanity. Her speech was as fluid as her body; she expressed her thoughts without restraint or artifice. I realize now that she was a mature, poised, and lovely person, complete as an individual and spiritually secure. She shook me into a realization of myself, and I remember every quiver of the shaking. I remember, in fact, all the things she did and how she did them, for I never again encountered in a woman those things or that way of doing them."

"It is fortunate that a man does not marry his first love," the Professor said. "For then he does not lose her. James Huneker said that. What became of the Woman?"

"During the next winter her mother died. She sold the house and left town. Infrequently she wrote me—from New York, Paris, Rome, Vienna, and finally England. There she married and there she died, in a little town on the Sussex downs, within sight of the sea. From the time she left Con-

147

necticut she was ecstatically happy. In seven years she was dead."

The Professor ticked quietly away, musing.

"And your friend," he said finally, "the Kid. What happened to him?"

"He died last year."

"So soon? He was young, was he not?"

"He was forty."

"Hmm. And you are thirty. You have no idea of following these friends, no morbid notion——"

"If I get out of this coffin alive," I said, "I shall live to be a hundred."

"It will do you no good whatever," said the Professor. "Your problem could not be solved in a millennium."

NINE

MEMORY is a dream in whose reality we believe because once we walked through it awake. Yet the things we touched and saw and put our lips against then, the words we heard, the pleasures we purchased, the disciplines we endured, the faces we watched and which watched us, are not in our recollection as they seemed in their happening. Nor is it what has been forgotten which changes their countenance; it is that which is remembered which induces mutation.

There is so much more in the moment now than existed at its impact. There was only, then, the strike of time and its reception, the event and its recoil, the meeting of experience and the merging with it: a pattern, a prejudice, an idea, a scene, rolled up to the instant and fell over its precipice, into self-consciousness. Called up, evoked, examined, it has altered its figure, furbished its garment—its voice has assumed intensity, its visage is spotted with implications, its gestures shimmer with meaning. It is no longer what once it was, a raw, unconditioned actuality, an incident existing in space and time, uninhibited and unjudged. It is part now of a particular mind, existing as thought, subject to the infiltration and the influence of every other thought with which it coexists in the particular mind into which it has fallen; affecting by its radiance the shifting, prowling pattern of that mind; arranging itself to receive the precipitation of new experience, which like a line of surf marks the meeting of mind and matter, the shore of form and dimension, the moment.

Only the moment holds man in the world. So long as he breaks, however softly, against the beach of time, he is aware of himself as existing, as human, as a sense-equipped extension into form, as an edge of consciousness rubbed against a limitation of itself. When the abrasion ceases he slips away from limitation; he drifts into depths without dimension; he moves backward toward laws which, though they sustain him, will shatter him if he comes too close. Only the moment is safe for him, and for his identity; he must return to it, however battering it may be, however wearisome is the continuous assault of duration and entropy.

He has learned through millennia to endure the instant and to meet it with skill. After long effort he can receive it and watch it simultaneously; he can move against it, roll with its impact, employ it in sequence, divert its force. The experience it has poured into him in the past he employs to arrange and control and forecast the experience it will bring against him in the future. Steadily, persistently, he widens his control over what has been and sharpens his cunning for shaping what will be. His awareness takes on strength, his dominion increases; depths without dimension seem less formidable. He has confidence in what he now perceives himself to be, a particular mind employing an organized, resilient, adaptable past to partially check and somewhat guide a future which ceaselessly pours toward him bearing infinite experience intricately differentiated.

He meets the future in the moment, swaying, countermoving, side-stepping, lunging, pulling it by him, throwing it into his past, where, if he has won the fall, it faithfully serves him. The combat ceases only for sleep and death; while it endures he creates himself. What his past is forcing on his future is what, in the moment, he is.

What I myself was at eight o'clock on the first Sunday morning in September, 1926, when I stepped on the platform of the Naugatuck station of the New York, New Haven and

Hartford Railroad, seemed at that instant largely negative. I desired to receive the future unconditionally, without reference to the past. A few abstractions and formulae were all I carried by way of instruments for education; what else I had studied was either now untrue or existed as fact, available in any library whenever needed, not to be stored in the particular mind, a dead weight in memory. The idola of my community I had rejected; the prejudices and politics of my race I had anathematized. The environment I was leaving was to me a picture—I can see the dew on the station lawn as clearly now as I saw it then. It meant nothing more to me than that.

My father, standing beside me on the platform, had the same practical view of geography. He knew our separation was to be partial, a matter of sensory perception. He would not see or hear me for a while, that was all; there was no odor or touch or taste of me to miss. Virginia was a postmark he would henceforth sort more carefully from other postmarks as he worked in the postoffice. Occasionally he would find a letter from me and carry it home to my mother; heretofore he had encountered me now and then as I emerged from the bank, fifty yards south of the postoffice, and walked home with me. The subtler break, the release of the son from the father psyche, had never taken place, had not been necessary. I had always been free; no bond of dependency existed to be cut. We had gone together that morning to early Mass, walking quietly, saying little, kneeling side by side, as brothers do. That was all.

It was a gentleman's duty, I thought, to give lip and pen service to sentimentality. The Virgin Mother, symbol of the purified soul bringing forth the hidden Christ, had suffered a long decline since Isis. Romance had given to every woman the qualities of both Eve and Mary; from their mixture had come puritanism and sentimentality, a worship of chastity for its own sake, a fantastic regard for the gestures of sex and a perverted abstention from the act itself, a succession of nauseating negative virtues, a cult of personal attachment based on a shared denial of life. But many whom I loved were sentimental; they knew no other exit by which their hungers might escape. So I had said what sentiment required, and written in careful precise epistles what it had dictated. None who listened or who received a letter believed that I was melancholy at leaving him or her, but it fulfilled a dogma for me to say so. What I was leaving was not a people or a place, but a shared future with that people and place, a communal interception of the moment. Our shared past would board the train with me; it existed nowhere but in my mind.

My mind was a small and anxious dominion. So far as we were able Joseph and I had secured and arranged it. What we governed was gathered and organized; what together we knew was prepared to act; what was to happen we did not wish to anticipate or influence; we wanted only to receive it without prejudice, without desire, and without a particular need. We were embarking not on an education aimed at preparing us for a career, but on a new approach to the central problem of our existence. In the womb our body had recapitulated biological evolution; through childhood, puberty, and adolescence we had simulated a synopsis of the emotional and mental history of our species, particularly that of the archetype of Western man. Now we were to trace the intellectual development of that archetype.

I would be at the moment, receiving the impact; Joseph would be in the retired, objective identity of the past, spreading himself to the edge of our dominion, extending its frontier, protecting its approaches. Our body would continue to bear us against the world. What practical use we could make of a university training was secondary; a writing job would be less onerous than most occupations we could envision. Its present importance, to us, was that it demanded a college education; a college education was an excuse for study and contemplation. If I said now that I intended to enter newspaper work—and I did say it—it was a promise which, Joseph and I knew, I might not have to fulfill. Something more agreeable might turn up, something which would allow us, under the guise of a career, to continue doing what we most wanted to do—study ourselves, the world, and God.

Our body was properly prepared and garbed for the journey. Since it was our threshold of temptation—physical appetite leads to emotional pattern and mental habit—we had inhibited certain of its reflexes; it was to be entirely subservient to us during the oncoming four years. It was clothed for our forthgoing in a gray, hair-striped suit made by Vito the Tailor, a happy Italian five feet tall. In the back room of Vito's shop I listened to dissertations on cloth and style and food and love. I first wore the suit on a minstrel night and for the occasion the Kid and I made a pint of whiskey. We used equal parts of grain alcohol and distilled water and added a few drops of coloring matter. Half an hour later in a dressing room backstage at the Gem Opera House I saw the Kid offer the bottle to a baritone. The baritone took a drink, then gasped in surprise.

"Where did you get that liquor?" he demanded. "It's the best I've had since prohibition began. I've got a pint right here that cost me eight dollars. Compared to yours it's rot-gut!"

The Kid winked solemnly.

"Private stock," he said. Then he whispered to me, "It seems to be all right. It didn't kill him."

The Kid was asleep now, along with most of the town. He had given me, the night before, some simple advice. "Study like hell so you can take it easy," he said. "Nobody ever died from rest or brains. Ignorance and work are what put a man in his grave." Then he tried to repeat the cockney proverb, "It ain't the 'eavy 'aulin' that 'urts the 'osses' 'ooves; it's the 'ammer, 'ammer, 'ammer on the 'ard 'ighway." Halfway through he gave up. "Let's sing," he said.

The stationmaster came out and stood with my father and me as the train rolled in. He shook hands with me; then my father gave me the kiss of reverence. I mounted the steps of the coach and went inside. As the train moved away I sat near a window and looked out. When the town was behind me Joseph exulted.

"We're over the hill!" he whispered.

For once he was out of hand; he made my heart pound and tightened my throat. I pulled him close to me and we huddled in our body, knees pulled up, back solidly against the cushion. The landscape trickled by. We had nothing to do now but wait.

The hills and fields were green yet. Now and then we swung near the river; it was thin-veined and muddy, in need of the autumn rains that soon would come. When the leaves turned color and fell there would be bonfires in the gutters at home. At night the wind would rustle across the lawns; the rain would fall gently.

"Why are you thinking of those things?" Joseph asked. "Are you going back already?"

"I was only remembering," I said. "I won't miss them."

The Woman was still asleep, her hair loosed and dark against the pillow. If all the town had been as lovely as she I could not have left it. I could not have left her, on that last night, had she not ordered it. I lay on the floor in the living room of her cottage, staring upward through broken light at the line of her chin, the edges of her nostrils, the flicker of her eyelashes. She had touched me, kissed me; there had been a changing and a lifting of the beat of my existence, a shift in polarity, an enlargement which edged into a more rarefied dimension, a dimension without standards of achievement or theologies of movement. The ecstasy had continued, humming through the molecular patterns of my body and mind. It had nothing to do with a deeper physical intimacy; it began whenever we met and continued until we parted; sustained indefinitely it would have accomplished complete escape from life.

She bent her head and kissed me, then put her cheek against my temple and bit the edge of my ear. Her hair threw itself over my face. "You should go," she whispered. "Why?" I asked. She quoted a phrase from Swinburne, "While time is with us and hands are free." I tried to consider the ecstasy which still possessed me, to ascertain whether I could break myself from it by an act of will. "Stumble not at the beauty of a woman," said the writer of Ecclesiastes, "and desire her not for pleasure. . . . Of the woman came the beginning of sin, and through her we all die."

Not this woman, but Eve, Maya-Shakti, she who weaves existence and is herself what she has woven, the spinner of the web of form and form itself, the artificer who delays and misleads and entangles the exploring spirit, and the inspiration which drives it on through death and resurrection to its ultimate destination as a soul. Through Maya-Shakti I had to proceed; it was her ecstasy I had to break. If I did not she would break it for me. None was held forever.

The Woman kissed me again and got up and walked out of the room and into the kitchen. I heard the outer door open and the sound of her footsteps along the driveway. I followed her. She said goodbye to me at the edge of the walk, at the place where we had met. "Remember me for this," she said. "A lot of people in the world will hurt you. I didn't." She turned and walked up the driveway. I watched her go, and stood where I was after she disappeared into the house, not wanting to move. That was thirty hours ago.

We were swinging along the Housatonic south of Derby. "Wake me up when we get to Bridgeport," I said to Joseph. But in my memory, if I let it flow without compulsion or specific demand, when I wake from that sleep I am in Virginia. It is the next day, I am in another coach, and the train is crawling toward Staunton.

I have suffered a shock; I have been hurled backward in time. Since Alexandria the train has been traveling in a previous hour, through a society which was broken sixty-one years before and which seems now to lie before me exactly as it then was left. The roads, the buildings, the distant farmhouses, circle through history and strike at me from the future. The red clay of the land has a wet look, as if the blood shed into it at Bull Run and Petersburg and the Wilderness had not all been absorbed and sent into the redbud trees.

It is only briefly unbelievable. Virginia, I realize, is precisely as I myself left her; I had never thought of her past Appomattox. I knew her from April, 1607, when the first permanent settlers landed at Cape Henry, until April, 1865, when the remnants of the Army of Virginia cut their horses from the guns and rode home for the first spring ploughing in five years. I had no notion of her since then. "Nobody knows you when you're down and out," the blues singers said.

When Charles II in 1660 received the crown which Cromwell had taken from his father—along with his father's head —he wore for the occasion a robe of Virginia silk, and he ordered that coins be struck to inform the people that henceforth his kingdom was to consist of "England, Scotland, Ireland, and Virginia." There had been a golden age in the Old Dominion; during the last quarter of the eighteenth century and the first quarter of the nineteenth she had given her civilization, her traditions, her energy, her great men— Washington, Jefferson, Madison, Patrick Henry, John Paul Jones, John Marshall—to the young republic. She colonized the South and the West. She sent John Randolph of Roanoke to Congress, where he said, "I am an aristocrat. I love liberty; I hate equality." On its Tidewater at Yorktown the Revolution ended; over its entire body, through the Piedmont and up and down the Shenandoah Valley, the Civil War was fought. After that I could recall only that Woodrow Wilson was born in the Presbyterian manse at Staunton.

Men from my town had fought in the Civil War; a few had been killed, a few wounded. A handful still rode in the Memorial Day parade. The names of the battles in which they participated were cut into the monument on the green. When I was small and played war the other side was always the South, and it always lost. Otherwise the struggle was a past thing, a few chapters in our high school textbook of American history. Except for veterans of the Grand Army of the Republic few people in Naugatuck remembered it; none had lost money or slaves or land because of it. In the town at the time of hostilities there was not a single Negro; there were only two now.

My grandfather left Boston and returned to Cahersiveen, County Kerry, Ireland, rather than take up arms against a people he did not know and whom he therefore could not dislike. What ill will he had was absorbed by the British; he was inclined to believe in the principle of States' rights upheld by the Confederacy; when the war was ended he sailed again for Boston. The incident, so far as he was concerned, was closed.

As I watched Virginia march past me I knew the flight to Ireland had not saved either my grandfather or me from identification with victory. In a war of attrition the industrial North had defeated the agricultural South; my grandfather and I had both lived on the spoils of battle, political domination by the North. Kerryman though my grandfather was born, he lived and died a damn Yankee. I was a damn Yankee. Part of my New England identity was a responsibility for the merciless battering of this country through which I was riding. It was as much a part of me as the freckles I had inherited from my father. Man makes history as he makes himself, with violence, hunger, and a dream in which he believes. The father both sustains and taints the son; I had eaten well since birth because of the Civil War.

I turn from the window as we approach Staunton in the dusk. I have been watching, off and on, the students in the coach with me, particularly the nervous, tense ones with new luggage, who are obviously fellow freshmen. A number of them have boarded the train in Virginia; they all have an appearance I associate with English people; there are no Lithuanian or Italian or Polish or Swedish or Irish faces. They are members of the society which lost the Civil War;

155

how well have they eaten since birth; how did their grand-fathers die?

There are a few upper classmen on the train. They have stickers on their bags and fraternity pins on their waistcoats. At Staunton they lead the way off the train. On the platform they make inquiries. We have missed the last bus to Lexington. A taxi driver says he will take us there at a flat rate of two dollars for each student. It sounds exorbitant to me. On the map Lexington is the next town south.

"How far away is the school?" I ask one of the upper classmen.

"Thirty-six miles," he says. "We'd better take this fellow's offer."

In Connecticut thirty-six miles is approximately the distance between Waterbury and Bridgeport. Along the way are Naugatuck, Beacon Falls, Seymour, Ansonia, and Derby, all busy, prosperous, industrial towns. I cannot imagine such a distance being deserted except for farmhouses and an occasional crossroads hamlet. My companions apparently consider it nothing unusual; perhaps they are accustomed to barren wastes.

It is dark when we leave Staunton and turn south on the valley road. One of the freshmen, a stocky, round-cheeked boy, dares to talk to an upper classman. The freshman has already accepted a fraternity bid and has been told to "come right to the house" on his arrival. The upper classman inquires as to the fraternity's identity. "Alpha Chi Rho," the freshman says. The upper classman is unimpressed. "I'm a Beta," he says.

We are riding down the Shenandoah Valley, pursuing the route General David Hunter followed in June, 1864, on his way to Lynchburg. A small Confederate force delayed but did not oppose his army on that foray. At Lexington Hunter found the bridge over North River burned. Confederate artillery struck at his column. He brought up heavy artillery and shelled the town, concentrating on the buildings of Virginia Military Institute. The cadets were gone; they had marched away under orders. A cannon ball struck the Campbell house, exploding in a crib from which an infant had just been removed. The Confederates retreated and Hunter entered the town. One rebel flag still flew, over the grave of Stonewall Jackson, who had left his professorial post at the Institute to assume a command under General Lee, and

156

whose sword lay now inside a piano in his Lexington home, hidden there by his widow.

There were three days and nights of looting and pillage. The institute was burned, homes were sacked, Washington College was robbed and mutilated. Hunter ordered it destroyed, but was persuaded to leniency by two of his officers, Colonel Rutherford B. Hayes and First Lieutenant William McKinley. Finally the Federals moved on.

Little more than a year later, with the war ended, General Lee came to Washington College to be its president. He was tired; the war had aged and broken him. The young men of the South flocked to the school to be near him. He built a chapel; he founded schools of commerce and journalism in the college, the first of their kind in America; in five years he was dead.

When he died the night filled up with storm and the river flooded. In haste when the strength of his illness was known three oversize coffins were ordered from Richmond; there was none in town long enough to hold his tall body. They came from Lynchburg by boat and arrived at dusk. They were unloaded and left at the wharf's end. In the night the General passed, the river rose, and the coffins were carried away. Next day men searched the banks for miles; one coffin only was found, the smallest. In it the General was laid; there was room for him, except for the heels of his boots. When the coffin was closed his boots were removed; he was buried without them, in the chapel he had built, from whose pulpit he had said, "Duty is the sublimest word in the English language."

Thus died a soldier whose mother was buried before he was born. The wife of General "Lighthorse Harry" Lee caught an illness brought by her husband from the Bahamas, whence he fled to escape jail for debt. She seemed to succumb, was robed for burial, and was placed in the family vault. A relative, arriving late for the funeral, went alone to view the body. He saw that it breathed. The family was called, the lady was revived, and soon she was well of her illness. Three years later she gave birth to a son, Robert Edward Lee.

Traveller, the General's white horse, outlived his master. He grazed on the campus lawns after the General's death and was petted by the students. When his last illness came and he lay on the floor of his stall a woman of the town

157

brought a great mattress for his comfort, and lying on it he expired, the only horse to die on a feather bed. His skeleton was preserved in the college museum and students wrote their initials on its bones for luck.

Washington College became Washington and Lee University. It had begun as Augusta Academy in 1749; it had changed its name to Liberty Hall in 1776. After the Revolution General Washington endowed it with two hundred shares of the James River Canal Company, a gift to him from the legislature of the state of Virginia in appreciation of his services to the Republic. With his consent the board of trustees transformed Liberty Hall into Washington College. The canal shares, converted into railroad holdings, were still providing the university with income in 1926.

"Slow up for the bridge," one of the upper classmen says to the driver of our taxi. We are at the entrance to Lexington. A covered wooden bridge crosses the North River, making a right angle with the road. The town is dark except for a block on Main Street, where light stains the front of a drugstore. The driver turns into a side street and feels his way for a few blocks, then makes a left turn and stops.

"You'd better get out here," one of the upper classmen says to me. "The dormitories are just up the hill."

I get out and walk up a mild slope. At its crest are two brick buildings; the one on my left is called Graham, the one on my right is named Lees. I enter Lees and look for the room assigned to me. It is on the first floor and the door is open. Inside there is a single bed with a set of springs, nothing else, no mattress, no furniture, not even a bulb in the light fixture. Such luxuries, I recall from the catalogue, can be purchased from the janitor. I set out to find him.

As I reach the second floor in my hunt a door opens and a black-haired, olive-skinned boy walks out, sees me, and comes toward me, his arm extended. We shake hands and he says something which is utterly incomprehensible to me, though I realize he is welcoming me as a fellow freshman and telling me his name. I tell him my name, but he doesn't seem to get it. I ask him about the janitor, explaining my predicament. Listening carefully, he seems to understand. The janitor, he says—I watch his lips in order to better detect the words he is using—is gone for the night, and will not be available until the next day after breakfast.

"Thanks," I say. "I guess I'll go to a hotel for the night."

"Reckon there's no need of that," he says. "You can stay with me."

It is a startling proposal to me, but it seems a natural act to him. He leads me into his room and points to a single bed complete with mattress, sheets, and a light blanket.

"If you don't mind a mite of crowding," he says, "you're right welcome."

I thank him, and we sit down and talk. Gradually I become accustomed to his slurred, soft, musical speech; I speak slowly, so that he can decipher my clipped, crowded New England phrases. His name is Leon Rice Robison; he is from Wetumpka, Alabama. He is a Baptist; when he is graduated from the university he intends to study for the ministry. He is interested in Connecticut; is it a land of great hardship and bitter cold?

By the time we decide to go to bed each understands a good part of what the other says. Crowding myself against the wall on the inside of the bed I thank him again for his hospitality.

"Shucks," he says. "No sense in going to a dag-nabbed hotel."

Just before I fall asleep the names flicker across my mind: Leon Rice Robison, black-haired, Baptist, Wetumpka, Alabama; Thomas Joseph Sugrue, red-haired, Catholic, Naugatuck, Connecticut.

All that is a single scene in my memory, without progression. The stage extends from my first glimpse of Virginia through the train window to the white wall of Robison's room, staring into my eyes as they shut. A moment which threatened to hold me was tripped and thrown, with others, into the past; a sense of schism, of being Irish in Connecticut and Yankee in Virginia, was avoided. Robison and I, in an oasis of peace provided by two great soldiers, had signified our intention to ignore the identities thrust upon us and to seek in common effort the impartial personality which is latent in every man, the wisdom which leaves among those who attain it no difference beyond the manner in which it was accomplished.

After that there is a period of sequence in the things I remember. I awoke with the feeling that an owl was staring at me. It was the head of a round-faced boy projecting through the doorway leading to the next room; the head was wearing horn-rimmed eyeglasses. Robison roused, spoke to

159

it, and introduced me. The head moved into the room, bringing a body, and I reached across Robison to shake hands. Head and body together were Hugh Lynn Cayce, of Virginia Beach, Virginia, another freshman. He talked with us while we dressed and went with us to breakfast. He was also interested in Connecticut; he had considered attending a New England college; he wanted to meet and know people in all parts of the country, he said. Neither he nor Robison mentioned the Civil War.

Robison and I decided to combine our inadequacies; either we would get a double room or combine two single rooms, using one for a bedroom, one for a study. Our trunks were delivered and we opened them. Robison, aware that he was going north, had purchased a heavy overcoat and half a dozen suits of long winter underwear. I, aware that I was going south, had filled my trunk with summer clothes and only at my mother's persuasion had included a topcoat. Moreover, I had not worn winter underwear since I was fourteen. Robison stated flatly that he did not believe this.

We both had tennis racquets, and after I made a deal with the janitor for a mattress and some furniture we went to the courts and played. The janitor was a short, pleasant Negro named John; he wore a moustache and gold-rimmed spectacles. While we talked I had for the first time the feeling of relaxation, of comfort, which comes over me always when I am near Negroes, particularly when they are doing a chore for me. It was not until years later that Joseph suddenly one day offered an explanation. "How would you feel," he said, "if you belonged to a race which had yet to commit its sins, which had been given the opportunity in this country of freedom and enterprise only to build virtue into its pattern by suffering slavery, by working as a menial, by living in poverty, humility, and gentleness?"

The next morning Robison, Cayce, and I joined a hundred other freshmen and went to Newcomb Hall to register. In the early September light the sweep of white colonial columns across the red brick front of Washington College was breath-taking. Down across the lawns, directly below the college entrance, was Lee Chapel, where the General and all of his family were buried. Freshmen from Georgia, Alabama, Mississippi, the Carolinas, Tennessee, Louisiana, Florida, Texas, and Virginia stared at the scene quietly; their grandfathers had served under Lee, or under Jackson or Beauregard or Longstreet or Forrest. Cayce's great great grandfather had fought in Washington's army.

The line moved slowly up the steps and through the building. We signed papers, made statements, selected courses, and shook hands with university officials. I finally reached the dean, Dr. Henry Campbell. It was he who, as an infant, was lifted from his crib and carried to another part of the Campbell house just before a shell from one of Hunter's batteries struck the nursery. He was a spare, tall man, bald and bespectacled. He asked me about my name. Was it French? I explained that it was Irish, in its present form an anglicization of O'Sioghreadha, which in turn was a gaelicization of two Danish words which meant, in the tenth century, when the family migrated to County Kerry, victory and peace. Dr. Campbell smiled and put a hand on my shoulder.

"I'm Irish too," he said. "This valley was settled by Scotch-Irish, Campbells and Grahams and McCormicks. We're always glad to see an Irishman. This is your university; it was founded by your people. Come and see me when you have time. I'd like to tell you about the history of the valley."

I moved away, stunned. It was the first time I had been welcomed to a place and told that it was mine; it never happened again. Afterward in a moment of doubt I considered that perhaps the dean, wise and diplomatic, had noticed that I was from Connecticut, and, unable to welcome me as a fellow Southerner, had asked me about my name, seizing on the Irish connection to make me feel at home. But this was not so. Dr. Campbell was from that moment a friend; he stopped often to talk with me; he described to me at length the settling of the valley by the Scotch-Irish; I went to his office with my problems and with the problems of other students; I enlisted his support when a group of friends decided to revive the undergraduate literary magazine, defunct since the World War.

On the day I was tapped for the campus leadership fraternity he was given a gold watch in recognition of his service to the school. He showed it to me proudly and I did not tell him that for the occasion I was wearing a borrowed suit. When I won the Santini essay medal I carried it to him, and he took it from its case and turned it over in his hand, and told me how he had won the same award forty years before, and how he kept his medal in a safety deposit box in a bank. "I liked what you said in your essay," he said. "I'm proud that you feel that way." The title of the essay was, "Of Religious Tolerance."

Once he helped me through an embarrassing situation with another member of the administration. After a squabble over technicalities involved in certain absences I wrote this official a letter which could only be termed offensive. I had either to apologize or be dismissed from the university. Dr. Campbell sent for me and explained the predicament.

"It is not a question of whether you are right, unfortunately," he said. "You are a student and the other gentleman is a member of our administration. Your letter is therefore a matter of record, an official document, and something"—he smiled—"of an indictment of the university's hierarchy. You shouldn't have written the letter; you should have told the fellow what you thought of him personally, and not in the presence of witnesses.

"But you didn't. You wrote the letter. He demands an apology. He isn't going to get it, but you aren't going to be dismissed either. Go home and write him a formal note. Say this—Dear Sir: I regret the unparliamentary language used in my letter of such and such a date. Yours very truly. Sign your name. Send it to him. He won't like it but he'll have to accept it."

He put his hand on my shoulder. "Next time don't write anything," he said. "Ask him to step outside where you can't be overheard. Then give him an earful." He smiled. "How are your eyes?" The student body had suffered an epidemic of pinkeye and my eyeballs had become ulcerated. "Did you see the doctor I recommended in Washington? I remember the time he operated on me. . . ."

When I left him that first morning and stood outside Newcomb Hall, waiting for Robison and Cayce and watching the lawn dip down to the chapel, I felt the first shivering premonition of an intense, radiant, unbearable happiness; but I could not yet believe that it would happen to me. When Robison and Cayce came we walked to the postoffice and to a drugstore on the opposite corner—it was called The Corner—and drank what Robison called a "dope," what Cayce referred to as a "coke," and what to me was a glass of shaved ice saturated with coca-cola. I liked it less than moxie, its New England counterpart, that first time, but by nightfall, having tried it several more times, I changed my mind.

We matched coins to decide which was to pay for the drinks. We bought freshman caps and put them on. We were students.

That night we went to the chapel to hear Dr. Henry Louis Smith, president of the university, instruct us in our duties as members of the undergraduate body. He was an old man, soon to retire, but except for white hair, thick and wavy, and a white moustache, he gave no signs of age. His face was young, his complexion ruddy, his step quick, his carriage magnificent. As he talked the white marble of Valentine's recumbent statue of Lee gleamed behind him. I had seen the statue earlier in the day. It represented the General asleep in his tent after a battle. He had not removed his uniform; a robe partly covered his body. His face was that of a patriarch; he had the countenance of a saint.

Dr. Smith walked back and forth as he talked. He wanted us to understand, he said, that there was a more important fact than our enrollment as college students. We were gentlemen of Washington and Lee: to that ideal we must surrender ourselves completely; henceforth our honor was to be the apex of our values.

Our school, he pointed out, was run on the honor system. No professor would be with us when we wrote our examinations; he would leave the room after giving us the questions. If we observed a student cheating it was our obligation to report him to the executive committee of the student government; the system was ours to keep or to abandon. An accused student could ask for a trial, to be held in the chapel, before the student body.

There were, he continued, traditions which were ours to carry on; in time they would become part of us. We were to speak to everyone we met, whether we knew him or not. We were not to wear sweaters or other casual articles of clothing—gentlemen about the business of knowledge did not attire themselves for a sporting match.

Gentlemen about the business of knowledge, meeting and mingling with the incomparable riches of the mind of humanity, should be and by nature were in a reverent mood, for though the presence of God is realized by faith the understanding of Him lies in the fathomless seas of consciousness which surround the soul and wash against it, the seas set forth by God to spawn the children of His love, as the seas of the earth formed and sent to dry land the creatures of

His design. The charts which mariners had made of these seas, partial though they were, crudely drawn, marred by error and cluttered by ignorance, contradictory to one another, plotted as often by legend and myth as by fact and gnosis, were gathered here in a university to be studied and examined for what they might have in them of truth and what they might reveal of error. Young sailors might learn from them how to navigate, but not what winds their sails would catch or what storms their ships would meet; and beyond the charts were waters none had known.

"I shall put it to you simply," he said. "You have come here to study how men before you thought, that you yourselves may learn to think. The substance of your thought is your own affair; there is no opinion likely to form in your mind which has not been held by someone before you, and which has not at some time in history attained respectability and evoked admiration. Your mission is to think, to be your own explorer on the seas of consciousness, sailing up the coasts of knowledge, seeking the Northwest Passage of truth!"

We were dismissed. Moving toward the door, watching the blue serge, checked cheviot, gray-striped, and brown-checked wool backs of other freshmen moving before me; noting absently their ears, hair lines, neck size, and shoulder length; I felt again the surge of exaltation which had rushed up in me that morning. Dr. Smith might have been Virgil, telling me that Beatrice, the countenance of Divine Wisdom, had ordained that I be saved, that I he led through the hell of action and the purgatory of reflection to the realization of heaven, with its eternal contemplation of the unraveling mystery of existence; and that all of this be accomplished for me in this Sacred Grove set aside for illusion and uncertainty, where the moment of now magically relaxed and stretched itself to the limits of man's remembrance, and beyond them to the monuments he made with his bones before he knew his name or his exile. So much did freedom of thought and assurance of the morality of that freedom do for me.

Outside the students moved naturally toward the post-office and The Corner. I walked with them. Above us the colonnade of the college was lighted, painting the sweep of the columns on the night. A freshman keeping step with me offered a cigarette. We stopped while I gave both of us a light and he began to talk. His speech was not Southern; his

164

voice seemed on the verge of laughter, as if his thoughts were in a state of glee.

"Stepping from one century to another is a basic pleasure of life," he said. "It should be guaranteed in the Constitution. From the chivalry of Lee to a theory from the School of Zeno is a delightful jump. We should now go to a dance hall and watch an exhibition of the Charleston."

We crossed the street to The Corner.

"Take note that Dr. Smith said specifically that we are to be encouraged to think as we please. He didn't mention acting as we pleased. Men have had some good thoughts from time to time but their actions have mostly been bad. Philosophy and history are the perfect dichotomy. Action must be restrained; it must proceed according to code. The code here is sensible and mature; my brother says he had fun and learned a lot while he was in Lexington. He's studying medicine now at Harvard. I tried Yale. So far I like this place better."

At the soda fountain he turned to face me and I saw that he was a Jew. His face, like his voice, seemed on the edge of laughter. He had a magnificent head; his hair was black, his eyes dark and blazing with intelligence. Leaning against the counter, relaxed, observing the crowd with a mixture of amusement and concern, he might have been a student from the Bruchion watching a street crowd in Alexandria, or a scholarly emissary come to town to sell a manuscript to Philadelphus. His attitude gave to his body an illusion of height. He seemed detached and a little above the scene about him, though interested in its activity and tolerant of its nonsense. He refused to match coins for our cokes. He paid for them.

"Education for enlightenment and service is old-fashioned in America," he said. "College is an investment, it has to pay off in money or it's considered a failure. Have you read Tawney's *The Acquisitive Society?* You can borrow my copy. We live by a simple syllogism. Man was given dominion over the earth; he was divinely ordained to administer his legacy; the more efficiently he does so the more approved he is in heaven. Make a lot of money and off you go to paradise. How can you make a lot of money? Prepare yourself for a career—get an education."

"If you can make a lot of money without falling in love with it you can still get to heaven," I said. "The effort of accumulation is lost and the time involved is wasted, but there is no positive harm."

It was an orthodox answer. I wanted to test his reaction to normal methods of moral evasion. He smiled.

"The first requisite for making money is to be in love with it," he said. "Fortunately for the South more is required for actual financial success than the first requisite. Love of money down here is a hopeless infatuation. The Civil War removed any possibility of pursuing the romance or achieving marriage. Education here is still for enlightenment and service—enlightenment is pagan and service is Christian. Success is American. The Southerners are not Americans. They are disfranchised; they are barred from success. Let us protest."

He put down his glass and laughed.

"You see what comes of being allowed to think as we please?" he said. "Logic and fact can prove anything. Only the improbable keeps us from mass insanity. The improbable happens all the time. It is the faith by which we live."

We walked outside and he casually said good night.

"My name is Elias," he said. "I'll see you around. Don't let me believe what I say. It confuses me."

The next day when I returned from the tennis courts he was sprawled on my bed, reading a book. He finished a paragraph before looking up.

"I brought you two problems," he said. "First, is time a dynamic sequence or a static whole? Second, how much does my identity as an individual depend on your identity as an individual, and on the identities of all other individuals?"

I took off my sweat shirt and regarded him. He was still solemnly on the edge of laughter.

"It depends on whether you have a watch or whether you ask me what time it is," I said. "If you ask me what time it is your identity becomes partly dependent on me. Without me you don't know what time it is, let alone what time itself is."

He was delighted. "I knew you would help me," he said. "I must persevere in my unbelief in all things. You can assist me. Apparently you believe in everything."

"I do," I said. "Everything exists, simultaneously and in all places. It is partially perceived in separate instants by incomplete and restricted mental organisms, though it can be believed in its entirety by a simple act of faith."

He leaned over the end of the bed. "A mystic," he said. "I feel a profound melancholy rising within me as a result of your completely imbecilic words. Light my cigarette."

I held a match for him while amazement trickled through me. I had spoken exactly what I thought on a matter of philosophy for the first time in my life. The silence which had existed since the beginning of my remembrance was broken. There was no shock; the remark had slipped naturally through an opening that was made, I realized, by what I had heard in the chapel the night before. Elias obviously was unaware that I hitherto never had said to another person what I believed about existence, reality, and mind. He need never know, I thought as I watched him draw away from the flame of the match, blowing smoke and shutting one eye. When he was gone Joseph said, "You can put the tennis racquet away until you really need some exercise. There is no more need to sublimate your energies. From now on you can use them for your own purpose."

Joseph was in a state of astonishment and ecstasy. His excitement and happiness reached toward me across our body; my heart pounded, my throat hummed, and I muttered songs as I moved about. What I had said to Elias had been spoken also by Joseph; dichotomy in that moment had disappeared. Joseph, near to me, happy, expressing himself, was the cause of my exaltation. In the narrow room of the red brick dormitory we were exposed before Elias as one, as a single voice, as a unified personality. Henceforth we would remain that way. Joseph was I and I was Joseph; there was separation only when I sat down to write letters home or answered certain questions in my classes. "What Elias has joined together let no man put asunder," was otherwise my motto.

I saw Elias and talked with him every day, either in my room or at The Corner or in the journalism building where we both went to work on student publications, or at the private residence in town where he roomed. He always had questions, theories, intellectual propositions; in addition to textbooks he had always under his arm the latest novel or nonfiction book recommended by the New York critics. He read while standing up, while walking, while sitting down, or while sprawled on a bed or on the campus lawn. When he was finished with a book he racked up its ideas in his mind and turned to a fresh volume. He criticized what he read, enthused over it, judged it, and visited it upon me. Whether he agreed or disagreed with my reaction was of no consequence; my opinion was another item to be racked up and marked for reference. He lived on top of the moment, enjoying the future as it struck him, disdaining to lean on the past.

People to him were complicated structures made up of what they had been, what others had been before them, what they had been taught, and to what extent and in what manner they had been disciplined; these experiences joined together to form personalities. The personalities reacted differently to the common stimulation of general events; because of this they were interesting to observe, to discuss, and to interview.

He was fascinated by people in general and he loved a large number of them in particular. He was enchanted by America; he knew its history, reveled in its present, and dreamed of its future. He was delighted and unperturbed by *The American Mercury,* wherein each month H. L. Mencken described Americans as "boobs and suckers."

"We can afford to be boobs and suckers," he said. "This is our Age of Innocence. Why not enjoy it? The common people who came to this country left their traditions and their cultures behind them; the rich and the aristocratic brought their intellectual and social environment with them —they couldn't leave it behind; it was their superiority and uncommonness. The vestiges of that imported social and intellectual environment are what laugh at the boobs and suckers, who are beginning a society that will outlast everything in Europe but the stench of her politics."

He was the ageless, intellectual, completely civilized Jew as he talked; a practical, dogged, opportunistic visionary. He loved and understood the boobs and suckers, and while he talked about them thousands of his people, in Hollywood, California, and on Seventh Avenue, New York, worked to speed up the basic stages of the boob and sucker society. In New York at the garment center they provided costumes available to all people in all parts of the country simultaneously and at approximately the same price; women in Massillon and Middlebury dressed as smartly and for as little money as their sisters in Manhattan. In Hollywood motion pictures were manufactured which demonstrated patterns of romance and social behavior for mountaineer and lobster fisherman, subway conductor and cowboy.

"Consider your personal religious dilemma," Elias went on. "You say you are a Catholic. But what kind of a Catholic are you? An American Catholic? No. There is no such thing as an American Catholic, because there is no American Catholic Church. America has Irish Catholics, Italian Catholics, German Catholics, French Catholics, Spanish Catholics, Polish Catholics, and Catholics from every other country in Europe. The church in each case came with the people, to serve them, but it came as an aristocrat, as a well-to-do aristocrat; it brought its culture and its traditions with it—the ritual and theology and canon law are the same in all cases, but national and racial manners and customs have created superficial differences which are obvious. You, then, are an Irish Catholic."

"I will die an American Catholic," I said. "It will take only a generation to break the tie with the old countries. The churches of which you speak were built by immigrants and are still largely attended by immigrants. A generation of Catholics born in America and educated in her schools will be American Catholics. The church is the people. . . ."

"You will die a heretic," he said. "Rome is stronger than you think. Let's get a coke. It's your turn to pay."

As we walked he swung his books with both hands, hitting each knee as it came up for a step. One day I watched him cross the campus swinging a new book. It was Tawney's *Religion and the Rise of Capitalism*. It was a long time before I got past the quotation from Bishop Berkeley: "Whatever the world thinks, he who hath not much meditated upon God, the human mind and the *summum bonum*, may possibly make a thriving earthworm, but will most indubitably make a sorry patriot and a sorry statesman." No wonder we are ruled by politicians, the earthworms of government, I thought.

Then I read Tawney's treatise on the separation of church and state, the division of business and ethic, the schism of private interest and morality. What once the Jew had been hired to do, lest Christians be stained with its sin, was now the noblest enterprise and sustaining achievement of Western society—the lending of money at interest. Theology did not condemn the hiring of money—borrowing a sum for a set fee—but interest, the gradual increase of debt on the basis

169

of its duration, was sinful, for it sold what no man owned —time. I hovered over this point; during my years in the bank I had spent hundreds of hours figuring interest and writing it in red ink on thousands of bankbooks. I recalled the European Jews of the Middle Ages, who were hired to trade in money and marked with a yellow arm band. Discover the sin of which the Jew is being accused, I thought, and the destiny of his accuser is revealed.

"Of what are your people being accused at present?" I asked Elias when he came to get my reaction to the book.

"Conquest of the world," he said. "We seek to dominate all nations by a secret hierarchy of money. We are no longer traders; we are jugglers of currency, masters of international finance. If we have our way you will all soon be in our power. Give me a cigarette."

I handed him a package.

"The only way to avoid such a catastrophe, obviously, is to beat you at your own game," I said. "Once we have achieved world domination through money it will not matter whether we achieved it in competition with you or as a natural result of our enterprise and intelligence."

Elias blew smoke at the ceiling.

"It will be the push of destiny," he said, "the thumb of the Demiurge pressing steadily on the neck of nationalism. The Jew will be up to something else then, probably colonization of the moon."

He closed his eyes and leaned against the wall.

"Actually," he said, "we are busy constructing a new religion for you. We gave you a religion two thousand years ago, a complete system for running your society, with an incarnated God for its capstone. You employed it for its proper purpose for a while; then you went into business— you can't resist imitating the Jews, apparently, any more than you can resist persecuting them—and your religion became a department of life devoted to the suppression of pleasure and the worship of virginity. A massive guilt complex developed from the suppression of the natural religious impulse to seek God and the substitution of a technique of evasion, propitiation, and bribery. A guilt complex is dangerous; it demands punishment. The sin must be expiated—but by somebody else. A scapegoat must be found. That means war, and with each side using the other as a scapegoat one war leads to another.

"So the guilt complex must be removed. There must be recognition, remorse, and reformation. These are religious operations. How then, is the Jew to perform them on the Christian? The answer is simple. He calls them scientific operations. He presents them as psychoanalysis, the invention of Dr. Sigmund Freud, a Jew. The real faith of the modern Christian is in science; therefore he accepts psychoanalysis. By accepting psychoanalysis and employing it he rids himself of his guilt complex without disturbing his conviction that he is a good Christian. He never becomes aware of his evil in terms of theology."

He yawned, opened his eyes, and stood up.

"To put it simply," he said, "we are assisting the Christians to be better Jews. Their irreligion has become a sorrow and a rebuke to us. Let's get a coke."

The sidewalk seemed, as we walked toward The Corner, somewhat below where my feet struck. It was not what either of us had said that lifted me up, but the fact that we had thus conversed, that we had discussed the world in terms of ideas, trends, theories, mistakes, and sins, expressing our own observations and deductions, our personal prophecies and judgments. There was joy in sweeping history into a little heap of errors; there was a heady inference in our recognition of the mistakes which men had made before our time—now that those mistakes were known they would not be repeated; in our time affairs would go well. In a few years, when we walked into it, the world would be bright with wisdom and busy with peace.

When we argued we smiled, pleased at each other's mental acrobatics. One day Elias gave me Hemingway's *A Farewell to Arms*. The next day he came back for my opinion. I knew he was enthusiastic about the book.

"It's primitive," I said.

He beamed. "Of course it's primitive!" he said. "It's American literature at the level of the American archetype. The prose is just right. It—"

"It's hieroglyphic," I said. "It grunts and groans. The story's as raw as a Cro-Magnon's steak dinner."

"Well, where do you think we are in civilization," he said, "at a dinner cooked by Escoffier? Are we ready to write like Dante or Sir Thomas Browne? What are the boobs and suckers in this country concerned with? Don't they worship the phallus and fear death? Don't they dress their whores in

171

black lace underwear and bury themselves in steel coffins to keep out worms? Don't they believe in magic, eating the flesh of animals to get the strength of animals? Don't they subscribe to transmigration of the soul, becoming Eagles and Elks and Lions and Owls? Don't they shoot, trap, spear, strangle, poison, or bludgeon every wild thing they can flush from the forests and swamps? Don't they dress and dance and court and mate like savages? Don't they use science to delay death and to enrich life? Don't they worship money and mammary glands? Don't they pay a million dollars to see a prize fight and set fifty cents a line as the top price for poetry?

"What do you expect of such people, epics filled with metaphysics and madonnas? Their hero is a guy with big muscles and active seminal vesicles who can tip a babe over by lifting an eyebrow and nodding his head. He can drink bad liquor all night, make money all day, and make love forever. He is honest, sentimental, simple-minded, and healthy."

I picked up the Hemingway book and riffled the pages with my thumb. I was not thinking so much of what Elias had said as of what he had suggested, the mediumistic function of the writer, the mirroring not of nature but of the human group in its moment of reaching for another segment of evolution.

"But how true is it?" I said. "The average American is not particularly strong, and some harsh things have been said about his proficiency as a lover. He might be able to run up a string of victories in open sexual competition but he seems more interested in getting away from the women with whom he is already entangled—his wife, his mother, his sisters, his girl friend. If he drinks too much it makes him sick; he doesn't make a lot of money and is usually in debt; the conditions which must be fulfilled before he is allowed to make love are so preposterously difficult, even when he is married, that inhibiting his natural desires is as normal to him as compromising with his ambitions. He is only honest because he is afraid to be dishonest. He is sentimental about people because he wants people to be sentimental about him; he wants friends who will weep at his funeral. He isn't simple-minded. He is lonely, frightened, unsure, and full of dreams in which he is popular, courageous, and certain of every move."

Elias waved a hand and smiled.

"Exactly," he said, "and his literature dramatizes those dreams. And that, as I contended, is wondreful. It's the sort of thing you ought to write. You're full of dreams."

"What sort of writing do you want to do?" I asked.

He flipped his cigarette through the open window.

"I shall write the great epic of the American citizen," he said. "I shall read carefully the most popular novels of our history, charting the virtues of their heroines and heroes. I shall then write a twelve volume saga of a man and woman who between them are without a single one of those virtues. It will be the ultimate classic of English fiction."

By the end of the week he had lost interest in Hemingway. A bootlegged copy of James Joyce's *Ulysses* appeared on the campus. He read it, at a rental rate of fifty cents a day. When he slept or went to class he gave the book to me, and I pursued the adventures of Leopold Bloom and Stephen Dedalus. A law student took the volume for the week end, at a reduced rate of seventy-five cents for two days and three nights.

"Well, what do you think of Joyce?" Elias said as we leaned against the counter in McCrum's on Saturday night. He was relaxed, detached, on the edge of laughter. He did not seem like a young man with a weak heart who as a boy passed long periods in bed devouring books and fighting rheumatic fever. He was a little older than I—we were both several years beyond the average age of our class—and he might have been, resting on his elbows and watching the crowd, a particularly healthy tennis champion, on the town after an easy match, with little on his mind or in it.

"Mr. Joyce seems to have beaten you to the punch," I said. "He has apparently written the ultimate classic of English fiction."

He did not hear me. One of the small, soft, fuzzy young girls of the town had walked past him, lifting and dropping her eyes in almost the same instant, and saying, in a low voice, "Hey!" He turned to acknowledge her greeting, to look at her legs, and to check quickly her hips, breasts, profile, hairline, and complexion. I ordered another coke, for the girl.

TEN

THE PROFESSOR stirred drowsily and sighted along his minute hand at Miss Iceberg. She was gathering things together, moving a pencil a little closer to a pen, arranging the chart, the drinking glasses, and the water pitcher in a geometric pattern. It was twenty minutes before three. The Professor smiled.

"It didn't take you long to find happiness," he said amiably. "How misleading that first flush of reason is! There is nothing so ethereally joyous or so completely deceived—not even a bride—as the student who has begun to think. All the thoughts which have gone before him are, as he meets them, his own. The essence of the best intelligences of history enters his mind through his eyes and ears and pops out, transformed into his own creation, through his mouth and his pen. There is nothing so intoxicating as the wine of a great man's mind. A university student has the choice vintages of five thousand years at the command of his taste. Some students, of course, select the most common labels—cooking sherry, usually—but most become connoisseurs of one type or another, experts in Rhine wine, or in Burgundy, or in Chianti. It does not occur to them at the time that the job in life is not to drink wine, but to make it, to press a liquor from their own minds instead of appreciating the vintages made by others."

He laughed. "You and Elias must have been a deluded pair, passing judgment not only on the present world but on history in general and God Almighty in particular."

"We were very drunk and we were very happy," I said.

The Professor sighed. "How easily time creates differences," he said, "in even the most abstract experiences of generations and individuals. Such matters as psychoanalysis, relativity, and the prose of Joyce are not at all to me what they are to you. Freud's first book was published in this country while I was at college, studying Kant and toying in a romantic way with

174

Schopenhauer. I remember encountering Schopenhauer's belief in pre-existence, and telling a Vassar girl that she and I had loved before and would go through this life joined in perfect understanding because of our previous adventures together. I was a junior then—the world would be mine in another year. She married a Texas cattleman and now she has more money and meat than the average city—feudalism is enjoying a happy and sanitary reincarnation in our Southwest. I have never ridden a horse, or wanted to; she has won prizes for horsemanship.

"I first heard of Einstein while I was on my honeymoon. We went to New York and I attended a few lectures at Columbia. One of them was on relativity. I slept through it. About the time you and Elias were discussing Joyce and Hemingway I was waiting for my appointment as assistant professor. I had received my doctor's degree finally, after working on it for seven summers. I had heard a lot about Freud and Einstein in the meantime, but only in conversation, and in jokes. I had read nothing about them or their theories. Joyce was a name I had seen and which I connected with Paris and a new literary cult. On the night my wife and I celebrated my appointment as assistant professor my largest block of knowledge concerned a few rather obscure months toward the close of the French Revolution. We had a very happy time that night—the orchestra played *Girl of My Dreams, My Blue Heaven, Side by Side,* and *Together.*"

"I remember those songs," I said. "They were an obbligato for many of my most earnest evenings of study. Every portable phonograph in both dormitories played them; now I understand that students prepare their lessons while listening to the radio."

The Professor nodded. "I learned to concentrate despite the sound of a mandolin playing, *Budweiser's a Friend of Mine* and *Cuddle up a Little Closer, Lovey Mine.*

"It was after I was made a full professor that I read some of Freud, looked into modern physics, and borrowed a copy of *Ulysses* from an instructor in the English department. One night at the Tennyson Club I heard a professor from the seminary read a paper on the Christian Fathers. It was staggeringly dull, a hodgepodge of heresiology. I found myself thinking of Freud and Jung and Adler. Suddenly it became quite clear to me that they were scientists only because the faith of our times is science—vitamins, not saints' bones, are the magic by which we are healed. I realized the simple religious nature of psychoanalysis—a technique for mental exploration and spiritual salvation in terms of the faith contemporaneously ascendant.

"Naturally I thought of the mystery religions, with their secret systems of self-discovery, under the guidance of initiates and masters. Christianity threw the mystery open to everyone, and simplified and legalized and dogmatized it until only the most obstinate and unrepentant sinner could miss both heaven and purgatory and land in hell.

"The long, involved, tedious, exceedingly difficult technique of actual self-discovery, requiring the patient guidance of a skillful and wise teacher, was lost. It was never for the many; it was always a voluntary adventure of the few. When it was rediscovered and restated in terms of the current faith it was openly taught and offered to the many, but it remained what it always had been, a voluntary adventure of the few. It required now not only time, patience, humility, and intelligence on the part of the neophyte, or patient; it cost him a sturdy sum of money. In a civilization compromised by materialism it offered for its aim a more successful and contented endurance of that materialism; its practitioners were specialists in the mind and the body, not the soul. Whereas the mystery schools offered to those who had the strength to seek God a way of finding Him, psychoanalysis offered to those who had the strength to conquer the world a way of enjoying that conquest. It answered, as all new religions do, the inner, spiritual need of a certain people in a certain time, or environment, or predicament. It reached out to help that people over an obstacle dangerous to the progress of its evolution.

"Those were my thoughts as I walked home that evening. I had in mind the mystery schools, the Assyrian, the Chaldean, the Egyptian, the Bacchic and Corybantic, the Mithriac, the Phrygian, the Samothracian, the Orphic and Eleusinian. I recalled a sentence from the Gnostic treatise, *Pistis Sophia*, or the Askew Codex, as it is listed in the British Museum—'I tell you that there will be found one in a thousand and two in ten thousand for the consummation of the mysteries of the First Mystery.'

"This seemed a fair guess as to the percentage of people being psychoanalyzed, I thought, and I was very pleased with myself for what seemed later to be an extremely ordinary deduction.

"As I walked I automatically returned the salutations of students who passed me. One of them stopped me to ask a question, and as I answered him I looked about and realized that I was in the middle of Fraternity Row. On both sides of the street illuminated porches dramatized slim columns, wide windows, and red brick fronts. Almost as if it were a common notion with me I thought, 'Here are the skeletons of the mystery schools—the Greek letter societies with their secret rituals.' I remembered joining one as an undergraduate; there was some florid prose about spirit and wisdom and the inner temple where Arthur draws the sword of his soul from the rock of spirit.

"We bury only our bodies, it seemed to me as I walked on. What we build with our minds we leave to rot, to deliquesce, and to jingle in the wind. It came to me that there were men in the world that night, alive, somewhere, who believed the most primitive explanation ever promulgated concerning the nature of God and their relationship to Him. Every superstition, every fear, every theology, still had its adherents. Only a small group, one in a thousand, two in ten thousand, pushed forward the frontier. They were like the first settlers of the West, of Oregon perhaps. Behind them for three thousand miles, all the way to Plymouth Rock, stretched those who were content with a partial journey, those who were disinterested in adventure and discovery, those who were afraid of hardship, and those who had made of the established settlements ornaments for their pride, supports for their egos, bastions for their fright, servants for their greed.

"When I arrived home I sat for a while with my family. I found myself examining my wife for evidence of spiritual malingering. I wondered if either of my sons would be psychoanalyzed, and if so, whether he would accept it as casually as I had accepted my first dose of sulfa drugs, or whether it would excite and fascinate him as the acquisition of a radio had excited and fascinated me.

"I thought of the physical wonders which had come into my daily living since my boyhood, which I had accepted without question and to which I had become accustomed without effort—electric lights, the telephone, the phonograph, motion pictures, the automobile, the airplane, radio. The subtler wonders, of course, came with them—relativity, psychoanalysis, nuclear physics. These I had also accepted; I had accustomed myself to them. But they did not serve me in

177

a simple, superficial way, without thought and effort on my part, and I did not find it necessary to seek them out for any particular help. They were not, so far as I could observe, easily convertible to public use, though in the long run I could sight great benefits deriving from them to all people. They were like the frontier lands, a source of future wealth and security for the nation, at present a subject for romantic speculation and daring enterprise. They might bring wealth or happiness or security to my sons or to my grandsons; they would bring nothing to me; I only knew they were there, come suddenly into existence at humanity's level.

"I sat thinking these thoughts and estimating the difference in personality between me and my sons caused by time, by the generation of history between their interception of experience and mine. The new technique of self-realization was not functional for me, I decided, and would probably not be functional for them. In the generation of their children it might be reduced to commodity form; by that time large groups would need and seek it, being unable to derive any help at all from the moribund Christian orthodox faiths.

"The matter, I thought, could not be hurried; its growth could not be forced, though a war might coax it, like a warm night, or a depression stimulate it, like a day of sunshine. In a time beyond mine it would blossom, and people would wonder how I in my era got along without it; they would not believe that I did not need it, that enough survived from the old technique to nourish and comfort me in my span.

"I wondered if, in the time of its strength, it would strike down its predecessor, as Christianity, in her triumph, struck down those which had preceded her—then robbed their corpses. Probably so, and the first move would be, as always, to establish the new cult as a state religion, in this case as a national program for mental hygiene, compulsory at first for all school children, then for all factory workers—under the joint auspices of their unions and employers—and finally for everyone. At no time would the word compulsory be used, of course. The word free would be employed; it would bring better results than compulsion and would assure the new religion of a happy and cooperative congregation.

"Whether it would be more enjoyable to live in such a time I did not know; I doubted it. Surely I would do nothing to speed the arrival of a period when psychoanalysis would be needed by as many people as now wore spectacles. I would not like to see every third man dependent for his con-

178

tent and security of mind on an elaborate ritual dispensed by priests disguised as medical men. Suppose every third man in the street walked with a crutch? It was enough that we could not exist without vitamins, could not depend on nature for our bowel movements, had so degenerated physically that our tonsils and appendices poisoned rather than purged us, spent more and more of our years eating with false teeth, and could not see past the end of our nose without artificial aid."

"Excuse me," I said, "but why is it that so many people wear spectacles?"

He paused, swallowed, and stared at me.

"Forgive me," I said. "It sounds like a foolish question, I know. We strain our eyes; we read a great deal and we do what we call 'close work.' But there is also the possibility that the eye is evoluting, is there not? It may be that we are straining to see more, that we are trying to expand our visual range and intercept more waves—waves that will, when transformed into images, give us a clearer conception of the world, even allow us to see more of it. We are being forced to sharpen our eyesight, to see objects which move more and more quickly—driving an automobile develops in the eye an observational and calculating skill not hitherto cultivated, does it not?"

"Nonsense!" the Professor said. "The Kentucky riflemen—"

"Were few in number," I said. "There are more expert marksmen in the country today than there were in the great days of the frontier. However, I will use your simile. In the days of the frontier a man needed a gun—in that time and in that environment he needed a crutch, and the gun was it. In this time and in this environment he also needs a crutch; a new technique of religion—or the resurgence of an old technique—is it. It doesn't exist except for the few; it is needed by the many."

"If that is so," the Professor said, "then the need will produce a technique for the many; fulfillment never lags far behind need in a practical country. I do not believe the need is large enough yet; it is still a specialized hunger."

"In your generation that may be so; in mine the need exists," I said, "though in many who are most hungry the knowledge of hunger does not abide; there is only a feeling of being unwell within, a sense of dissociation from the main stream of life. The fact is that Christianity began the

179

mass initiation of a Western society into the 'mysteries,' which are the successive layers of realization which the mind reaches as it expands toward ultimate enlightenment. The present period has broken into another layer of realization. It is called, variously, electricity, the unconscious mind, relativity, quantum physics—whichever way the mind faces it encounters something new. The mind must adjust itself to the new layer of realization. It must explore it, colonize it, and develop techniques for subduing and employing it. You regard it as a faraway frontier country to which you will never go and which will never in a serious way affect your life. You are of the opinion that it will not greatly affect my life, and that I should peacefully go about my business without concerning myself over the new frontier except to read news of it in the morning paper."

"I consider that a reasonable and a civilized procedure," the Professor said. "You are obviously a personality designed for a stable society, one which is dynamic and positive. You were born into a society undergoing change, a society being pushed forward so rapidly that it feels uncertainty about the future, nostalgia for the past, and general instability. Some members of that society—perhaps I am one of them—hold back from the future, clinging to what they know in preference to what they have not experienced, cannot too clearly discern, and are not enthusiastic to embrace. Others —and you are of that band—want to gather all of us together and leap wildly into the future. You are victims of curiosity; you have a mania for acceleration; you are impatient with the past because it was not part of your pleasure and did not give you security. But mainly you suffer from the uncertainty incident to tradition, and you therefore wish to push forward quickly until a position of stability is reached. Perhaps I also dislike uncertainty; that may be the reason I hang back from a program of acceleration. Perhaps I want, so long as I live, to remain in sight of what is familiar in the past, and what once, in that past, was stable, or at least seemed so to me.

"It may be that we both desire the same thing, and that only the difference in our generations gives to our desires an illusion of difference."

He smiled; he was bright again, optimistic and professionally reassuring. His minute hand tilted cheerfully upward, like the words of a Rotarian song. Only five minutes remained now until three o'clock. All the repressed irritation of the

180

past five hours and fifty-five minutes broke through my relaxed will and boiled through my being.

"It is not a question of desire," I said, "nor even of necessity. It is a matter of safety, of survival, of moving with history or being crushed by it. The new layer of realization is no further removed from you than it is from me; I need a gun on my hip in this new wilderness and so do you. No discovery of this magnitude is singular or partial; it involves every man whose soul is not an embryo or a fossil. It is a movement forward on the rim of the spiritual wheel, a step toward God, from the cool shadows of reverence and faith to the hot sunlight of reality and remembrance, from contemplation to activity. You must move on to this new layer of realization with the rest of us, or be lost as a part of the collective awareness of mankind, the evolving ego, the growing soul."

"I am in no danger," the Professor said smugly. "I have only to put a date on everything which transpires; what it is, why it happened, what it accomplished, do not concern me. I am the moment, the marker, the milestone, the monument, nothing more."

"Then mark this," I said. "Put a date on it. The new religion is offered to America as an integral part of its evolving democracy and an inspiration to its declining Christianity. The decision to accept it or reject it is not to be made by officials of the government or the hierarchy of the church, but by the population, the people, the congregation. It is a matter of accepting a new awareness, a new phase of realization, a new revelation of spiritual responsibility, or refusing it. It is a question of acting in a manner which will strengthen, develop, widen, and secure democracy, and reanimate, revitalize, cleanse, clarify, and perhaps even consummate Christianity. If the decision is no, then the new religion will be accepted elsewhere, perhaps in Russia, when her revolutionary phase is finished. That's why every individual's acceptance or rejection of it is important. It's like a national election. The votes will never be counted, of course, but some day it will be apparent that more people voted yes than voted no, or vice versa."

"What's the difference?" the Professor said. "One way the United States will dominate the world for a long time; the other way she will fairly soon be a second rate power, which is perhaps all she deserves, considering her average intelligence."

"Damn it!" I said. "It isn't a question of world power! It's a matter of spiritual progression! It concerns the advancement of the soul of this frigid vixen who is nursing me, not the nationality or personal wealth of her great grandson!"

I looked at Miss Iceberg.

"Do you think Simon Magus was Paul?" I said to her. "He might have been."

She smiled with half of her mouth.

"The stretcher will be here in a minute or two," she said. "You'll soon be upstairs."

She walked past me and into the corridor, where she intercepted someone. They talked, and I heard a voice which I recognized as Miss Yellowhead's ask a question I could not quite distinguish, except that it was about me. "Only slightly," Miss Iceberg said, "and not for long at a time."

The Professor spoke. "Let us consider your case critical for the present," he said. "We'll take it up again when you return—if you have the courage to try another treatment."

Miss Iceberg and Miss Yellowhead came into the room, followed by two orderlies pushing a stretcher mounted on a carriage. Miss Yellowhead touched my brow and smiled.

"I hear you have been a good patient," she said. "I hope the treatment will help you."

She took a blanket from the stretcher, lifted the cover of the cabinet, and deftly covered me. The diathermy machines and the battery of electric bulbs had been turned off by Miss Iceberg. The orderlies lifted me to the stretcher.

"So long," I said to the Professor.

He flicked an arm in farewell. "Should I not see you again," he said, "and should anything—uh—happen to you, give my mother my regards."

"Your mother?" I said.

"Eternity," he replied.

Mary was waiting for me in my room. I told her I felt fine, that the treatment was certain to help me, that everything would be all right soon. She said the baby was fine, that she herself was all right, and that things at home were going smoothly. I believed her and she believed me. We were both lying a little. I had remained at home while she went to the hospital for the birth; on the day she returned, bringing our daughter in a basket, I left for the hospital to begin the first and unsuccessful series of fever treatments, given by injections of typhoid vaccine. My reaction to the vaccine was negligible; after that the cabinet was suggested. There was nothing to do but say yes. An ill man does not argue with science.

The floor nurse came in and reminded us that my temperature still was high, and that it would not be normal for several hours. Mary accepted the nudge and left. I lay wrapped in blankets until six o'clock; then I was bathed, fed, and left to my own supervision. I got out of bed and walked. I found that I did not need a cane, and that I limped only slightly; I felt neither stiff nor heavy. So far so good. I got back into bed, turned out the light, and tried to sleep.

Outside, New York was on its way to the saloons. Times Square threw a shout of light into the sky, a reflection of its bonfire of pleasure, its pile of mixed trash burning by the aid of repeated injections of kerosene. The reflected light fell through my window and was pale and still on the floor. I heard the ticking of my watch. What was it the Professor had said?—"Psychoanalysis offered to those who had the strength to conquer the world a way of enjoying that conquest." It was a quasi-truth; the Professor had a quick, slick way of presenting personal opinions and proceeding from them as if they were solidly established truths. Psychoanalysis was a technique for entering into life, the mystery religions were a way of escaping from it. That was a quick and slick comparison too, but nearer to fact.

What a tremendous effort early Christianity made to leap to heaven with humanity in its arms! The fall back to earth was long and hard, the reaction to the fall was an overcaution; the Christian now was so theologically and dogmatically protected, so provided with indulgences and mantras, that he was rocketed into eternity with complete confidence on the part of all concerned. Where he landed nobody knew, but everyone felt certain it was not far from the throne.

How faithfully the Christian had followed the Jew! He had designated Jesus as the Messiah promised in the Old Testament; he had insisted that the Dying God, common to all mystery religions, was singularly, particularly, and divinely the unique possession of the Jews; he had declared that all truth discovered in pagan religions—and he was dismayed to find so much of it—had been placed there by the Devil and consisted, as Justin Martyr described it, of "plagiarism by anticipation." He had battled to build his position into orthodoxy, and he had succeeded. Later he had followed the Jew

183

into trade and finance, declaring a convenient exemption of his business career from the jurisdiction of his church. Now he was preparing—after the usual period of sneering, smiling, and snubbing—to accept a Jewish rediscovery and restatement of the mystery technique of self-discovery by remembrance, examination, analysis, recognition, and acceptance, the mystery technique he had previously rejected and condemned. The Jew was his pioneer, his permanent Magellan, his mystical guide, his hunting dog of the soul, kept active, lean, and eager by persecution, discrimination, and distrust.

The new link between Christian and Jew was forged just as the old one broke, servered by biblical higher criticism, which proved everything Marcion of Sinope, a bishop and the son of a bishop, contended in 150 A.D. Marcion painstakingly pointed out the difference between the God of the Old Testament and the God of the New Testament, and asked how it was possible to reconcile Christ, who preached a doctrine of salvation for all mankind, with the Messiah predicted for the Jews, a conquering King of the world. He rejected the Gospels except for a version attributed to Paul; this, with some of Paul's letters, comprised what he considered authentic in Christian documents. He was, of course, excommunicated, but for a time his opinions were popular, his churches thrived.

Where had I first read of Marcion? It was in the library at Washington and Lee, in the west room on the second floor, at the long table before the window, where I went to read because I could rest my eyes occasionally by looking across the ravine to the athletic field and beyond it to the hill where the walls of Liberty Hall still stood. There I regarded all of history with my mind and felt a sickening lurch in my soul. Such a small way had mankind come, and by such dissimulating means.

ELEVEN

AFTER the first term at Lexington my eyes were always tired. When midyear grades were released I went to Dr. Campbell and asked for permission to enroll for extra courses, with the hope of completing my undergraduate work in three years. He glanced at my record, nodded, and said, "So long as you maintain this average you can take as many courses as you like. If your grades drop you'll have to return to the regular curriculum. If you get C in any course I shall consider that you have failed it."

It was not the additional courses, however, which put a burden on my vision. It was the fact that they caused me to visit the library more often, and that the library had more temptations per square inch than the female torso.

There was Elias, too; he brought me a new book every few days, and I had to read enough of each to fomulate a condemnation, if Elias was enthusiastic, or an endorsement, if he was skeptical. There was also Cayce; I found books on his study table which I was unable not to read: F. W. H. Myers' *Human Personality and Its Survival of Bodily Death*, Sidgwick and Gurney's *Phantasms of the Living and the Dead*, James' *Varieties of Religious Experience*, Hudson's *Law of Psychic Phenomena*. Cayce often talked all night— he slept in class, his head bent, a pencil poised at his notebook—about religion, destiny, morality, existence; he had a habit of reasoning himself to the brink of a conclusion, then retreating from it; he seemed intent, at times, on arguing himself out of everything in which he believed. Robison, an excellent listener, occasionally would say, "Cayce, you don't believe that." "Of course I don't," Cayce would answer. "I'm just trying to find out whether you do." "I'll believe it for fifteen minutes, just to accommodate you," Robison would say.

A curious frustration took hold of me whenever I entered the library; I wanted the contents of every book in the building transferred to my mind, but the thought of reading them all, of burying myself in the stacks, made my head ache and my feet drag. I never got past the shelf of new books without stopping; I was acquainted by way of Elias and the literary supplements with critical opinion regarding them, and I tried to skip through the important volumes, spotting and reading the recommended passages. When that was done I went to the stacks to get the books assigned by my instructors. Here another delay ensued. I could not read, or even skip through, the items on Fichte, Kant, Hegel, Spinoza, Hume, Locke, Nietzsche, Spencer, which attracted me, but I had a way of dealing with them which partially satisfied my hunger. I opened each book to its index, then looked for specific subjects—mind, will, reason, soul, destiny, memory, deity, desire, responsibility, emotion, resentment, sacrifice. In an hour I could compare the opinions of a sample batch of philosophers on several aspects of the problem of man's identity. By then the afternoon was half gone, however, and I had still my reading to do for English or history or some other course. In the west room on the second floor I hooked myself to the table by the window in such a way that if I fell asleep with my chair tilted backward I would not tumble to the floor. Then I was ready for work.

I tried to train my eyes to see an entire page at once, to photograph it, and to soak up its sense in a few seconds of contemplation. I was never successful; the effort hypnotized me; I put my face against the pages of the opened book and dozed, inhaling the fragrance of the paper. I loved the odor of books, the feel of them, their shapes, their type. I never put them out of my bed at night; I tucked them under the pillow's edge, or placed them where the bed met the wall, so my left hand could touch them as I slept. They gave me sensuous pleasure; they inflamed my mind with desire. Each had a perfume particular to itself, but all of them, to me, smelled of musk. Like women, they drenched me with a desire they could only partially fulfill. I wanted more than they contained—the complete story of man and his adventure, organized, synthesized, and reconciled. Drowsing in the west room over the *Cambridge History of English Literature* I counted what I knew of the tale thus far.

In the beginning Vishnu lay asleep on the quiet sea of his essence during the cosmic night. Markandeya, the Hindu sage, fell from Vishnu's mouth and saw this; he was quickly swallowed again, as he had been swallowed at the end of the cosmic day, and he remained within the god with the rest of created things, suspended in activity, until the long night ended.

Then Vishnu, rousing, stirred the waters with his hand. Ripples rose and raced after each other; the space between them moved, and in its ether wind was born. Wind whipped the sea of essence, broke and spun it about, until the friction caused fire. Heaven was made, and into it Vishnu thrust the thousand golden petals of his new lotus, with Brahma, the Son, sitting at its center. Into Brahma Vishnu had put his mind. Brahma spun creation for him, the web of Myra, the illusion of diversity, the dream in which I was awake.

Said the Bible: "In the beginning God created the heaven and the earth.

"And the earth was without form, and void; and darkness was upon the face of the deep. And the Spirit of God moved upon the face of the waters.

"And God said, Let there be light: and there was light.

"And God saw the light, that it was good: and God divided the light from the darkness."

Said science: "In its primitive state matter was a gas indefinitely diffused. There was first gravity, chemical action, and a concentration of the diffused gas into one or more nebulae which appeared as luminous spots on the dark space of heaven."

Said the Bible: "And God said, Let there be a firmament in the midst of the waters, and let it divide the waters. . . .

"And God made the firmament, and divided the waters which were under the firmament from the waters which were above the firmament: and it was so."

Said science: "This primitive nebula was divided into smaller nebulous masses and thus was formed the visible or lower and starry sphere."

Said the Bible: "And God said, Let the waters under the heaven be gathered together unto one place, and let the dry land appear: and it was so. . . .

"And God said, Let the earth bring forth grass, the herb yielding seed, and the fruit tree yielding fruit after his kind, whose seed is in itself, upon the earth: and it was so."

Said science: "The nebulous masses concentrated into stars and our sun became one of them. From the sun the earth was formed, or thrown off. It was at first self-luminous, a tiny sun. It cooled, a crust formed; water and land appeared, and first life appeared—infusorial plants and protophytes."

Said the Bible: "And God said, Let there be lights in the firmament of the heaven to divide the day from the night; and let them be for signs, and for seasons, and for days, and years."

Said science: "When chemical action subsided the earth lost its photosphere and the sun and moon became visible. There were nights and days, seasons and climate, and protozoa."

Said the Bible: "And God created great whales, and every living creature that moveth, which the waters brought forth abundantly, after their own kind, and every winged fowl after his kind: and God saw that it was good."

Said science: "Then came the sea animals, fishes, reptiles, birds. There were land plants, and the coal beds were laid down. These were the Paleozoic and Mesozoic ages."

Said the Bible: "And God made the beast of the earth after his kind, and cattle after their kind, and every thing that creepeth upon the earth after his kind: and God saw that it was good.

"And God said, Let us make man in our image, after our likeness. . . ."

Said science: "Now the higher animals appeared, the mammals. There were carniverous beasts, cattle, and herbiverous animals. This was the Tertiary age. In the Quaternary age which followed man appeared."

Said the Bible: "And God saw every thing that he had made, and, behold, it was very good."

Said science: "Material creation was now finished and a moral world emerged. It was the time of man."

So man was made. The fire of spirit took residence in his heart, then descended through the higher worlds of his mind to the unstable, watery, lower world of his emotions, and fell beyond it to the dense, stolid, insensitive body of his flesh. His blood turned warm and red; his brain stirred, blinked, vibrated. The long process of pouring creation into his consciousness began; he saw gods before him, and propitiated them; he heard music, and was frightened.

So the holy sacrifice of involution was begun. Divine Love and Divine Wisdom were joined, and brought forth Divine Mind, the Archetypal Man, the Word, the Son, the Christ Consciousness, Brahma, Balder, Osiris, whose Father was the Godhead, Vishnu, the Absolute; whose Mother was Sophia, Isis, Frigg, Mary, Beatrice, Eve; whose birth was brought about by the first cross; whose destiny was crucifixion.

The cross moved, and the Son began the long spinning of the new cosmic day. He limited Himself in form, He scattered and dimmed His divine brightness by differentiation and confinement, by incompleteness and separation; He placed His image in dark places, where realization was to begin its long growth; He carried man to the place of his becoming and sealed Himself up with the child in the womb.

Then Balder was slain, Lemminkainen went to kill the Swan of Tuoni and was cut to pieces, Set tore the body of Osiris to bits, Dionysius was dismembered, Eurydice was lost, Persephone was raped, and the kali yuga, the fourth and bitter age of evil and sorrow, of pain and redemption, began. The Golden Age when man lived in the spirit, the Silver Age when he dwelt in the mind, the Bronze Age when emotion was his life—these were ended. He was on the edge of darkness, at the hard rim of the world. Dharma, the sustenance of order, was at its ebb; now was the age of choice, of will, of temptation, of morality; now was the time of man. Involution had ended; the Fall had transpired; the Word had descended into flesh and was buried in desire and sense, too deeply for the instincts to discern.

Thus Hoder, who is instinct, was blind. When the other gods, knowing Balder was invulnerable, amused themselves by shooting at him, Hoder stood at the edge of the circle, doing nothing. Loke, who is desire, disguised himself as an old woman and went to Frigg, who as Wisdom had ordered the laws of creation not to hurt the soul. "Is it true," asked Loke, "that all things have sworn to spare Balder?" Then Frigg told him she had excepted from the oath a twig called mistletoe, or mind, because it seemed too young to take an oath. Loke found the twig and brought it to Hoder. "Why do you not shoot at Balder?" he asked the blind god. "Because I cannot see him," said Hoder, "and because I have no weapon." Loke gave him the mistletoe for a weapon, and guided his aim. Balder, struck by the twig which had not sworn to spare him, fell dead.

But the mistletoe had become engrafted on Loke; from its stimulation he developed a separate will; the war against discipline by natural law began; there was generated a willful stubbornness of the new self, of the limited, lower, evolving consciousness for whose birth the Archetypal Man had shed His blood. Evolution had begun. Ahura Mazda fought Ahriman, Oannes taught his disciples, Isis collected the fragments of Osiris, Orpheus sought Eurydice, Mithras slew the Bull, and Moses on a mountain top received from the Demiurge the laws by which the journey back must be made, the plan of the return of the Archetypal Man, who was to be raised up by the humanity in which His slain body lay.

"When he (the soul) shall have passed over as the image to its Archetype, then he will have reached his journey's end," said Plotinus.

In the Bhagavad Gita, Krishna, an incarnation of Vishnu, told Arjuna, the personality, how to make the journey. In the Law of Zoroaster Ormazd set down the precepts of salvation. Buddha revealed an eight-fold path; Lao-Tse provided a way of life. There were the mystery religions; there were the Therapeutae and the Essenes; there were the Greeks—Democritus, Pythagoras, Socrates, Plato. Slowly creation dripped into the consciousness of man. There came Jesus the Nazarene, and after Him Paul; there were the Marcionites, the desert monks, the Gnostics—Naaseni, Peratae, Sethians, Docetae, Carpocratians, Basilidians, Valentinians.

There were the Neo-Platonists, who while the heresiologists battled Arians and Manicheans passed on to Christianity through Augustine and Dionysius the Areopagite the mysticism of Plato and the symbolism of the mystery schools. There were Origen and Gregory the Great, and in the Dark Ages John Scotus Erigena. There were Bernard of Clairvaux and Hugh of St. Victor, Francis of Assisi and his biographer Bonaventura; Aquinas, Dante, Meister Eckhart, Tauler and Ruysbroeck, Jacob Boehme, Thomas à Kempis, the anonymous author of *The Cloud of Unknowing,* Teresa of Avila and John of the Cross, Brother Lawrence and William Blake. All of them, if each group and school were limited to a single representative, could have gathered in the west room with me. But they were the wool of a single white thread in a tapestry of gray and black, a thin bright line marking a steady way through the dark cloth. The rest of the pattern was more difficult to see.

There were black edges where in dim remembrance and debased symbology men ate their gods, fed them blood and virgins, prayed to them for strong seed. There were young, weak egos frightened of the spirits at work in trees and rivers, propitiating them for fear of being possessed by them. There were maidens who thought themselves ravished by gods who swooped from their subconscious. But as creation dripped more and more into self-consciousness these fragile egos saw less of alien identities, their personal selves grew stronger and reached further. As gods and demons drifted from sight superstition and idolatry diminished. The pattern brightened. In the West the black turned to gray.

Jesus opened the mystery to all men. He revealed the way; it was He. If a man could be as Jesus he would be as the Archetypal Man; Christ would be risen from his soul, the crucifixion accomplished, the ego shed, the journey safely made from the cross to the crown, from the sacrifice of involution to the redemption of evolution. The sweet, subtle ectasy of recognition, which begins when the soul first stirs and murmurs in the mind, would be consummated. What had seemed for so long to be the identity would be a dream, and what had been for so long a dream would wake and be the identity.

"Let not your heart be troubled," said Jesus to His disciples. "Ye believe in God, believe also in me. . . . Believe me that I am in the Father, and the Father in me. . . . And whatsoever ye shall ask in my name, that will I do. . . . If ye love me, keep my commandments. . . . If ye keep my commandments ye shall abide in my love; even as I have kept my Father's comandments, and abide in his love. . . . This is my commandment, That ye love one another, as I have loved you. . . . These things I have spoken unto you, that in me ye might have peace. In the world ye shall have tribulation: but be of good cheer; I have overcome the world."

The Archetypal Man, the Son, had risen from the soul of Jesus; the ego of the carpenter had been crucified, buried, and resurrected in the consciousness of Christ; the agent of the universe had been nailed to the cross of matter, immersed in the darkness of humanity, freed by a particle of that humanity, a man from Galilee. Others could do as He had done; through His example all men could accomplish the redemption. It was necessary only to believe in Him and to obey His law, the esoteric counterpart of the exoteric Decalogue received by Moses, the higher rule of conduct by

191

which discipline of the ego is achieved, the deceivingly simple set of precepts contained in the fifth chapter of St. Matthew, the Emancipation Proclamation of the soul:

"Blessed are the poor in spirit: for theirs is the kingdom of heaven. . . . Blessed are the meek. . . . Blessed are the peacemakers. . . . Whosoever therefore shall break one of these least commandments, and shall teach men so, he shall be called the least in the kingdom of heaven. . . . Agree with thine adversary . . . resist not evil: but whosoever shall smite thee on thy right cheek, turn to him the other also. And if any man will sue thee at the law, and take away thy coat, let him have thy cloke also. And whosoever shall compel thee to go a mile, go with him twain. Give to him that asketh thee. . . . Love your enemies. . . . Be ye therefore perfect, even as your Father which is in heaven is perfect."

It was done, it was finished, it was won: the chapter was read, the faith was firm, the brother was embraced; the world was enrolled in the mystery and all men were redeemed. What man could not be perfect with the vision of Jesus to lead him, and the promise that He would return in His glory, perhaps that very day, to rule over the world in peace and righteousness? In the desert, in the cities, in the caravans, men dropped their work and lifted their arms to meet the embrace of heaven; they stood on the peaks of their faith and tried to leap through the gravity-bound atmosphere of evolution to the free space of the spirit beyond. They spoke with tongues, they heard voices, they were struck down by visions. Behind them, with argument and cunning, with wisdom and opportunism, the church developed. Authority was established, ritual was devised, the mystery was secularized, popularized, advertised. Confidently it crossed the Mediterranean and took up its task, the spiritualization of the Western world.

Behind it lay the first great effort of the Orient, which had carried monarchy to its peak—monarchy political, economic, and spiritual. The time of the great good kings was done—Hammurabi, Asoka, David, Solomon, Ikhnaton. The mystery was no longer for the few, for the select, for the chosen. Jesus had proclaimed it a democracy, wherein all men were free to seek the center, yet bound to each other until the quiet of the hub was reached. The goal of evolution was a fire on the altar of every church; the sacrifice of involution was bread and wine for the faithful at every Mass: this and the commandment of love were incorruptible; they were the ring and its stone in the marriage of man to his soul. The irreverent said that a Christian was better off than a pagan; he could eat his God and have Him too.

The Roman Empire had declined; it had finished its first phase, conquest of the physical world (there is first a life of the body, then a life of the mind, and finally a life of the spirit; this is the image or reflection of the life of God, which is first in the spirit, next in the mind, or Son, and lastly in the body of creation). The emissaries of Christianity followed the arteries of the empire; they strung together on a framework of salvation and spiritual promise the infant nations of Europe. The life of the spirit came first and suddenly to people still living in forests, still drinking blood; it appeared to egos still frightened of demons, still haunted by vampires and succubi. The mystery was to them a dream, and they believed in dreams; this great new dream protected them, and exorcised their enemies. They lived in magic and died in Christ.

In the darkness which came over Europe from the sixth to the ninth centuries the mystery was an only light. In Christian monasteries the dying mind of the Graeco-Roman world was tended and succored and confessed of its sins by monks who were themselves forgiven a venial sin for every manuscript letter they copied. Then the hunched and shriven ecclesiastics began to nibble at the mystery's flesh. Erigena translated Dionysius the Areopagite, who became Saint Denis. Abelard brilliantly attacked the nominalists; Anselm of Canterbury proved God by reason. Aristotle came up from Spain in the interpretations of the Arabian scholar Averroes. There were Bonaventura, Aquinas, and Duns Scotus. There was finally William of Ockham, whose reason broke through the ring of faith toward skepticism. The mind of Europe came out of its dream, shook off the pursuing werewolves, and looked at the world. What had been the philosophy of a society disintegrated into the opinions of individuals. The second phase of the Roman Empire—now called Christianity —began; its birth was called the Renaissance. Europe set out to develop its mind. It questioned the mystery, pointing to the corruption surrounding it. There were quarrels; the Council of Trent was a failure at reconciliation; lines of disagreement were drawn.

The mind of the Orient, mature and jaded with existence, understood the mystery and appreciated it as a technique for realization of the soul. The primitive peoples of Europe believed the mystery as a fable, sensing intuitively its truth and huddling at its core. The developing individuality of Europe, feeling in its adolescence far from death and contemptuous of demons, werewolves, and purgatory, questioned the mystery as fable and denounced it as a totalitarian system for the ordering of daily life. It might be the way to a better afterward; it was the plague and poison of an enjoyable present—unless, of course, you were one of the jolly monks; they ate well and did nothing. So the mystery was set aside until its proper time was come, until it was discovered by the Western mind as it had been discovered by the Eastern mind, in the normal course of seeking. Meanwhile it was placed in a convenient spot, handy but out of the way. The Western mind had other things to search out.

It found them. Science, philosophy, ethics, logic, skepticism, psychology, economics, all set out, like the bear who went over the mountain, to see what they could see. Each found a trail and followed it. The oppressed and the poor also found a path, a physical one; they sailed to the New World, to America. They were Christians squeezed out of their environment by economics and intolerance; they founded a theocracy; it grew into the second democracy, the state of the politically free. This second democracy flourished as the green bay tree; it proclaimed the third democracy, the state of the economically free.

My eyes looked quickly; they oversimplified the pattern; they blurred the fine lines of detail. But they saw the general outline and they caught the undulating evidence of waves; they observed how tides had mixed the colors and pushed the edges of the pattern on. The East rolled up to Greece; the Macedonians under Alexander swept over the Orient; the Jews washed back and forth between Egypt and Babylonia; the Romans conquered the world; Christianity took over Rome; Islam raced up to the Pyrenees and Byzantium; the Crusades flowed out to wrest the Sepulcher from the Saracen. When trade replaced faith as a cause for war the fleets of England, Spain, Portugal, and the Netherlands searched and fought for new lands and fresh slaves. The dispossessed and the unwanted of Europe sailed to America.

Americans, on the first of the modern Crusades—there would be more—rushed to France on troopships in 1917. In California in 1910 an army of revolutionaries was secretly trained; it was smuggled across the Pacific to Sun Yat-sen, who used it the next year to establish the first Chinese republic. The second democracy had reached Asia. Half a dozen years later, over the Urals in Russia, a curious counterwave broke out against all three democracies, spiritual, political, and economic. It demanded not freedom but equality. Its argument paralleled the legal negativism of Christianity—all who embraced the faith and followed its rules shared equally in the glories of heaven; all who joined the party and obeyed its mandates shared equally in the riches of earth. Heaven was made for Christians; the world was made for Communists. Christian democracies, with a positive, vital economic system, and a negative, legalistic religion, were embarrassed. Communism invited them to Christianize their economics and to revitalize their religion, to be democratic or give up the claim to democracy, to put up or shut up. The spindrift of that wave blew even to the campus at Washington and Lee. "What do you think of Russia?" the student lawyers asked each other at The Corner. "A banana peel," Elias said. "If we don't watch our step, we'll slip on it."

There was one thread in the pattern which alternated its color, going from red to white and from white to red, from prostitution to virginity and from virginity to prostitution. Man was of two minds about the symbology of woman: she was Mother Earth, whose fertility was humanity's sustenance, whose belly must annually be filled with seed; she was Divine Wisdom, the Virgin of the soul, who brings forth from her stainless womb the Son of Man, the salvation of the world, Jesus Who is the consciousness of Christ. The Daughters of Aphrodite offered themselves at the temple to passing strangers; the children of Mary were told to throw inkwells at employers who threatened to kiss them.

In the West now the color of the thread was white. When the mind of Europe ceased to see gods it made a goddess of woman; she became the symbol of the soul, the maiden for whom the exiled and wandering ego sought the Holy Grail, that chalice from which the sacrificing god drank the consciousness of the world, and from which the world thereafter drank the consciousness of the sacrificing god. The worship of the symbol was called romance; in the church it became mariolatry. Woman, who was Mother Earth as well as the Virgin of the World, divided her life to accommodate the duality of her symbology; she fulfilled romance in the time before marriage; as a bride she offered herself to the stranger who was her husband. In time romance made inroads on marriage; the husband became less a stranger, the wife became more a goddess; there was more searching for the Grail, less planting of the seed. The white thread caught shadows from the black line of puritanism, which followed it closely, jealously.

Where the thread was red a silver line pursued it—yoga, the Hindu technique of the mystery by which kundalini, the sleeping fire of life, is guided up the tree of the spine to the centers of illumination in the temple of the skull. Puritanism was not a technique; it was a rejection, a negation; the sacred fire was renounced, abjured, shut up: the effort to endure the heat of a blaze trapped in the hold caused the vessels of puritan virtue to sail constantly on all seas and to set upon any strange craft. Once in New England they entirely wiped out a strong strain of clairvoyance.

Near the black line which pursued the white thread there was now a new, uncertain, gray line. It was psychonalysis, a Western yoga, a modern technique of the mystery.

Somewhere in the pattern was a detail too small for anyone to see; it was myself, floating on the surface of my generation, a microorganism in the tide, plankton in the surf. I exhibited reactions which could be foretold; I felt hunger; I was aware; I became tired; often I slept in the library.

I never left the building without stopping at the large dictionary which rested on a stand in the main reading room. I looked through it until I found some words to take with me; I put them in my mind as sometimes I put raisins in my pocket, to chew on as I walked—paludal, rimous, proteiform, scansorial, transilient, viviparous, xenelasia, mundungus, gobemouche, epithelium, berm, aseity. One night I finished my reading assignment about nine-thirty. After stopping at the dictionary I walked into the May night and set out across the campus toward the postoffice. There had been a light rain; the fragrance of the lawn was heavy. I stopped and pulled a blade of grass from its sheath. I held it under my nose; I drew its tip across my mouth.

"You are lanceolate!" I whispered.

While I stood there a girl came down the path, a professor's daughter not long in high heels; she wobbled a little as she proceeded. I walked home with her, helping her up at curbstones—she could have cleared them by a foot with a standing jump, but not in high heels. As we walked she talked, her small head darting at me occasionally, her hands carving gestures in the dark.

"I s'pose you've been up to the library doin' all that ol' readin' Daddy puts on you. I reckon it's all right, seein' as a man has to learn a heap o' things so he can make a mite o' money now an' then, though it'd be so much nicer if everybody could just dance around an' pitch woo like the ol' pagans an' ol' Greeks, though I reckon folks'd think that was right sinful nowadays, though I don't see why. Shucks, I'd like to dance on the lawn right now, in my bare feet, but they'd come an' put me away like I was touched. Some day maybe I'll marry a real rich banker an' have a big lawn like this all my own, an' then I'll jus' dance and dance and dance on it every night. Will you come and dance with me?"

I said I would.

"But what I'm really jus' fascinated by is destiny. I think it's the nicest thing for every person to have a destiny all his own, though I reckon I wouldn't care to be like Whiskey Willie Jones an' have a still blow up an' kill my whole family an' three prize hogs. That was Whiskey Willie's destiny, because he was in jail when it happened, for stealin' a mule an' tellin' the judge he was glad it wasn't a woman 'cause stealin' a woman wasn't worth goin' to jail for but stealin' a mule was, and that's why it was Whiskey Willie's destiny, 'cause he was in jail an' escaped, an' if he hadn't been in jail he'd have been jus' killed, an' it wouldn't have been destiny at all. I think that's interesting. They were fine hogs that Whiskey Willie had; I saw them at the County Fair last fall. Do you think about your destiny quite a bit, like meetin' the woman whose name is goin' to be engraved on your tombstone? That was the most romantic proposal I nearly ever heard about, when John Carter Bond said to Mary Randolph Dixson, 'Mary Randolph, how would you like to have your name engraved on my family tombstone?' Mary Randolph said she never was so thrilled. I think about my destiny all the time. Don't you think destiny is a fine thing?"

I said destiny was a fine thing and that I thought about mine quite a bit. We reached her house and turned in at the gate; I followed her up a walk to the front porch. On the way we passed a wisteria bush; it was drowning in its own perfume, a languorous, saccharine odor that drugged reason as it bubbled up in the mind. At the porch we stopped.

197

"I s'pose you'll be a damn Yankee an' not kiss me," she said.

I kissed her, and through the sticky rouge on her lips felt a warm membrane. Her arm lightened around my neck. The odor of wisteria was stifling. In my mind the girl lost her identity; I could think only of the South, a soft, patient, incredibly friendly South, looking for its destiny on a spring night, loving its enemy, giving him not only its other cheek, but the full moist warmth of its mouth.

A nation which is defeated in the flesh must find its victory in the spirit. The South had been forced to look within itself for the triumph which slipped from its grasp at Gettysburg. It had seen, looking within, the spirit and the shadow which lies always across the spirit, making it an imperfect soul—the ego. Some of its people had embraced the shadow, the ego, and were lost in its darkness. They were the warriors forever wounded, who borrowed the blood of their fathers and grandfathers and used it to stain their personal defeats; they were the paranoids who charged their inadequacies to the armies of Sherman and Grant. They were also the few, the Ku Klux Klan members, the lynchers. The many were quiet in the comfort of the spirit; they had learned to love their enemies; they were free of what had been taken from them. They were an embarrassment to hypocrites, a preplexity to fools.

In Virginia they were friendly; they were soft of speech; they had time for each other. They had time also for what God had put about them, in the valleys and on the hills. They regarded each man as a creature dear to his God, and they had reverence for the power which moved him. Their manners flowed from this; they were thoughtful, courteous, and left judgment to heaven. They were good companions, complete friends. What had made them poor had made them gentle; what had been taken from their hands had been given to their hearts.

Their women were assured and feminine, shyly frank, carefully trusting, designedly helpless, edging slightly toward the matriarchal, softly and irresistibly inspiring, implacably determined. After the harsh, open matriarchy of the Irish this dissimulation, this pretense that as man I was a superior being, was pleasurable. The pretense was not true, any more than the Irish mariolater's version of me as a lusting, grape-fed pagan was true; but in the electrical interplay of the sexes nothing was important but the ultimate purpose, the constant, sweet abrasion which wears away the two and builds the one, and in this matter good manners and good tempers were a joy. For it was not a single woman with whom a man had to mix for the knowledge of his dilemma—that was romance, and that particular woman, his mate, was the symbol of his soul—but all women, who together formed the veil of Maya-Shakti, Mother Eve; they were his to study, to brush against with his thoughts, and to contemplate. A man without friends who were women was lame in one leg of his mind.

All of them now, Virginians, virgins, and vixens, painted their lips. Was it evolution, whispering in their intuition? How long would it take for the sacred fire to lift itself up the spine and lick at the mouths of lovers, until by a kiss the womb was quickened, while the testes, like the appendix, became vestigial? It would require millennia of necking, and the first girl made pregnant by a kiss would have a skeptical audience for her story. Perhaps it would not happen until the new cosmic day, when such a mechanism for mating would emerge as a normal part of the pattern of the new and more spiritualized race.

There was a legend which said that when man descended into flesh the sacred fire separated, part going to the base of the spine, for generation, part lodging in his throat, for articulation. Kissing was an articulation of affection, a sign of spiritual union; the kissing of lovers simulated mating; it might, if nature so ordered things, be mating in actuality. Suppose nature, after centuries of preparatory necking with sensitized and aphrodisiacal lipsticks, decided to pull the switch on a certain night and shift the center of mating to the mouth. By midnight a generation of virgins would be ravished. When the metastasis was known every mouth would be covered. What then would be revealed and rouged?

"I reckon you're jus' obliged to sit down an' hold my hand a little bit now," the girl said. "What's so funny? You look as though you'd eaten a canary, like my cousin Georgie May, only he took the feathers off first an' cooked it."

"I'm happy and I like being with you," I said. "That's all."

She sighed. "It's almost like meetin' my destiny," she said, "only I've got so much homework to do for school and I haven't even looked at it yet."

I rubbed the back of her neck, at the place where a kitten likes to be scratched. How much of her would I have to unravel to find a common force, something I knew to be both her being and my being, the eternal face which lies under time? Wound about that face were layers of race, religion, environment, heredity, community, family, and beyond them the accretions of experience on her will; the selection, judgment, and interpretation that was her personality; her desires, her dreams, fears, longings, hates; her understanding, her ambition, her sex.

"What are you going to do when your schooling is finished?" I asked.

"Oh, I'll jus' be like the rest o' the Lexington girls," she said. "I'll sit around on the porch cussin' the damn Yankees an' hopin' one o' them'll ask me to marry him."

She looked up at me and laughed. "Would you like a piece o' cake an' a glass o' milk?" she said. "Yankees have to be fed, I'm told."

We went into the house and she brought cake and milk to the living room. While we ate I did her trigonometry problems. Then I kissed her again and said good night. There was a crumb of cake on the side of her mouth.

"I don't know when I've enjoyed doin' my homework so much," she said. "I think it was real nice of you t'be my destiny this evenin'."

The postoffice and The Corner were closed. I walked to the dormitory and joined the argument in Cayce's room. It went on all the time, like a continuous card game. The participants changed, Cayce and his roommate Bill Meredith left the double room and went to classes or the library or the postoffice, but the battle continued. The sandwich man arrived at night and forgot to leave; Robison gave up studying to defend his sociological and theological convictions; older students came in to stop the noise and got into the discussion.

The subject normally was philosophical, religious, or scientific: the reality of God, the nature of man, relativity (with diagrams on the whitewashed walls), women, hell, sin, telepathy, virginity, the Ten Commandments, the Pope, Protestantism, the double standard, Catholicism, clairvoyance, ghosts, morality in general, morality in specific instances, prostitution, necking, dreams, premonition, incontinence, drinking, smoking, the church as a career, love, marriage, divorce, the fidelity of women, the infidelity of women, death, resurrection, pre-existence, immortality, purgatory, heaven, history, whores, hypnosis, self-discipline, the speed of light, radio (could it tune in on the dead?), romance, reason, instinct, reflex action, fate, the future, phantoms, happiness, destiny. The contenders stood in the middle of the room or sat on the backs of chairs, their feet on the seats. Spectators lounged on the beds, choosing sides and offering advice.

No agreement was ever reached on any phase of any subject at any time. Opinion normally was almost evenly divided; only on the question of prostitution was there a semblance of unanimity. I and the Angel of the Hills, a black-haired banjo player who ended his songs by stomping his feet and shouting, "All policemen have big feet," were the only upholders of the oldest profession. I contended that it was the standard of puritanism which made prostitution a sin; it could be condemned on the basis of a complete rejection of sex, not otherwise. From the viewpoint of the Oriental techniques it was an expedient—an evolutionary expedient—for the channeling of uncontrollable and potentially dangerous energy into an impersonal and symbolical repository. So long as man was sexed for spiritual advancement as well as for physical reproduction it was necessary that such a symbolical repository be available; it was the insistence of Christian romance that a whore be personalized and that sex be denied except for reproduction which tranformed any woman whose impulses were general into a harlot.

That there was a class of women below the level of personal selection and romantic fidelity was obvious; that these women performed a religious service basic to the preliminary stages of the technique of raising and controlling the sacred fire was never denied in the Orient, however the abuses to which the service was put. The Western suppression and rejection of the sacred fire necessitated the declaration that prostitution was unnecessary to any portion of Christian life and was therefore a temptation to sin rather than a release from it.

I quoted from the fifth chapter of St. Matthew: ". . . whosoever looketh on a woman to lust after her hath committed adultery with her already in his heart." When lust came how many women thus were ravished in the mind before the blaze was confined to the hold and the hatches battened down? The prostitute offered, at the most, a single brief sin in place of a multitude of night-long, infinitely detailed sins. If the words of Christ were believed by a Christian, how could he anathematize a prostitute, who offered him a means of shortening his purgatory? He could only denounce her by assuming hypocrisy, by declaring that he was above the power of lust, which he was not.

My argument was denounced and rejected by everyone but the Angel of the Hills. He decided that his chances of finding, winning, and holding a desirable woman were poor; he therefore preferred to depend for the fulfillment of his needs on the general affection of a professional class.

The threefold nature of Jesus Christ was another recurring topic. I never entered this particular discussion, pointing out that it was a matter of personal understanding, and that since division was man-made, for his partial and progressive apprehension, only the unitive principle was unchanging. God was God; man's imperfect realization of Him constantly detected His countenance where only His shadow had passed. One night the differences of theory were so many and so sharp that an opinion from me, any opinion whatever, was demanded. I stood in the middle of the room and drew a vertical line through the air with my hand.

"That represents the division between the Father and the Son," I said.

I drew another vertical line through the air, without changing my position or shifting my arm.

"That represents the difference between the Son and the Holy Ghost," I said.

I drew a third vertical line, also without moving or shifting my arm.

"That represents the difference between the Holy Ghost and the Father," I said.

I stepped aside and looked at the space through which I had been moving my arm.

"Where are the lines?" I asked.

The Angel of the Hills laughed.

"That's easy," he said. "The lines are in our heads. We saw you draw them but we can't see them now, so they only exist in our minds, and since we all saw them from a different angle each has a different picture in his head."

"So far as I'm concerned that's where the Trinity exists," I said, "in your heads. And each one has a different picture."

The others continued the argument without reference to what I had said; my opinion, though given at their request, was considered worthless, having been delivered by what they referred to as the "Irish section" of my mind—my sense of humor. Cayce contended with them, though he was as disinterested as I in the upside down pursuit of truth, the attempt to gather knowledge by reading from the back of the book forward, beginning with the last page. We theorized that if Calvary as a date was taken as the apex of involution and the nadir of evolution, the lower tip of the caduceus, the base of the spiritual spine, the completion of the crucifixion in matter, then the Orient and its religious techniques were concerned with helping the slowly forgetting subconscious to remember its origin, while the psychological, scientific methods of the West were engaged in stimulating the self-consciousness to discover its goal: the Orient returned an unrealized ego to the forgetfulness of Nirvana; the West drove the ego onward until in an ecstasy of realization it made the sacrifice which brought forth the consciousness of Christ from its soul: in the Orient a man set out by himself to lose himself: in the West a Christian set out with others to discover himself.

It was not as simple as that: there was no East or West actually, no before Calvary or after: space and time were illusions, parts of a process of development, as were forgetting and remembering. In the East and West, before and after Calvary, there were souls involving and evolving, minds pushing ahead to what Myers called "preversion," the accumulation of "characteristics assumed to lie at a further point of the evolutionary progress of a species than has yet been reached." There were also souls reverting, slipping back into the accumulation of the subconscious, living on money in the bank. Creation dripped steadily into the mind of man, but after his self-consciousness was weaned he went to forage for himself. In the West he had discovered, along with internal combustion, electricity, radio waves, and molecular architecture, such apparent human talents as clairvoyance, telepathy, psychometry, precognition, clairaudience. These evidences of preversion he found, for the present, difficult to assimilate, since they could be used neither to illuminate a house nor to bolster skepticism, the prevailing intellectual mood. They were also of no use as nourishment to the church; orthodoxy had decided to get along on a diet which excluded hearing voices, speaking in tongues, and seeing angels. They lay thus still outside the realization of Western man, while their modern history piled up to staggering heights in such places as the files of the London Society for Psychical Research.

That was why Cayce and I needed a theory; we wanted a reason for the temporary lag in absorbing a scientific technique for measuring and studying the rate, method, incidence, and characteristics of contemporary preversion; we wanted an excuse for considering the lag as a normal period in evolutionary chronology; we didn't want to believe there was something wrong with the spiritual progression of our times. The lag bothered Cayce; he spent entire nights describing trends and citing individual cases in an effort to prove to himself that the lag was being overcome, when he knew quite well that it wasn't. The lag bothered me, too, but not a great deal. The world, I was sure, would change, now that I realized it needed to change.

Not all our arguments were serious. One night Robison bet me I couldn't do seventy-five pushups. I did them; I needed the money. Once Cayce, during a discussion of the power of mind over matter, offered to bet me that I could not compel him to perform an announced, specific act, without the use of physical force. I accepted the bet. On the wall over the mantel of the Cayce-Meredith room a Virginia Beach pennant hung.

"I will compel you to take that pennant down without touching you or it," I said.

The next night when he and Meredith went to the post-office I opened Cayce's trunk and removed all his trousers, giving them to Robison, who hid them with an acquaintance in Graham dormitory. I locked up my trousers and Robison's. The other boys on the floor were so much taller than Cayce that it would have been impossible for him to wear their pants. I set my alarm clock for five-thirty; after Cayce returned to his room I spent all of the study hours arguing with him, sitting between him and his trunk. When he was safely in bed, his trousers flung over a chair near the door, I went to my room and slept. When the alarm went off I got up, walked quietly to Cayce's room, opened the door, and took the trousers. He woke, saw me, and made a futile grab for his pants. By the time he got to my room I had them locked up. He went back to his room and looked in his trunk, then began a search in the other rooms for something to wear.

204

It was imperative that he attend classes. He had taken more than his allotment of cuts and was on probation; one more cut without a medical excuse and he would be dismissed from the university. He demanded a pair of pants of Robison; Robison explained that I had taken all his trousers and locked them up.

"Put the snatch on me, son," he explained. "Dogged if I knew what he was up to until I found myself plumb down to what I got on."

Cayce turned to leave, then lunged suddenly at the laundry bag. Protruding from it was one leg of a pair of old trousers Robison wore when he played tennis. I had not seen them. Before Robison or I could move, the pants and Cayce were gone. They were short for him, and so soiled I was certain he would not wear them to class, but he did. That afternoon he circulated through the dormitories the promise of a generous reward for the return of his pants. Before dinner he had them.

Next morning during a free hour I went to Rice's drugstore and asked the pharmacist to prepare a mixture of the most evil-smelling liquids he possessed.

"I want something that smells so bad no one will be able to remain in the same room with it," I said.

The pharmacist was delighted with the opportunity; in a few minutes he handed me a six-ounce bottle filled with a brown mixture whose odor staggered me. I corked it tightly and went to the dormitory. Meredith and Cayce were at class. I asked two freshmen to witness my act; I wanted evidence that I had not touched the pennant. I stood on the mantel and carefully poured the brown liquid over the red and gray cloth. The freshmen gasped and fled. I jumped to the floor, threw the empty bottle in the fireplace and went to my next class.

When I returned a crowd had gathered in the hall outside Cayce's door. In the room a violent argument was in progress. Meredith and John McKimmey, a tall boy from Arkansas, were demanding that Cayce remove the pennant from the wall, the room, and the building. Cayce said he would not take the pennant down; he admitted that the odor was bad, but contended that it would gradually disappear; he was prepared to endure it for as long as it lasted.

"I'll move out," Meredith said.

"Go ahead," Cayce said.

The windows were open and John, the janitor, was quietly standing by, smoking his pipe and holding a trash can ready.

"Take it down," McKimmey said, "or the whole damned floor will have to move out."

"I won't touch it," Cayce said.

"Then I will," McKimmey said.

He put one hand on the mantel, jumped, and pulled down the pennant with his other hand. Instantly he dropped it in the trash can.

"Thank you," John said, and went out.

Cayce turned to me and smiled.

"You lose," he said. "Pay up."

Robison, Cayce, and I made a laboratory study of the church services in Lexington; one Sunday morning I took them to the missionary chapel which served the handful of Roman Catholics in the town and the few cadets and students who were of the faith. It was a small, bare building, poorly and starkly furnished, in an undistinguished section of the town, halfway up a steep hill. A priest came from Staunton to say a single low Mass each Sunday; the Mass was read at eight o'clock; a bell without tone or resonance proclaimed its imminence. Seldom did I meet anyone as I walked across the campus. Yet as I knelt on one of the incredibly hard benches, following the mystery from the *Et introibo ad altare Dei* to the *Et verbum caro factum est*, I felt a fresh, strong tenderness for the Mass, for the incorruptible ring of the mystery and its stone, for the church which carried it to such remote and improbable places. Where I had known the church, in New England, it was rich, strong, and in no need of help from me. Here it was poor, lonely, wretchedly housed, and with a bell not fit to speak for God, His angels, or even His saints. Here it needed me; here I could love it and aid it.

But that was a personal feeling; I could neither explain it nor transfer it to Cayce and Robison. They sat politely through Mass and afterward asked me polite questions, as I had asked them polite questions about the services in their respective churches, the Presbyterian and Baptist.

We were not reticent because we feared to hurt each other's feelings. It was something else. We had seen the church in action, Protestant and Catholic. There was nothing to say except the thing we did not want to say, but which we clearly saw, and which hurt us to know. Christianity was not doing its job. If spiritual evolution was proceeding it was doing so without ecclesiastical sanction or help.

TWELVE

ON A MAY NIGHT when we should have been studying for examinations Cayce and I sat talking about apports, teleportation, poltergeists, wraiths, possession, and other infringements of what is called natural law. Since there is no unnatural law we were forced to discuss our subjects on the basis of a break in natural law, a perversion or freak, or an infiltration of events normal to another environment but strange and upsetting to ours. I listened to story after story, relishing each weird episode as another crack in the thin wall of predictability, knowing that eventually Cayce would get around to clairvoyance and the subconscious; he couldn't stay away from those two things. I knew also that he would answer, glibly and with an air of authority, almost any question I asked. When I requested proof of his statements, or the names of books in which I might find them corroborated, he would wave his hand and say vaguely, "Anywhere. Just look in the library." If I pressed him further he would become annoyed, wave both hands, and say, "How do you expect me to remember the name of every book I read?"

On this night he said, at one point, "There is no mystery in clairvoyance. The subconscious mind of any person is capable of getting in touch with the subconscious mind of any other person. In environments beyond ours that is the manner in which individuals communicate; it is as simple as calling a person on the telephone and beginning a conversation. In our environment the conscious mind is a barrier against that easy method of intercourse. By hunches, by telepathy, by sudden feelings of like or dislike for persons just met, the subconscious mind does communicate with other subconscious minds, but the echo in the conscious mind is very faint. Only in clairvoyance is the communication clear and understandable."

He went on to describe the types and degrees of clairvoyance, and the two main types of clairvoyant, the sensitive and the intuitive. The sensitive clairvoyant did not go into trance; while awake and fully conscious he was able to concentrate on another person and see the subconscious pattern, particularly the disturbed detail which was causing a physical manifestation of illness. Some sensitives not only saw the subconscious pattern, they felt the disturbance in their own patterns and reproduced the symptoms of illness in their own bodies. Intuitive clairvoyants went into trance and were told by their "conductors" what persons to find and examine. They were able to reach any person, at any distance, so long as the person's name and whereabout were known and given to them while in trance. They reported at length and in detail on whatever aspect of the person was designated—general health, mental outlook, emotional mood, or the history and present state of a specific ailment. After emerging from trance the intuitive clairvoyants recalled nothing of what had transpired, knew nothing of what they had said.

"I'd say they were better off than the sensitive clairvoyants," I said. "They don't know what they are seeing and feeling, and considering the misery and pain they are asked to investigate, they are fortunate. Where did you say I could find out about that golden age of clairvoyance you've been talking about, when people all over Europe went to what they called 'somnambulists' rather than doctors?"

"Anywhere," he said. "Just look in the library. There are a lot of books about it. It began with de Puysegur and lasted until the middle of the last century. Of course, diagnosis by clairvoyance was opposed by orthodox medicine."

"You can't expect any man to accept the evidence of the inner eye against the evidence of the outer eye when he has no sight in his own inner eye and has no reason to believe that it exists, in himself or anyone else," I said.

"Well," Cayce went on, "if people with clairvoyant powers were tested by scientists under laboratory conditions and records were kept and reports—"

But this time he was not going to get away from me.

"Never mind about the scientists," I said, "and don't tell me again about a lot of books in the library on clairvoyance.

Just tell me one thing—the title of a book containing the statement you made a while ago, that the subconscious mind of any person is capable of getting in touch with the subconscious mind of any other person. I want an authority for that. Everything proceeds from the general to the particular—if we go back far enough all of us not only are able to communicate with each other, we intermingle, lose our identities, and return to unexpressed spirit. At a certain point in the retreat from self-consciousness we still retain our identities and yet intermingle with other identities; that is reasonable; humanity is a single experiment being performed by interdependent members. But where is that point of communication—directly behind the waking state of consciousness, or as far back as the ego has power to protect itself from the reach of other minds? I want to know. I want to read in a book the statement you made, and I want to read everything else in that book. What's its name? Where can I find it?"

Cayce got up and walked around the room. His face showed pain. He drummed on the study table with his fingers. Then he returned to the chair, sitting on its back.

"I can't tell you the name of the book," he said, "because so far as I know it doesn't exist. There may be a book somewhere containing that statement, but I don't know where it is or what it's called."

"Then who made the statement?" I asked.

"My father made it," he said. He stared straight at me. "My father is a clairvoyant," he said, "—an intuitive clairvoyant."

He was suffering; I had to say something quickly.

"Why didn't you tell me that before?" I said. "May I meet him some time? I'd like to see clairvoyance in operation. You're lucky to have an experimental laboratory in your own home."

"I want you to meet him very much," he said eagerly. "I'd like you to visit us at the beach when school is finished. You'll like the beach. There is a new concrete sea wall and promenade running for three miles along the water, and all summer there are ten girls to one boy—"

"I'll go," I said. "But now I want to hear about your father. Tell me the story."

He looked at his watch. He was relaxed, smiling with relief.

209

"It will take quite a while," he said. "It's not a short story and I may ramble."

"We're not due in class until eight-thirty," I said. "It's only two-thirty now. You have six hours."

He began to talk.

Shadrach Cayce lived in Powhatan County, Virginia. He had a brother named Archibald who emigrated to South Carolina and founded the town of Cayce in that state. He had a son named Pleasant who went to Fulton County, Kentucky and founded the town of Cayce there—it was later the home of a locomotive engineer called Casey (for Cayce) Jones. He had a son named George who went to Illinois, where he sued a man named Abraham Lincoln over some fence rails. He had a son named William who went to Christian County, in western Kentucky, and settled there on a farm near Hopkinsville, not far from the Tennessee line. William named his sons after Presidents—George Washington, Thomas Jefferson, James Madison. Thomas Jefferson Cayce named his sons Edgar, Clinton, Matthew, Leslie, Lucian, Delbert, and Robert E. Lee. Leslie married a neighbor, Carrie Major, who lived in a house made of bricks and timber imported from England. Leslie and Carrie had four daughters, Annie, Ola, Sara, and Mary. On March 18, 1877, a son was born to them. He was named Edgar.*

When Edgar was a child he had invisible playmates; as a boy he was fascinated by the Bible and resolved to read it through once for every year of his life. One day while musing over the story of Manoah he had a vision. He saw a beautiful lady; she asked him what it was he wanted most of all. "Most of all I would like to be helpful to others," he said, "and especially to children when they are sick." The lady smiled and vanished.

He was drowsy and inattentive in school, a poor student. One night at home while studying his spelling lesson he put the book behind his head and took a nap. When he woke he knew how to spell all the words in the volume; as his father asked them he saw in his mind the pages on which they were printed. He found that he could sleep on any of his school books and when he woke recite from any of its pages. He became the school's most dependable pupil.

---

* See *There Is A River*, the Story of Edgar Cayce, by Thomas Sugrue, Henry Holt and Company, 1943.

When he was seventeen his family went to Hopkinsville to live. He worked in a bookstore, taught Sunday School, and became engaged to a girl named Gertrude Evans. When he was twenty-one he lost his job and moved to Louisville to find another. When he was twenty-three he went on the road as an insurance salesman. He caught a cold and lost his voice. It did not return. For a year medical specialists attempted to cure his aphonia; they failed. Then it was discovered that under hypnosis he could talk; but post-suggestion that he retain the ability to articulate after waking was unsuccessful. On waking he was again speechless. During one experiment a Hopkinsville amateur hypnotist named A. C. Layne asked him to give his own explanation for the aphonia. In a clear voice the sleeping young man said: "In the normal state this body is unable to speak, due to a partial paralysis of the inferior muscles of the vocal chords, produced by nerve strain. This is a psychological condition producing a physical effect. This may be removed by increasing the circulation to the affected parts by suggestion while in this unconscious condition."

Layne suggested that circulation in the throat area be increased; gradually Edgar's upper chest and neck turned pink, then red. After a while he spoke to Layne again.

"It is all right now," he said. "The condition is removed. Make the suggestion that the circulation return to normal, and that after that the body awaken."

Layne made the suggestions; Edgar's throat and upper chest resumed a normal color. He woke, sat up, coughed, reached for his handkerchief, and spat blood.

"Hello!" he said in a normal voice. Then he smiled.

"Hey!" he said. "I can talk! I'm all right!"

Apparently he had slipped, as had other hypnotic subjects, into a state of clairvoyance. The phenomenon was first observed in 1794 when Victor, a French peasant boy, while being "magnetized" by the Marquis de Puysegur, fell into a deep trance and began to diagnose the physical ailment of a person sitting next to him. With Victor began the fad of diagnosis by "somnambulism," which because it ignored time and space, sensory observation and medical learning, was doomed to condemnation. Edgar Cayce, when he was told what he had done, was disturbed in his conscience; when he was asked to do it for others he refused.

Layne at last prevailed upon him, however; Layne was himself ill, and needed, so he said, Edgar's help. Edgar gave

211

it and was horrified to see Layne take medicines which he, Edgar, had prescribed while asleep. With his ninth grade education how could he possibly know, even in a dream state, what would relieve his own or any other man's aches and pains? But Layne's health improved, and he begged Edgar to use his clairvoyance for the assistance of others. Edgar fled to Bowling Green, Kentucky, and there opened a photographer's studio; he had studied photography in Hopkinsville during his year of enforced silence. He married Gertrude Evans.

Layne pursued him. There were people now who declared, so he said, that their only hope was a diagnosis by Edgar's clairvoyance. Again Edgar gave in; he was afraid, but he could not resist a request for help. A group of young doctors in Bowling Green became interested in his clairvoyance; they studied it scientifically, matching the results of their own examinations of certain patients against Edgar's opinions given while in trance. He never saw the patients, never knew who they were; the doctors read off names and addresses while he was in trance; he "found" the patients and reported on their health. The doctors gave him a perfect score on diagnosis; they were confused at the mixed nature of the treatments he suggested; he drew freely from the homeopathic, allopathic, naturopathic, and osteopathic schools of medicine, and usually added psycho-therapeutic suggestions. Whatever would help in relieving the patient's affliction was described, whether it was a modern drug, an ancient mixture of herbs, a massage, a brisk walk before breakfast, or the removal of an offending part by surgery.

The doctors took many "readings," as the dissertations which Edgar gave while in trance were called. They made a great many notes; they came to no conclusions. Edgar tired of their skepticism; he was irritated and worried by his curious talent, as was Gertrude. They both wished it had not been discovered, and they hoped eventually to be able to abandon and forget it.

In December, 1906, Edgar's photographic studio was destroyed by fire. In March, 1907, Gertrude bore him a son, who was called Hugh Lynn. In September of the same year the new studio burned. When his debts were paid Edgar returned to Hopkinsville. There he became nationally notorious; a homeopath named Wesley H. Ketchum had reported his talent for medical diagnosis in a paper read before the American Society of Clinical Research in a meeting at Boston. The newspapers, including *The New York Times,* seized on the story. Nearly ten thousand letters came to Edgar asking for his help, many of them heartbreaking in their recitation of the failures of medical specialists to discover the cause of their ailments or give them relief from discomfort and disability. Ketchum convinced Edgar that he could not ignore these pleas; he agreed to give two readings a day, so long as he could also conduct a photographer's studio and thus "honestly" earn a living. The readings were given in the studio; what Edgar said was recorded in shorthand by a stenographer and later transcribed on a typewriter. Some people came to Hopkinsville to hear their readings; most did not. They received the stenographer's typed report. Normally it contained a diagnosis, suggestions for treatment, dietary precautions, and answers to questions submitted. Among those who came and heard a reading was Dr. Hugo Münsterberg, professor of psychology at Harvard.

"I would hesitate to pass my opinion without a long and thorough examination," he said when Edgar had wakened. "But if it is a trick I am convinced you are not yourself aware of it."

"If it is a trick, doctor, I would like to know about it before I go too far and cause some harm," Edgar said.

One day Dr. J. B. Jackson, a local physician, called Edgar to his office. Gertrude was ill, and Dr. Jackson was attending her.

"There is nothing more I can do for Gertrude," he said. "She has tuberculosis. Her brother died of it; you know that. I've had other doctors look her over—we agree on what she has. So far as we can see there is no hope. I don't know how long she will live; perhaps another week.

"You've been doing things for other people. If there's anything in that monkey business, now is the time to try it. It's your only hope. We've done all we can. You'd better get a reading."

Gertrude had never asked for a reading, and Edgar had never offered to give her one; he knew how deeply she distrusted clairvoyance. Now he gave a reading on her condition for Dr. Jackson. There were other doctors present; one was a tuberculosis specialist called from Louisville. When Edgar woke after the reading the specialist said, "Your anatomy is fine, fine. Your diagnosis is excellent. But your *materia medica* is rotten. The things you suggest are what we make medicines with. We don't use them as they are.

They won't make a compound. Heroin, you say, mixed to make a liquid, given in a capsule, and manufactured only three at a time, because after three days the compound will disintegrate. That's just weird!"

"Did I say she could get well?" Edgar asked.

"Yes, you did, but . . ."

There was a little more argument, largely for the sake of professional honor, then it was decided to follow the suggestions of the reading precisely. Dr. Jackson informed Gertrude of the decision. She agreed meekly. In a few months she was on her way toward being well. When she was entirely recovered she went with Edgar to Selma, Alabama, and there they opened a photographer's studio. Edgar had broken his contract with Ketchum; the pain of his conscience had become intolerable—he could not yet believe day after day in a talent he was never aware of possessing and which so far as he knew was uniquely his own among living men. But in Selma, Hugh Lynn burned his eyes with flashlight powder, and when the doctors said they would have to remove one of them Hugh Lynn said, "If you had a little boy you wouldn't take his eye out, would you?"

"I wouldn't take any little boy's eye out if I could help it," one of the doctors said. "We're only trying to do what is best for you."

"My daddy knows what is best for me," Hugh Lynn said. "When my daddy goes to sleep he's the best doctor in the world." He reached for his father's hand. "Please, daddy, will you go to sleep and see if you can help me?" he asked.

"Go ahead," the doctor said. "We can't offer much. We'll listen and do what we can afterward."

The reading was given in the photographer's studio. While asleep Edgar said that the solution being used by the doctors was helpful, but that to it should be added tannic acid. When he woke the doctors said tannic acid was too strong for use on the eyes, but after a while they agreed to try it; they believed sight was already gone.

When the bandages were removed at the end of fifteen days Hugh Lynn looked up at Edgar and Gertrude and said, "I can see."

After that the letters which continued to find their way to Edgar from all parts of the country were answered. Readings were given regularly, and Gertrude acted as "conductor"; she read to Edgar, while he slept, the names and addresses of the people for whom the readings were to be given, and asked him pertinent questions; she gave the suggestion that he wake up when the reading was finished. Edgar put himself to sleep; he had discovered after the first few experiments with Layne that it was by his own will that he went into trance; he did not need the aid of a hypnotist.

In 1918 a second son was born; he was named Edgar Evans. In 1922 a Selma stenographer, Gladys Davis, took an interest in the readings and studied the manner and style of Edgar's speech until she was able to take down accurately what he said while asleep and transcribe it with the inflections preserved and the meaning clear. One day a man from Dayton, Ohio, visited the studio; he wanted to obtain a set of readings on philosophical subjects. Edgar had never attempted anything beyond medical diagnosis, but he was willing to try, now that Gertrude believed in his talent.

The readings on philosophy shocked everyone but the visitor from Dayton, whose name was Arthur Lammers. As casually and as confidently as he had described the ailments of hundreds of physical bodies Edgar talked of the mystery, of the sacrifice of the Archetypal Man, of the consciousness of Christ lying hidden and dreaming in the soul, of the cycle of death and rebirth, of the herculean effort of evolution, of the interdependence and inter-identity of the units of humanity, of the sacred fire and the ladder of illumination, of the gnosis, of the resurrection of the body of the slain God from the awakening soul of the world.

Edgar had been raised as an orthodox Christian; he was a Campbellite, a member of the Christian Church, which was an offshot of Presbyterianism. He had been taught to interpret the Bible literally, and he had for a quarter of a century been teaching a literal interpretation of it to his Sunday School classes. He and Gertrude had finally come to believe in the reliability of his clairvoyance; now that clairvoyance informed him that what he believed about God and salvation was primitive, over-simplified, and in many details untrue; it assumed a more difficult spiritual path for the soul than Edgar had imagined; it ignored the schism between daily life and Sunday life so carefully arranged by Christians; it acted as if the Gnostics had not been defeated by orthodoxy in the battle that raged along the Mediterranean seventeen hundred years before; it proclaimed a Christianity so long condemned that to Edgar it sounded like the liturgies of Lucifer, the Articles of Confederacy of the damned. Only by its constant reference to Christ as the apex of truth and the realization of every soul did it give him comfort. This and his knowledge that the medical diagnoses had always been accurate kept him from renouncing the clairvoyance forever. He accepted an invitation to visit Lammers in Dayton.

There he met men from New York who were interested in both the medical and philosophical aspects of his talents. They suggested that he move East, where they could study his work; they planned a hospital for the treatment of people who received medical readings. Edgar went to New York for a visit. Then, in 1925, he moved with his family to Virginia Beach, where the hospital was to be built. A non-profit organization for the study of psychic phenomena was incorporated in the state of Virginia.

The New York men who were interested in the plan were, naturally, Jews. They accepted without question not only Edgar's clairvoyance, but the metaphysical system set forth in the readings; it was a plan for the soul which they intuitively recognized and understood. The Cayce family, on the other hand, swarmed with theological guerrilla warfare. Hugh Lynn particularly refused to believe the metaphysical doctrines of the readings. He set out to prove them false. Yet he believed sincerely in his father's clairvoyance in the matter of medical diagnosis. How he was to reconcile this dichotomy of faith he did not know; at the university he hoped to find a solution.

It was dawn when he finished the story; at breakfast I was still asking him questions. A few weeks later, when school was finished, we set out together for Virginia Beach. I liked the flat Tidewater land through which we rode and the bright streak of sand which raced south from Cape Henry to form the beach. The Cayces lived at Thirty-fifth Street, two blocks from the water. Edgar was standing in the doorway, tall, lean, smiling, an expression of such friendliness around his eyes that I felt more at home with him than I did with Hugh Lynn. He was a shy, humble, uncertain man, natural in his hospitality but eager that it be accepted. He offered me a cigarette; he took me to see his chickens and his garden. We picked strawberries and looked critically at some tomato plants. He asked me if I would care to witness a reading; two were given each day, the first in the morning at ten-thirty, the second in the afternoon at half past three. Gertrude came out and joined us. She was slight, black-haired, talkative, anxious that I be at ease. Edgar Evans, the younger son, rode up on his bicycle; he was tanned and wore a round, small cap on the back of his head.

The house was large and it was filled with people. Miss Davis, the stenographer, was a permanent resident; so was Leslie Cayce, Edgar's father, now a widower. Dr. and Mrs. Thomas House and their son, Tommy, were visitors. Mrs. House was Gertrude's aunt. When her son was an infant he was near death from convulsions. Her husband took a reading from Edgar but was nervous about administering the medicine suggested; it was belladonna, a deadly poison. "Then bring it to me," Mrs. House said, "and I will give it to him." The dosage was small; Dr. House prepared it and Mrs. House fed it to the child. The convulsions ceased. The boy was a high school student now; he was spare, about my size, laughed easily, and whistled through his teeth. His mother was a buxom, motherly, handsome woman; anyone near her was tended and comforted. Dr. House was mild and frail, with large eyes; now and then he swore bitterly at some evidence of human stupidity in the newspapers or in the spate of news which several times a day he managed to flush from the monstrous radio in the living room. He was to be in charge of the hospital when it was built, the hospital for people whose ailments were diagnosed by the readings.

Dinner consisted of eating and argument. The subject under discussion was pre-existence, or metempsychosis, or rebirth, or reincarnation, depending on the particular speaker's taste or the terminology employed in the reference work from which he was quoting. Everyone presented evidence both for and against the theory of previous earthly experience for the soul; each felt obliged to believe whatever Edgar said while asleep, but none could accept what he said of the architecture of individuality and the mechanics of spiritual evolution. They asked my opinion. I did not want to shake their doubt, and I did not know, so I suggested that pre-existence might be both true and not true; it might be, I said, like time and space, an arbitrary separation of existence into successive lives, necessary for human understanding but actually an illusion; it might be an artificial breakdown of a single experience into different phases of that experience, as the spectrum was an artificial breakdown of the sun's light into its component parts. If that was so, then Christianity's limitation of earth life to a single incarnation was also both true and not true, since in discarding the spectrum it declared that the light of the sun not only appeared to be but actually was composed of a single hue.

No one seemed more than politely interested in this notion but I liked the simile of sunlight and the spectrum and I went on with it. The component colors, I said, could not be regarded as existing one before another in time; they existed simultaneously and together formed the single personality of the sun's light.

"Would you like some more black-eyed peas?" Gertrude asked.

The next morning I went into a small room near the kitchen and witnessed a reading. Edgar took off his tie, loosened his shirt cuffs and shoelaces, and lay down on his back on a narrow couch, his hands folded and resting on his solar plexus. Gertrude sat near his head. Miss Davis settled herself at a table and opened a stenographer's notebook. Edgar closed his eyes and went to sleep. When he was breathing deeply Gertrude began to read from a small memorandum book: "Now the body is assuming its normal forces, and will give such information as is desired of it at the present time—now you have before you the body of"—she read the name and address of a man in Manhasset, Long Island— "and you will go over this body carefully, examine it thoroughly, and tell me the conditions you find at the present time, giving the cause of the existing conditions, also suggestions for help and relief for this body. You will speak distinctly, at a normal rate of speech. You will answer the questions I will ask."

Edgar mumbled over what she had said in a tired, plaintive voice—it sounded almost Chinese in its inflection—and repeated the man's name and address several times. Then he cleared his throat and said, distinctly and easily, "Yes, we have the body." He described a minor spinal injury as the result of a fall from the front steps of the man's home several years before. He suggested a method of treatment—it included osteopathic adjustments and a diet—and answered several questions which the man had submitted. Then he said, "We are through for the present," and Gertrude, reading again from her memorandum book, gave suggestions for a gradual awakening without ill effects to Edgar's body from the nervous strain of the clairvoyance. In a few minutes he woke, sat up, and said, "Did you get it?" Miss Davis nodded. He went into the kitchen, then returned and said to me from the hallway, "Let's go see the chickens."

We walked through the back yard to the hen house. He was eating a cracker.

"When I wake up my stomach is empty," he said. "A cracker and a glass of milk fix me up. After that I feel fine."

Then he said, "What did you think of the reading? I hope you'll be frank with me. All my life I've been trying to find out whether I'm fooling myself. If I am I want to know it."

I said I didn't think it made much difference whether he was fooling himself or not, so long as he helped people. Quite probably the majority of the principles on which orthodox medicine was based were wrong, but so long as the treatments prescribed in their name were efficacious the theories didn't matter. They would be revised, altered, and finally discarded in favor of new theories, also wrong but nearer, perhaps, to truth.

"In talking with your son and in reading material on psychic phenomena in general," I said, "I have observed a fundamental misconception with regard to information obtained in a supersensory way, as in clairvoyance. It seems to be a common belief that if this information is actually obtained through the psychic rather than the sensory centers of the body, it is infallible: if it varies from truth then it was not psychically obtained. It seems to me that the chance of truth in information obtained psychically is about the same as the chance in information volunteered by the conscious mind.

"Information obtained psychically apparently comes by way of the subconscious mind, which is by no means omniscient. Hugh Lynn tells me that in one of your readings it was stated that the subconscious mind of a man is capable of communicating with any and all other subconscious minds."

"That's right," Edgar said, "and my mental and physical apparatus has a kink in it somewhere which makes it possible for my subconscious to come through while I'm in a hypnotic sleep and deliver information."

"Information obtained from other subconscious minds," I said. "That means it is limited in its source of supply. It cannot go beyond the mind of man. It can go backward as far as his thought extends, and it can go forward as far as his intelligence observes; it is apparently free of space and time; but it cannot penetrate beyond man's realization, and only beyond man's realization does unqualified truth exist."

Edgar walked over to the strawberry plants and squatted on his haunches. I squatted beside him and we picked and ate the ripe fruit.

"Maybe that's it," he said. "Maybe that's it."

"If you are limited to the mind of man in your clairvoyance," I said, "there is no need to worry about the truth or falsity of pre-existence. If your subconscious was dipping into the general basin of man's metaphysical speculation it would naturally pick out pre-existence and declare it true. The theory of rebirth has emerged again and again in history, usually at the apex of a society's culture. Your subconscious mind would find it considered as a superior and ultimate speculation on the problem of man's spiritual evolution in a time-governed environment. It is basic to Hinduism; the Buddhists accept it; the mystery religions taught it; Plato took it from Pythagoras—it is discussed in *Phaedrus*. There is every reason why it should have been a fundamental part of Christianity, and among the Gnostic sects it was. Why *samsara*, the wheel of life, was discarded, and *moksha*, salvation, retained, is confusing to us, but the popular appeal of early Christianity was based on its promise of immediate *moksha* and its repeal of *karma*, the law of retribution and rectification which keeps souls chained to the cycle of lives. *Karma* was replaced by the vicarious atonement of Christ: also, the society of Europe which Christianity converted was young; pre-existence is a theory for mature minds and subtle imaginations; among simple egos it causes fear, despair, and social stagnation.

"But there is every reason why your subconscious mind, searching through the collective realization and meditation of man, should bring it forth. That does not mean it is true. It means it is one of the most civilized and intelligent metaphysical doctrines which the human mind has devised, that is all. The point is, does it help people?"

Edgar stood up and reached for a cigarette. "I think it does," he said. "The readings we give on a person's past embodiments—there haven't been many such readings—we've just begun—seem to be of use as vocational guides; they are character analyses, really, with the former personalities of the individual supplying the reason for defects, talents, inabilities, physical traits, and other idiosyncrasies."

He smiled. "I'll give one for you this afternoon. Maybe you'll recognize yourself."

He seemed pleased with the things I had said; I had gone a long way around to avoid expressing open skepticism. Obviously his clairvoyance was genuine, consistent, deep, and of a wide range. But it was not, I knew, any more infallible

than the mind of man is infallible; its range was the subconscious, the intellectual record of humanity; its advantage
was freedom from space and time. In medical diagnosis it
could describe accurately existing physical conditions, since
those physical conditions were reflected in the subconscious
of the person being examined. In suggesting treatment it was
limited to the collective mind of man; no magic medicine
plucked from divine law could be prescribed. In searching
for answers to philosophical questions it could go only to the
barrier of man's realization.

I did not recognize myself as I listened that afternoon to a
reading on the record of my ego, yet everything Edgar said
fitted me. He described a set of personalities engaged, every
one of them, in religious teaching, writing, and study—one a
Hindu, one a Mediterranean mystery school student, one a
Moslem, one a Christian. My impulse in the present was to
reconcile these separate experiences, so Edgar said.

Such a record might, I realized, have been read from my
subconscious; such a group of personalities might be pressing
against me, lying just behind Joseph, out of his remembrance
and beyond my observation. If so, what were they to me,
what was their share in my identity, or mine in theirs? How
could we have successively endured terrestial incarnation and
maintained the spiritual simultaneity of timelessness, unless
the terrestial personality itself was illusory, a finger of consciousness held against the wheel of time? In that case the
record of such personalities was also illusory; the only
reality was the area Joseph governed, the field of realization
reaching out to the unconquered wilderness of unqualified
truth and the frightening brightness of cosmic law. If in that
area these personalities existed, they had been broken up,
scattered, reduced to their values as experience, as the personalities of my childhood and boyhood had been broken up,
scattered, and reduced to their values as experience. They
might be part of my handicap, and of my strength; if so
they shared in my realization. I did not remember them. If
they were my record in history then I was a forgetful,
repetitious, inept and unsuccessful oaf, not far advanced in
the discharge of my Father's business. That I could believe.

On the other hand, my personality, reaching back toward
its general source, might be meeting and mixing with these
other personalities at the point where its own identity weak-
ened and dissolved. The personalities, including mine, might
be different editions of the same pattern, each suited to a

221

particular room in time. Whichever relationship was real, one point was obvious. My movement, like the movement of all humanity, was forward. Behind me lay extinction, the nothingness from which I had proceeded; before me lay creation, pouring steadily into my mind, heated and served to me by a blazing, friendly star.

That week end several of the New York men concerned in the hospital's building plans visited the beach. They arrived on a train which left New York at midnight and ejected its passengers at the sumptuous Cavalier Hotel at the north end of the beach in time for breakfast. Most of them brought wives. Later in the morning they gathered in the living room of the Cayce house; the sheen of the city was in their clothes and manners. I was presented to them, but there were many names and they slipped into and out of me as I said, "How do you do."

One couple were newlyweds; she was an actress, he a business man. Later I identified them as Lucille and David Kahn; for convenience in the confusion of introductions I separated them from the others as the Lady and the Gentleman. He wore striped trousers and talked easily, confidently; she was a fragile, brief, beautiful thing, with movements and inflections which suggested a tenacious, dormant intensity. She detached herself from the group gathered around Edgar and talked to Hugh Lynn and Tommy House. I went to the porch and sat in a swing.

After a while she came out and sat in a chair near me. I turned to look and found her regarding me with the objective concern of a scientist's eye at the lens of a microscope. Just before she spoke she smiled, and the reins of my mind were pulled sharply. "Be careful," Joseph whispered.

"Hugh Lynn has been telling me about you," she said. "What do you think of Mr. Cayce's work?"

I said I didn't know, I couldn't tell, I had witnessed only two readings; clairvoyance was a subject too uncertain for judgment or even opinion; there was a latitude to the readings which was intoxicating to the mind, and a limitation which was sobering; clairvoyance was a supernormal event, in that it was a mental operation beyond the laws of space and time, but it was not supernatural. A dead man, for instance, might be aware of himself in his subconscious—such a condition might be the state described as purgatory—whereas a living man was aware of himself in his self-consciousness.

That did not mean the dead man was possessed of supernatural intelligence.

She interrupted me.

"Hugh Lynn says you intend to become a writer—"

"A newspaperman," I said quickly.

"Why not a writer?" she asked. "Wouldn't you prefer to be creative rather than reportorial?"

"God is creative," I said. "If I can accurately report His activities I shall be content."

She smiled. "I think you'll be a creative writer," she said. "Are you planning to work on a newspaper in New York?"

Joseph was frantic. How could her questions be evaded; how could she be told that any career in which I expressed interest was a sham, a device, a pretense, a veil behind which I hoped secretly and in freedom to pursue what constantly beckoned my thoughts, the widening of the gap through which creation poured into the consciousness of man?

I tried to match her smile.

"I don't suppose it ever occurred to me that I might work anywhere else," I said. "When I think of a city the city is New York. When I think of a newspaper the newspaper is the *Times* or the *Herald Tribune* or the *World*. Is there any other city? Are there any other newspapers?"

She looked bored.

"You Easterners are impossible," she said. "I'm from Oklahoma, and I happen to like Chicago, San Francisco, and New Orleans, but never mind that. What do you plan to do after your newspaper work, for a really serious career? Newspaper work is delightful, but you'll get tired of living on so little money."

There it was. What are you going to do to make money, son? How are you going to accomplish the great American dream? You want to be a success, don't you, lad? You want to get a million dollars and coronary thrombosis at forty-nine, don't you? Just step up and sign your name on the dotted line. We get your happiness, your peace of mind, your health, your days and nights and week ends; you get the money, the apartment on Park Avenue, the ulcers. Your wife gets an electric icebox, an electric stove, an electric washing machine, an electric reducing cabinet, a maid, a mink coat, a separate bedroom and your insurance. You want your wife to be financially secure should anything happen to you, don't you? Well, take out a lot of insurance, and if you work hard enough to keep up the payments something will surely happen

223

to you. Remember that in the eyes of your wife, who is a typical American girl—clean-minded, virginial, and devoted to her home, God bless her—the measure of your manhood is the money you bring home. So step up, son, and sign on the dotted line; all you can lose is your life and your soul; maybe you'll win a mansion, a bronze coffin, and a front page obituary in the *Times*.

"Does the creative writer make a lot of money?" I asked.

She laughed. "I see your point," she said. "Well, such decisions can wait, though it does no harm to think about them. Perhaps you'll stop in New York on your way to Connecticut. I'd be glad to take you sightseeing, unless you consider yourself sufficiently acquainted with the city, or too sophisticated to be seen with an Oklahoman."

Acid trickled from her smile.

"I know how to get to the Polo Grounds and the Yankee Stadium," I said, "and no one can lose me in Times Square."

"I'll show you the museums," she said. "They are educational."

I didn't want to return to Connecticut; I didn't want to go back to the multitudinously schismatic life of Naugatuck, the stratified social, economic, racial, and religious existence of New England. I didn't want to exile Joseph to the loneliness and the silence from which with such ecstasy he had so recently been liberated. But I went. A week later on a night filled with the levitation of early June, I walked up Kelly Hill carrying a suitcase, stopping occasionally to speak to the Irish families gathered on their front porches.

The next morning after breakfast I started toward town, but at the edge of the hill I stopped. I could see the factories, the river, the railroad yards, and the face of the clock in the tower of the Town Hall. The factories were busy, the river was polluted, the railroad yards were filled with freight cars, the clock in the tower of the Town Hall was five minutes slow. I could not face all that just yet. I turned and walked the other way, toward the rim of hills at the southern end of the valley.

All morning I climbed through a fir-shaded glen where under moss and rock there still lay patches of winter ice. The water of the brook threading its way through a mass of glacier boulders was so cold that it numbed my fingers. I tried to stop at spots I had long known and loved, but I could not. I had to keep walking. I followed the brook upward until I reached a road near the top of Hunter's Mountain. By then it was late afternoon. When I arrived home it was suppertime. I took a bath, changed my clothes, and started walking again. This time I went down into the town, where I met the Kid. He went with me to Lake Quassapog and until midnight I danced steadily, never leaving the floor, tearing ten cent tickets off a long strip and handing them to the guard at the door between numbers. Fortunately my partners were not interested in conversation; they hummed the tunes to which we danced and sang phrases from the lyrics—*Ain't She Sweet, Russian Lullaby, My Blue Heaven, Muddy Waters, Make Believe, Girl of My Dreams*.

After the last dance the Kid and I rode to Waterbury on the trolley, ate hot dogs with chili and diced onions, and hitchhiked to Naugatuck. I walked up Kelly Hill slowly; I was finally nearing the end of my physical strength. As I crawled into bed I began falling asleep. I did not think. The pain at the back of my head was eased. I muttered a prayer of thanks. In the morning when I woke everything was all right. Joseph was where, in New England, he belonged; behind me, separated from me, undetected, mute, and in pain.

THIRTEEN

"GOOD MORNING!" the Professor said. "I am delighted that you have decided to continue the series of treatments. In your small way you will aid science to demonstrate the efficacy of one of her discoveries. It was thoughtless of nature not to provide the human body with a proper reaction to arthritis. You are fortunate that intelligent, objective, imaginative men have found a way to provide artificially the proper reaction in your body."

His voice had the heartiness of men who get up and write in their diaries before breakfast.

"I can hear you quite well," I said. "Perhaps if you spoke in a lower tone your thoughts would have more depth."

Miss Yellowhead was tucking me into the cabinet. Miss Iceberg was checking her supplies—salt water, fresh water, orange juice, thermometer, face towels.

"This time it will not be so bad," Miss Yellowhead said. "You know what to expect."

"I wish I didn't," I said.

She smiled, and Miss Iceberg stared at me, estimating the chances of trouble.

"A few hours after the last treatment I could walk without help," I said, "but all day yesterday I slipped gradually back to stiffness and lameness. This morning I am just as I was when the first treatment began, except for the four pounds I lost in the cabinet. If I lose four more today that will be eight. I lost weight when I took the typhoid treatment, when I took the sulfa treatment, when I took the baths and diathermy and massage, and when I dieted. If I keep losing weight how will I know whether the arthritis is getting worse or whether I am just getting too weak to walk?"

She smiled.

"Soon you will be feeling better and the pounds will come back like the leaves in spring," she said.

The Professor was impressed.

"She is a remarkably warm and liberal-minded woman," he said. "She considers you as alive and deserving of sympathy as a tree."

Miss Yellowhead went out and the Professor and I regarded Miss Iceberg. She was slick, cool, and sealed in her white envelope of uniform, stockings, and shoes. Her ankles, I noticed now, were a little thick. A faint odor of bath salts and shampoo emanated from her body. On the back of her neck was a small mark where the collar of her coat had rubbed.

"I wonder what happened to Dorothy Arnold?" the Professor said. "This young lady reminds me of her, somehow. It was in 1910 that she disappeared, while walking through Central Park. She went in, I believe, on the Fifth Avenue side. She never emerged. Now it seems to me—"

"She was turned into a swan," I said. "She is living on a lake in the park."

The Professor nodded. "It's just the sort of thing you would believe," he said. "And that reminds me; I've been making some notes on your case. You'll forgive me I hope for eavesdropping while you were trying to go to sleep night before last. Your return to Connecticut was important to my study of possible symptoms. I'm afraid you have never reconciled

226

your quarrel with New England, and that we must consider it as one of the prime causes of your spiritual melancholy. Connecticut is the place of your birth and your upbringing; it is your home. A man cannot leave his home and be free of it unless he goes from it in peace and understanding; otherwise it remains a basic and unsolved problem in the development of his personality. You did not leave Connecticut in peace and you satisfied your craving for a homeland by falling in love with Virginia."

"Go right ahead with your notes," I said, "but it will do you little good to consider either Connecticut or Virginia as my homeland. It is true that I accept creation as the temporary environment of the particularized self-consciousness and subconsciousness which is myself. I am dangled from superconsciousness by a rather long thread, which it is my pleasure and privilege to wind up. As I do this I wind creation around my self-consciousness and subconsciousness, and eventually I reach superconsciousness.

"Connecticut is a place of low, intimate hills and faraway, tightlipped people. Virginia is a place of distant, high mountains, and warm, voluble people. But if you insist that I choose a homeland, make it New York, the caravan city of the world, the jeweled eye of Mother Earth, the wet-edged lips of civilization in the West, the—"

"By the way," the Professor said, "did you stop in New York on your way to Connecticut after that nonsense at Virginia Beach about clairvoyance?"

"You consider it nonsense?" I said. I was not warm enough yet for an argument.

He smiled tolerantly.

"I see no harm in so-called scientific investigation of psychic phenomena," he said. "I don't believe such investigations can be scientifically controlled, and I doubt that the aberrations and subconscious leaks of one sort and another which result in precognition, clairvoyance, telepathy, and other paranormal demonstrations can be employed to help or advance or illuminate or inspire man, or to prove that his personality survives death. I sympathize with your hope that man will rediscover God by means of the instrument of his present faith, which is science, but I do not believe it will transpire. The investigation of psychic phenomena cannot be a true science; it cannot be exact. The experiments with cards at Duke University, by which students are tested for telepathic powers, are interesting but inconclusive. What is the name of that professor at Duke, and what does he call his studies? He has written a book, something called *New Frontiers of the Mind*."

"Rhine," I said. "Dr. J. B. Rhine. He intended to study for the ministry when he went to college as a student. He found that he couldn't continue in theology in the face of the evidence science had piled up against what he was expected to believe, teach, and preach. He went to Duke as an instructor in psychology the year I returned to Lexington as a sophomore. He calls his laboratory experiments in extra-sensory perception parapsychology. There is a *Journal of Parapsychology*. It is scholastic, difficult, and for those not interested in extra-sensory perception, formidably dull. You would enjoy it. Dr. Rhine has proved rather conclusively that extra-sensory perception exists and is not uncommon among ordinary people. The detection of this evolving faculty and the study of its range and depth and frequency, parallel psychiatry and psychoanalysis. It is impossible to underestimate the importance of parapsychology—Dr. Rhine at Duke, Whately Carington at Oxford, Dr. Gardner Murphy at Columbia, are pioneers in a sense which I fear is beyond you."

The Professor laughed. "Precisely," he said. "It is a sense which is beyond me—an extra sense. I am not disturbed when you ramble on about pre-existence; it is civilized and amusing to discuss historical trends in metaphysics and to note their persistence in what Jung describes as the 'collective unconscious.' That they bob up in such contemporary spots as your friend Cayce's clairvoyance is interesting. Seems to me I've heard of him, by the way. One of my colleagues had a daughter who was quite ill; he took her to a clairvoyant after the doctors failed to help her. The clairvoyant had a hospital at Virginia Beach. The girl improved, got well in fact. Probably the sea air helped her."

"Probably," I said.

"Precisely," he said. "Now where was I? Oh, yes. Cayce's subconscious does not differ from yours or mine. It is a well extending into the collective unconscious. Consciousness flows up in it to the general level of consciousness in the earth. You and I and other people take our awareness off the surface, where the consciousness in the well meets the environment of space and time. Cayce has a trick whereby he is able to dive deep into the well, reach the general basin of consciousness, and either draw from it or penetrate into other wells and observe their conditions and situations.'

"It's a good trick. It turns up every now and then in history. It will continue to turn up, just as will other paranormal phenomena. A so-called scientific study of these phenomena may eventually result in the declaration that survival and the soul, which are man's oldest hopes and dreams and uncertainties, are laboratory facts. That will constitute achievement of what you want and what you also dread; it will sweep science into the realm of metaphysics and put orthodox religion in the museums—unless, of course, orthodox religion is opportunistic enough to capitalize on the new 'discoveries' of science.

"But when all this has happened and the new tide of faith has reached its high-water mark, and the ebb has set in, what then will have been accomplished for man and his purpose? There will be a flat surface of historical events, a piece of tiling set next to hundreds of other pieces of tiling, each with its hieroglyphs of time, place, and personality, victor and vanquished, heretic and saint, slave and satrap. There will be also a swelling of the contents of library shelves, an addition to the literature of speculation, contemplation, and observation. There will be a fossil architecture and the usual remnants of manners and styles. Historians will be amused at the problems which occupied you and me and our contemporaries. They may quote, for humor's sake, from some of my textbooks. You are wise to remain a reporter; you will not share my immortality as a buffoon in a footnote. Keep your childish notions on pre-existence to yourself; the illusion of sequence may be overcome in the—" he hesitated—"well, I am forced to say in the succeeding society, since that is the way it appears to me."

"That is also the way it will appear to the historians you fear," I said. "Otherwise they will not be writing about an age which is past. Sequence is part of our environment; future societies will endure it as we endure it. The simultaneity of eternity, entering our environment, is broken up into sequence. It is perhaps a gradual conditioning, proceeding as awareness moves through subconsciousness toward self-consciousness. Our memory works in this fashion. We recall events in our experience by exorcising them from our subconscious and breaking them into sequence. Sometimes it is difficult to rebuild accurately the sequence—we remember

229

two separate happenings, but we cannot distinguish which occurred first."

"Oh, nonsense!" the Professor said. "That is only faulty memory. Things seem to happen to us in sequence and they remain thus in sequence in our minds. It is not that men will cease to endure separate and sequential experiences, but that they will learn to regard them laterally, as parts of a single large experience, each dropping into its proper place. The change will come slowly; common knowledge will greatly precede common practice. We still speak, for instance, of the setting of the sun, though we know the sun does not set, or rise, or go south in winter; it is only the earth which moves, rotating on its axis and circling the sun.

"There is no pre- or post-existence. There is only now, constant and, we hope, able to endure the change of environment we call death. Take that now from man and he is extinguished."

"You are an apt pupil," I said. "I did not anticipate that you would force my own opinions upon me so soon.

"There is only one life, indeed. It consists of creation passing through the eye of now, pouring into the mind of man. Memory is only real when it is repoured through the eye of now; precognition, prophecy, are anticipations of what is to pour through the eye of now—previews, previsions, advance information obtained by means of an underground system of communication. What has poured through the eye of now is technically past, what is yet to be seen is technically future. Actually, what is past is at the command of the eye of now; it is potentially the present. Eventually all of creation will have passed through the eye of now, into the mind of man; it will be potentially the present, a static, available memory. The single life of humanity will then be finished; the eye of now will be fixed on the source of creation; there will pour into it the Archetypal Man, the Godhead, the Essence, the Pleroma, the Absolute."

"Please don't rush me into these things," the Professor said. "If you want to meet your God rush on ahead and get it over with, but don't take me with you. I like a more leisurely pace. I enjoy activity. I am not interested in Nirvana."

"Nirvana is not the end of evolution," I said. "It is the beginning of involution, the nothingness from which we proceeded, the womb to which new and frightened egos yearn to return. After evolution is begun the dream of the soul is activity, participation in creation, rather than flight from it. The orthodox heaven of complete rest is a nostalgic memory of minds on the descending, or involutionary wave; it represents young intelligence, mental immaturity and laziness, and an absence of the vision of spiritual realization. The mystical union of saints, the degrees of initiation in the mystery schools, the theories of pre-existence and of karma, and even, in a negative but courageous way, the skepticism of agnostics, are part of the evolutionary dream of participation, of responsibility, of realization.

"The only idea of heaven which beckons me is a vision of intensified, magnified intellectual activity and expanded spiritual responsibility. I cannot imagine union with the Godhead, and I therefore do not want it. What I can imagine and what I do want is the job of supervising a star during its birth, during the shucking of its planets, and while life is being introduced to one or more of its cooling satellites."

The Professor smiled.

"A star doesn't need supervision," he said. "It is itself an intelligence. However, I'll go along with you on that notion, since what you really want is to force yourself to the forefront of the collective mind of man so that you can see and report what is going on along the frontier.

"Let's say we agree, and that we don't care how many simultaneous or sequential personalities are dangled from the thread of a single soul, or awareness, or ego, or being, or whatever the unit of spiritual and conscious perception which operates as man may be. Let's agree that the unit of perception, biting its way through creation, is alone important, and that the past is significant only insofar as it has dimmed or sharpened, widened or narrowed, deepened or made shallow the unit of perception in its eternally present activity."

"You have learned the lesson well," I said. "But there is one danger which must not be overlooked. It is possible for the unit of perception to become snagged on a passing moment and dragged into the past, away from the eternal now. 'Living in the past' is a common phrase for a common affliction. The function of evil is to tempt the soul to tarry in its journey, to entice it into inactivity; some of the webs of evil are spun of such subtle thread that only humor can detect them; morality stares at the trap and sees a clear passage.

"No immorality is apparent, for instance, when an ego clings to the manners and fashions of a past era, the Victorian or Edwardian, for example. In fact it is common prac-

231

tice for persons jointly to endeavor to perpetuate and to extend to others the customs and habits of their group, piously pretending that these customs and habits comprise a moral code. Satire is the best defense against this particular device of Satan.

"But the moment which snags the unit of perception need not be contained in the present lifetime of the ego. It may be a portion of the past, a part perhaps of the soul's pre-existence, if we wish to accommodate that theory. A man may be utterly immersed in a minor phase of Greek history, or the reign of a particular Ptolemy, or the French Revolution—"

I stopped talking suddenly and closed my mouth, almost biting my tongue. For a moment the Professor looked angry; then he laughed.

"I'm sorry," I said.

"You are forgiven," he replied. "What are professors trained, hired, and paid to do? What is their job? It is to immerse themselves in the past, to reanimate that past, and to transform it, for the student, into contemporaneity. The faculty of a university is theoretically prepared to expand the consciousness of the student until it includes all of history. That goal may be far from the mystical ideal of bringing to each soul remembrance of all things past, even to the foundations of the world, but it is a reasonable, intelligent, and practical method of civilizing and maturing successive waves of savage adolescents. It is what thrilled and exalted you when you attended Washington and Lee."

I was embarrassed. I looked at Miss Iceberg's neckline, at a smudge of ink on her thumb. The first joint of her thumb was shorter than the second. She lacked initiative; she would die for logic, but not for love.

"I did not have professors in mind when I spoke," I said. "I have found university instructors and professors more contemporaneously active mentally than almost any group I have encountered. Their knowledge of the past, and their interest in it, breeds a natural concern for the future, which is forever being realized in the present. I had in mind, in fact, telling you today about a particular professor, about my friend Fitz, who teaches English at Washington and Lee."

He did not answer at once. He regarded Miss Iceberg, who was preparing to strike at me with her thermometer. He was trying to keep his head above his hurt. Finally he said:

"Do you mean that large, joyous-looking man who visits you upstairs in your room and who reads Shakespeare to you? I thought he was a writer, or an actor. With such a voice he could speak in a stage whisper and fill an amphitheater. It seems a shame to waste such talent on mere teaching. What is he doing in New York? Spring vacation?"

"Yes," I said. "He visits me between theater hours. Personally, I would rather listen to his description of a play or a musical comedy than see it myself. No person I have ever known so completely enjoys, absorbs, understands, and articulates the happy experiences of life. He has an infinite sense of play. His sense of humor discovers and exposes the most commonplace departures from reason. His tenderness digs up tragedy where only the hard surface of normal conduct is apparent to the average man's discernment. He has that tolerant wisdom which lies over the hill from skepticism, beyond the reach of most minds. He has no need to consider a career as an actor or as a writer; he makes teaching an art."

"In what subjects did he instruct you?" the Professor asked.

"In every subject," I said. "I sat in many of his classes—English Literature, The Comic Spirit, Eighteenth Century Literature, The English Novel—but I also walked with him through the countryside on spring and autumn afternoons, sat with him in his study during winter evenings, drank tea with him on Sunday afternoons—"

"Drank tea with him?" the Professor said. "Is he an Englishman?"

"He is a Virginian," I said. "His father was a Presbyterian minister; his grandfather was a Confederate officer. As a student he went to Washington and Lee on a scholarship which he won in competition with other Virginia high school students; as an undergraduate he was elected to Phi Beta Kappa and won a Rhodes scholarship; at Oxford he won Firsts in English Literature; after a year as an instructor at Stanford he was invited to join the faculty at Lexington— he began as a teacher the day I began as a student.

"His lectures from the beginning were a wonder and a delight to us. Teetering in a cane-bottomed chair, pacing back and forth on the narrow speakers' platform—sometimes in his preoccupation he overstepped its length, but he never allowed the mishap to interrupt so much as a syllable of his remarks—he poured out not only his love for the English language and his knowledge and understanding of

233

the great writers who employed it, but his enchantment with the entire fabric of existence and his appreciation of its duality of loveliness and laughter, good and evil, reason and ridiculousness."

"I love that last word," the Professor said. "It rolls and sloshes like the human mind. I am beginning also to love this Fitz. What is his full name?"

"Fitzgerald Flournoy," I said. "He is a full professor now, and two years ago I went to New Haven in June and watched him receive his doctorate at Yale. We celebrated the event with a pub crawl. It was our plan to drink a glass of beer in every tavern in New Haven along a direct east-west line. We had permission from our wives, who were poor mathematicians. Naturally—"

"Never mind that," the Professor said. "Let's get back to Lexington. I gather that not many students cut Instructor Flournoy's classes."

"He had remarkably few absences to record," I said, "and he stimulated a genuine concern for literature in boys who otherwise might have confined their reading to the sports pages of the newspapers and an occasional venture into Hemingway or Sinclair Lewis. What he did for those of us who had a natural interest in reading and writing is incalculable.

"He invited a few of us—Elias and Cayce were included— to meet at his home on Sunday afternoons to read plays and generally to amuse ourselves with talk about books and their authors. It was then that we drank tea with him. During my freshman year we read all of Shaw.

"During my second year the group decided to revive the student literary magazine, *The Southern Collegian,* defunct since the World War. We put our own money into the enterprise, and eventually it was successful. I remember the first essay Elias submitted to me. It began, 'From the left comes a cry of "No standards!" The right rumbles an answer, "Values or nothing!"'"

"You were the editor of the magazine?" the Professor asked.

"The group elected me while I was imprisoned in the home of Stonewall Jackson, now the town hospital, suffering from influenza. I had a difficult time getting well. The other patient in my room was Mike Seligman, one of Elias' fraternity brothers. Mike was from Mississippi; he was big and good-natured and he called me 'Sugar.' He was suffering from a leg burn—he was captain of our wrestling team—and it was almost healed. The doctor ordered his medicine stopped. Our nurse got the names mixed and stopped my medicine instead of Mike's."

I paused and stared at Miss Iceberg. She was looking at my chart. "I have not been in a hospital for treatment since that time," I said, "until this illness developed. I hope a mistake won't be made again."

The Professor assumed his heartening look.

"You'll be out of here in two weeks," he said, "and you'll be skipping through the lobby as you leave. Forget about mistakes and hospitals and medicines. Let's get along with our psychotherapy. At this rate we'll never finish those golden undergraduate years with Fitz and Elias and Cayce and Robison. They came, I presume, to an end?"

"Yes," I said, "they came to an end. I will tell you about it."

FOURTEEN

LEXINGTON was so small a town I felt that I could hold it in my arms. Its streets and houses were old and full of weather; their aura shed softness and warmth; they were shaded, quiet, and accustomed to the rhythm of human life; they were casually confident of their appearance, like a woman who has ceased to look anxiously at her face, having discovered what is in her heart.

In the shops along the streets were barbers who knew me by my beard, tailors who identified me by my measurements, drugstore clerks who recognized me as the student who used a baby size toothbrush and liked lemon in his coke. The lady who worked in Boley's Bookstore sympathized with my lust for books; she let me sneak new titles from the counter and read them while I sat in a corner. Often Dr. Easter, the assistant dean, sat next to me. He customarily carried a pocket knife, a steel watch, and an

235

apple; when he sliced the apple he offered me a piece, and I always accepted it. Dr. Easter loved fairy tales, a circumstance which caused Dr. Campbell once to accuse him of being superstitious. "But I only believe in fairies!" Dr. Easter protested. "It is you who are superstitious, Harry. You believe in the Westminster Confession of Faith!" On the day Dr. Campbell received his gold watch from the university he set it by Dr. Easter's steel watch. "If they ever ask you, Harry," Dr. Easter said, "tell them I'd prefer a sun dial."

When I lived at the Phi Kappa Psi house Fitz was my neighbor. I could walk through our side yard into his side yard and go to his study by a back door. Sometimes I rode with him to or from classes. He had a Model T Ford which he had driven across the continent from Palo Alto, California, to Lexington. When the A Model Ford was issued he accepted the transition and purchased one. The change from pedal to gear shift didn't bother him, but frequently after a lecture on Dryden or Milton he got into the A Model and stared uncomprehending at its operational mechanism, his mind two hundred years removed from internal combustion. When he was reoriented to the third decade of the twentieth century he inserted the key in the ignition lock, turned the switch, and put his heel on the starter.

If I walked home after a morning class I stopped at Marshall Penick's gift shop near the Dutch Inn. Marshall was the youngest of the university treasurer's three daughters. As a child she spied on Fitz when he, as an undergraduate, dated her oldest sister Emily. During the dates Fitz played on his violin while Emily accompanied him at the piano. Mary Monroe, the middle sister, was absent from home, a mysterious, romantic figure playing on an organ in a Fifth Avenue church.

Marshall was fragile, but not deceptively so; her bones actually broke under a hard grip; her efforts to remain comfortably and normally invested in flesh were medical adventures of heroic proportions. Curious things happened to her; she was bitten by a horse; a ghost shook hands with her. She had long blonde hair and large blue eyes and her voice was like spring licking at the ice of winter—warm, patient, and steady. "The doctors say it seems as if my body just wants to melt away," she told me one day. "Do you reckon it's my overpowering love for just everything and everybody that's causing it?" Her knowledge of things and people reached everywhere. She bought antiques as shrewdly as she traded horses. She kept a trusting, cunning eye on local real estate; she told long, fantastic, completely unbelievable stories which invariably turned out to be true.

She was being courted by one of my fraternity brothers, a young man of short stature who engaged in various dormitory feuds involving, at different periods, the discharge of a shotgun loaded with tacks, a battle with fire hoses, and a unique duel with natural elements. He and Marshall rode horseback; often I saw them returning from an afternoon in the fields and on the paths, Marshall in the lead. "John has a bad seat," she told me. Years later he suddenly entered the ministry. "All my men either turn to God or go to Paris," Marshall said. She took up ballet, taught Sunday School to the children of mountaineers, and decided she wanted to die in the air. She was undecided about cremation.

There was a Lexington lady who died and whose body was cremated. After the funeral two of her friends discussed the event over a cup of tea. One of them was melancholy. "I couldn't bear it," she said. "Melanie was always so strong, so resourceful, so courageous—and then I saw her reduced to a handful of ashes in a tiny urn!" "Nothing of the sort," the other said sharply. "Melanie was a full quart, with half a pint to spare. I measured her myself."

When I left Marshall's shop and turned toward town I was likely to see Elias standing on a Main Street corner talking to Ollie Crenshaw, an instructor in history. Ollie was tall and lean, the best tennis player in town, and he habitually carried a staggering number of books under his right arm. He stood quite still and listened while Elias talked, gestured, and reached down to drum on his knees with whatever volumes he carried. If I passed a grocery store and saw Mrs. Barclay, our house mother, shopping among the vegetables, I stopped and offered her my suggestions for the dinner menu. At the fraternity house there was time to sit on the porch and listen to Perry, the house man, sing quietly in a rich, nimble bass at he set the tables. Babe McCorkle might ride by in her topless Model T touring car and wave a hand. Babe was everybody's friend, a blonde with a turned-up nose who came from West Virginia to visit her uncle, who lived at Timber Ridge, nine miles from town, in an old and beautiful house which had its own graveyard. Whole fraternities were engaged in attempting to narrow Babe's affections from the entire student body to one, or at least to a few, of its members. They never succeeded.

Once on a spring afternoon as she rode down Main Street in her Ford Babe finished a cigarette and flipped it over her shoulder. It landed on the rear seat cushion, whose inner contents were partly disgorged and trembling in the wind. They immediately took fire. Smoke and flame came from the tonneau as Babe passed McCrum's drugstore. Students along the street, seeing her predicament, called and waved. She waved back. Students farther down the street, appraising the situation, stepped off the curb and held up their hands. Babe held up her hand and swept past them, laughing. There was nothing to do but give chase. Roadsters swept north in tandem, manned to the trunk racks. The Ford was not easy to catch on the twisting, humpbacked road, and the smoke pouring from it was a hazard to the drivers of the roadsters. On a straight stretch a Reo Flying Cloud managed to pass the Ford; then it slowed its pace, forcing Babe to stop. Brave hands seized the burning cushion while other brave and more fortunate hands assisted Babe from her perch. "Imagine that!" she said. "I was a ball o' fire and didn't even know it."

One autumn night I dated Babe at her uncle's home on Timber Ridge. The tall old trees, the weathered brick of the house, and the white shafts in the graveyard took just enough light from a new moon to make shadows. Babe met me at the door. She carried an oil lamp in her hand. I followed her into the library; she set the lamp on a long table and we sat on the floor before an open fire. The walls of the room were lined with bookcases; in the dim light the volumes looked small; all of them were bound in leather. After a while I examined some of them, while Babe held the lamp at my shoulder. I did not find a single title published later than 1862. When we sat down again a mixture of melancholy and guilt assailed me. The library, the house, the grounds, were as General Hunter found them when he rode down the valley toward Lynchburg. Time could be stopped, I thought, and by other hands than those of God.

But Babe was not stopped. She rode through the seasons at Lexington as if they were fields of blue grass; she grew prettier and more popular with every prom and fancy dress ball. When finally she married there was a general shattering of hearts. One of her admirers, a fraternity brother of mine finished with schooling and established in the grocery business, brooded over the selection of a wedding gift; nothing available quite matched his feelings. One day he received from a food company a carload of premiums for his customers;

238

among the shipment was a barrel of sugar bowls. He wrote a brief note—"This is how sweet I think you are—," nailed it to the barrel head, and sent the sugar bowls to Babe.

In the afternoons Elias and I worked in the journalism building, writing and editing copy for *The Southern Collegian;* material was scarce and we contributed fiction, essays, poetry, and letters to the editor, using various pseudonyms. We also contributed to the student newspaper and to the yearbook. The yearbook contained a humor section, and one of my jobs was to compile or compose the material contained in it. Once I spent a long and happy day writing an archeological report on our civilization. It was dated 10,000 A.D., and one of its sections described the discovery of certain sites of religious worship in ancient America, among them various churches and two outdoor temples for the celebration of the rites of the Baseball Mysteries—Yankee Stadium and the Polo Grounds. It was clear from a study of the stadia and the churches, the archeologist wrote, that normal religious dichotomy obtained in the republic of the United States. The population as a whole worshiped the sun; most of the churches contained the traditional altar of sacrifice; many of them harbored representations of the golden disc; there were statues of priests holding miniature suns; there were chalices for the drinking of blood; there were altar stones containing human bones; there were no books or engraved tablets of any kind, though in some churches stories were told in pictures. The general populace obviously was illiterate and practiced human sacrifice.

The intelligentsia, as in all societies, worshiped the mystery. Annual rites were conducted, beginning in the spring and culminating in an October festival called the World Series. The symbology of the Baseball Mysteries was based on numerology and the progress of the ritual was revealed by mathematical formulae understandable only to the initiated.

"So cunningly were the secrets of the mystery disguised," the archeologist wrote, "that no student has yet been able to decipher the paper tablets found in such profusion in the stadia. Such hieroglyphs as 'Ruth, l.f.,' and 'Gehrig, 1b.,' still tantalize the research expert. The basic symbology of the ritual itself, however, is obvious and easily understood, being traditional.

"The altar stone, called home plate, was a square with a pyramid surmounting it—the four-fold problem of the world solved by the trinity. The priest, or pitcher, stood on a raised

239

spot of earth sixty feet from the altar. Adding, for the length of the altar, another foot to this distance, we have a total of sixty-one feet—six and one, or a total of seven, the number of rungs on the solar ladder of the soul. The priest threw the cosmic egg of life, the baseball, to the sacrificing ego, the batter, who stood at the altar holding a bat, or phallus. When the phallus struck the egg the sacrificing ego was precipitated into life, or creation. He entered on the base paths of involution and evolution. Midway on the diamond-shaped field of play, at second base, involution ended and evolution began. Return to the altar, or home plate, ended evolution and brought the sacrificing ego back to his source. Seven centers of illumination, or fielders—four lower centers, or infielders, and three upper centers, or outfielders—sought to prevent this consummation. Each sacrifice ego was aided in his progress by the succeeding sacrificing egos, who by propelling, or batting themselves into life, advanced those who were before them toward the mid-point of evolution and beyond it to the ultimate goal of home plate. The bases were 90 feet apart, the journey around them totaling 360 feet. Thus the playing field, or diamond, squared the circle."

There was a great deal more, and the symbology became obscure and strained. The summary described the final victory of the soul in the World Series, and the conclusion stated that the birth of the historical Jesus would have to be set forward at least two thousand years, since it was clear that he was not known to Americans of the period of the Baseball Mysteries except as a mythical Dying God, perhaps under the name Ruth, which might have been derived from either Rex or Ra. I showed the manuscript to Elias, forgetting in my enthusiasm that he had flunked freshman mathematics six times in six consecutive terms. It was the only one of his courses in which he did not receive A.

He read the essay carefully, then said, "What is its purpose? Are you writing for ecclesiastical magazines?"

"It's for the humor section of the yearbook," I said.

He shook his head and handed the sheets back to me.

"That's the trouble with you," he said. "No one knows when you are going to be funny and when you are going to be metaphysical. Neither do you. You seem to have an outrageous notion that humor and heavenly mechanics belong together, like women and giggles."

"They do," I said. "Humor is a spiritual law, operating

to save man from follies too subtle and transitory for morality to inhibit. It is as much a part of metaphysics as is sex."

"Perhaps," Elias said, "but I counsel you to separate your humor from your metaphysics; you will get along more easily in the world and stay out of state-maintained institutions longer. Keep one in front of you all the time, as a protection; hide the other in your room, behind an incense pot. If you become a good newspaperman you won't need metaphysics. When you die you will go to Paris and work on the *Herald*."

This latter information we had on the authority of our instructor in journalism, Professor Roscoe B. Ellard, a large, amiable Missourian who had the wisdom to let us alone while we went through the chameleon stage of writing, changing style with each new author we admired. His advice to us was simple and sound. "Sit in front of a typewriter long enough," he said, "and something will come out of it that's worth printing." He didn't bother with examinations. "If I'm not intelligent enough to discover your capabilities as writers and reporters in four months of classes I'm too stupid to find them in a set of examination papers," he said.

One afternoon Elias called me on the journalism school's telephone. He was at The Corner.

"Do you want to meet a fellow who's met James Joyce?" he asked.

"Yes," I said.

"I'll bring him over," he said, and hung up.

In a few minutes he entered the building. With him was a handsome young Jewish boy who had large, melancholy brown eyes, and who seemed friendly but embarrassed and a little confused.

"This is Jimmy Pollak," Elias said. "He's going to tell you what happened in Paris."

"Nothing happened," Jimmy said. "Nothing really happened at all. I just went to a café with some people—Martha Foley, Whit Burnett, Elliott Paul—"

"And you met Joyce," Elias said. "Nothing happened and you met Joyce."

"Joyce was there," Jimmy said. "We sat at his table. After a while I said, 'Mr. Joyce, I read *Ulysses* but I didn't understand all of it.' 'No reason why you should,' he said. 'You need a key. There is an accurate one available, written by a man in Chicago.' 'I particularly didn't understand the chapter at the lying-in hospital, where the style keeps changing,' I said. 'No reason why you should,' he said. 'Get the key.'

That's all, absolutely all. Nothing else happened, nothing at all."

"Just another thick-headed Irishman," I said, meaning Joyce.

But Elias was unperturbed. He gave Jimmy the only comfortable chair in the room, then questioned him for the rest of the afternoon on Joyce's appearance, his gestures, his costume, his cigarettes, the drinks he ordered and who paid for them, the *décor* of the café, the number of customers, the weather and the precise time at which Jimmy said good night to Joyce, left the café, and returned by taxi to his hotel.

In spring and autumn when the afternoons were warm we broke our work and went to Whistle Creek, crossing fields and skirting limestone sinkholes until we reached a place where the water, working its way through terraces of rock, fell to a quiet, dark pool, where the current paused to meditate before meandering on. At the lip of the plunge, where the stream huddled itself for the jump, there were two stones, smooth, firm, and well-laced, to which we could cling, one by one, while letting ourselves into the white leap of the water where we were turned, caressed, shaken, embraced, and pummeled by the childish torrent. Fitz christened the spillway Arethusa, after the maiden who was turned into a waterfall, and we cheerfully gave ourselves to the spellbound female whose loneliness for human lovers must be, we estimated, immense.

She was, in her eager, ruffian way, a perfect mistress. Her entity could be completely penetrated, and all of her was engaged in the tumultuous, intuitive, multitudinous activity of instantaneous seduction and continuous ecstasy. She shut out the slower-moving world, raided and raped and stunned the senses, broke over the barriers of consciousness, and drowned remembrance and awareness in her racing, incendiary blood. She was Maya-Shakti, the spinning, leaping form of creation, holding her lovers with arms which could be felt and touched but not held and examined; casting them, when they tired, into the pool of purgation, of remembrance, of meditation, of regret. One by one we gave ourselves to her, then, releasing our hands from the rocks, fell, like the doomed souls whom Dante saw at the river's edge of hell, downward into the pool.

And as the late leaves of November fall
  One after one till on the earthen floor
  The ruined bough looks on their funeral,
So by that river Adam's seed impure
  Cast themselves from the wharf, one after one,
  At signals, as the bird goes to the lure.

I watched Elias fall, then took his place in Arethusa's arms. While she bathed and battered my body and fingered away my senses I knew nothing; I could not watch or know the things she did to me. Only when I dropped, sank, and drifted upward to the surface of the pool, seeing above me the arched lances of the tall trees which stitched the bank, did I catch running through my mind, wet and shaking with delight, the moments which had mixed with Arethusa.

Lying in the sun on the rocks above the pool I one day moved in my awareness upward toward the sun and a little to the left. I did not know what had happened and I did not care; the joy of release was supernal; if it was death, then death was a consummation devoutly to be desired. I saw, removed from me, what I had thought was I and what I knew to be Joseph. They worked in unison, one within the other, receiving, observing, arranging, reflecting, the outer rim quick and unselective, the inner hub slow and thoughtful. They were recorders, collectors, archivists; I could obtain from them, whenever I wished, whatever they possessed. They worked within the body, building up, atom by atom, the magic by which consciousness, in the ultimate hour of my journey, would levitate me from the geometry of form.

It lasted only a short time, perhaps a minute. Then I settled back into the normal dichotomy of my being, felt the sun on my legs and face and torso and the rock against my back and skull and heels. The taste of Arethusa was in my mouth, and I knew at last that I was an awareness, a point of observation, an entity beyond the trinity with which I had invaded earth, or into which I had been exiled in the time stream of the world. I sat up and looked at Fitz, who was descending into the mist and narcosis of Arethusa. When he rose to the surface of the pool below, an incarnation would be ended. So little was a life in the love dream of a soul, an instant that never quite awakened, a sensation that could only hazily be recalled. I ached to swing out to longer immersions in the shock of experience, to leap into swifter streams of time.

When spring moved on through May one year Fitz turned his ankle and could not walk through the uneven fields to be in the arms of Arethusa. Late in the month, on an afternoon full of bosom and warmth, he called to me as I sat in the side yard reading Boswell's, *The Life of Samuel Johnson.*

"Let's ride out to North River for a swim," he said. "I'll have to walk through only one field. There's an old tree with a great spread of limb just at the water's edge. We can lie in the grass and talk."

"What about Boswell?" I said. "I've got to finish him before the examination tomorrow."

He hesitated, seeming to regret that he could not, as a friend, repeal what as a teacher he had assigned. His courses were difficult—Boswell was only one of the outside reading assignments in Eighteenth Century Literature—and his examinations were thorough and probing. A question I remember particularly was: "Discuss Shakespeare as a comic artist. This should take you at least three hours."

"Bring Boswell with you," he said. "You can read by the river."

We entered the Ford and down the street picked up Munsey Gleaton, the university Y.M.C.A. secretary, a mountain man who had walked fifteen miles to school each day as a boy and who, having worked his way with enthusiasm into the ministry, was now in the process of working his way, with the same enthusiasm, out of it. Somewhat north of the covered bridge we turned away from the highway to Staunton and ran briefly along a dirt road. When we stopped only a hundred yards of field separated us from the river. We found the old tree with the great spread of limb; its shade went almost to the water's edge. I lay in the grass and read Boswell while Fitz and Munsey swam, sun bathed, and talked. After an hour ants found my arms and legs. I killed them, and then the steady prose made me drowsy. I nodded as I read: "In the month of January, his mother died at the great age of ninety, an event which deeply affected him. . . ." I shook myself, stood up, and decided to disperse my lethargy by swimming. I took off my clothes—we did not wear bathing suits unless our company was mixed—and slid down the bank into the water. While I drifted or stroked against the current the four-oared crews of our boat clubs went by. When I climbed up the bank I stood in the sun, shaking the water from my skin. Along the dirt road a Model T Ford moved slowly, going toward town. In the front seat next to the driver a large woman in a black dress sat very straight; her profile was stern and matriarchal. I watched the car until it was out of sight, then relaxed by the tree and returned to my reading.

Some time later I heard a rustling in the grass. I was reading Johnson's remark to Boswell—and agreeing with it—"Sir, you have but two topicks, yourself and me. I am sick of both." The rustling was repeated. Suddenly I heard a shout.

"Don't move!" a voice cried. "We've got you! Stay where you are!"

I looked up and saw Fitz and Munsey staring incredulously at the entire Lexington police force—two men, a chief and his lieutenant. They had crept across the field on their hands and knees. They were heavily armed.

"You're under arrest for indecent exposure!" the chief said, triumph and righteousness mingling in his tone.

I saw temptation flicker in Munsey's face. It would be fun to throw the cops into the river.

"Was there a complaint?" I asked. "Did a woman in a black dress tell you we were here?"

The chief smiled at me. He knew his trade. He wouldn't talk. He took out a notebook and asked our names. We were summoned to appear in court at nine o'clock the next morning to answer the charge entered against us.

"Where is court held?" Fitz asked. He was controlling his mirth.

"Upstairs in the fire house," the chief said.

On our way home we agreed that it was fascinating to be arrested for indecent exposure, but inconvenient. The examination for the course in Eighteenth Century Literature was scheduled for eight-thirty in the morning. I said I would help Fitz write the questions on the blackboards, so that as soon as class was assembled we could leave for court. Once in court I would have to remain until the case was settled while the time allotted for taking the examination ticked away. That worried Fitz.

Ours was a seldom-met opportunity to strike against prudery, to cut at the shackles of our puritanical manners. We could assemble and Fitz could deliver unassailable arguments against degrading the human symbol of creation, the lower end of the mind, the wick of the lamp of life, by decreeing that its disclosure in a natural setting at a distance of one hundred yards from a public thoroughfare in a bad state of repair—due to nepotism, chicanery, and possible miscegenation in high places—was indecent and offensive (sic) to female eyes. But the presentation of such a defense would take time, during which my chances in the examination would diminish. I wanted to risk it but Fitz refused to put me in jeopardy. He decided that the only safe procedure was to plead guilty with an explanation.

"You have a straight A in the course so far," he said. "I cannot endanger that mark by making it impossible for you to finish the examination."

At eight o'clock the next morning we went to the classroom and wrote the examination questions on the blackboards. When the class assembled at eight-thirty Fitz called the roll and explained certain aspects of the questions. Then he and I hurried to the firehouse. The courtroom was filled with students; they even stood against the walls and outside the door. Obviously they anticipated entertainment. The mayor of Lexington, who was presiding as judge, also looked expectant and pleased. I was sorry that because of my predicament all were destined to be disappointed.

Our case was called first and we pleaded guilty. Fitz offered his lame ankle as the reason for our proximity to the road. He spoke casually of the body pores as nostrils of the spirit, needing to breathe now and then the open, unstrained air which never was denied the lungs. He mentioned sunlight, and how in the atmosphere of earth it breaks into myriad jets of magic, nourishing to the body and to the soul. He talked of nudity, the most innocent of garbs, and of modern female clothing, the most erotic of raiment. He pointed out that at one hundred yards we could not have had, for an observer, more reality than a Greek statue. He suggested that what mischief took place did not transpire in us; if one had looked upon us and lusted after us, were we, then, adulterers in our hearts?

The students stirred and the mayor leaned forward in his chair. But suddenly Fitz stopped. He had caught sight of me and had remembered the examination. He said no more, and since neither Munsey nor I had anything to say there was nothing for the mayor to do but sit straight in his chair and agree with us in our plea of guilty. He was disappointed, and he ordered us to pay a fine of five dollars and costs. I wrote a check for seven dollars and then Fitz drove me back to the classroom. I finished the examination with a few minutes to spare; I received A for the course.

After the hospital was finished and in operation I spent two summers at Virginia Beach. I worked in the basement of the new building, which stood on a high dune at 105th Street, half way between the Cavalier Hotel and Cape Henry. My job was to study the readings on metempsychosis and compare their theoretical material with what I could find on the subject in Hindu and Buddhist literature, among Greek and Gnostic fragments, and in treatises on the Jewish Cabala.

The Cayce readings, concerned as they were with detailing the component parts of particular personalities, only occasionally mentioned a general operational scheme. Each reading did, however, stress one point: the past or receded personalities combined in the present personality were only a selection from the total record of an ego's pre-existence. They represented a group of unsolved problems brought together for restatement and a new attempt at solution. Added to the group was a leaven of pre-accomplishment, sufficient to propel the ego slightly forward spiritually, providing the debt of problems first was solved. The inoperative personalities of the ego's pre-existence dwelt in recession in the subconscious.

The present personality was to the total ego, then, as a day's jaunt to Manhattan was to a Westchester housewife's total life. There were things to be done—bills to be paid, friends to be met, a lecture to be attended, a medical treatment to be endured, commodities to be purchased, aging relatives to be visited, cocktails to be drunk, dinner to be eaten, something as yet unplanned to be enjoyed before train time. All this might go off smoothly; it might go off badly. Either way the housewife would return to Westchester a little changed, slightly sadder or happier or wiser, ready to resume the larger portion of herself which temporarily she had put aside for the sake of errands which had to be done and duties which had to be faced. In the same manner of simile the ego's excursion into the solar system was to the complete adventure of the soul as a leisurely trip around the world was to a student of sociology—personal observation of and experience in conditions hitherto known in theory but not realized and felt.

I typed my deductions and filed them with the readings; every few days I added new similes, fresh deductions. Generally, the theory of an ego probing three-dimensionality with selected portions of its awareness, keeping the remainder in recession, seemed sound as a basis for techniques of self-help such as those which the Oriental religions had devised from it. Its drawbacks were obvious; it stimulated dreamy and romantic notions of self rather than concern for that self's predicament; it provoked navel-admiration rather than navel-contemplation; it bred inertia, self-indulgence, rationalization of ineptitudes, dissociation from the common effort of humanity, indifference to a spiritual evolvment known to be intricate, tortuous, and extended. Only the vigorous, the resourceful, the humble, and the intellectually nimble enjoyed and welcomed it. As a therapeutic device for patients in the hospital it was successful. It offered a logical and comforting reason why peculiar and baffling afflictions preferred one person to another. As an explanation for the details of any personality—ugliness, talent, irritability, stupidity, loveliness, grace, virtue, ambition—it was disturbing. It upset the rationalizations erected by the conscious mind to discount defects by stating flatly that the defects were the result of errors of omission and commission in pre-existence. The mistakes of a man's soul were visible to everyone; few people enjoyed this thought.

I lived within sight of the hospital, in a house on the water front. Early in the morning army planes from Langley Field woke me as they flew along the beach. I watched them from my bed, remembering the lectures of my history professors, Dr. Bean and Dr. Helderman, on the tactics and diplomacy of the World War. Another conflict was inevitable. How long would it take to develop? Measuring and mixing the opinions I had heard, feeling a little sick that murder in the human pattern was so far from being exorcised, I fell back to sleep. It never occurred to me to get up and go swimming. That was for late in the afternoon, when the sun was a safe distance away. I had no desire to lie in the building light which burned and freckled my skin, sealed my eyelids, sickened my stomach, and broiled my brains.

At night we dated the girls in the cottage line, substituting the gentle interplay of opposite polarities for the sleep which older folk were under the impression we required. The girls were clean, brown, odoriferous, playful, clad in bright cotton dresses, high-heeled summer shoes, and jingling silver bracelets. We danced with them, took them on beach parties, talked endlessly to them in the easy banter which nibbles away the edges of restraint, watched them stain red the cold edges of coke glasses in Sammy Benstock's drugstore—Sammy was the Manhasset man whose reading I had heard; he was so impressed by the description of his fall down the front steps that he moved to Virginia Beach and opened a pharmacy, so that the hospital might obtain promptly whatever medicines it needed. Sometimes we drove to an old cemetery where cape jessamine grew against the headstones; the girls put the white, perfume-heavy blossoms in their hair and piled them up behind the seats of the car, so that our lungs were soaked in their odor as we drove slowly over back roads, nosing toward the sea.

On beach parties we built a fire, then left it to swim when the tide ebbed, floating on the smooth, slick, restless belly of the sea, staring at the stars. Aloft on the endless amniotic ocean the aura of my maleness vanished; about me I could see undulating shadows that were females of my species, their sex washed from them as they lay in the impersonal womb of the common mother, their egos soaking up forgetfulness. Back on the beach there was a period of drying and combing, while the sexes were separated and quiet. Then slowly polarity and orientation returned and the intermingling of talk and laughter had again its restfulness, its light flick of the flame of ecstasy.

Beyond the talk and laughter was the waiting, restless ground of practical execution, the bodies which brought the radiations of polarity to a focus. The manners of our period dictated that we confine our activities to the subtle radiations of average proximity and occasional nuzzling and rubbing against prescribed sections of the fleshly periphery. The girls were our friends; they had a single uncertain chance in life and we had no desire to spoil it; departure from virginity, experimentation in sexuality, were theirs to choose but not ours to impose, advise, or even insinuate. As males we were expected by the idola of our society to be unmoral, aggressive, and insatiable. Some of the girls may have heard such nonsense, but none of them believed it. We were their friends; our ambitions represented our uncertain chances in life, and they had no desire to balk us. Whether by persistent titillation a girl might have accomplished seduction and forced a marriage is improbable; several tried, and laughed when they failed. They understood that a boy often had more and better reasons than a girl for saying no. His capitulation was as calculated as hers; he chose for it, if he could, a woman whose need was only the thing for which with soft and stricken eyes she asked.

The girls we dated were too young for that. Their legs were still growing and many of them yet wore cotton pants.

One afternoon when we lined up on the beach for touch football a slim, long-limbed child of fifteen who swung from the hips as she walked and carried her head high, said to me, "Tell me how to tackle a man." She was on my team.

"Leave your feet and hit him at the ankles," I said.

Then I threw the football toward the other team, which was captained by Fitz, who came down from Lexington each summer to spend his vacation in the sun. I aimed at one of the girls, calculating that she would fumble, but an offshore breeze carried the ball toward Fitz. He caught it, and then I saw my long-limbed girl, who was far in advance of the other members of our team, leave her feet. When her body was in the air she put her legs together—she was an accomplished diver and swimmer—and reached forward with her hands, closing them around Fitz' ankles. He went down as if bludgeoned. The girl got up quickly, spat sand from her mouth, and said to me, "Is that what you mean?"

"Yes," I said, "but this is touch football. You need only to slap the ball-carrier's arm."

She was disappointed that she could not continue tackling, but the next summer, having grown into a woman, she was so helpless that I had to help her take off her beach shoes before we went for a swim.

When we rode at night along the asphalt ribbons which made a lace among the dunes I wondered what I felt for the girl who sat beside me. Her name changed often, and normally she was a house guest of Cousin Corinne Mosby, the Alpha Tau Omega house mother at Lexington, who during the summer conducted the finest cottage at the beach. Cousin Corinne's meals were unsurpassed and the prettiest girls in Virginia flocked to her, knowing that any Lexington students within a radius of fifty miles would turn up at her dinner table. I never questioned her selection of dates for me, nor was it ever necessary; she gave the girls to me in trust and I returned them unscathed, except for an occasional set of injured feelings. One night a girl who had been strangely quiet during our ride struck at me when I reached for a blossom of jessamine which lay behind and past her head. The implication so irritated me that I pulled her across my knees and whacked her until my arm hurt to the elbow. Hugh Lynn, who was driving, did not turn around, nor did his date. The front seat of the car was one world, the back seat was another.

250

Years later, on the eve of her marriage, the girl wrote me a letter. She had been recalling some things which happened to her before the now oncoming hour of climax; the most exciting scene which rose to her mind, she said, was a memory of the night I whacked her; it was so romantic to be lying over my knee, she thought, screaming with pain and choking with the fragrance of jessamine which poured down over her from the flowers in her tumbled hair.

When it happened I thought that perhaps all love was parental or filial, and that I had a paternal interest in these almost formed, not quite ripe young women; but I know now that my indifference was because I compared all of them, and every other woman I encountered, to the Woman, who was an incomparable treasure I allowed to slip from me without knowing the loss I sustained. Other women helped me count it, helped me remember that her lips broke open my mind like sleep, that her flesh was as soft as the endless prayer which rose without sound in the chapels of my mind, that her voice had the whispering quality of wind which is not in a hurry, which has time to caress and to talk, and which does both with the same breath. She never moved except in a way I somehow had anticipated she would move; her gestures seemed liquid, part of the drifting of air in the room where we sat or the field through which we walked. Our minds lay with each other as stillness lies with the night, or mixed like sunset and the dusk. I felt the unruffled union, but I did not know its worth, not until I had looked for it through hundreds of nights with other girls, and found not even its shadow.

Then I knew that a man's search is for a woman to whom he can give his mind, not his body, and that such a woman is rarely found. She is the Virgin of the World; she is the symbol of Holy Wisdom to whom Everyman offers the sign of his virtue, the intelligence with which he carries forward the labor of his resurrection; with her alone he is safe; in her arms he can rest, his weapons put aside; she will not betray his soul or stop his heart while he sleeps. He must be certain it is she, however, before he capitulates, just as a woman must have marriage before she gives up the entrance to her womb, for if he is wrong he is lost. That is why a man may lie all his life with women and never give his mind. He gives his body as he gives kindness or friendship, or bread, but the chalice of his thought is kept for the bride of his soul; if the lips of a courtesan touch its rim the man is dead.

One night at Virginia Beach we stopped on a back road by a bay where an old wharf had worked its way into the moonlight. My girl that night had black hair tied in a small knot at the nape of her neck, a white oval face, and a mouth thin and soft and lightly painted. We walked to the end of the wharf and the sky darkened and it rained softly. She lifted her face and I watched the drops strike her skin and catch in her hair. She put her arms around me and we stood in the warm, affectionate mist, and for those moments she was like the Woman. But the car horn blew and we left the wharf, and half an hour later we were dancing at the casino. After that we ate hot dogs and drank cokes and jabbered.

The hospital in summer was filled with patients; Edgar gave readings for them and Dr. House and his staff administered the treatments suggested. On week ends the New Yorkers and their wives came to the Cavalier. There were plans now for a school; foundations were built near the hospital.

"Are you still planning to come to New York," the Lady asked me one day, "or have you decided to teach at the school?"

I had just returned from Mass at the Star of the Sea Church, a low, lovely red brick building within sight of the ocean but bordering a small, fresh water lake. I was depressed at the usual Sunday sight—hundreds of men and women in elaborate rainment giving half an hour and almost no attention to the mystery, impervious to its symbology, considering their attendance as payment on a salvation which, if the rules were kept, was guaranteed.

"If the school is to fulfill its announced purpose it will require a faculty composed of the greatest minds in history," I said, "and most of those minds belong to dead men."

"Perhaps a little money will bring them to life," the Lady said.

Perhaps it will, I thought. There seemed to be no end of money in those days, and no limit to its power. Perhaps money could create another Bruchion, nourish again the gnosis, revive the techniques of the mystery schools. But where were the books? They had long ago been burned. Where were the teachers? Were they available in a society in which millionaires were revered as were once the saints? Could money create them, even in 1929? I did not believe that it could.

252

On a Saturday evening late in May of that year 1929 we gathered in Lexington at the Dutch Inn for the annual dinner of Pi Delta Epsilon, an undergraduate journalism fraternity. When dinner was finished we stood outside in the twilight. Examinations were scheduled to begin on Monday. "I should go home and study," Elias said. But he stood on the curbstone, teetering and twirling his watch chain. He moved with us when we walked a few yards up the brick-paved street to the Sigma Chi house. He laughed at something Bill Plummer said. Ben Eastwood's yellow roadster rolled down the hill from the Alpha Chi Rho house and stopped beside us. Campbell Hutchinson moved through the group and said to me, "Are you going to the hop at V.M.I.?" I hesitated.

Elias couldn't attend the dance; there was an agreement between the senior classes of Washington and Lee and Virginia Military Institute which stated that members of both classes were invited to the social functions of each. That was as far as relations went between the two schools; long before our time the impracticality of athletic contests between cadet and student teams had been demonstrated, and dances indiscriminately attended by both undergraduate bodies were obviously unwise. The same girls were courted by students and cadets and were invited to dances at both schools. They were as much in favor of restriction as were their suitors. The senior classes had come to terms after long discussion; the agreement was based on a mutual belief that both groups were composed of complete gentlemen, and on the unmentioned fact that all parties concerned would soon be leaving Lexington and were therefore not apt to interest themselves in such elementary nonsense as student feuds. Because my three-year plan had culminated successfully I was a senior. Elias, proceeding at the orthodox pace, was a junior.

"I'm going home and study," he said when I did not answer Campbell.

"Are you going to pass freshman mathematics this time?" Campbell asked.

Elias shook his head and laughed.

"No," he said, "but I'm going to pass Greek and Microscopic Crystallography."

"Are you sure you want to study?" I said.

"Yes," he said. "I have examinations on Monday, Tuesday, and Wednesday. I've got to start reading my notes."

The roadster was gathering a crowd—Pat Jones, Rowland Walker, Mosby Perrow, Bill Plummer.

"Let's be off," Campbell said.

We said good night to Elias.

"See you around third base," he said.

The dance was a success for the cadets; our dark, severe tuxedos were no match for their bright colorful dress uniforms. I danced with the little destiny girl; she was grown now, poised and lovely and a little shy. One of the senior cadets was in love with her.

"He's quite deadly about it," she said, closing her eyes as she spoke. "Quite deadly. His name is Dudley and I call him Deadly Dudley."

After the dance I walked alone along the shaded street which separates the two schools, crossed the university campus, passed Lee Chapel, and at the Episcopal church turned east toward the Phi Psi house. At Main Street a car swung to the curb, blocking my path. Jimmy Pollak leaned out from it.

"They want you at the hospital," he said. "Step on the running board and we'll drive you there."

"I can run," I said, "it's just up the street." I was throttling my heart, preparing it; in my mind I opened a way for shock.

"We'll drive you," Jimmy said.

I stepped on the running board and the car began to circle the block, going away from the hospital before approaching it. Jimmy put out a hand and held my arm. He began talking in a low voice about an accident. Ben Eastwood's car had turned over on the way back from a dance at Natural Bridge. Some of the boys had been hurt. Elias was one of them.

Then he had not gone home to study. My mind said: I should have known that he would not go home; I should have known that he would not go home.

At the hospital I stepped to the pavement. Someone touched my elbow and guided me into the basement, where the emergency room was situated. It was Mike Seligman. At the end of the corridor we stopped at a narrow cubicle hardly long enough for the stretcher carriage it contained; on the stretcher Elias lay. He was covered to his neck by a sheet; I saw no marks on his face. He was waiting for surgery, I supposed, unconscious from his wounds or drugged by ether. I began to talk to him after Mike went away. I told him how easy it all would be, what a simple matter it was to get well as opposed to the complex task of passing freshman mathematics. A nurse walked by and heard me. She stepped to the other side of the stretcher and stared at me anxiously.

"You mustn't talk to him," she said. "Please don't! I know how you feel, but—"

"How bad is he hurt?" I said. "When are they going to operate on him?"

"Didn't they tell you?" she said. "Don't you know that he's dead?"

"He isn't dead," I said. "There isn't a mark on his face. How can he be dead?"

She came to where I stood and took my arm.

"The whole back of his head is broken," she said. "He was dead when they brought him in. Please come away! Please don't talk to him!"

She led me into the corridor, and then I saw another cubicle with another stretcher carriage and on the stretcher lay Bill Plummer.

"Is he dead too?" I said.

"Yes," she said. "He's dead. But the others are still alive."

I turned from her and went to the emergency room. Dr. Reid White, the university physician, was working on Pat Jones. Ben Eastwood lay on another table. Dr. White looked up quickly, saw me, shook his head in despair, and went back to his task. I walked into the corridor and Mike put his arm around my shoulder and we went outside and stood on the sidewalk. I heard students quietly telling other students what had happened. It was on the long, dangerous curve of the Roanoke road, the one we all feared. The red clay shoulder caught the wheels and pulled them. The car staggered, leaped, and turned over. Elias and Plummer, sitting together in the rumble seat, were crushed as the compartment closed on them. Ben Eastwood, sitting on the collapsed top, was thrown high in the air. When he fell his head struck a rock. Pat Jones, behind the wheel, was trapped. Rowland Walker and Mosby Perrow, sitting in the front seat, were thrown clear and seemed unhurt, though cut and bruised.

We stood on the sidewalk until dawn. Jones and Eastwood were still alive when we went home. In my room I fell asleep and woke up not believing what had happened. On Monday the student body walked to the railroad station and sang *College Friendships* while the coffins were placed in the bag-

255

gage car. Mike went north with Elias. I saw him turn into the coach as my lips moved to the song.

> *Our college friendships soon must sever,*
> *And fade as does the dying day;*
> *Our closest bonds must all be broken....*

Jones and Eastwood were still alive, but they had not yet regained consciousness. We kept a twenty-four-hour vigil at the hospital, in two hour shifts. We took our examinations.

One night I went to Cayce's room in the dormitory and borrowed the textbook for Dr. Helderman's course in American Foreign Policy. I did not myself possess a copy of the book; it was large and it cost six dollars. I intended to spend the night reading the borrowed copy, finishing by eight-thirty in the morning, in time for the examination.

Suddenly at eleven o'clock I stood up, took the book in my right hand, and pitched it through an open window, forgetting that it was not mine to throw away. I walked to the Phi Psi house and went to a room where students who had completed their examinations were dipping corn whiskey from a half-gallon fruit jar. I joined them. At three o'clock I was standing on a table reciting Swinburne's "The Triumph of Time"; at four I gave the traditional speech in the upper house by Senator George Washington Tallahatchee on the occasion of an attempt to change the name of Arkansas to Ar-kansas.

At eight-thirty as I walked up the campus I saw, behind Washington College, a group of workmen engaged in argument. One broke away as I drew near, and when he was a few yards along the road he put a hand to his head. There was a noise, and he fell on his face. I saw a pistol barrel gleam as his body dropped. He had been away from the job for a while, and on returning to it had been fired. He always carried a gun. He was dead.

After receiving the examination questions from Dr. Helderman I went, with his permission, to the journalism building and wrote my answers on a typewriter. I paced myself; each time I finished three pages I walked to The Corner and drank a coke flavored with spirits of ammonia. On one visit I met the chairman of the Student Publication Board. He reminded me that Elias and I had been recommended as candidates for editor of the yearbook in the spring elections. I had withdrawn as a candidate and Elias had been elected without opposition. Now the board wanted to name me his successor.

"It depends on whether I come back next year," I said. "If I win a graduate scholarship I will return, otherwise I won't."

I sipped my coke. The way things were going I wondered if I would even get my degree; a scholarship seemed remote. But a few days later I met Ollie Crenshaw as he emerged from a faculty meeting and he told me I had been awarded the fellowship for which I had applied. I could return in the fall and work on a master's degree. While we talked about it Dr. Helderman came out and asked me to step into his office.

"I want to speak to you about your examination," he said.

When I stood before his desk he smiled and handed me the paper I had submitted.

"I thought you might care to keep it," he said, "and I wanted you to know how much I enjoyed reading it."

I looked at the mark he had written on the first page—A++. Under it was a remark: "This is the finest paper ever written by a student in this class."

On the morning of commencement some salesmen for printing and engraving firms, eager to close contracts for the yearbook, visited me before breakfast at the Phi Psi house. Somehow I didn't eat and left for Lee Chapel with only two sips of corn whiskey for nourishment. Jan Garber stood under the trees with his musicians and played a march as we walked along the paths. Dr. Smith handed me my diploma, but I only stared at him and could not think the things a graduate should think.

That afternoon a special meeting of Phi Beta Kappa was held, at which I was initiated; I had been in Washington taking treatment for ulcerated eyeballs when the general induction took place. I stood quietly while the symbology of the key was explained and while the story of the founding of the society, in a room in Raleigh Tavern in Williamsburg, on December 5, 1776, was related. Dr. Campbell showed me the secret grip, which I soon forgot, and when the meeting was ended we walked out of the building together and down across the lawns. At the Phi Psi house I put the key on my watch chain and dipped it three times into a jar of corn whiskey, explaining to the freshmen that victories of the mind must be cleansed in the spirit, lest they rust as they lie in the soul.

Then I walked out on the porch and stood looking north to the throat of the valley. In the living room behind me a girl known as Fo' God O'Shanahan demonstrated a dance called the shag and assured each new partner that, "Fo' God I'm jus' obliged t' be in love with ol' han'some you." At the hospital Jones and Eastwood were still unconscious. For the first time in Lexington I heard a cock crow. The sound came from high on the rim of the eastern hill, just at the edge of the town.

FIFTEEN

SO that is the way it ended," the Professor said, "with the crowing of a cock. I am sure that if there had been no cock to crow at that hour you would have imagined one. You have a sense of melodrama worthy of the time in which you were born, but not of the era in which you are living."

"There was another year after that," I said, "a year of anticlimax. I read history and English and wrote a thesis on the heroic couplet for my master's degree. I remember the tapping finger of Dr. Helderman and the nervous, penetrating eyes of Dr. Bean, and their voices quietly lacing together the threads of human foolishness. Some of our students left school in February, though they had passed the January examinations without difficulty. Others made quick trips home and returned without their roadsters. Senior law students put aside their copies of *The Saturday Evening Post* and became experts on the financial panic. Cayce told me that the backers of the hospital—several of them were brokers—were thus far not part of the Wall Street wreckage.

"By spring the situation was worse for everyone. Members of my class regarded the oncoming commencement with gloom. I wondered if we would be emancipated from the moral obligation to become millionaires. I hoped so. I remembered the fantastic market values of certain bonds carried on the books of the Naugatuck Savings Bank in 1925 at a par value of $100 each. Things were getting healthier, I thought, but even in Lexington I dared not express such an opinion. In those early months of the depression people who had made a great deal of money on the stock market, and who were losing it, had an ugly, dangerous look. The evil they had committed possessed them.

"The beauty and strength of automobiles soared to an apex that year, and the road gangs finally finished their conversion of the winding, narrow, humpbacked highways of the Shenandoah Valley into straight, four-lane stretches of macadam. On my last ride north the car in which I was riding reached Washington in four and a half hours. My first trip, in 1927, took nine hours.

"Commencement exercises were long that spring. Dr. Smith was retiring, and there were many gifts for him, and many speeches. He was, some people said, old-fashioned. They were the sort who smiled when Dr. Smith suggested that the university sever athletic relations with a rival school whose football coach habitually cursed at his players. I did not agree with their opinion, nor did most of the students. They loved and respected Dr. Smith. He did not expect them to go into the world and become millionaires."

"How do you know that isn't precisely what the students wanted to do?" the Professor said. "Aren't you judging their desires by your own? Most young men, it seems to me, are quite enthusiastic about trying to make a lot of money; they admire those who have managed to put together a fortune."

"In some cases pleasure at making money is a natural taste," I said, "and often it is accompanied by a natural skill in satisfying that taste. For most men it is an acquired taste, and the skill at satisfying it is grudgingly learned and unwillingly exercised. You have no idea how acutely the average student suffers from the obligation which is thrust upon him to prove his worth by a standard which is foreign to his moral, intellectual, and spiritual standards."

"If he has any," the Professor said.

"He has them just as the student of the Middle Ages had them," I said. "The student of the Middle Ages was under an imposed compulsion to succeed or fail as a theologian, as a juggler of abstract ideas. He might or he might not have a talent for such matching and improvisation. He might be offended in his soul by the intellectual posturing of scholasti-

259

cism. That did not matter. The standard remained, and by it he was judged."

The Professor nodded and smiled.

"And in that time and by that standard you would have achieved a large and easy success," he said. "In this time and by a standard which prizes a skill you do not possess, you are a failure, and as such you wish to set forth for yourself an alibi. Since you incline to include everyone who is about you in whatever misery confines your ego, your class at Lexington must of necessity be composed of fragile souls who loathe the material world and who are crushed by the need to enter into it and to be rewarded for labor according to its rules.

"In our society every man is free to choose his vocation and to exercise whatever talent he possesses. If he succeeds in the enterprise he selects he will be materially rewarded; wealth is a result of success, not success itself. If some people desire only money, they are a gross lot and few in number. As for yourself, your wish is to hide the fact that you did not want to participate in life by pretending that the only result of such participation is either material wealth or lack of it, depending on whether the participant succeeds or fails. Were it not for a preposterous personal dissatisfaction with the modern, sensible, utilitarian, businesslike attitude of your church you would during adolescence have fled from life to the womb so conveniently maintained by that church for such deserters, the monastery. You would have returned to God, to Nirvana, to nothingness—I give you back your own words—rather than face the adventure set before you in creation.

"Had you done this, a part of your apology for flight would have been a careful contempt for the world, a studied disdain of its problems and its pleasures as matters beneath the dignity of the soul. That you did not run off to the cloister was due to a concern for the comfort of your opinions and a thirst for extravagance in metaphysical speculation; the comfort of your opinions was only safe in secular life, and only in secular life were your metaphysical sprees tolerated. So you looked for a combination of monastic retreat and secular tolerance and comfort. You found it at Lexington. You enjoyed it for four years. You disported yourself in the university atmosphere with physical glee and mental abandon. You played at being an intellectual, a philosopher, an artist, a man of the world. You borrowed the wisdom of better men and used it to weave a pattern of easy living for yourself; you set out on a melodramatic search for whatever your pleasure preferred, disguising the journey as a lonely, tragic quest for truth. As an added touch you wrapped your Galahad-at-Golgotha figure in a mist of Confederate tears; even the South's defeat, which succored the Republic from schism, was not safe from you.

"Then in your hour of darkest need, when there were no more defeats in which to cloak your negation and selfishness, the nation and the world plunged into an economic depression. By that tragedy of hunger and suffering you were saved. Now the society whose system of cooperative labor and shared responsibility opposed your personal, inverted tastes in living, was unable to offer you a place in its plan. You were free once more to evade what normal men embrace as a privilege."

He was obviously bilious. I waited for him to finish talking. He soared into a splutter and descended from it slowly, muttering. He stared at Miss Iceberg's shoulders, a neutral point of anatomy, and refused to look at me. I went on with my story.

"That summer I worked at Virginia Beach for the hospital, but plans were being altered as the depression deepened and metaphysical research was marked for abandonment, as was my secondary job of writing and putting together the hospital's promotion material. In September I went to New York and offered myself to every newspaper, magazine, and publishing house in the city. None accepted me. In October I returned to Naugatuck and went to work on the *Daily News*. There was no job for me on the staff, so I labored as an apprentice; I covered reportorial assignments and wrote a daily column and was paid nothing. At Christmas I was given a bonus of fifty dollars; it was all the money I earned until the following August.

"One of my assignments was a series of stories on local industries. I hoped that by studying production methods and observing operations in the plants I would discover the excitement and fascination of manufacturing, and perhaps even understand what had happened to it in the depression. But as I walked through the rubber factories and iron foundries I saw hundreds of men and women I knew, dozens of boys and girls who had been my schoolmates, people I had seen walking to work for years without knowing where it was they went or what it was they were hired to do. As I passed they smiled at me and waved; they were busy and glad at tasks requiring skill, patience, and stamina. As I sat in the *News* office and wrote stories about them I saw their faces and felt the pattern of their days and nights and years. I realized that they were content, and that their contentment was as far beyond my understanding as were the excitement and fascination of manufacturing and the reasons for the misfortune which had overcome it, abstractions which soared beyond the reach of my mind. I had simple ideas about craftsmanship, home industry, communal culture, and cooperative nurturing of the psyche. The complexities of national distribution and interchangeable parts eluded me."

The Professor lifted his glance in mock pity.

"You saw only people who were not individuals because they made nothing by themselves, shaped no artifacts with tools turned cunning in their hands," he said in the high, rhythmic voice of old-fashioned preachers. "You saw only workers who did not gather together for festivals of song, but went separately or in groups to the movies. You spied no poet, no sculptor, no teller of tales. You saw only a lost, forsaken, inadequate, groping, imprisoned and blind-souled set of slaves!"

"My discontent seemed quite as removed from their comprehension as was their content from mine," I went on. "My column was a continuation of the sort of copy I had written for *The Southern Collegian,* except that certain subjects were of necessity sent into exile, along with Joseph. As a university graduate I could, in New England, write boldly and critically about a large number of things, and I did, inviting my readers to disagree, to present their own views, or to inform me of their concurrence with mine. Since I was expressing myself on a number of test subjects—politics, literature, history, war, women—I wanted to ascertain the reaction of people I had known since childhood. No one wrote to me; during all of that autumn and winter the column received not a single letter. Then one cold day a note addressed to me was delivered at the newspaper. It was not signed. The writer said she was a woman who enjoyed my opinions; she was, however, a neighbor, and therefore did not wish to reveal her identity.

"At first I was amused at the New England characteristic she so aptly demonstrated—praise is an abnormal act which must be committed, like a sin, in secrecy and anonymity. Then the entire weight of Puritan repression, rigidity, formality, and austerity, which had been lifted from me by Virginia and Washington and Lee, fell on me. I could not write another column."

The Professor managed a small, knowing smile.

"You will forgive me," he said, "if I enter in my notes the truth of these matters rather than your highly colored and obviously contrived versions of the motives behind your acts. You realized quite suddenly that your childish perorating and your literary mimicries were tolerated and overlooked in Lexington as a natural effluvium accompanying the birth of your mental body. When you invited the citizens of Naugatuck to applaud you for waving an intellectual rattle and saying 'ga-ga,' they were polite. They looked the other way and pretended it wasn't happening. When you became aware of your exhibitionism you stopped it, but you blamed its foolishness on the people who with good manners had endured it. The result, I suspect, was that for some time thereafter you were inhibited in your writing with regard to the use of the first person singular and in the matter of expressing opinions on abstract ideas.

"What was not inhibited, I am sure, was your romantic attachment for Lexington as an island of ideal existence. Disillusion, in fact, would strengthen the legend you had begun to build around Elias as the first of a band of adventuring knights braving the forests and jungles of environments beyond the earth, setting a signal fire which you, when the world pressed too hard against you, might answer by your own death. It is unfortunate that New England could not shame you from this hallucination also."

"Perhaps," I said, "it did. One evening late that autumn I read in the *Daily News* of the death of a schoolmate and fraternity brother in an airplane crash in West Virginia. I was reminded of a Saturday morning in my freshman year; it was the day of our football game with the University of Virginia. At The Corner Elias called me to a group of students with whom he was conversing; they were all editors or assistant editors of the various student publications—Ike Lebow, Tommy Thames, Bill Plummer, and Jairus Collins. I joined the conversation, someone bought cokes, and we went outside to soak up the November sunlight and discuss freedom of the press in a self-governing student body.

"On Monday Lebow went to the hospital with a sore throat. On Wednesday he died of a streptococcic infection. During the summer following my second student year Thames died at his Ohio home. Elias and Plummer were killed the following May. Now Collins had crashed in his own plane, which he purchased as a commencement present for himself. That left me.

"One night that winter I was riding in a car along the road from Southbury to Newtown. At Sandy Hook a bridge swings over the Housatonic at a right angle to the road. It was a cold night; the highway was frosted with fresh snow. At the turn the car skidded, broke from control, and leaped over the bank. My face struck something and I lost consciousness.

"When I regained it I was still sitting in the car, which was resting, wheels down, on the ice covering the surface of the river."

"The ice didn't break?" The Professor said.

"There were great cracks leading away from the car but no water appeared," I said. "I do not know how thick the ice was but it had sufficient depth to hold an automobile dropped from a height of thirty-five feet. With the other occupants, two friends, I got out of the car and climbed the embankment. People in a nearby house gave us shelter and sent for a doctor; he sewed our cuts by the light of an oil lamp. None of us was more than bruised and gashed. My watch was missing. It had been torn from my wrist; there were lacerations where the metal band broke.

"I was sorry to lose the watch. It was a gift from Elias. His last letter to his mother reached her after his death. In it he asked that she buy a watch; he wanted to give it to me at commencement. When I visited the family during Christmas holidays that year Mrs. Elias took me into her sitting room and showed me the letter. Then she gave me the watch.

"During the week following our tumble down the embankment I rode to the river in daylight and thanked the mother of the family which had sheltered us. 'Did one of you lose a wrist watch?' she asked. I said yes, and she went to a mantel in the kitchen and picked up something and brought it to me. She opened her hand and said, 'Is that it?' I said yes. The metal band was torn open at its middle. 'One of my boys found it on the river frozen in the ice,' she said. 'He didn't believe it could have come from your car but I said it might have. It was three hundred yards upstream. It was stopped but it began to run when he wound it.'

"That's all there is to the story. I would not have mentioned it in my recitation except for the need you exhibited to record a cure for my romance—a word you employ and intend in its most degenerate sense—with Virginia. You may set down in your notes that New England in its cold, impersonal way effected a homeopathic cure. Or perhaps the cure was symbolic. I fulfilled the pattern of the other five in the doomed group, and the watch, symbol of my immersion in three-dimensionality, was torn from me and flung away. But the ice did not break, so that I was not drowned, and the watch was returned to me. In Virginia there would have been no ice; I and the watch would have sunk in the stream. New England held us both on the surface, against the moment, at the edge of space and time. It would not allow me to evade the normal sequence of experience for which I was washed into breath and hunger."

"Don't attempt to agree with me," the Professor said. "Your posturing is absurd, whether you play Saint Paul or Pagliacci. It is ridiculous to plunge in an automobile thirty-five feet down an embankment to a river and to wake up sitting comfortably in the tonneau, unhurt. Your imitation of Elias and the other dead students was a parody, something to be expected of you, an act from the 'Fireman Save My Child' school of melodrama, complete to the flinging away of your watch, which was a ham gesture of your subconscious.

"I shall enter in my notes that during the winter of 1931 the death wish was discernible in you to some degree, but that it was not as strong as the ice in the Housatonic River, which means that it was thin stuff."

He raised his eyes until his gaze passed over me. He was lifting himself to the judgment seat, from which, with careful scholasticism, he would deliver my damnation.

Miss Iceberg gave me salt water to drink.

SIXTEEN

"THE DEATH WISH was strong in Naugatuck that winter," I said. "There were funerals every day when the cold weather came, and wakes every night. I went to the wakes; it was a service I could perform no better than the next man, sitting with the dead, but I did it. There were men in the town in their late forties and early fifties who had worked in the local factories for thirty or more years, winning gradually to positions of responsibility and salaries of size; one by one during 1930 these men were discharged from their jobs—they were too old and they were being paid too much; that was the philosophy which dictated their release. During the winter of 1931 all but a few of them died. A doctor said to me, 'I write pneumonia on their death certificates but they die of broken hearts.' He was a sentimentalist, but he was right. They died because they had faith in the American industrial system and no contract to guarantee that their faith would not be betrayed. They did not belong to a union; they had worked their way upward from office boy to paymaster, from stock clerk to superintendent. They were fired without notice because their salaries were large enough to attract the attention of the experts in charge of reducing the costs of operation at the various factories. I sat in the kitchens of their homes and saw, in the pattern of old and new furniture—kitchen ranges and electric refrigerators—the proud and gradual rise of their standard of living."

"There are two things which can be spared from this discussion," the Professor said, "—a defense of labor unions and a description of an Irish wake."

"I sat in the kitchens of their homes," I went on, "and felt the warmth of the fires in their kitchen stoves. Wherever on the Kelly Hill the wake was held the warmth of the kitchen was the same, the men who sat in it and quietly talked were the same, the women who came into it and

266

prepared a lunch after the midnight rosary were the same. One of them put the kettle on and its simmer joined the talk. Those who planned to sit up through the night ate food sent in by neighbors.

"Always one of the women in the kitchen was Deborah Quirke, a girl I had known since we entered kindergarten on the same day and were seated in adjoining chairs for the lesson in cutting out paper dolls. She was superior to me in cutting, tracing, drawing, and coloring, and she was able to talk continually and without effort. In fourth grade we enacted the roles of Mr. and Mrs. Santa Claus in the Christmas pageant. Deborah grew to be pretty, buxom, witty, and with a heart as wide and as soft as a summer cirrus cloud. She was married now to Al Kazemekas, who adored her, who was handsome, and who, as nature demands in such cases, was quiet. Deborah attended all wakes, funerals, weddings, and bridal showers. She was a natural actress, and was starred in the productions of The Valley Players, a local amateur dramatic group. Throughout rehearsals she carried on a verbal war with the group's director, Francis O'Connor. O'Connor was her equal in mimicry and wit, but he could not outtalk her. They were inseparable antagonists."

"What has this to do with anything whatever which concerns us?" the Professor said.

"The Kid and I were members of The Valley Players," I said. "The group originally was called The Saint Francis Dramatic Guild and was one of our church organizations. Our pastor shut up the hall where its rehearsals were held and where its productions were staged. He was an old man; he said there was no need for Catholics to indulge in parish activities beyond the practice of their religion.

"In a way The Valley Players practiced religion in their acting that winter. Their productions were sponsored by charitable organizations and the proceeds were used to feed and clothe and warm such as were in need. It was a small contribution, but the plays, when they were produced, provided a reason for the people of the town to gather together and to commonly aid their anonymous poor. Everyone was helping someone else that winter, but beyond this personal, family-to-family, friend-to-friend bolstering of the barriers of security there was the common effort of aid for the community's economically disabled, for which little theater productions, minstrel shows, raffles, dances and group suppers were the front, the mask, the facade behind which the giving

267

hand was extended and the receiving hand held up and opened. No one said, 'I give.' No one said, 'I receive.' Yet there was giving and there was receiving."

"Precisely," the Professor said. "The economic pride of even the lowliest citizen was upheld by the common effort of all the citizens, for each man in his heart prayed that whatever the depth of the catastrophe, Lucifer would be upheld—dependence of man upon man for salvation in the earth must never be avowed; those who gave of their goods gave to anonymities; those who received the goods were faceless, nameless, and ashamed. They had sinned; they had broken the New England commandment: Thou shalt be thrifty. Charity was a tolerance of their transgression but not a forgiveness. Tell me, was there in your church, at one of the side altars, a basket of coins bearing this legend: 'Take What You Need'?"

"No," I said, "there was not."

"Were sums of money delivered to the local grocers by the churches, so the grocers could say to certain customers, 'Your bill is paid'?" His voice was soft, his face gentle, his eyes narrowed and bright and hard.

"No," I said. "That was not done."

"I must have dreamed it," he said. "I must have dreamed what I seem to remember. There was a meeting of all the churches, and the meeting was attended by officials of the labor unions and by delegates from the political parties, including the Communist party. It was decided that all groups would co-operate to succor the needy, create employment, and dissipate anxiety, and this was done. It was a great and sincere and successful effort; its most enthusiastic supporters were the clergy of your church, officials of the labor unions, and leaders of the Communist party. These were indefatigable and in harmony; they were close to the people and knew their needs and ministered to them."

"It was a dream," I said, looking away from his gaze. "I had one like it. My church on the green, which in the years of my absence had continued its labors—in my mind, where it lived, its stones had weathered and its ivy reached higher—sent its priests and priestesses into the town to find the ill and the destitute and to care for them. Its dormitories were filled with homeless men and women and children; its priests and priestesses slept on the floors of the library, the study, and the laboratory. Meals were served to all who came to the refectory; the priests and priestesses ate when everyone else was fed, sharing such food as was left.

"All night a bonfire blazed before the gate and a priest walked back and forth beside it, waiting to welcome any who came to be warmed, and to lead him, if he wished to go, inside. By day there were lectures on the history of economics, the industrial revolution, the metaphysical symbology of money, and the relation of physical, emotional, and mental hunger to the general and larger hunger of the spirit. There were expeditions to the farm on the mountain top, where trees were felled and cabins were built which were to house the homeless in the spring, when they were to take over unused land and cultivate it on a cooperative basis.

"None but the children were idle on any day, and by night there were consultations, study, meditation, and vigil in the chapel.

"But all of that was as the meeting you seem to remember. It was a dream."

"Precisely," the Professor said, "except that I, even in my dreams, should have known better. Your church, the Communist party, and the labor unions are like three outwardly beautiful women competing for the same man. Each knows the weakness of the other two and could destroy their chances by attacking it, but she dare not do this, for the weakness is also her own. So she criticizes, instead, the taste of her rivals in clothes, in cosmetics, or in perfume. Their motive in seeking to win the man she does not mention, nor their methods, since their motive and their methods are her own.

"Could the officials of the labor unions or the leaders of the Communist party criticize the hierarchy of your church for the use of its funds? Could they denounce a cardinal for taking a million dollars to Rome as a personal gift to the Pope? Could they comment later on the fact that certain appointments suggested by the cardinal are confirmed by the Vatican? Could they deplore the spurious democratic base of your church, which so carefully pyramids to totalitarianism? Even at this moment, do the contending elements in the Spanish Civil War speak out, in their denunciations of each other, the truth? Does not each cry that it is the salvation of the people, and are not both grimly intent upon possessing the people? Is not one a reflection, an imitation, a debased copy of the other? Are they not both contrivances of Lucifer, monstrous images of Mother Eve, intent not upon liberating man but on making him a husband, a lover, a deceived and willing and happy slave, a support and bastion, a source of comfort and material wealth, an adoring, bemused, and exploited servant?"

"Communism is the purgatory of the church," I said. "The church believed it could legalize and dogmatize the entire mass of humanity into heaven, a position from which it finally and sensibly retired after murdering, burning, and breaking on the rack untold numbers of men and women who contended that salvation was a gradual and personal process which could not be artificially consummated by low cunning. Communism is convinced that it can legalize and dogmatize the entire mass of humanity into an earthly paradise, and it shoots holes through those of its adherents who consider that such a destiny may demand for its realization more than a faith and a system, and may be, when achieved, of dubious worth. The cases are parallel, and Communism sets its goal at the level of desire which the church, by its compromise with usury and its support of capitalism, condones and by implication applauds. Communism, in fact, is a perfect image of the church by inference—the inference which the average man is free to draw from the contradictory mixture of attitude, activity, affirmation, and assent which makes up the church's countenance. Labor unions are another such reflection, and labor unions and Communism, since they are reflections of the church, must be assumed by those who have drawn them to be reflections of truth. Thus they comprise the church's purgatory; in them the church sees itself as others see it."

"And slaps what it sees in the face for such honest reproduction," the Professor said. "The lady is indignant when, looking in the mirror, she sees before her the image of a courtesan. The Virgin who aspired to mate with heaven is enraged that her body reflects the comfort she has taken from a hundred earthly lovers, and she is frightened that her daughters, setting their ideals in the pattern of her conduct, proclaim the comfort of earthly lovers as the end and apex of existence."

"Perhaps it is only the wash and rub of the tides of evolution," I said, "the tides which rise and fall in the consciousness of man, in the blood which carries the imprint of his soul. Sometimes their movement irritates and infects the soul. Man's remedy for this illness is simple and, by modern standards of medicine, old-fashioned. He lets his blood. When

270

he is stricken, fever and fear infest him. He is filled with delusion—the way to salvation is revealed to him, and he sets out to share it with his brothers, afraid lest they perish in ignorance. When the fever is finished and the fear subsides he wonders at the smashed and broken bodies of those who did not instantly accept his revelation, pondering how he let their life into the gutters in the madness of his certainty, which now he sees as a frenzy of his bothered being, an effort to escape the sickness which beset him. Such blood-lettings must continue, I suppose, until man acquires a more civilized technique of medicine, a habit of better health, and, eventually, freedom from his body."

"They will continue so long as he regards the bodies of all men as portions of his own body," the Professor said. "It is one thing to regard men as spiritually of a piece; it is quite another to reckon humanity as a group ego, with a single, undifferentiated mind which can be instructed and governed as a unit, and with a form which can be fed and put to labor and pleasure as a single body. That is the superstition which sits at the center of your trouble, the hub on which infallibility and totalitarianism turn. Because the soul of the individual is all-important to the church his mind and body are of no worth. Because the soul of the state—the ideal of comfort and welfare for everyone—is all-important to Communism, the minds and bodies of the component parts of the state are of no worth. In Spain the fight is not for freedom, but for vassalage—vassalage to Rome or vassalage to Moscow. The contesting ideologies are not tides of evolution; they are ripples in the backwash. The tides have moved on; they have crossed the channel to England, and they have crossed the Atlantic to the United States.

"England is not a group ego; it is a group of individual egos, operating as a unit by free agreement, cooperating in the conduct of an orderly and profitable community so that each member, the exasperations and dangers of existence lessened for him by being dissipated among many, is free to pursue the peculiar path which in his hour and time and longing bears toward his contentment, his happiness, his dream. 'Let us work together,' says the Englishman to his fellow Englishmen, 'in order that we may leave one another alone.'

"What is true of England is true of the United States. The purpose of union and order is freedom and isolation for the individual. There are pools from the group egos of Europe in our country, but they break and run off into the earth and the patterns their cohesion made are gradually lost. There are fresh, temporary pools of individual egos forming in cities, in suburbs, in towns, on rich strata of land; but they will also break and run off into the earth—their patterns will be preserved in novels and in plays, in fashions and in figures of speech. The important thing is that no large, permanent, national pool will ever be formed, flooding the surface of our identity, giving it a single, shining face. Individual egos rain down on it, enter its earth, and nourish the profusion of differentiation which cooperatively flourishes over our landscape when the season is ripe and the weather is fair. 'Let us work together,' says the lily-of-the-valley to the maple, 'in order that we may leave one another alone.' "

"You are anticipating the fulfillment of democracy's ideal," I said. "The liberation of the individual ego from group egos has been announced in proclamation and provided for in law, but its realization is a personal accomplishment which few have achieved. The immigrant pools of group egos are breaking and running off, but pools of community, economic, genealogical, employment, educational, and religious egos take their place, and if these in turn break and run off they are replaced by others. Men do not gather together for physical security, but for the security of their identity, for the safety of their awareness and the assurance that it is real. They tell each other their thoughts and describe to those who will listen to them the shape and intensity of their pain, hoping their pain and their thoughts will find likenesses in the pain and thoughts of others, so that they will not be alone in their suffering and their contemplation. They reach eagerly for common beliefs, common enthusiasms, common doubts and anxieties, common ailments, common remedies. Doctors do not treat individuals who are ill; they treat diseases which affect various physical bodies of the group ego. Teachers do not instruct children; they guide the group ego from one stage of awareness to the next.

"Occasionally an individual ego detaches itself from the group and strikes out for itself. It feels strong enough to resist the pull of the group egos of nature, the forest and river spirits from whose enchantment it long ago fled into community with others of its kind and weakness. It is unafraid of the demons of the subconscious, the limits of the group which pose as the laws of the universe. It is attracted

272

by something which lies ahead, a strange fire leaping along the far rim of the mind. If it is able to live beyond the group and alone, if it recognizes the strange fire as the outer flame of the superconscious and is stirred to move toward it, it becomes a saint.

"That is the ultimate test of individual ego; if it is truly able to live beyond the group and alone it is ready for the journey to the superconscious; if it is not truly able to live beyond the group and alone and attempts to do so it will fall prey to the group egos of nature; it will lose its awareness, forget its identity, fall away from the moment, and walk off into a dream, becoming an eccentric, a fanatic, or a madman. Democracy as an ideal envisions a society of individuals truly able to live beyond the group ego and alone. Democracy as a reality constructs a framework of society within which individuals are free to prepare themselves for the effort to live beyond the group ego and alone, and wherein they are privileged to make the effort whenever they wish to do so. A democratic nation in theory is a collection of co-operating I's; in reality it is a pattern of interpenetrating, interdependent, constantly colliding we's. It follows, in fact, the pattern of all forms of life; it is composed of atoms, but the atoms are gathered into molecules; they do not operate independently as parts of the form in which they are incorporated."

"That," said the Professor, "is a lot of damned nonsense! I was born in this country and I have lived all my life in one or another of its towns and cities. Its communities are made up of individual egos living together for purposes which bolster, heighten, and accentuate the singularity of each. That is the genius of America and you know it, and were it not for your sullenness and frustration you would admit it. Americans are people who live together not from necessity, but from choice. It is not that they need each other but that they like each other; it is not that they depend on each other but that they enjoy helping each other. That is why, if I may quote a horrible example, you were a member of The Valley Players in the winter of 1931, and why members of your community left their homes on cold nights and paid money to see you act."

"It may be that we both are right," I said. "Movement within the group ego, a continual friction and abrasion, sharpens and strengthens the individual parts, conditioning them for expulsion. There were symbols of this in productions of

273

The Valley Players. In one of the comedies we produced I played the part of a worthless, educated cad. My wife, a fine but misguided woman, was portrayed by a lovely young thing named Helen Daly, the bride of a colleague of mine on the *Daily News*. During rehearsals she confided to me that there was an invisible member of the cast, someone who turned out to be, later on, John J. Daly, Jr.

"One of the props in the last act was a wheelbarrow filled with apples. During the second act it was rolled into position in the wings. Early in the third act Helen, after a scene with me, walked into the wings. A few speeches later she was to call me from offstage, something she had never failed to do in rehearsals. The first thing she saw when she walked into the wings was the wheelbarrow full of apples. She had been longing for an apple all that day, all the day before, and all the day before that. She took one from the pile, sat on the edge of the wheelbarrow, and began to bite. The time for my cue passed. On the stage I ad libbed with another actor. After a long minute O'Connor, the director, called to me in a high falsetto from the wrong side of the stage and I accomplished my exit. Helen was still sitting on the edge of the wheelbarrow her eyes glazed, her jaws moving steadily, a look of quiet ecstasy on her face. I sat down beside her and wondered why it had not occurred to me to say to the other actor, when my cue was missed, 'I think I'll go along after my wife.' "

"It wouldn't," the Professor said. "Your only reaction to a crisis is to ham it up."

"I determined to be more resourceful in the future," I went on, "and I was. In our next presentation I was the hero. In a scene with the heroine I demonstrated my emotional turmoil by engaging to help her with some teacups and by dropping one on the floor. The next set of speeches concerned the breaking of the cup. In dress rehearsal I dropped a cup, it struck the thin carpet covering the set, and broke.

"Next day the heroine's mother, examing the set, expressed distaste for the thin carpet. She had it removed and replaced it with a thick rug from her living room. I did not know this, and in the excitement of performing before an audience that night I failed to observe the softness and resilience of the terrain underfoot. When I dropped a cup it bounced. I picked it up, ad libbed a line, and dropped it again, this time propelling it with my fingers so that it fell with speed. Again it bounced. I picked it up, took a saucer from the table, and beat the saucer against the cup, ad libbing sounds of emotion and embarrassment, increasing the power with which I brought the cup and saucer together until, after a particularly violent collision, both broke. Then, as the heroine and I proceeded with the scene, my hands became wet. I closed my fists and embraced the heroine, pressing her to me with my wrists. The scene ended and I got into the wings before any of the blood leaked through my fingers. There was not much of it and it clotted quickly. The cuts were superficial."

"Precisely," the Professor said. "They were deep enough for melodrama but shallow enough for safety. It did not occur to you to step on the cup while it lay on the carpet. That would have been a practical act, but undramatic. It was not the solution of an Irish martyr, the man who dies a thousand times a day, the hero ever-breasting the flood of adversity, his burden constantly increased, his labors never appreciated, as on and on he struggles, and nobody cares."

"There was not a lot of that in Naugatuck during the winter of 1931," I said, "though it is found in certain types of Irish, as it is found in certain types among all peoples. Generally there was a quiet tolerance of trouble and a mutual appreciation of what peace and warmth and nourishment were left, along with a discovery that in each case the amount was considerable.

"What bothered me was the return of my predicament to its former status. I was still in Naugatuck, with Joseph in exile and with no way of escape. The memory of our temporary liberation in Virginia only made our return to confinement more painful. The failure of our effort at expression in the *Daily News* depressed us. Joseph was melancholy and I was sullen.

"The Mass we attended on Sunday was the only break in our frustration, yet its brevity and the haste with which the congregation fled the church when it was finished served to deepen our sadness and heighten our irritation rather than fasten us with peace. God labored for six days, and on the seventh He rested. The seventh day was the day of man, the time of his labor, his effort, his destiny. But man, like God, labored for six days, and on the seventh, proud of his divinity, he rested. Thus God waited for man to work out his salvation and man waited for God to accomplish the task. The situation remained static; nothing moved, nothing happened."

"What you mean," said the Professor, "is that you did nothing and that nothing happened to you. You demanded salvation on your own terms and your terms were not met. You stood on a street corner and waited for the world to translate and to glorify you."

"Perhaps I did," I said. "There was a lot of company on street corners in 1931. On cold nights the speakeasies were crowded with men who sipped whiskey, sucked at their pipes, and talked quietly of their work or their lack of work. They never knew how many days during the week the factories would allow them to labor—one, two, or three. 'I had three days last week but I've been sent home every day this week,' a man would say, and I would notice that after that when the man ordered a drink the bartender took the money the man placed on the bar and rang the cash register and put back on the bar in front of the man an assortment of coins equal to the amount he had picked up.

"One night the Kid and I left a speakeasy and walked home through a fall of snow that reached almost to our knees. We crossed the river bridge and reached the overpass of the New York, New Haven and Hartford Railroad. Normally in winter the walk below the underpass is streaked with ice, due to a steady drip from the trestle and a lack of sunlight. Kicking my way through the fresh snow I forgot this. Suddenly my feet leaped forward; I sat in the soft flakes and slid down the gentle slope of the walk into a gutter.

"It was a wonderful ride. Snow went up the legs of my trousers, up the arms of my coat, down my neck, under my hat, into my mouth and nostrils and ears and eyes, into my pockets, into my gloves, and into my shoes. The Kid came and sat down beside me in the gutter and together we laughed. It was funny, but we laughed beyond its humor. We laughed, though we did not know it then, at its symbology. It was the end of the depression for us."

The Professor snorted.

"It was the end of your concern for the suffering of others," he said. "You were tired of the melodrama of want, particularly as the action of the plot was not to your taste. Since you were young and without responsibility and basically selfish, you abandoned the situation to concentrate on your personal dilemma."

"I tasted the snow and melted it with the heat of my body, and remembered that humanity moves through the mind of God and that booms and depressions are the breathing of economics, which is a natural law domesticated to the use of man," I said. "I remembered the ultimate end of man and the penultimate act of his ego's crucifixion. I remembered certain lines from John Donne's *The Progresse of the Soule.*

> But if my dayes be long, and good enough
> In vaine this sea shall enlarge, or enrough
> It selfe; for I will through the wave, and fome,
> And shall, in sad lone wayes a lively spright,
> Make my darke heavy Poem light, and light.
> For though through many streights, and lands I roame,
> I launch at paradise, and saile towards home. . . .

"I remembered also what Elias had said about separating my humor from my metaphysics: 'Keep one in front of you all the time, as a protection; hide the others in your room, behind an incense pot.'

"I remember nothing else about that winter except the laughter of Deborah, the searing wit of O'Connor, and the voice of the Kid singing, 'Were you there when they nailed Him to the tree . . .' After these things the weather in my memory turns warm and I am walking up a street in the Bronx, looking for a house in which a policeman killed by a gangster is being waked."

"According to the record," the Professor said, "you joined the reportorial staff of the New York *Herald Tribune* in August, 1931. Your city editor was Stanley Walker. Your salary was twenty-five dollars a week. You were twenty-four years old and five feet eight inches tall. You had hazel eyes and auburn hair which was rapidly thinning. Let's stick to facts. I've seen *The Front Page* and I've read about James Gordon Bennett and Adolph Ochs. I am acquainted with the legend which newspapermen, dedicated to the exposition of truth, have shamelessly fastened on their profession.

"As a reporter in what is variously called, by your colleagues, Bagdad-on-the-Subway, modern Babylon, Gotham, the Big Town—why do you wince?—you accomplished the dream of every street corner loafer and every town gossip. You were able to attend accidents, parades, trials, funerals, political rallies, banquets, receptions for distinguished guests, fires, celebrations, inaugural ceremonies, and all the other festivities and catastrophes which attract the curious, the idle, and the rude. Once on the scene you were privileged to push up front, ask questions, and generally make a nuisance of yourself. Afterward it was your duty to describe what transpired, and this description was printed next day in a newspaper read by several hundred thousand people. Now and then your name, in large type, preceded the description, thus proclaiming you as its author. You were therefore not only paid to pursue the life of a morbidly curious vagrant, you were respected and publicized as such a purposely worthless person.

"You were sent to interview politicians, men and women of letters and the arts, murderers, musicians, taxi drivers, centenarians, eccentrics, gifted children, subway guards, and others whose opinions were considered of value and interest. You met ships and trains, wrote obituaries, listened to sermons, attended meetings, visited the zoo, talked to widows and other victims of misfortune, and generally participated in the foam of each day's wave of events. Every assignment was fresh and different, but all were expeditions of impudence, purposely planned to fit the talents of a Paul Pry. I am sure it made no difference whether you were sent to the Bronx or the Barbizon-Plaza, the Lower East Side or the Waldorf Astoria; so long as you were meddling in someone's private life you were happy."

"No," I said, "it did not matter where I was sent or what I was asked to do, any more than it mattered what I wore, when I ate, or whether I slept. During that August of 1931 and throughout the year which followed I was sustained above what happened to my body and what took place in my mind by an immanence which shone from the quiet lying underneath my being, beyond Joseph and far away from me. Its radiance penetrated and strengthened my aura, so that everything which approached was softened and made pleasant before it reached me. Nothing could injure me, nothing could make me unhappy. I was in a community at the edge of the group egos, where individuals who desired to live beyond the groups and alone gathered to test themselves for the strike into personal identity. They were free of the rub and mutter of their inherited and environmental patterns; they were like molecules thrown off from heated water, soaring into a form less dense, moving in a freer sphere. Nothing held them now but their own limitations—their own courage, their own vitality, their own talents.

278

"There was an illusion that time and space had been conquered; everything seemed to happen in New York, everyone seemed to come to New York. Here the frontier of the mind of man was slowly pushed back; here the barriers of understanding and accomplishment were constantly assaulted; here the pioneers of identity, recognition, and realization came to report their discoveries, organize fresh safaris, compare experiences, publish observations, refurbish their courage, and inspire others to ape their daring. Here the suburbs of knowledge, skill, tolerance, understanding and charity grew steadily larger and pushed resolutely in new directions. Here the archetype of America grew, studied, labored, and was nourished, taking into itself the egos of those who broke from the groups, feeding on them, reflecting their essence."

"Oh, rubbish!" the Professor said. "New York is a brawling metropolis of seven million people, not one of whom knows why the city exists, any more than you do. Manhattan reflects America in its immigrants, its skyscrapers, its unlimited opportunities for success, its appreciation of talent, its tolerance of all people and all philosophies, its fantastic wealth, its conglomerate population, its casual acceptance of leadership among cities of the world, its concern with and delight in changeability, its mixture of practicality and daring, cynicism and naïveté, shrewdness and idealism. The best of our young people go there and it uses their intelligence and vigor in giving back to us our culture, such as it is—our costumes, our opinions, our literature, our fashions in prejudice and humor and aspiration. It is the Big Town. It runs us. It dominates our ambitions and certifies our accomplishments.

"It does not house our archetype, it reflects it; the image is distorted, magnified, and mounted on a scaffold illuminated by alternate teams of electric bulbs. As Americans we do not achieve success or fail to achieve success; we achieve success in New York or we fail to achieve success in New York. The standards are high, the rewards are large, the initial price to the aspirant is his integrity. There is nothing spiritual in the process and the ego is never strengthened, it is only expanded.

"Let us stick to facts. You joined a profession which fits square pegs into round holes, which utilizes some of the most debilitating characteristics native to the human pattern. You wandered about the town poking your nose into other people's business, and you did it for pay. You acquired a knowledge of Manhattan's geography, an acquaintance with

279

her police and politicians, a friendship with her restaurants, an ease with her people and her greatness. You ate and drank at Jack Bleeck's Artists and Writers Club with men from your office, reporters from the *Times,* editors of *The New Yorker,* and decent men of more honorable callings who behaved well and did not charge their drinks against next week's pay check. After a time you came to fancy yourself quite a fellow. The chameleon of your vanity, having lost the hue of Lexington, with its high lights from the great minds of history, took on the coruscating color of New York, accepting the dimensions of the city's intelligence and wealth as the measurements of your personal worth.

"Our problem concerns the connection between your mind and your body. It has nothing to do with your career as a reporter, particularly since your thoughts at that time were not inhibited by the editorials which appeared in your newspaper and your body was not damaged in line of duty. Let us get on with the job. You can paint the glamour of those years later, in a book for students of journalism, God pity them."

"There is not much to paint," I said, "and the colors are not bright. The glow which comes from them is a reflection of my personal content. The *Herald Tribune* building on West Forty-first Street seemed to exist in 1931 more in my mind than in reality. What you have said is true—I could not imagine being paid for what I did; it had to be a dream, in a place beyond life, where desires, for the sake of faith, are fed for a while on honey. I sat at my typewriter in the city room and watched the process by which the reflection of the community and national and international archetypes is each day assembled, and I thought to myself, 'This is a fine thing and I am a fine fellow to be part of it.'

"Each afternoon the staff assembled at half past one and received its assignments. Activity among group and individual egos in the community was scrutinized by the city editor and his assistants, and reporters were dispatched to observe the more alarming, significant, tragic, humorous, and traditional manifestations. Toward night the reporters returned, opened their typewriters, and wrote in compressed, stylized prose, careful accounts of what they had discovered. Meanwhile cable and telegraph editors sorted and edited dispatches from domestic localities and foreign capitals. Members of the editorial staff finished their essays of opinion, sports writers came back from the ball games, and the drama critic decided which of the plays scheduled to open that night most deserved his attention. By seven o'clock a hum of planned frenzy filled the large room; the vibrations gathered around my spine and shook me with pleasure. Deadline for the first edition was nine o'clock; at eleven the presses turned. A few minutes later copies of the next day's paper were being piled into trucks. Reporters sitting in Bleeck's saw their stories in print before their dinners were finished.

"Sometimes I walked down to the pressroom and watched the paper being printed—editions were run off each hour from eleven until two the next morning. More often I went into the library at the west end of the city room and browsed among the encyclopedias, prepared obituaries, dictionaries of biography, and the thousands of envelopes of clippings, each containing the newspaper record of a man or woman or organization or movement or disease or holiday or nation or animal or disaster. Dozens of copies of the paper were cut up each day by the library staff; every story printed, however brief, was filed under the names mentioned in it and the human disturbance it described. Thus the initial steps in translating happening to history were accomplished: reporters converted occurrences into chronicles, editors arranged the chronicles in general contemporaneous patterns, librarians broke the general contemporaneous patterns and rearranged the chronicles in specific biographical journals.

"Reporters constantly referred to the cross-indexed clippings for background on their assignments. On dull afternoons the city editor's small, nervous figure prowled among the green steel files, threading together association and remembrance and circumstance, weaving from what had happened notions of what might occur. Editorial writers sat at tables, patiently examining the public records of politicians. Once I looked up from a volume of the *Catholic Encyclopedia* and found Geoffrey Parsons, our chief editorial writer, staring at me but not seeing me, his eyes jarred from focus by something in his mind. It was near the time of an election in Germany. Before him on the table were half a dozen envelopes of clippings, bearing such names as Paul von Hindenburg, Adolf Hitler . . ."

"Precisely," the Professor said, "and forgive me for interrupting. You are determined to recite the story of your romance with the *Herald Tribune* down to the final vulgar and perfumed details, the dousing of the boudoir light and the rustling of silk being shed in the dark. I am determined not to listen. I shall merely enter in my notes at this point: *et cetera, ad infinitum, ad nauseam."*

He stared coldly at Miss Iceberg. She looked at me.

"Please try not to roll your head," she said.

SEVENTEEN

WHEN the fever was gone again I lay in my room in the dark and counted the streets south and east to the place where first I lived in New York, a brownstone house at 35 East Twenty-second Street. On the second floor in the two front rooms, paying six dollars each every week for rent, were three art students, one of them Marion Junkin, a Washington and Lee graduate and a resident of Lexington. The others were Frank Crittenden, who came from Georgia, and Bob Skemp, a Pittsburg boy who liked to draw ships and cowboys. Crittenden and Junkin had studied under George Luks, whose studio was down the street a few doors toward Broadway. They painted in the front room each morning; from four in the afternoon until midnight they worked as cashiers in Childs restaurants. Skemp was apprenticed to a successful painter named Charles Baskerville. There was not space in the rooms for another art student with his easel and canvases and brushes and palette and rags and turpentine and temperament, but since my only equipment was a typewriter, and since I did not go to work until afternoon and was available in the morning for posing, I was welcomed.

Crittenden and Junkin were deep in the Luks technique of painting; they lunged at the canvas, used a lot of paint, and labored to put humor into their subjects. They got up early enough to work in the morning light and usually I got up with them. We ate breakfast in an Automat; toward pay day we sometimes had to pool our funds so that all three could be nourished. Once in a while on pay day I had no money at all; then I slept late and did not eat until the pay

282

envelopes were distributed. As a result of these occasional fasts I discovered a fact disconcerting but not serious: I was afflicted with hyperinsulinism, which kept my sugar reserves burned up and was apt to make the missing of a meal a nutritional crisis.

After breakfast we worked steadily for several hours. Often I looked up from my typewriter and found that I was being sketched by one or both of the artists. Later fresh fruit would be painted over me, or a nude woman—models were hired with pooled funds and treated with icy courtesy—or one of the female members of the Callaway family of Georgia; there were a lot of them, they were pretty, and they were in town often.

We did not talk while we worked, but at breakfast and very early in the morning as we sat around the fireplace we discussed interminably the problems of genius, self-expression, discipline, artistic integrity, form, style, aesthetic, and the future of honesty in any field of creative effort. Junkin, son of a Presbyterian missionary, was a disciplinarian; he followed the yoga technique of pouring the greatest possible force into the smallest possible opening; he put all the effort of his being into the execution of his canvases, and nothing that was not basic to existence or imperatively necessary was allowed to dip into his energy. Crittenden was quiet and inclined to dream; he had a shy smile and hummed to himself. His painting, despite the Luks technique, edged toward softness; his subjects had auras, peripheral fields of color which perhaps he saw when he looked at them. Both boys were dissatisfied with whatever was finished; each new canvas was an experiment, a search for further skill and fresh understanding. At my typewriter I practiced paragraph architectonics and sentence patterns, testing words for rhythm values and osmotic strength.

Because my word arrangements were already in commercial use Junkin and Crittenden were inclined to theorize that my integrity as a writer could dwell unharmed in a dichotomy whereby the shallow end of my mind made a living in journalism while the deep waters worked to express themselves in literature. They did not believe, on the other hand, that they, as artists, could engage in magazine and advertising illustration without losing their ability to paint in the pure, uncompromising fashion of fine art. When a painter compromised his style, they said, he compromised his art; with a writer this was not so.

So long as my writing was reportorial I agreed with them, since art is only reporting in depth, with interpretation gradually added to observation. My stories in the *Herald Tribune* were like their paintings of New York streets and back-yard groups; they were observations of contemporaneity without interpretation, but with accent, accent provided by arrangements of fact and choice of words. Junkin and Crittenden achieved accent by arrangement of objects and selection of color. My writing and their painting would continue to be reportorial, gaining depth and adding interpretation; my writing, like their painting, could lose its integrity by departing from reporting to concern itself with deliberate untruth. One form of deliberate untruth was popular magazine fiction; it employed a formula diametrically opposed to the normal pattern of human behavior, a formula dedicated to romance, mariolatry, and the proposition that conflict between the sexes precedes rather than follows marriage, and is ended rather than begun by the virgin's sacrifice to life's need for amplification and continuation. I could not write such fiction any more than Junkin and Crittenden could illustrate it; I proved that I could not write it; I tried seriously again and again—a few hundred dollars in 1931 would have cleansed a lot of anxiety. Every effort ended in burlesque; humor pointed out the unreality of everything I set down. I sat at my typewriter in the mornings and wrote:

She was the sort of girl who went in one ventricle and out the other, and sometimes she wondered why. She had a little thing she said to her dates when they were slow in reaching for her left hand, the one she kept soft and perfumed and, as she confided to her intimates, "handy." "Don't be a smartery," she would say to her escort. "Let me in your artery." One day she met a tall, apparently impregnable young man from Mississippi, and as she sat beside him in the front seat of his handsome automobile a basin of warmth spilled over inside her and she realized that she was in love. She did not know—she could not have known —that some of the best blood in the South had turned to water in his veins. She never drank water except with whiskey. Later she died of acute alcoholism.

There was once a young man who above all things in the world wished passionately to meet a pure and handsome woman and to win her love and devotion. He met many passionate women who offered him love without devotion, but these he refused. One day as hope seeped from him like blood working its way through a bandage he heard a woman say to a beautiful, thin, quiet girl, "Who is freezing to death in your heart now?" The girl did not answer her tormentor, and the young man said to himself, "She is the one for me; she is pure," and he went to her, feeling like a message which at last has been delivered. They were married, and on their wedding night, lying beside her, he shook himself to death. He died, the coroner said, of exposure.

Terry Fleglip leaped up the steps of the Avonend Country Club and walked straight to her father, who was sitting on the porch. Elihu Fleglip was a writer whose talent was too small to be neglected, and he was therefore enormously rich.

"Pa," said Terry, "that dirty little snot Francie Pingwhup is saying nasty things about me again, and so is everyone else at the club."

"Pour the poison of gossip into a single ear," said her father, "and it comes out through a hundred mouths."

Terry gave him a look which slit his poise from ear to ear. Then she turned to her mother, who was drunk. She bent and gazed imploringly into the countenance of her dam.

"Who the hell are you?" said Mrs. Fleglip.

In the basement of the adjoining brownstone there was an Italian restaurant which served an excellent meal for seventy-five cents and which sold a bottle of passable red wine for a dollar. Its proprietor was a young Roman named Mario who longed to sing in grand opera. His best customer was an editor of encyclopedias, a Scotsman who spoke twenty languages and who drank two bottles of wine every night. At ten o'clock Mario locked the front door, served free wine to the patrons who remained, and sang. Once on his day off Junkin sat with the Scotsman and me while Mario performed. Later, when we returned to the front room, he said gloomily, "I suppose that's the way it will be with me; I'll run a restaurant and bribe the customers to look at my paintings." I knew that would never happen to him—he had too much talent and too much drive—but I said, "Mario is a very happy man. He sings for anyone who will listen and he need only be concerned with pleasing himself. If five thousand people had heard him tonight and applauded his singing, the important thing would still be that Mario expressed himself. A larger audience would have strengthened his pride, but not his spirit."

Junkin groaned. "I knew I would never be able to escape theology," he said. "I ran away from Calvin and bumped into Aquinas."

We sat in silence.

"Even Shakespeare," I said, "gained more for his soul from the writing of his plays than has been gathered from them in understanding and perception by all who have read them since his time and all who have seen them performed."

Junkin shook his head. His eyelids drooped and Calvinistic rebuttals gathered on his brow.

"It was already gained," he said, "or the plays could not have been written. The writing of the plays was the act of passing the understanding and perception on to others. That is the painful thing about being an artist, the compulsion to externalize in a form which is recognizable to others an understanding and perception which are abstract, nebulous, and personal. If the understanding and perception could be endured without expression they would be a source of happiness to their possessor."

We were silent again. Then I said, "It is the difficulty of obeying the compulsion which causes pain. It is not easy to imitate creation. First of all the matter of it must be exorcised from the subconscious, from both personal and impersonal memory, by meditation. Whether the patterns in which it appears to our self-consciousness represent a system of order and reason in the subconscious we do not know, but for our self-consciousness the patterns are unsatisfactory. They do not conform to the systems of association, chronology, and intensity by which the self-consciousness devises judgments of logic and wisdom and beauty. It is the task of the self-consciousness to discern in the exorcised patterns the understanding and perception of multiple dimensionality, and to translate this understanding and this perception into new patterns, patterns common to three-dimensionality but immanent with the understanding and perception of multiple dimensionality."

Junkin's eyes were almost closed. "Simplify it," he said. "Simplify it."

"It is the basic operation of creation," I said. "A skilled, purposeful awareness translates raw force into simple patterns of energy, then into complex designs. Following each operation with a logical successor it crystallizes groups of designs into primitive centers of awareness, which in turn begin to shape raw force into simple patterns of energy: the raw force is observation, the simple patterns of energy are images, songs, stories. The primitive centers of awareness grow in the image of the primary awareness which formed them, and seek to imitate the skill and purpose of that primary awareness."

"Simplify it, simplify," Junkin said. His eyes were completely closed.

"It is the actual labor of creation which is difficult and painful," I said. "Dreaming about it, imagining it, understanding its purpose and glimpsing its goal, are easy. It is the accomplishment which tires the body, disappoints the mind, and frustrates the ego—the ego puts up the original investment of vitality and perseverance and its expects a quick and handsome return. Creation for man is a long, tedious, involved, enervating task, and its finish invariably is a combination of satisfaction and dissatisfaction, blended, like a woman's body, in a manner calculated to halt him with pleasure briefly and then to send him on to another of its kind.

"But consider the body of this next woman, this next creative goal. First glimpsed, first desired, it projects the illusion of perfection and the sequential notion that embracing it will achieve participation in that perfection. In imagination the embrace is quickly achieved: the woman's robes fall from her and her face is lifted up to yours with a look of drowsy, joyful surrender. But in actuality the embrace is far away and a wilderness of difficult labor and deliberate postponement lies before it. The woman must be met, she must be courted, she must be entertained, flattered, plied with gifts, deluged with demonstrations of esteem, decorated with corsages, salved with courtesies. Her confidence must be won, then her affection, then her love. When all this is achieved the embrace is attained, but it is only somewhat as it was imagined to be; it has a surface more harsh and an edge more rough than sight could discern in a dream. But there is another woman, with another body, a soft and luminous body, not far beyond, at the rim of another wilderness, and in imagination her robes fall easily from her and her face is lifted up with a look of drowsy, joyful surrender."

Junkin opened his eyes, turned back his head, and laughed.

"That's simple enough," he said, "but remember that the time of joy is when the woman begins to give you her trust and affection. That is when you are past the spade work, in the midst of anticipation, but not at the climax. For me there is a period when each canvas is going to achieve just what I planned for it; that is when I am happy. It is the period just before I finish, before I make the last brush stroke and realize the truth of the old football motto: Practice doesn't make you perfect, it just makes you better."

We were quiet again. Then I said, "I suppose art is the step before mystical contemplation. By successive stages we fear, placate, worship, bribe, implore, and explain God. Then, in the creative processes of our arts, we imitate Him. Finally we seek Him. The ego reaches its peak in the imitative period, realizes its limitations and its inadequacy, and takes on the humility which precedes crucifixion. It is worth the effort to become a great artist if the reward is true humility."

Junkin leaned forward in his chair.

"What else is there to do but try," he said, "when you can't live with yourself if you don't?"

As a reporter I exorcised the matter of my prose from the people I interviewed and the events I investigated. There were sometimes more facts than I needed for a tidy piece, sometimes not enough. Riding back to Times Square on the subway I assembled the first paragraph, or lead, in my mind, gathering the facts which had to be included, arranging and rearranging them for rhythm and emphasis, setting them in motion by inserting the vibrating little Anglo-Saxon words which, with the pentameter line, make up the genius of the English language. When I walked into the city room I was ready to write: Mrs. Elphine Dishue at 2:30 P.M. yesterday struck once at her husband Artifact with a twenty-five cent kitchen knife as they fought in the parlor of their three room apartment at 879 316th Street, and stabbed him in the heart. He was dead when police from the West 312th Street Station under Sergeant Costello O'Toole, answering a complaint of excessive noise, arrived. Mrs. Dishue was held on a charge of disorderly conduct. "I meant to cut his ears off," she told reporters. "I always was a lousy shot."

Normally the facts of a happening accumulated their own attitude. Humor, like a vapor always present in the air, seeped into a number of stories, testifying that life, like a maiden's prayer, proceeds toward God at a slightly ridiculous angle. The city editor found that I did this type of assignment well, and that I also had a gentle touch with funerals. Things that were either dead or funny were set aside for me. Apparently what I hid in my room behind an incense pot was not well concealed. Once the city editor, introducing me in Bleeck's to a Hollywood writer, said, "He's all right but I suspect he's a mystic."

On a Saturday in the winter of 1932 I covered the annual luncheon of a society of middle-aged men and women who every other year went somewhere together on a cruise, meanwhile accumulating passage money by a system of dues. The luncheon cost five dollars a plate. I sat at the press table and watched the members pick at their food; much of what was served they left untouched. All of them were overweight. While the program of speeches proceeded they listened politely, eructating gently. When their president, a female, stepped to the rostrum, they applauded. She smiled on them and announced that the 1932 cruise would take them through the Panama Canal and north to Hollywood. She congratulated the members on their faithfulness and regularity in the matter of paying dues. She spoke modestly of her executive duties.

"I think of myself as a little dynamo," she said, "and you are my dear electric bulbs. I send out a message and you are lighted up by its news."

When I returned to the office another assignment was given me before I had time to hoist the cruise society on its president's petard. A baby was dead in Hell's Kitchen, poisoned by food from the city's home relief agency. I walked to the address; it was in the West Fifties near Ninth Avenue. The family lived in a rear flat on the third floor of a tenement. An Irish policeman with blue eyes and black hair was sitting quietly in the kitchen. The father of the dead child, an unemployed bellhop, paced back and forth between the sink and the stove. He answered my questions. His son, eighteen months old, was dead. His daughter, three years old, was at Polyclinic Hospital; his wife was with her. There had been nothing in the flat to eat that morning but a can of Argentina corned beef, the last of the supplies

289

received by the family from the home relief agency. It was fed to the children; the parents ate nothing. Very soon the baby became ill, and while the father went for a doctor the daughter doubled up with pain.

"I can't stay here any longer," the father said when I put down my pencil. "I can't stand the waiting. I'm going to the hospital."

When he was gone the policeman and I sat without talking while I went over my notes and drew a line to separate the facts of the baby's death from the cruise society's luncheon. When I looked up the policeman was staring at me, his eyes very wide. He got up and walked to a bedroom and beckoned to me. I followed him and he pointed to a crib where a small purple body lay. When we were in the kitchen again he said, "I thought you ought to see him, so you can put the details in your story. If I was your editor I'd print it on the front page in letters a foot high."

"We're saving that big type for the second coming of Warren Gamaliel Harding," I said.

"I'm ashamed of myself," the policeman said. "I'm ashamed of myself before God for that poor dead little fellow."

Back at the *Herald Tribune* I said to the city editor, "Can't these stories be run side by side—the five dollar luncheon and the baby who died of poisoned food from the home relief agency?" He smiled at me, and for the first and last time in my service under him I saw him look wistful. "I'd love to do it," he said, "but this a newspaper and I'm an editor and you're a reporter. Just write hell out of both stories and try not to hate yourself for being alive and well fed."

I wrote hell out of both stories. I labored over a half column describing the cruise society's luncheon until venom dripped from every syllable. I worked on a column describing the baby's death until fingers of accusation pointed from every phrase. One story appeared on page five, the other on page thirty-six. About and between them, running through the pages like a stream of rectangles, were the other news stories of the day, clustered according to their subject, sweeping through the supplements in a cunningly planned pattern which kept the postures and pretense separated from the facts and failures. Each page had its eyes lowered, lest it see what preceded it and what followed, for though almost every story was a faucet pouring forth an effect of the

290

basic sin of the economic system, the trapping of man in time, in the service of the sin and for the sake of its perpetuation each pretended not only that the others did not exist, but that it did not exist itself.

Conditions and situations were declared to be the illusions of unreliable clairvoyants, the fears of radical alarmists, the apprehensions of timid defeatists. Hunger was treated as an isolated phenomenon, a misfortune which struck one person at a time, and for personal reasons. A murder was reported as if murder had never before been done, as if Cain had only yesterday, in a speakeasy on the Upper East Side, struck Abel. The past, except for the sinking of the *Titanic,* the blizzard of '88, and various conflagrations on excursion steamers, was regarded as a happy and almost perfect time. The future was expected to brink the millennium—tomorrow no one would die, or go hungry, or be murdered. Only the moment was troublesome.

It was taken for granted that readers of the newspaper were concerned solely with the best in music, the theater, books, and the graphic arts, and the best was described for them by the best critics. The society page told nothing of the coupling of common folk; it listed only the matings of blooded stock, males and females bred for income, holdings, and genealogy. Such men as died at a "good" address were announced on the obituary page, with their directorships, their ancestors, and their survivors prominently mentioned. Banquets and ship sailings were celebrated in print, along with holidays, the birthdays of dead heroes, the rites of spring, conventions, meetings of indignation, funerals of prominent citizens, testimonials to politicians being retired for senility or theft, and gatherings of ecclesiastics at which the sufferings of man were delineated and the perversity of man blamed for them. The reports of all such occasions listed the important people present and spelled their names correctly, with titles before or after and mates in their proper places. No matter what happened the reader of the *Herald Tribune* woke up with his hat on.

All this was what we wanted to be, what we pretended to be, what we hoped others would believe we were—borrowed music, derivative and imitative art, literature seminally rich, cerebrally promiscuous, and spiritually barren. Radio, the fertile, unmoral actuality of our culture, the common denominator of the archetype, was ignored; its programs were announced on a back page and no critic appreciated them.

291

Radio denied the sophistication which strutted through the rest of the paper; radio exposed our national taste for what it was—low, bathetic, and solidly common. It was, I thought, the best thing which had happened to America since the indifference of Howe and Cornwallis. The culture which some citizens, certain newspapers, and a few magazines pretended was a possession of the people was definitely shown by radio to be the property of a vigorous and individualistic few. The culture of the nation was lounging against a fence, chewing a blade of sweetgrass, strumming a guitar, humming a hymn in celebration of the discovery that man is sexed without season, made for pleasure as well as for labor and sleep. Radio, its vast electrical anatomy hired out for keep and concubinage to advertising, knew this; it would always, in fact, by the nature of its function, know where our culture was, and would supply unto surfeit what it wanted, and would therefore stimulate its taste buds to hunger for new titillations, to seek among savors for rare and subtle veins. Radio was a clinical thermometer kept always under the nation's tongue. "In ten years we'll all be working for it," said John Lardner, the reporter who sat next to me in the city room.

The news, penance and purgatory for our obstinacy in sin, ran across the top half of the paper's inner pages. Along the bottom half and creeping up the far side were the pleasures of our deadly transgression, the advertisements setting forth what money could buy. Most of these purchasables were for women, and the majority were appurtenances of plumage—fur coats, dinner gowns, breast harness, aphrodisiacal underwear, jewelry, silk stockings, girdles, perfume, shoes, and nightgowns as foreign to sleep as a maiden at moonrise. Unbelievably beautiful young ladies exhibited the merchandise in sketches and photographs, each model artfully displaying the new secondary sexual characteristic she had been developing for the last decade, her legs. The top of the page usually balanced the bottom: the temptation, the consummation, and the consequences of the sin were on view together; you paid your money, took your choice, and got your just deserts. Everyone looked at the bottom of the page, wanted what he saw, and hoped to obtain it without the penalties listed above.

There was news of the churches here and there in the paper; religion was treated respectfully, noncommittally, and with neither vigor nor humor, as were certain rich old men who had stolen fortunes and were now, in their dotage, turned pious. Seldom was there mention of prohibition, the curious law which came into existence because of sanitation. When water was for reasons of health unsafe to drink children were given small beer and mild wine with their meals. After civic progress cleansed the wells, built reservoirs, and installed plumbing, water was declared the only liquid fit for the human body. Alcoholic beverages, no longer fundamental to civilized existence, became, like religion, a special taste. Large quantities of whiskey habitually placed inside a working man reduced his efficiency and worth as an economic unit. Drunkenness, hitherto merely questionable from a standpoint of good manners, was proclaimed immoral. As gluttony it was already listed, in yoke with lechery and sloth, among the Seven Deadly Sins. It now took on a new and proud significance, an importance among evils so great that measures were taken to save men from it. Alcohol, its cause and sustenance, was exiled, banished by law from the land.

Prohibition was like forbidding sexual intercourse in marriage, lest ecstasy seize upon too many and a plethora of babies smite the land; the law had no more chance of success than would attend such a mating ban. By decree it extinguished the most delicate uses to which grapes and grain had been put by man. The entire population of the country set out to quietly, persistently, and good-humoredly drink it into oblivion. The movement became a crusade; women and children joined it, and the aged and infirm.

It was a chore to perform the labors of the crusade— bootleg whiskey, gin, beer, and wine were equally unpalatable, and had to be imbibed with the firm purpose of taking in a maximum of liquid and demonstrating a minimum of effect. The first time I drank Manhattan cocktails, at the insistence of a reporter back from Hollywood with a fur coat and a Rolls-Royce, I remember lifting the fourth round from the bar. When the glass reached my lips it had turned into a spoon. I was sitting at the press table in a banquet room of the Knights of Columbus building in Brooklyn, drinking soup. A pretty girl sat on my right. I turned to the reporter on my left and said, "Who's the dame?" His eyes widened. "Don't you know?" he said. "You brought her."

It was true. She told me about it later. I stepped off a subway train at Eighth Street and asked her to help me get to Brooklyn, where I had an assignment. I had been on four trains and each one had returned me to Times Square. She explained that they were South Ferry trains, which do not go to Brooklyn but loop around and around Manhattan Island. She lived in Brooklyn and was on her way home. She would take me with her.

"You insisted that I have dinner with you," she said, "and I accepted and here we are. After the speeches you can escort me home and tomorrow you can take the pledge."

But prohibition was the only crusade in which the people as a whole were engaged, and it was a fight for a sign, not a reality. The essence of grape and grain is a symbol of spirituality, the blood of creation: too much of it pitches a man back to his subconscious and even beyond it; enough of it opens the wells of longing and rubs at the soul's desire. What I wanted was a crusade which would keep open the wells of longing and build the abrasion of the soul's desire into a raw and immediate passion. There was no such crusade; there was only a lust for security, for flesh, for possessions, for separation from responsibility, and for forgetfulness of the circling periphery of death.

EIGHTEEN

WHEN I finished reading the paper that Sunday morning in the winter of 1932 I went, as I did each Sunday morning, to Saint Patrick's Cathedral at Fiftieth Street and Fifth Avenue, seat of the archdiocese of New York, the largest and richest see in the Roman Catholic world, to cover the eleven o'clock solemn high Mass, at which Patrick Cardinal Hayes presided. The service lasted ninety minutes, only twenty of which were consumed by the sermon. Seventy minutes were given to the mystery. When the Host was raised light fell down to it from the reredos and rolled over the altar steps, through the rail and along the aisles, touching in its soft descent the prostrate Cardinal, the sanctuary boys behind him, the kneeling nuns in the early pews, the congregation, the bowed heads of the ushers, the gleaming coins on the money tables beyond the benches; each outward succeeding ring from the immanent hub of the mystery to its hard periphery was brushed, softened, and illuminated.

This in that time and in that year was my church. The money on the tables in the vestibule was illegal; it was an offense against canon law to charge a fee for attendance at Mass; under the guise of pew rent the practice was condoned throughout the American hierarchy. In the great Gothic cathedral, architecturally perfect, carvernously beautiful, three thousand people could sit, a thousand more could stand. Hanging from a wall was a rack three feet high and two feet wide; in it were various pamphlets on aspects of the faith, written at a level somewhat beneath the twelve-year-old mind, for sale at a price less than the admission fee for Mass. In all the vast masonry which filled the block from Fifty to Fifty-first Street between Fifth Avenue and Madison Avenue there was no place where a man might find a book or a priest to whom, without bending his knee in Confession, he could talk. There were no libraries, lecture rooms or meeting places, no priests learned in law and medicine waiting to advise the poor who were stricken and beset.

Behind the cathedral, facing Madison Avenue, were the rectory and the Cardinal's residence. Reporters were never allowed in the Cardinal's residence; in the rectory they were let into the reception hall, and sometimes they were taken into one of the sitting rooms. Their questions were received with smiles of tolerance and answered with evasions. The rector disliked the public press; it was, in his opinion, ignorant and inaccurate. He himself was an historian; he knew a lot of dates. He and his staff delivered, each Sunday, sermons which began with daring observations of fact, moved into traditional designs of logic, settled on a base of dogma, and melted gradually into desuetude. Sometimes visiting priests, noted for their oratorical talents, talked at the solemn high Mass.

One, a handsome young man, did not leave the church when his sermon was done. Fifty minutes later, when parts of the dissolving congregation flowed into the curve behind the main altar, he was to be found pacing back and forth before the Lady Chapel, a cape flung carelessly over his shoulders, a breviary in his hand. He always seemed startled when admirers, most of them women, surrounded him. He always had a copy of his sermon handy, and he was willing to point out for me its important sections. In the pulpit he proceeded from one point of logic to another until his objective was in view; then, taking off from his last syllogism, he flew to his goal on the wings of emotion. I searched the texts he gave me for hidden steps of logic, but none were there. I found it difficult to explain to him that the *Herald Tribune* could not report in its Monday editions that a flight of emotion was the most important event transpiring at Saint Patrick's Cathedral on Sunday.

The prince of the archdiocese was known as the Cardinal of Charities, a designation which might have implied a lack of the favorite virtue of Saint Paul in the Sacred College heretofore had it not been so obviously an admission that the spiritual leader of the wealthiest congregation in the world was offering his labors as a penance for the sin of economics in which the faithful under his care were entangled. When Christians engage the majority of their labors in a condoned connivance with evil, a deliberate delay of spiritual advancement, an obstinate refusal to move forward toward God, charity becomes an anaesthetic for the conscience. Catholic Charities in New York, organized by Cardinal Hayes, himself a native of the Lower East Side, raised a million dollars each spring. During the remainder of the year social workers distributed the money among the worthy (sic) poor. You wrote your check in April and you were free in your mind and heart in May when you marched in the Communion breakfast parades, in August when you took your vacation and stayed an extra week at the beach, in October when you attended the World Series, at Christmas when you gave your wife a mink coat and took her to Midnight Mass. Salvation for you was certain, a lead pipe cinch. You had only to fill out the forms, send the money, attend Mass on Sundays and holy days of obligation, abstain from serious sin, and take the sacraments once during the Easter Season.

When I left the cathedral after solemn Mass there was a sucking heaviness in my mind, and if the weather was fair I walked down Fifth Avenue to build up a leaven. I bought a gardenia from the old woman in front of Saks and pinned it to my lapel. I stopped to examine the books in Scribner's and crossed the street to browse along the windows of Brentano's. I looked at the lions lying before the public library at Forty-second Street. I admired the dignity and the quiet of the bums in Bryant Park. By the time I reached the office I felt less grieved. The proper part of me was showing; the rest, the larger portion, was hidden.

But the dichotomy now was more difficult to maintain; it caused a pressure in my head and a stiffness in my neck. It was an unnatural state, and because now in New York it had to be enforced only in certain situations and with certain people the effort to bring it about produced physical tension and nervous irritability. As often as possible, even in the city room, I released myself from it, bending over a book or a sheaf of clippings while I let down the barriers of my awareness and allowed Joseph to pour in. Then together we dreamed of a warm, bright morning when men and women in great companies set forth from the outpost of the group egos toward the faraway flaming rim of the superconscious; together we pictured a cold November dusk when priests went into the streets seeking those who were homeless and hungry and took them into the cathedral to be fed and warmed, and taught them, while they rested, the anatomy of the mystery; together we envisioned a meeting of theologians, scientists, philosophers, poets and lay representatives of all Christian sects and all monotheistic religions, a meeting which went on month after month, year after year, while truth was sought and unity planned and tolerance proclaimed and practiced, while in the assembly room of the delegates a tall candle burned continually before an altar into which was cut the legend: There Is But One God; Seek Him.

One day as I sat looking at a thesaurus, not seeing its pages, the presence of someone near me circled my awareness and moved in toward its center. I set in motion the effort to restore dichotomy but it was hardly begun when I raised my head and saw an enormous pair of brown eyes staring at me from an incredibly delicate face, the face of a young woman. The eyes were warm, like the turned turf of a field in a spring sun at noon. Under them a slender mouth had moved a fraction of an inch beyond the dimensions of the Mona Lisa smile. The young woman seemed as perishable as the Cheshire cat, but less real.

"I understand you would like to review books," she said.

"Yes," I said, "I would."

"I will send you one," she said.

Then she was gone. By the time my dichotomy was restored I realized the young woman's head had not been attached to a body, and that the happening was an illusion. But later that day I received a book from the review section on the eleventh floor, and clipped to its dust jacket was a note from Belle Rosenbaum, assistant to Irita Van Doren, the review section's editor. Was Belle the head? Were hers the large eyes, the slender mouth? More books were sent to me, and one day I went to the eleventh floor, pretending I was confused about the deadline for a particular review. The young woman's head was there, behind a desk, and the young woman was indeed Belle Rosenbaum. In an adjoining office Mrs. Van Doren, slimmer by half than the chair on which she sat, looked up from a sheaf of galleys and washed me with a smile. The only visible human solid was Lewis Gannett, the daily reviewer, who sat in a corner office with his shoes off, his feet on the opened lower drawer of his desk, a pencil in his mouth, his eyes sweeping through someone's prose like a scythe cutting August wheat. When I returned to the fifth floor I realized that the head named Belle still had, for me, no body. Over the years she grew one, beginning with shoulders and working downward, but it was not until I met her one day on Fifth Avenue that she acquired legs and feet. I realized then how wonderful it is to fall in love with a woman from the top down; I realized, in fact, that there is no other way in which to fall in love with a woman.

I liked to go to the eleventh floor to talk to Belle and to smell and handle the new books. "Would you like to work here?" she said one day. She was asking a question, not offering me a job. "No," I said. "If I worked with books I would have to give up people. I wouldn't be able to write stories about Cavalliere Prisco."

Cavalliere Raffaele Prisco was the hero of Mulberry Street, the boulevard of Italian Manhattan. He had come to the city from Italy in 1899 and set himself up in one room at 64 Mulberry Street to sell steamship tickets and service immigrants who wanted to send money home. Twenty-five years later his Prisco State Bank, the only marble building on Mulberry Street, was dedicated. Early in the depression the bank failed. Cavalliere Prisco and his three sons were prosecuted. The three sons said the fault was their; Cavalliere Prisco said the sins of a son are the sins of his father. He was sent to prison on Welfare Island, but only for a short term. "It is not his fault," said the people of Mulberry Street. "His sons have American ways, but he has not. He is like us. We trust him. Let him go free and let him return to us."

He was released on September 6, 1932. On September 7th he opened, again at 64 Mulberry Street, a new business in steamship tickets and money transmission. I had to push my way through a crowd to reach him. Glass had not yet been put in the counter windows and people were thrusting their arms through the frames, holding money toward the Cavalliere. He was weeping, and one of his sons, standing aside from the customers and his father, was also weeping.

Each year on September 16th Mulberry Street begins its annual three days festival in honor of Saint Gennaro, patron of Naples, who with four of his friends was beheaded in 305 on a charge of practicing magic. The five had been placed in an amphitheater and exposed to lions, who licked the hands of Gennaro and did not molest his companions. This obviously was sorcery, and execution was the only course of action. In the cathedral at Naples the blood of Gennaro, kept in a phial, liquefies every year on the anniversary of his decapitation, so the faithful say. In Mulberry Street each year an image of the saint is taken from the Church of the Most Precious Blood on Baxter Street and carried in procession to a throne at the corner of Hester and Mulberry Streets, where for three days it reigns, with ribbons flowing from its base to which supplicants and penitents and admirers pin paper money in various denominations. In 1932 Cavalliere Prisco, who was president of one hundred and three Italian societies, led the procession. It became a celebration in honor of his homecoming.

In the office at 64 Mulberry Street I helped him select several sashes from the multitude on the walls. He put on the chosen few and we had a drink together, holding the glasses between thumb and second finger, the forefinger held upright and away from the glass to show what sort of men we were. Then we went outside and poined the procession. The Cavalliere put his arm around my shoulders and announced that I was co-leader.

"My damn good frien' Mist' Grue, *Herl' Tribune*," he explained.

We marched off to Park Street, our route taking us from Park to Pine to Mott to Hester to Baxter. Along the way friends called to the Cavalliere. Now and then he halted the procession and took me into a shop or club, where I was introduced to an entire fraternal organization with a single sweep of the Cavalliere's hand, and where toasts were drunk to Saint Gennaro, to the Cavalliere, and to Mist' Grue. At the church a solemn high Mass was sung; then we marched to the site of the throne, stopping occasionally for a toast. When the saint was ensconced the Cavalliere and I returned to 64 Mulberry Street, put the sashes back on the walls, and had another drink, our forefingers again upraised.

Then the city desk called me. That morning Federal agents had raided a series of speakeasies on the Bowery. I was nearby. Would I check the situation and find out whether any of the places which had been raided was open again for business? I left the Cavalliere and walked through Chinatown to the Bowery. The first of the raided addresses was open and filled with customers. So was the second; so were the third, the fourth, and the fifth. There were no locks on the doors; there had never been locks on the doors. I had no trouble buying a drink. Beer was a nickel, whiskey a dime. The bartenders were angry about the raids.

"Nobody wants these places closed," one of them said to me. "The saloons on the Bowery do more for the bums than all the social service agencies in town. Every saloon serves free lunch, and that's all most of the bums get to eat. In an hour we'll feed fifty men in here, and we won't give them pretzels and cheese. They'll get a meal. Go into the kitchen and see for yourself."

I went to the back of the saloon and looked into a small kitchen. Great pans of frankfurters, sauerkraut, and potatoes were cooking on the stove. I walked back to the bar and the bartender pointed to a row of men sitting in cafeteria chairs along the wall.

"Our dinner guests," he said. "They haven't even a nickel for a bottle of beer."

I looked down the line of faces. There was trust in every countenance; each man was relaxed, without responsibility, a soul free of the sin of economics, a parasite on the conscience of capitalism, a failure. What each might have been in a less competitive system, in a more cooperative society, in a civilization built on craftsmanship rather than mechanical cunning, was forever lost. They were part now of the reflection which man the profit-maker sees when he looks in the mirror of his environment.

"I would like to buy them a drink," I said.

"Drinks for the house!" the bartender shouted. His assistants went to his aid; in a few minutes the men along the wall were served. Thirty-six glasses of beer were lifted in a toast to me. I paid the bartender a dollar and eighty cents.

It was the end of a hot, difficult summer. The Childs restaurant management had informed its cashiers they would have to work twelve hours a day instead of eight. Since this made it impossible for Junkin and Crittenden to paint in the mornings they quit. Crittenden returned to Georgia, Junkin became a Childs waiter. He found a studio for himself on the far west side and I went to live in the Peter Stuyvesant Hotel at Eighty-sixth Street and Central Park West with John Lardner and his cousin, Dick Tobin. Dick was also a *Herald Tribune* reporter; by the time he joined the staff the starting salary had dropped to twenty dollars a week.

In June Governor Roosevelt of New York was nominated for President at the convention of the Democratic Party in Chicago. At a Catholic Charities luncheon that April the Governor and his predecessor at Albany, Alfred E. Smith, flanked Cardinal Hayes on the dais, but the archbishop, if he made the attempt, failed to bring Smith to a docile acceptance of Roosevelt's candidacy. Al continued to want the nomination, and to believe it was rightfully his. The next time I saw him, in August, his expression had changed; he was bitter.

He was standing in front of an apartment house on the East Side, dressed in formal morning attire, waiting to act as honorary pallbearer in the funeral of Marty McCue, Democratic leader of the north end of the 12th Assembly District, a man who had worked his way from prize fighter and bartender to Assemblyman, in which role he had worked for the poor, fostered the widows' pension bill, and become the hero of his constituents. There were other honorary pallbearers, all Democratic politicians from Tammany Hall. They formed two lines, with Smith at the head of one and John F. Curry, leader of Tammany, opposite him at the head of the other. While they waited Curry, a sartorially immaculate man, put on a pair of gray gloves. The other men, except Smith, did likewise. Curry glanced nervously at Smith a few times, then said, "Al, aren't you going to put on your gloves?"

Smith continued to stare straight ahead.

"I haven't got any gloves," he said.

"Oh," Curry said. "Then I won't wear mine."

He took them off, and the other men took theirs off.

The funeral Mass was sung in Saint Agnes Church, on East Forty-third Street near Lexington Avenue. After the Mass

301

Monsignor John P. Chidwick, rector of the church and former chaplain of the battleship *Maine,* stepped forward and began to speak.

"It is not customary," he said, "for our church to eulogize the dead."

Everyone knew this, and the reporters, suspicious, wondered why the custom was being broken. We took notes while McCue's career was described. The account closed with the statement that Martin G. McCue was "a devout neighbor of the church, loyal and faithful; a man who knew that God was to be loved, adored, and obeyed; a man who kept himself ever humble.

"Would to God," the monsignor added, "that every public man who stands as an example to young men, who is regarded as a hero in their eyes, would be careful to understand that he is not only an official but a guide and an inspiration, and lead a clean and pure life.

"He"—meaning McCue—"never permitted his wife to become an object of scorn and another to take her place in his affections. He never branded his children with the scorn of a father who forgets his home. He was faithful, strong and honest, and his public life stands out as a marvel of integrity."

Outside we gathered in the middle of the street and discussed the obvious question—was the eulogy a condemnation by the church of the private life of Mayor James J. Walker? Gossip concerning the Mayor and Betty Compton, an actress, was common, constant, and, until now, condoned. The Mayor was under pressure from secular sources for his conduct as an executive, but unless Tammany or the church deserted him he was in little danger. Was the church withdrawing from him its approval? Monsignor Michael J. Lavelle, rector of the cathedral, had been in the sanctuary during the funeral Mass, representing the Cardinal. Did that signify that Monsignor Chidwick spoke for the Cardinal?

One of the reporters asked Al Smith whether he knew the eulogy was to be delivered. Smith shook his head. "You could have knocked me over with a feather," he said. Did he think any particular city official was being criticized? He shook his head again. He didn't know.

At the office I presented the story to the city editor. He called the managing editor. The managing editor went to Geoffrey Parsons. Geoffrey spoke to Ogden Reid, the editor and owner of the paper. There was no way to judge the importance of what Monsignor Chidwick had said. The story could not be pointed up without assuming an implication which might not exist; it could only be printed for what it was, a report on the funeral of Marty McCue. Before the month's end Walker resigned. Later Monsignor Chidwick confided to friends that the criticism in his eulogy was leveled at a minor city official, and that he had been careful to mention children, lest it be interpreted that he meant Mayor Walker, who had no children. He was amused, as were others in the hierachy, that the blast blew Walker out of City Hall.

Such in 1932 was the power of my church and the manner in which it was used. There was another religious power abroad that summer; I watched it one Sunday for seven hours in a Harlem dance hall.

A Negro named Father Divine was released from jail on Long Island after the judge who sentenced him to a year and a day for maintaining a public nuisance in the town of Sayville died. The release had nothing to do with the judge's death, but the followers of Divine, a short bald man who declared that he was God, would not have it so. Their leader had killed the judge, they said, and let it be a lesson to others who doubted the Father's divinity. On the day after Divine's release they gathered in Harlem to welcome him. The singing and praying and testifying began at dawn; by the time Divine arrived at four o'clock in the afternoon three thousand people were on the edge of hysteria. When he stepped on the platform a huge woman wearing a pink silk dress dropped to her knees and washed his shining brown button shoes with her tears. The crowd sang to him:

> *God will hold me in the hollow of His hand.*
> *God will hold me in the hollow of His hand.*
> *He will make me understand*
> *Every word of His command.*
> *God will hold me in the hollow of His hand.*

I had been listening to the voices for six hours, begrudging each moment they were still. The apparently limitless resources of timbre and pitch which are the Negro's natural treasure transformed simple, even banal hymns into miracles of music, and the pyramiding frenzy of the undulating, quivering thousands pumped blood into every note. Now Divine began preaching and voices began their antiphons, increasing the tempo gradually until polyphony was established.

Would the Lord show the way? He would; He would indeed. Had not He always shown the way? Who said He hadn't? Had not He suffered? He had. He was bruised. Oh! He was crucified. Oh! He died. No! No! No! He was laid in a tomb. Oh! But He came forth from it. Yes! Yes! He rose. Rose! From the dead. From the dead! For you. Oh! For me! Oh! For all of us. All of us! That we may follow Him. That we may know. Yes.

They wanted to know. They wanted to understand. They wanted to realize. There was something within them that banished their pain, something of comfort they could not explain. All that they knew was that it was within. Everything troublesome was now driven out. But all that was out must be carried within, all that was troublesome must be made still. Jesus would show them how this could be done. He knew the trick of it. He knew the way.

They looked up at Him from the nadir of the caduceus, from the end of involution, from the beginning of the ladder of logic and reason, of intellectual comprehension and creative apprehension. A new wave of the mind was moving, a surge of emotion pushing its base, a thin crest of awareness cutting the atmosphere above. When the surge of the base slowed the top would whiten, bend, fall, and break into patterns of detail. How far would the substance of the wave be carried before its perception perished? What beach of golden, gleaming sand would slow the surge and suck its crest to ruin?

That fall there was economic penance for the editorial staff. New contracts had to be negotiated with unionized compositors, typesetters, and linotype operators. Wage increases were demanded by union officials and, following discussion, were granted. After the contracts were signed a general cut of ten per cent was announced for all editorial workers; they were not organized. My salary, which had been raised to thirty-five dollars a week in September, after a year's work, was cut to thirty-one dollars and fifty cents. At that wage I set out to cover, six days each week, various aspects of the autumn political campaigns.

Fiorello H. LaGuardia was running for Congress, opposing Tammany; he toured his district in a truck, speaking from its rear end; I noticed that wherever a crowd gathered to

304

hear him fire engines went by and kept going by until he was finished and had moved on. John P. O'Brien was Tammany's candidate for Mayor; he was a good family man; that was his platform. In November LaGuardia was defeated, O'Brien was elected, Herbert H. Lehman became Governor, and Governor Roosevelt won the Presidency.

"Well, we're stuck with him for four years," one of the *Herald Tribune* editorial writers said. "I suppose we might as well make the most of it."

"You'll make the most of it for eight years," Geoffrey Parsons said. Then he added, by way of rubbing salt into the wound, "At least."

Tammany Hall was curiously gloomy on election night. Al Smith sat on the edge of a table watching photographers arrange Mayor and Mrs. O'Brien, Governor and Mrs. Lehman, and the John F. Currys for a group picture.

"Come on, Al, get in the middle," Mayor O'Brien said.

Smith stared at a long cigar he was holding in the fingers of his right hand.

"I do not belong in any picture tonight," he said. "I was not a candidate for office. I won nothing. I lost nothing. Leave me out."

Governor Lehman, Curry, and the photographers tried to coax him, but he was obdurate.

"I don't belong in the picture," he said. "I won't get in it."

After the inauguration in March gears were shifted and the country moved to another valley in the enchanted land of economics. The New Deal was an exodus, a migration of the havenots to the land of haves, a mass teleportion achieved by the magic of debt, an adaptation of man's fundamental theological error, the illusion that souls can be legislated into heaven. It was a step in the natural evolution of the republic; the majority got what it wanted, which was, as always, what the minority did not want. The minority, irritated, forced to share part of its goods, moved on, seeking further valleys, climbing in its trek over higher values. The archetype had a new frontier.

The theology of Franklin D. Roosevelt was simple. He transferred the penance of the sin of economics to the government and declared the pleasure of the transgression to be the privilege of all. He erected a scapegoat with multiple heads bearing mumbo-jumbo names; he proclaimed the dogma of security by faith without works. With casual sureness he gave the majority what it wanted and the minority what it did not want. The minority, aware for the first time of the irksomeness of material wealth and contemptuous of the majority for wanting it, began to dream of possessions which could not be taxed, expropriated, or even shared. When it found them the majority would want them also. Thus little by little, pressure by pressure, hunger by hunger, the population would approach the beatitude of poverty in the spirit and the miracle of understanding in the mind. Roosevelt, like Jefferson, let democratic political evolution proceed at its natural pace, the lowest common denominator of the majority vote; when the populace had suffered sufficiently for its decisions it would change them. Fresh forms of foolishness would then transpire; there would be further fumbling toward God, larger dealings with Lucifer.

The task of selecting a penitential hierarchy and devising a machinery of expiation turned Washington into a pismire of bureaucracy. So much copy came from our Washington bureau that news of the city was crowded from the paper. Interviews, feature stories, reports from the zoo, descriptions of derring-do on the savannas beyond Brooklyn, went into overset. I found a woman who was in love with a cigar store Indian; the romance was in the paper every day for a week until press time; each night it lost out to a column of New Deal propaganda; it never was printed. There was not much for me to do now unless someone died.

That June Jerry Danzig came down from Dartmouth determined beyond dissuasion to be a newspaperman. At night we rode through the pleasantly quiet streets of Manhattan in his roadster, top down, the forced air cooling us, our dates insisting that we light cigarettes for them in the wind. Jerry had the constant smile and the relaxation of Elias; like Elias he was poor in the spirit. What he possessed of the world had no grasp on him, nor did he keep a hand upon it, even lightly. He was interested in the trinity of human needs—bread, circuses, and salvation; he enjoyed the interplay of opinion, posture, and prejudice which spattered the fringes of the group egos like a steady fall of rain; he was fascinated by individuals who broke through the texture of controlled reactions and dashed for the far rim of the superconscious. He had a simple solution to the problem of stimulating more assault upon the texture.

"Write a play about salvation," he said. "Produce it as a circus. Turn the profits into bread."

"That," I said, "is what Shakespeare did. He dramatized man's break from medievalism to modernism. It was the question of his time—is man's destiny in the hands of the gods or is it his to shape and propel? As history proceeded the gods lost out; man took his destiny away from them. He did what he could with it; he put it on wheels, wired it for sound, and gave it a balanced diet. There is nothing left for him now but to return it to the gods, of his own free will and at the insistence of his wisdom."

"Time for another Shakespeare," Jerry said. His date looked up at him admiringly. "Not me, baby," he said, "and not you. Somebody else. We're just people."

She laughed and turned away, the Fifth Avenue street light running a soft, quick hand over her body, tightening its grip where silk was drawn over her tibia. American girls were lovelier than ever that summer; they moved along Madison Avenue and Fifth Avenue with the mellifluous but vital swing of people who are free.

"Wouldn't it be wonderful if women really did get to be people?" Jerry said. "There would be twice as many folk from which to choose friends."

Friendship in New York had little to do with propinquity; in a population of seven million its basis was direction; people moving toward related goals, recognizing a single origin, a mutual longing, and an eventual common identity, fell naturally into step, into mental harmony, into sublimation of personality differences. My bond with some friends was an interest in extrasensory perception; with others it was the problem of articulation in the arts; with a few it was social service; with many it was the desire to splice a yearning for self-expression with the business of making a living. I had no central theme of my own; I was at home with many sets of friends, but not with myself. I loathed the constant pressure of maintaining dichotomy, of hustling Joseph into the back room of my mind when certain people came in sight. My neck ached and I was tired in my body most of the time. I wished I were like Denis Tilden Lynch, a veteran *Herald Tribune* political reporter, who was accosted in Times Square one day by Ben Robertson, one of the younger members of the city staff.

"Denis," said Ben, "what in the world are you doing in the middle of Times Square at high noon on a hot day, leaning against a light post in your shirt sleeves?"

"I am doing two things," said Denis. "I am contemplating a line of Aeschylus, magnificent in its poetry, perfect in its understanding. I am also minding my own business. Now run along and let me be."

One day a letter from Hugh Lynn Cayce asked me to look up a man named Harold J. Reilly, a physiotherapist. Edgar, in a reading for a New York man, had referred to him. Suggestions had been given for the man's health involving physiotherapy treatments. When Gertrude asked, "Where in New York is the best place to get such treatments?" the answer was, "Reilly's." Subsequent readings for other New Yorkers continued to recommend Reilly, and said he was to be found on upper Broadway. There was a Reilly's Health Service at 1908 Broadway. Was this the right Reilly? Yes, said Edgar, it was.

The gymnasium and baths were on the second floor of a wooden building on the northeast corner of Sixty-third Street. I climbed the steps and walked into a small reception room. A pretty blonde, trapped behind a desk, smiled at me. When I explained my mission she went away and a pretty red-head replaced her. The walls of the room were covered with photographs of opera singers, actors and actresses, writers, and radio performers. All the pictures were autographed to Harold J. Reilly, in gratefulness for health, vitality, and various other states of well-being. Here and there between the photographs were small oil paintings, mostly landscapes. They were signed Elvira Reilly.

I turned around and met another pretty blonde. Behind her was one of the most handsome men I have ever seen— not too tall, not overdeveloped, with a profile which combined the best features of Greek and Roman pulchritude and a countenance Irish below the nose and Nordic through the eyes. He was Harold J. Reilly.

"I'm glad you came," he said. "When the first man walked in here with a Cayce reading I didn't know who was crazy, Cayce or the customer. The suggestions were sensible and I followed them; they were helpful. Since then I've seen a number of readings; I can't vouch for their diagnostic accuracy, since I'm not a physician, but what I'm asked to do, though in each case the details differ, is basic physiotherapy and gets results. People have been sent to me by their doctors, their dentists, their psychiatrists, their astrologers, their barbers and hairdressers, their chauffeurs—Beniamino Gigli, the tenor, was nagged into coming here by his chauffeur—

but this is my first experience with a clairvoyant. I'll give you a treatment if you'll tell me about him."

It seemed a fair exchange so I accepted. I talked while I undressed and while he worked on my arms and legs. When his fingers reached my neck I was quiet; the pain was gagging. Then he began to talk—about the connection between the mind and the body, the pressure on the nervous system of noises and quick-moving objects in modern urban life, the debilitating effect of sedentary occupations on muscles trained for 50,000 years to varied and constant movement, the need for compensatory exercises to offset the drudgery patterns in physical labor, and the importance to the body of relaxation, elimination, and normal circulation.

"The same blood which flows through your intestines flows through your brain," he said. "Yet people who do mental work attempt to subdue the body instead of working with it; they oppose it instead of harnessing it. We're developing a philosophy of sickness in America instead of a philosophy of health. People expect to feel bad. They expect colds every winter and a week or two of illness every year. Their bodies have become a burden because actually, except for pleasure, a body is no longer functional. You could get around New York a good deal more quickly and do your work more easily if you had only a mind."

He turned me on my face and his amazing hands—they seemed to be inside me, working on my skeleton—fingered the tension in my back.

"But the less we need our bodies the more trouble they become to us," he went on. "We neglect them, fail to exercise them, overfeed and undereliminate them, overtax their supplies of nervous energy, and end up on a diet, in a padded cell, or under ether."

He rolled me over again and I sat up.

"Spend as much time exercising your body as you would in walking a dog and you'll find yourself straining at the leash," he said.

I talked some more then, about mediums and clairvoyants, their limitations and eccentricities, and the fact that they seemed intent on catering to the orthodox notion of afterlife—a reflection of our better suburban areas, with effort, conflict, hunger, and competition removed. It was, I thought, an indication that clairvoyance was not only confined to the mind of man, but in most cases to the subconscious of the clairvoyant. Reilly nodded.

"The average American's idea of heaven is earth without a body," he said. "Everyone is rich, everyone is healthy, and no one is interested in stealing anyone else's wife. A massage and a colonic irrigation will give you the same feeling without putting you to the trouble of dying."

When I was dressed we walked through the men's department and reached the reception room again.

"Who were the pretty girls I met?" I said.

"My sisters," he said.

"All three?" I asked.

"I have five sisters," he said.

I looked at the oil paintings again.

"Which one," I said, "is the artist?"

"My wife is a painter," he said.

A short, strong, pleasant-looking man came in and I was introduced to him. He was Bill Eigan, Reilly's associate.

"Not a member of the family, eh?" I said hopefully.

"He's my wife's cousin and he's married to one of my sisters," Reilly said.

He walked with me to the stairway. Down the corridor leading to the women's department I glimpsed a small, slim figure in gym clothes. She waved and called something to Reilly.

"Which sister is that?" I asked.

"That is my mother," he said.

By the time I reached the office I was in a state of euphoria. Reilly's fingers had eliminated the tension in my neck and back, and I felt so stimulated and cleansed that I was unable to consider anything an obstacle or anyone an adversary. I felt far too well in fact, for competitive life. It was several days before I was tense enough for effort and sustained concentration. After a week I went back to Reilly's and reported my findings.

"It will take a while to get accustomed to feeling well," he said. "You're like a person who's been favoring one leg. It requires an effort to walk normally again."

He was good-humored about the matter of health, without fervor but with a tremendous interest in the body's place in the pattern of man. He realized that good physical condition was an acquired characteristic, and that the process of acquisition was for most people not enjoyable. For him it was a pleasure, but he didn't expect others to agree with him.

Singers and actors, he told me, exercised willingly because

their professional success depended in part on their vitality, physical appearance, and continuous freedom from illness. Others worked in the gym because they realized the investment was sound. Reilly, a native New Yorker, grandson of a Mississippi River steamboat captain, former wrestler, weight lifter, boxer, track athlete, and jujitsu expert, worked with them because he liked to see people looking well and because his own body enjoyed movement. Later, when he moved to Rockefeller Center and had 8,000 square feet of space studded with the finest physiotherapy equipment available, he said to me one day as I tried to avoid taking a Scotch douche, "If anyone leaves here feeling no better than when he came in, it will be over my dead and highly toxic body." I took the douche.

In the free time bestowed on me by the excess of news from Washington I experimented with magazine articles, particularly the curious form which sets out to reveal the contributing aspects of a man's personality in terms of facts which any fool can detect as misleading. The arrogant scientific virtue of magazine editors, who forbade deduction and generalization, was religious in its intensity; the satanism with which they juggled documentary evidence to build an implication or support a personal prejudice was also religious; it was, in fact, all the religion they had.

One of my biographical sketches concerned a local detective named Bill Quaine, who was known as "the toughest cop in New York" because he considered gangsters, thieves, and other parasitical riffraff beneath the dignity of a mechanical weapon. He ignored their pistols, knives, and blackjacks and subdued them with his fists. Now anyone who has been brought up in proximity to the environments which breed stickup men, crooked gamblers, blackmailers, and racketeers knows that nothing so humiliates, frightens, and unnerves these mock heroic characters as a grownup equivalent of the spankings from which their bodily growth so recently has liberated them. Quaine, who had been a student at the University of Dublin, knew that if he used a gun against the hoodlums it was his task to shepherd they would be enormously flattered. They would consider themselves his equal, cease to fear him, and probably shoot him. He kept his health and their respect by using his fists.

The editor to whom I submitted the piece sent for me a week later; he talked to me in the cold, soggy, dismal reception room grudgingly maintained for visitors to the magazine's offices. He was a thin-faced man with a small moustache and shell-rimmed spectacles.

"The piece is all right," he said, "except for one thing. You have failed to bring out the main point about Quaine's character, which is that he is a sadist."

I felt ill. I saw visions of wracks and dungeons. Had psychotherapy come so soon to dogma, infallibility, and inquisition? ("I am a sadist!" cried Quaine in an ecstasy of confession as the flames leaped at his throat.) I tried to explain the simple psychological basis of Quaine's technique. The editor shook his head.

"He must be a sadist," he said. "There is no other reason for a man to strike other men with his fists. Unless you bring that out in the piece I am not interested in it."

The next editor who saw the sketch bought it and printed it without change. I then worked on a study of Cardinal Hayes for the thin-faced editor; while I was writing it one day at the Peter Stuyvesant Hotel a girl went by my window and fell on the courtyard below, a suicide. When the editor sent for me to discuss the manuscript I saw on the margin of one of its pages a penciled question, "What is a Mass? Explain." I dared not look at the editor; he was intently studying a sentence which he considered elliptical. Years later I discovered a curious fact about this odd man. He was a prizefight enthusiast; he seldom missed a bout at Madison Square Garden; around town he was an accepted authority on pugilism, the art of physical punishment.

One afternoon I received a note from the fiction editor of a small publishing house; he had read some of my stories in the *Herald Tribune* and he wanted to talk to me. Perhaps I had thought of writing a book? I showed the note to Stanley Walker. I didn't care about meeting another thin-faced editor. "This fellow has round cheeks," he said. "Go and see him."

I took Dick Tobin with me; we walked into a reception room smaller, darker, but cleaner than that maintained by the thin-faced editor's magazine. We asked to see Clifton Fadiman. We were admitted to a green-walled room smaller than a New England pantry. Fadiman and a desk occupied one end of it. Fadiman's face, chubby and malleable, was arranged to reflect discomfort. His right hand rubbed his stomach.

"Feeling bad?" I said. He made a grimace which agreed with me and said something about a long and apparently poisonous dinner the night before. Dick and I sat down. Fadiman turned his revolving chair slightly and stared at me.

"I have a feeling that you ought to write a funny book," he said.

It was the first time Elias' advice had boomeranged. Operating behind a visage of humor had its advantages; finding the visage mistaken for the manipulating intelligence was not one of them. I said nothing. Suddenly Dick spoke.

"I think you're entirely mistaken," he said to Fadiman. "I believe that some day Tom will write an epic poem."

Fadiman's countenance mirrored waves of nausea.

"Really?" he managed to say.

How did Dick contrive to see through the back of my head, I wondered. Now both ends of my mind were visible. I felt like a woman in a gown with a low neckline and a long skirt, caught suddenly in a freakish updraft of air. I leaned forward to engage Fadiman's tottering attention and began to talk.

"I do not think it is possible for me to surgically remove humor from life and put it in a book," I said. "Some people can do it, just as some people can write books about food, or morality, or fishing. I believe any book I write will contain some amusing material because humor is one of the driving forces of life. But to write just a funny book, as you call it—"

Fadiman groaned slightly.

"Write a book," he said faintly. "Just write a book, any kind of a book."

We realized that we were adding to his suffering so we left. There were other notes from other editors after that. On a January morning in 1934 Beverly Smith invited me to lunch at the Dutch Treat Club with his employers, the editors of *The American Magazine*. Halfway through the meal Summer Blossom, the editor in chief, turned to me and said:

"How would you like to take a trip around the world and write some pieces about it for us?"

I put my fork down quickly. What welled up in me was not going to be easy to control. Joseph was clawing at my vocal chords.

"It would be an interesting assignment," I said quietly. "I would like to try it."

Blossom nodded casually.

"Good," he said. "Can you leave in two weeks?"

NINETEEN

THE PROFESSOR examined his notes while Miss Yellowhead tucked me in the cabinet. Miss Iceberg, her back to me, arranged her paraphernalia and patted her hair.

"How many of those wicked germs we must have killed by now!" Miss Yellowhead said. "You will be going home soon to see your new daughter."

The Professor looked up and frowned. The arrogance which infects a man when he inspects information he has himself gathered pulled his nose and his mouth askew.

"The woman is a fool," he muttered. "Why does she take it for granted that you are a sentimental slob whose only pain is caused by separation from an infant you have seen but three times?"

"She is very much like you," I said. "She meets people at her own levels of intelligence and emotion, not theirs. It is a common characteristic, an inelasticity of the ego suffered by so many people that it is normally considered a natural trait, not a personality fault."

"Precisely," the Professor said. "It is similar on a small scale to your insistence that the world be more actively about the business of seeking God, a Person in Whom you believe and Whose business you feel qualified to manage."

"There is nothing I can do to accelerate or retard humanity's penetration of general awareness," I said. "I wish only that the fact of this penetration might become part of the personal awareness of more people."

"An evasion," the Professor said. "You are full of them. Now let me see . . . according to our record you sailed from New York on January 28, 1934, on the *Europa*, and landed at Cherbourg four and a half days later. In Paris the cafes were filled with the first refugees from Hitler Germany. I must tell you some time about my theory of Nazism. I believe it to be a cancer in the body of European nationalism, composed of cells of personality turned to sports, driven wild by the constant irritation of politically devised differences, artificial economic hungers . . ."

"An interesting deduction," I said. "I haven't heard it lately, though. It seems to have fallen from fashion."

He went on with his notes. "You visited San Marino, in Italy, the smallest republic in the world—continuously free for sixteen hundred years, I believe. You stopped at Venice, then went to Budapest, and from there rode the Orient Express to Istanbul. Leaving Turkey you traveled by boat to Athens. You sailed from there to Haifa by way of the Mediterranean islands."

"When you want me to talk," I suggested, "just ask me."

"I am trying to avoid being met at your level of familiarity with Europe instead of my own," he said. "I have been there a dozen times—I conducted student tours for ten summers—and I have taught the history of every one of its countries but Ireland, which is not a country but a Catholic seminary supported by agricultural slaves owned by a Protestant landlord.

"You arrived at Haifa early in March and set out the next day for Jerusalem, riding in a Dodge car driven by a Moslem named Ahmed. You reached Cana and paused to consider the miracle of the wedding feast, the changing of water into wine. Then you went on to—"

"Please!" I said. "Let me point out the symbology of that miracle. Blood is the sign of consciousness, the mark of life laden with awareness. Christ, the Archetypal Man, the Word, is the Consciousness of creation, the Mind of God in action. Sacrificed, immersed, poured into differentiated forms, He transforms the cold, colorless unconsciousness of their existence into warm, bright awareness. He changes water into wine. Life is born from water, grows into blood, and is twisted and burned and beaten into spirit by the experiences of consciousness.

"Ahmed and I were separate collections of experiences of consciousness, and each of us yet had some water in his blood. Ahmed believed the blue beads he had wrapped around the radiator of his car would protect him from the malice of the Evil Eye. I believed that by going to Jerusalem I could learn something about Jesus."

"Precisely," the Professor said. "So you proceeded to Nazareth, where you had lunch, and where you visited the churches built over the grotto of the Annunciation and the workshop of Joseph. Did they inspire you?"

"In the Church of the Annunciation," I said, "I listened while a Franciscan monk described Mary's Grotto as a typical inner room, or sleeping chamber of the period. He was addressing a group of tourists. At the group's fringe one Englishman said to another, 'What sort of church is this, d'you know?' The other said, 'Catholic, I s'pose.' The first said, 'That's odd. Chap was a Jew, wasn't He? Jesus?' "

The Professor nodded, ladling a grin from the left side of his mouth.

"You liked most of all the well in the center of the town, Mary's Well," he said. "It was still being used, and you were struck by the fact that meeting someone at a well in Palestine—a happening described often in the Gospels—is like meeting someone on a village green in New England, or at a corner drugstore in any American town. It is a typical tourist's reaction. You sat by the well and watched people come to it, observing how they paused to rest and to visit with one another. Now, you said to yourself, when I read of Jesus meeting a woman at a well, I shall know precisely how it happened.

"With that ordinary thought tucked away in your mind you went on to Tiberias. The Sea of Galilee, a fair-sized lake, was being whipped by a spring wind. You were sensible enough not to look for historic spots, but to stand and let the wind blow over you as it came off the water. That was an experience you could share with the fiseshermen disciples, and with Jesus Himself—in fact through all of the Holy Land there is nothing worth while for the pilgrim to experience beyond the touch of warm sand on his bare feet, the odor of dawn, the damp taste of dusk, the sounds of the towns and cities by day and by night. These have not changed in two thousand years.

"It was night when you reached Jerusalem. You stayed at a small hotel run by a literate and friendly Arab named Abu Ali Omar, a charming, well-to-do man who during the World War had been a scout for T. E. Lawerence, the Englishman who was called Lawrence of Arabia. In that connection—"

"I should like to report," I said, "that when Ahmed turned the car into the quiet street containing Abu Ali Omar's hotel I experienced an overpowering sensation of familiarity. I knew the car was going to turn left, and I knew how the street would look, even to Abu Ali Omar standing on the sidewalk. The room to which he escoted me, the curious little lobby, the intimate dining room—none was strange. I felt—"

"Excuse me,' 'the Professor said. "That entry is on another page." He thumbed through his notes, nodded, and read from a mixture of scrible and personal shorthand: "Among the more common and superficial reactions described by pilgrims to Jerusalem is a sense of familiarity, a feeling of having been in the city before. The obvious explanation is that drawings, photographs, and descriptions of the city have since childhood stimulated Christians all over the world to daydream of the Holy Land and to identify themselves with the adventures of Jesus, particularly those events which marked His final days and hours. A pilgrim who has in childhood meditated on the image of a holy spot will experience a sense of recognition when he actually visits that spot, particularly if he happens to see it from the same angle and distance from which the photograph or drawing was made.

"The proof of this lies in another common and superficial reaction experienced by Christian pilgrims, a sense of shock and disillusion at finding the Church of the Holy Sepulcher owned by the Moslems—they could lock it up if they wanted to—and the Greek Orthodox, Coptic, Syrian, Armenian, Abyssinian, and Roman Catholic churches dividing ownership of the other holy spots, each being unfriendly to the others. It is a situation of which the average pilgrim arriving in Jerusalem is unaware; it is not part of the idea of Palestine he has constructed in his mind and it shatters the hypocritical pretense he houses that Christianity is an accomplished fact rather than a sentimentalized ideal carefully placed beyond his own and his fellow man's grasp, excusing them from the attempt to reach it, requiring only a bend of the knee, a coin on the plate, and acceptance of the fact that it is there, above and comfortably removed from them."

"Ownership of the holy spots by Moslems and quarreling Catholic groups did not bother me," I said, "though I could not help thinking how some of my Irish-Catholic townsmen would have stared to know there were so many Catholic churches. I liked the small mosque on the Mount of Olives, built by the Moslems over the rock on which Jesus stood to ascend into heaven.

"It has six inches in its circular wall, one for each of the six Catholic groups, which are allowed to say Mass on the spot once a year, on Ascension Thursday. In the niches the groups place their altar stones, and separately they celebrate the mystery."

The Professor nodded. "It is peculiarly fitting," he said, "that on the spot which symbolizes the supreme unity, the return of the Son to the Father, the ascension of the risen Soul, the flight of the resurrected God, the climax of evolution, the disunity of Christians should be so sharply displayed. I am glad the Protestants hold nothing in Jerusalem but the Y.M.C.A."

"There is the same disunity at the spot which symbolizes the beginning of the spiritual journey," I said. "In Bethlehem the church built over the manger belongs to the Greeks. To the left of its altar is the spot where Joseph was sleeping when the angel appeared to him and told him to flee with Mary and the Child to Egypt. Beyond it is the cell of Saint Jerome, held by the Franciscans. A narrow carpet runs across the altar of the church; it is for the Franciscans; it is their pathway to and from Saint Jerome's cell. They must not stray form it."

The Professor looked at his notes. "I have an entry here concerning medieval anatomical symbology," he said. "It was made when I first visited Palestine twenty years ago—something about Jerusalem being the symbol of the brain. The hidden Christ comes forth from Bethlehem, the heart, where peace has been won. It moves up the backbone, that spine of road which covers the eight miles from Bethlehem to Jerusalem—part of it is like a neck, you will recall—and begins the trials of consciousness which are climaxed on Golgotha, the place of the skull.

"I can't make much out of what I put down; the rest was in my head and I've forgotten it. I scribbled a few sources—Origen, Gregory the Great, and Saint Paul. I suspect I meant their references to the heavenly Jerusalem. There's a detached phrase here—'meaning of the tonsure.' I suppose I pondered whether the monks shaved their heads to signify that the gate was open for the soul's ascension.

"Well, anyhow, the idea was that each of the holy spots in Jerusalem corresponds to a part of the brain governing a faculty which must be controlled and subdued by the adventuring ego. I remember that it seemed very clear at the time, an interesting vestige of scholasticisms's confusion of science and theology."

318

He stopped, puzzled at his forgetfulness, and stared at Miss Iceberg's fingers, which were swinging a pencil back and forth.

"That girl is getting nervous," he said.

"In the Church of the Holy Sepulcher,". I said, "I looked at the tombs of the Crusaders, Godfrey of Boulogne and his brother Baldwin. I noticed that the Romans hold the spot where Jesus was stripped, and the place where He was nailed to the cross, but that the Greeks own the spot on which the cross stood. At each station of the cross a priest of the controlling group waits to collect offerings. Most people, the guides told me, are a soft touch. 'They have guilty memories and fat pocketbooks,' Abu Ali Omar said.

"I suppose you remember that beneath the place where the cross stood is the legendary tomb of Adam and that a drop of blood from Christ's wounds fell through the earth—the ground was opened by a quake—and wakened Adam."

"Of course, of course," the Professor said. He was smiling now. "The blood, or consciousness, of the dying God fell on the drowsing flesh, the Adam cast out of paradise into creation, stirring it to a realization of its spiritual nature, its heavenly home. There is a lovely legend which tells how the cross to which Jesus was nailed was made from the tree of the knowledge of good and evil, which grew on the same spot."

"The tree of life," I said, "the caduceus, the spine—down which the blood of the dying God descends to waken the sleeping Adam, who climbs upward to resurrection and ascension."

"That's it! That's it!" the Professor said. He was delighted. "Helena didn't miss a thing when she went in search of the holy spots," he said. "She found Adam's tomb along with the true cross and the place where the soldiers cast lots for His garments."

He laughed. "Perhaps," he said, "she hired clairvoyants to help her in her search."

"The antechamber of the Sepulcher was dark," I said. "When I stepped toward the lighted vault my foot came down on something soft and yielding. At the same time I heard a sound of moaning. Then I heard weeping, and whispered prayers. As my pupils widened in the dark I saw black forms moving below me. They were nuns, Negresses, and they were crawling over the floor, kissing it.

"I walked between them and entered the narrow vault. Along one wall lay a rectangular box with a heavy slab on top. A Greek priest stood by it. He threw rosewater at me, and continued to throw it until I realized his purpose and gave him some money. By that time I was damp on one side and heavily odoriferous."

The Professor thumbed through his notes again. "I must revise an entry," he said. "I accepted the statement that you were not dismayed by the mixed ownership of holy spots and the manner in which these spots are exploited. It is obvious now that you were more than dismayed. You were sickened for a while, then hardened by disgust."

"You are speaking of yourself," I said, "not of me. It was you who went to Jerusalem with a brittle, sentimental faith, not I. The flagrant exploitation of holy spots, the variety of Catholic churches, the dirt and noise and stench of the city, the Jews writing messages to God and hiding them in the Wailing Wall, the Mosque of Omar on the site of the Temple of Solomon, the shouting, bargaining hodgepodge of people representing twenty-four nationalities, the beggars and cripples and lepers, the hashish houses and Jewish schools, the ancient gates—all of these excited and thrilled me. They were my first experience with Christian and biblical reality. My faith leaped up and tied its flame to them."

"You went from one hope to another, that was all," the Professor said. "Churches covered the field of action, but the interlacing space and the people inhabiting it were unchanged. Caravans still came through the gates, donkeys plodded up the streets, and although the city, resting on the ruins of its former selves, was thirty feet higher than it was at the time of Christ, its people dressed and traded and gathered in bazaars and generally lived as they did two thousand years ago. Because life in America changes its face every ten years you considered this biblical countenance of Jerusalem evidential and exciting, forgetting that an industrial revolution—a chewing gum factory and a medium-sized steel mill—would erase it in six months."

"I walked down the Via Dolorosa one day," I said, "and crossed the Brook Kidron to Gethsemane on the Mount of Olives. There is a church there, built over the rock to which Jesus clung in His agony, but there is also a garden, sown with violets, with narrow paths and a place to sit. I looked across to the city and down the valley toward Bethany and Jericho. Tourists washed into the garden and were swept

320

out by their guides. The Franciscan in charge of the flower beds told the tourists that each might pick two violets. I saw an American woman turn her back to him and snatch three handfuls. She hid them in her handbag. As she scuttled away, her buttocks flipping her skirt, a nausea swept in on me from the circumference of my being. I was sick at the thought that I must follow the woman back to the United States, where Christianity had degenerated to the mockery she personified. I wanted to stay in Jerusalem, where all religions, like the people of whom they are composed, are brazenly imperfect."

"You preferred," said the Professor, "the reality of no religion at all to the muddle-headed, well-meaning idealism of your countrymen and countrywomen, who are, in a sense, an unconscious band of Robin Hoods, stealing and giving without knowing they do either. The woman who stole the violets probably wanted them for friends who deserved them, people whose charities perhaps supported the Franciscan whose whim of doling out the flowers forced the thievery.

"However, that is of minor importance. The incident merely brought to its peak a desire for escape which had been building since you entered the city. I expected it; Gethsemane was a logical setting for the climax."

"That may be so. As I sat in the warm sun after the woman had gone I thought about the things Abu Ali Omar had told me during our conversation the night before. He once had been engaged to marry an American girl. He broke the engagement because she expected him to live in America on money made by her father, who was a wealthy manufacturer.

"She did not understand why he could not do this. He tried to explain, to imply delicately the Arab's philosophy of marriage, but she was only bewildered. His own wealth—he owned several hotels, some groves, and ran a flourishing guide bureau—was to her a point of amusement.

"He said to me: 'A man proves himself to a woman by his conquest of their mutual environment. Normally the environment is a test of the man's physical prowess, mental agility, and spiritual strength. In America, which has an economic environment, the conquest demands cunning, opportunism, and a fanatical belief in the supreme importance of material goods.

"'A man proves himself to an American woman by his ability to make money. That is an unnatural basis for judgment. American men who are poor, or who are unsuccessful in their careers, must be very unhappy. Their charm, their wit, their virility, mean nothing to their wives. Always, in the thoughts of these women, there is a longing for something else, a magic in their men for making money, a magic which translates itself, in the women's dreams, into the simple ability which all men but eunuchs possess, and which beggars most deeply enjoy.'

"He smiled at me and sipped coffee from a small cup. 'It is a very versatile magic,' he said. 'It is hereditary, and it can be passed on from father to daughter, changing sex as easily as it changes generations. American heiresses shop for husbands as if they were men, and in their feelings and reactions they are men, for they possess the magic, the seed of life, which in your country is money and which elsewhere is the male sperm. Is it not true that in America husbands and wives limit the number of their children according to the size of their income? How craven your men must be, and how ashamed! Each must buy his place beside his wife at night with success in the world by day.'

"He set down his cup and said, 'America is a curious country. So much is done and so little is accomplished. I visited the research laboratories in the plant of the man who was to be my father-in-law. The scientists told me how they and their colleagues throughout the nation were pushing forward the frontiers of knowledge, approaching ultimate truth. I asked them if this would mean more poetry for the American people and they were annoyed.'

"He got up and we went outside and walked up the street toward the center of the city. He said, 'You see, the frontiers of knowledge have been pushed back before. The explorers found djinns and dragons and devils and gods. The scientists in America are finding the same things, but they are calling them different names—elements, chemicals, drugs, laws of relativity, quantum physics, electricity, internal combustion, blood transfusion, vacuum tubes. What is the use of it, beyond pleasure and novelty? In the end their discoveries will be superstition; that is the fate of all knowledge.'

"He lighted a cigarette and said, 'Would it not be better if you were a nation of poets? I looked for poetry in America and I found that all of the things about which poetry is written are disbelieved, so that there is only a laughing and a sneering poetry, and another kind which lies about what it believes, and which sounds as loud and shallow as the whistles on your factories.'

"He pointed across the street to a small motion picture theater. 'That is your only poetry,' he said. 'It is a simple tale, told over and over again with hardly a variation. It was long ago prefected in *A Thousand and One Nights*. Now the passionate, greedy will of your country has a Scheherazade, telling tales to stave off her destruction and win the love of her master.'

"I laughed, thinking of cold, practical, megalomaniacal Hollywood as Scheherazade, and we talked of something else. Abu Ali Omar had a house outside the city, with gardens and a grove and a library. He wanted me to visit him there, and to instruct him in English poetry. He was fond of Chaucer, and asked me many questions about *The Canterbury Tales*. Why was *The Cokes Tale of Gamelyn* not completed? It had a more exciting beginning than most of the other stories, he said. There was an apprentice who gambled and drank and danced, and who was finally dismissed by his master, whereupon he moved his belonging to the home of a friend who shared his appetites.

> *And had a wyf, that held for contenaunce*
> *A schoppe, and swyved for his sustenaunce.*

"I said I had never thought about the matter, but that perhaps Chaucer found he had devised too excellent a plot. His mind's merest hazard at what might happen when the apprentice moved in with his friend and was introduced to his friend's wife may have sent his talent reeling and reduced him to helpless wonder and delight.

"Abu Ali Omar said that was probably so; the plot was too ingenious. 'Your American civilization is like that,' he said. 'Perhaps it also cannot be finished.'

"He spoke then about the dead civilization in Trans-Jordan, and about his expeditions to Petra, and about the pleasures of archeological excavation for a man of imagination. It was unfortunate that I had to return to America, he said; there was a great deal in Palestine to occupy a person of taste, and much of it could be engaged in at a profit."

The Professor ticked with impatience. "If Abu Ali Omar was not goaded into that last remark then I am a Michaelmas goose," he said. "Once again you saw a way of escape, and you rushed toward it. What could have suited you better than a gentleman's status in Jerusalem, a business calling for the exercise of your morbid desire to dig into man's religious past, and an economic environment demanding a modicum of enterprise and utilizing only a substratum of energy? Abu Ali Omar did not offer you this way of escape. You asked for it."

"I did not ask for it," I said, "but I thought of it. I sat in Gethsemane and looked down the valley toward Bethany and Jericho and remembered sitting on a stone at the edge of the Jordan, letting the water run over my hand. Some sheep came to drink, and a black lamb stood close to me and put his forefeet in the water.

"The land all the way down to the Dead Sea seemed a worthless desert to me, yet the sight of it filled me with an ultimate content. Joseph sat in the front of my mind and saw everything; there was no dichotomy, no tension, no effort within me balancing a pressure from without. The quiet in the hub of my being had moved out during the weeks in Jerusalem, and now its tranquillity pierced the periphery and extended beyond it, so that nothing reached me without entering my environment and submitting to the atmosphere of my judgment and understanding.

"Hitherto I had jutted into the environment of the world, and things had reached me in terms of the world's atmosphere. Now I pervaded myself entirely, and surrounded my area of existence with an aura strong enough to impose such conditions as it chose on any experience which entered it."

"A pleasant state of egotism," the Professor said, "full of peace, pleasure, and presumption. Why did you abandon it? Why did you leave Jerusalem? You discovered while you were there that your employers expected you to describe your journey in the first person singular. You did not want to do that; you could not write about yourself without betraying your dichotomy, your division into funny man and philosopher, poet and practitioner of the pratfall. You had either to devise a fictional character and represent him as yourself or abandon the job. You wanted to abandon the job. Why didn't you?"

"The geography which provoked my contentment explains why I did not abandon the job," I said. "As I descended from Jerusalem to the Dead Sea I went over the rim of the

West and down toward the East. My contentment was made of remembrance, abandonment, irresponsibility. It signified a turning toward Nirvana, the heaven of undifferentiated form from which I came forth; it symbolized a return through the familiar pastures of involution to the nothingness which disgorged me. It meant an abandonment of self to Self, not a transformation of self into Self; it was a refusal to face evolution, a signal that I had given up the adventure in consciousness of my will and my identity, an announcement that I preferred annihilation to realization."

"Grandiose!" the Professor muttered. "A pompous dream!"

"In Jerusalem the downward spin of spiritual involution stopped and the upward swing of spiritual evolution began," I said. "Christianity declares man's return to God by way of the realized self, the resurrection in the soul of the crucified God. It proclaims a translation of self into Self by the salvation of humanity. Thus no man achieves himself without somewhat achieving all men. He cannot seek God without looking for Him in humanity, where He lies hidden and sown, asleep in His tomb.

"The Christian is instructed to go to God the long way, in the company of all other men. He should not desert and return home in the night. He should not rush forward by day to be first at the next encampment. He should move with the column, pressing firmly at each step, that the mass may receive from him what strength he possesses beyond the needs of his personal march. I need not tell you this; if you did not know it your blood would be colorless and cold.

"I left Jerusalem. I took a morning train to Cairo. I sat in a compartment with a flat-faced English girl who had thick ankles and six tennis racquets. I thought that again I would need to play tennis for something beyond exercise. My neck was stiff and my stomach quivered with nausea.

"At Lydda I changed trains. I bought a small bottle of brandy and got into a compartment with three men who were wearing caps and a woman who was eating a banana. They were Americans. One of the men was a minister. He had fallen off a donkey while riding around the walls of Jerusalem. He laughed when he told me about it. One of the other men had fallen off a camel.

"I offered them a drink of my brandy. None accepted. They did not drink, they said. They were members of a temperance league. They were pleased about prohibition.

"I dank some of the brandy and my stomach felt better. I looked past the minister's cap and through the window at the desert racing by. My return had not even the value of a symbol. There was historical movement everywhere, but except in the sight of the wide, high eye of God movement of the spirit was at a pause; the soul of man was a river turned to ice, a glacier shimmering in the sun, firm to its face at the edge of the sea, breaking off bit by bit and drifting away, each section still valiantly solid, denying the liquid nature of its being."

"Oh, come!" the Professor said. "It's not as bad as that, even from your melancholy and maladjusted viewpoint. You were returning to economic competition, religious authority, moral stability, and a kind of intellectual activity in the arts and sciences in which you were not capable of participating. That is why I do not understand your decision to leave Jerusalem. You were content there, and you had no reason to return. There was nothing for you to do here. You fulfilled no useful purpose; your job was a task better left undone; you supported no one; you were functionless in democracy, a malcontent with an incipient martyr's complex. You should have stayed."

"I could not stay," I said. "I had to return to being functionless in democracy. It was a compulsion and I do not expect you to consider the compulsion reasonable. Man was made to be content only while moving toward God, at however slow a pace. I could not accept the contentment I felt in Jerusalem because it accompanied a backward movement, a retracing of ground already won, a remembering, a nostalgia, a surrender. I had to find contentment in movement which was forward from the furthest frontier.

"If I could not find that movement; if at the last encampment the soldiers were huddled in their tents; I would have to get along without contentment."

"You are," said the Professor, "a damned fool."

"Let us get on with the story," I said. "I experienced one day a moment of supreme content when I sat on a rock at the edge of the Jordan and let the water run over my hand. On another day I left Jerusalem. Late that night I arrived in Cairo."

TWENTY

I WOKE in a corner of the Hotel Metropolitan. I walked out on its balcony and looked down into the street. Across the way was a large red brick building. Along its front in gold letters six feet high ran a title—THE MANURE COMPANY OF EGYPT, LTD. After breakfast I stood on the steps of the hotel and listened to the sounds of the city. A pleasant-faced Arab who was doing the same thing spoke to me. He was Mabrouk, chief of the hotel's guides. We talked amiably for a while and I made a date with him for the next day. Then I walked to Shepheard's Hotel and to Cook's, just beyond it, where I picked up my mail.

It was not until I turned a corner and saw Shepheard's before me on the left that I realized I had asked no one the way. I had meant to inquire of Mabrouk, but our conversation was enjoyable and I forgot about it. I stood still and considered my route. I had followed the line of least resistance; I could have gone no other way without taking to a narrower street, something a foreigner on his own in a strange city seldom does. I felt better when this was ascertained; I walked on, and then suddenly someone was keeping step with me, addressing me as if we were old friends. It was Mabrouk. He was on his way to Shepheard's to interview one of the guides on business. On the sidewalk in front of Shepheard's he introduced me to his nephew and to several cousins. There was something curiously familiar about Mabrouk, but I shook off the feeling and went on to Cook's.

In the following days the feeling of familiarity returned, but I charged it to the fact that Mabrouk and I spent a lot of time together. We attended Coptic funerals, went to Egyptian vaudeville shows, inspected the Tutankhamen collection in the Cairo museum, sailed in a felucca on the Nile, and prowled through tombs. One tomb was the property of a young sheik who was also one of Mabrouk's

327

cousins. He asked me to spend a few months with his people in the desert, or perhaps a year.

Several of Mabrouk's friends conducted a perfume business. They offered to prepare a scent for my wife, my mistress, or my sweetheart. When I confessed that I possessed none of the three they were disappointed. They suggested that I choose a woman from those available in Cairo, one who would not be repulsive to me in certain circumstances. They would prepare a scent which, when she received it from me and pulled the stopper, would cause the woman to be instantly infatuated with me. Capitulation would be inevitable; I could pick my own time and place. Since the only women I knew in Cairo were wives of English army officers I asked the cousins to hold the offer until someone more deserving of so dubious a fate turned up.

In the morning while waiting for Mabrouk I read *The Egyptian Mail*, an English newspaper which reported local news in brief, terrifying paragraphs. Its readers were informed that:

Four epidemics were reported raging in Egypt: cholera, typhoid, smallpox, and cerebrospinal meningitis.

A woman was stabbed seven times by her brother, who asked her for money and was refused.

A baker of sixty murdered his son-in-law and tried to marry his daughter.

A man murdered his daughter for not bringing home enough cigarette butts.

A camel bit off his master's arm at lunchtime.

A bomb was found under the home of a local prince.

After several weeks of sightseeing I was invited one day to lunch at Mabrouk's house in Mena, the small native village at the foot of the hill on which the Great Pyramid of Gizeh stands. We arrived from Sakkara by camel; as we rode over the sand long ribbons of green edged the Nile on our right and the pyramid on its plateau of rock loomed ahead to the left. Crouched below it, looking from a distance like a fed dog drowsing in the sun, was the Sphinx. As we came nearer it reared proudly; sand had been cleared from its base, giving it the dignified appearance of something cared for and respected.

The symbolism of its form and the meaning of its riddle were simple to see from the gently swaying saddle on which I sat with a knee hooked around the pommel—out of the lower nature emerges the higher. The Sphinx has the body of a lion, the breasts and head of a woman, and wings: from the appetites of the animal grow the emotions which foster the intellect which discovers the spirit. The riddle of the Sphinx asks what creature it is that walks on four feet in the morning, on two at noon, and on three in the evening. The answer is man, who goes from animal group consciousness to egotistical self-consciousness to spiritual superconsciousness. As a child he crawls; in youth and maturity he walks upright and unaided; in his latter days he uses a staff to insure his progress.

It was noon as we swung past the great figure and came alongside the hill of the pyramid. We rode into one of the streets of Mena and my camel stopped before the gate of a two-story house. As I dismounted a number of people gathered to watch. Mabrouk explained that they were his relatives; he and various branches of his family occupied the entire street.

We walked through the gate and up a flight of steps to living quarters on the second floor. In the yard a woman in black was bent over a household task; she seemed to be sewing and she seemed old. Mabrouk pointed to her. "That is my wife," he said. The two were, I knew, the same age, thirty-five. They had married when they were fourteen and much in love. He had no other wives; four were allowed him by Moslem law, but he was content with his one.

In the main room of the living quarters we sat down to a meal of rice, chicken, and lamb. The food was heaped on a large silver platter. There were no individual plates, no knives, forks or spoons. There was nothing to drink.

Mabrouk smiled.

"You begin on your side," he said, "and I will begin on mine."

We ate with our hands, reaching into the platter for what we wanted, working toward each other slowly through the pile of food.

"When we finish," said Mabrouk happily, "we will wash our hands."

My thirst became unbearable and I asked for water. Mabrouk spoke to the servant, who filled a tumbler from an old-fashioned cooler which sat on a stand in a corner. I took the glass and drank from it sparingly, throttling a desire to drain it at a gulp. I set it down and Mabrouk picked it up and drank from it, also sparingly. He set it down and the light from a window struck it, illuminating the greasy print of my fingers and reaching toward them from the other side of the glass, the print of Mabrouk's hand.

Later, when we were finished, I drank again from the glass, and Mabrouk did also. Then we washed our hands in a basin and lighted cigarettes. Mabrouk showed me his wardrobe—the robes were of broadcloth, each one carefully tailored—and talked about the guide business, the perfume business, the trade in scarabs, liaison between guides and tourists, and how all these enterprises need imagination, organization, and leadership. We went down the steps and walked along the plateau, squinting up at the soaring mass of stone. The rear end of a large woman in knickers was disappearing into the entrance passage, which in 2170 B.C., when the pyramid was built, pointed to Alpha Draconis, then the polestar, at its lower culmination. I asked Mabrouk if he knew the mathematical facts of the pyramid.

He recited them with a casual reverance, as if he were saying his beads. The height of the pyramid was to a circle whose circumference equaled the perimeter of the pyramid's base as π or 3.1416. He drew a circle in the sand for illustration. "The length of the four sides of the base," he said, "is the circumference. The height is the radius. The circle is squared."

The height of the pyramid, he explained, if multiplied by ten to the ninth power, became the sun's mean distance from the earth. The pyramid inch, 1.001 of the modern inch, is exactly one five hundred millionth of the polar axis of the earth. The number of days in the solar year is set in the measurement of the pyramid's base perimeter, a hundred pyramid inches being given to each day. The gravity of the mass of the pyramid multiplied by $10^{5 \times 3}$ is equal to the gravity of the earth as a mass. The pyramid sits at the exact center of the earth's land area. Its summit points to the sun at noon and at midnight of the autumnal equinox in 2170 B.C. it pointed to Alcyone in the constellation Pleiades, the center of the universe, around which the sun

330

and its satellites wheel. Said God to Job, "Canst thou bind the sweet influences of Pleiades, or loose the bands of Orion?"

Mabrouk stopped talking and we stared at the clean lines of the great mass of stone. The pyramid had long since been stripped of its smooth outer facing and thirty feet of its top had been knocked off, but its magic and its beauty were intact. A single point of spirit, the summit, broke as it neared the earth into four descending lines of force which anchored themselves in the foundations of flesh—mental faculties, the emotional pattern, the body's vitality, the body's form. From these foundations the differentiated spirit rose back toward itself; the soul flew in from the polestar and worked its way in darkness to the shining goal of the Pleiades. In the pyramid's inner chambers, according to legend, students of the mystery religions were initiated; Pythagoras, so the faithful said, was one of them, as was Plato. Said Isaiah, "In that day there shall be an altar to the Lord in the midst of the land of Egypt . . . and it shall be for a sign and a witness unto the Lord of Hosts . . ."

I asked Mabrouk if he knew the prophecies of the pyramid, particularly those based on measurements of the inner passages, with a solar year assigned to each pyramid inch. He nodded absently.

"All prophecies end with this century," he said. "You must know that. Students of prophecy come here and ask me what the pyramid says, because they have discovered that neither the predictions of Nostradamus nor the list of popes of Saint Malachy goes beyond 2000 A.D. The same is true of the pyramid measurements, of course, but the students of prophecy are so unhappy—though none I have known is young enough to live past 1960—that I tell them there is a legend among the people of Egypt that when Armageddon is finished the first of the survivors who enters the pyramid will find, released from its hiding place by the shock of battle, a new Ark of the Covenant, with prophecies and spiritual laws for the new age. The students of prophecy are cheered when they hear this; they seem certain that they will be among the survivors of Armageddon. I feel that it does no harm to tell them of the legend. It makes them happy."

He looked at me and smiled. "Besides," he said, "it is true."

I said goodbye to him after a while and returned to the city by myself. At the hotel there was a letter from Abu Ali Omar. He was driving to Cairo in a few weeks, he wrote, to interview some archeologists about a trip to Trans-Jordan. Would I care to ride back to Jerusalem with him?

That night I answered the letter. The next day I booked passage for England on a boat scheduled to arrive at Port Said from India on April 1st, several days before Abu Ali Omar would get to Cairo. My train left Cairo for Port Said at seven o'clock in the morning. I ordered breakfast, including a large pot of coffee, sent to my room at six, and went to spend the evening at the bar of the Hotel Continental; I could not leave Cairo, I knew, except under anaesthesia. I returned to my room at five o'clock and fell asleep. When the waiter brought breakfast an hour later I sat up, swung my feet to the floor, and reached for the coffee pot. I poured half a cup and drank it quickly. It was tea.

"The gentleman does not drink tea for breakfast?" the waiter said. He was astonished.

I reached the train and the boat and the upper bunk in my stateroom. It was the next afternoon before I felt well enough to sit at the open end of the aft saloon and sip a mixture of brandy and port, which the bartender assured me would settle my stomach. It did, but there was a discomfort in my head which continued and the tension in my neck had returned. That night I slept without a pillow. In the morning I put my neck on the metal safety rail which ran along the bunk's open edge and let my head hang over; it was the only way I could ease the tightness along my spine.

There were no other Americans on board. Most of the passengers were English civil servants returning with their families from various parts of the Empire for a holiday at home. There were a few Indians, and there was the Aga Khan, spiritual ruler by divine right of the Ismaili Moslems, a god whose bath water is bottled and sold to the faithful. His wife, a slim, pretty French girl, walked the deck in a leopard skin coat. She shared her American cigarettes with me and introduced me to her sister, who spoke English well. One night the Aga Khan sent for me and I talked to him in his cabin. He lay in his bunk, a very large man, and complained about the ship's food and service, the Mediterranean weather, and the economic state of the world. He asked me about the United States. How much were they worth now as a nation? What was the best stock to buy? How were the Rockefellers and Morgans getting along? Had I seen them lately? No, I said, I had not seen them lately. Soon he lost interest in me and I left.

One afternoon in the lounge the ship lurched as he rose from a chair and he fell to the floor. I left the desk at which I was writing and helped him to his feet. It was not an easy task, and I appreciated the zeal of his followers, who every year give him, as a mark of their faith, a gift of his weight in gold. When he was safely on his way I wrote in my journal: "3 P.M. God fell down and I helped him up."

My cabin mate was a friendly, round-faced London engineer named Frost, an Englishman raised in Lancashire. He laughed a lot and was kind to me. None of the other Englishmen spoke to me, but I met a girl named Cynthia who had been sent on a vacation to the East to get over an affection for a not quite acceptable young man, and she was kind to me because, on the ship at least, I was in the same unfortunate social position as her disqualified suitor. We walked around the deck until we were tired, then stood together just below the bridge, watching the prow break open the sea.

We reached Marseilles and set out for Gibraltar. The chief steward jumped overboard and was lost. One night as I stood below the bridge with Cynthia, waiting for the moon to rise and light the water, I admitted to myself the reason for the return of tension to my body and faced the fact that the discomfort in my head was no better and probably was not going to improve. The reason was simple. Joseph was gone.

He was no longer with me in any part of my being. I existed only on the periphery of awareness, jutting into the world, meeting experience in terms of the world's atmosphere. There was nothing now between me and the shrunken, faraway quiet at the hub of my being which so briefly ago had encompassed me. There were no secondary levels of perception, no descending depths of realization to cushion my thoughts like sleep. I was alone at the edge of the moment, a rim moving over existence without spokes and with no axle at my center, a hoop rolling aimlessly through sensation, kept moving by the natural slope of time. I knew what had happened. I knew why Joseph was gone. I had found what he wanted to do, what he wanted to be, what he wanted to know, what he wanted to discover, and I had abandoned these things. Joseph was my arm stretched out to the spirit. I had cut him off. Since childhood he had been the left hand of my mind, and he had trusted me. His blood was on the hand of my consciousness that remained.

"Let's walk some more," I said to Cynthia.

She reached into my pocket and gripped my fingers and set out again to circle the deck. So long as my body moved or there was someone to whom I could talk the pressure and the discomfort stayed behind me, but when I was alone and still they closed in, stiffening my vertebrae and beating against the base of my brain. How long this would go on I did not know; I wondered if it would be always.

I had no patience now with the long view of a soul plunging into darkness at the finish of spiritual involution, feeling lost until the first flicker of the beacon of spiritual evolution is sighted. That was all very well for saints; John of the Cross could aptly call it, "the dark night of the soul." I was not a saint; I was only ill and lonely and uncertain, without the solace of the single wealth I had possessed, a bass string on the instrument of my mind which gave the low, full tones of meditation to thoughts which struck it, and which filled the continuous and empty caverns of my subterranean awareness with pleasant and echoing sounds. I was at last a mature and responsible man, without mystical leanings, philosophical theories, or religious ideals. I did not like myself. I did not trust myself.

With Frost and Cynthia I played skittles and shuffleboard and table tennis. I walked the deck until I staggered. I ate a great deal and slept heavily. I was introduced to some of the English men and women on the ship, and after I had been presented they spoke to me when we met. The women, I found, were only shy; the men apparently considered it bad taste for the American Colonies to have done so well for themselves since 1776. They disliked the United States because they were rich.

One morning after breakfast I found a group of them staring at the bulletin board. The news from London said that Chancellor of the Exchequer Neville Chamberlain had announced the first treasury surplus since the World War. It was a small surplus, only five million pounds, but it was, the government stated, cause for rejoicing throughout the Empire. Just under this announcement on the board was a dispatch from Washington; several members of Congress, when informed of the surplus, had suggested that it be paid to the United States as an installment on England's war debts. The man standing in front of me took his pipe from his mouth and said, "What arrogance!" Another man said, "We won't pay them a shilling! They're too bloody rich already."

I walked away. If the man in front of me had turned around while I stood there I would have spoken to him, and there would have been trouble. Without Joseph, without anything but a nervous awareness on the moving edge of sequential phenomena, I was subject to the pull of identities beyond myself—group possessions, group angers, group prejudices, nuclear forces providing the comfort of a center for unstable, insecure egos, holding them in an orbit, chaining but warming their frightened clusters of thought. I was losing my objectivity. Unless I held securely to the periphery and fought back toward the quiet at the hub of my being, replacing Joseph with a self-consciously woven texture or interlaced and cushioning webs of reason, I would lose myself.

We paused at Gibraltar, then bucked the Bay of Biscay and went on to land at Plymouth. In London I looked up Dick Plummer at the *Express* office in Fleet Street. His wife, Beattie, was at their house in Sussex, and the next day I went there with Dick for a week end. The house was fourteenth century, and except for plumbing and electricity had been left in its natural state by the new owners. The floors tipped slightly, the fireplace was enormous, and a brook ran through the yard.

Across the road and over a hill lay the way to the town where the Woman had lived, and where she died and was buried. I had ascertained its position from a map; I had not mentioned its name to my host or hostess. I did not want to go there; I did not want to stand at the Woman's grave, or walk nervously around it, unable to settle back in my mind to the place where we existed together and from which for so long had come a steady throb of comfort, muffled in its beat when I was otherwise concerned, steady and strong when I turned the face of my mind to it and put the cheek of my thought against its ecstasy. The place had vanished from within me; it had gone with Joseph, to whom it belonged. It was he whom the Woman had loved; always she had looked through me and lifted her mouth to him.

Back in London I walked the streets and shuffled through museums. When my legs tired I sat in cinema houses. One afternoon I saw a newsreel featuring Neville Chamberlain, who sat at his desk and read an official announcement of the treasury surplus. When he was finished reading he looked up and said, smiling, "I assure you this money will not be sent to the United States, as has been suggested by several of the gentlemen in Washington." The audience around me broke into loud applause.

The steady procession of Anglo-Saxon and Celtic faces in London puzzled me; I had never been in a city made with so few racial strains. I missed the Slavic, Latin, and Scandinavian physiognomies of New York and Naugatuck. The Semitic varieties of Jerusalem had not been strange to me; the Teutonic monotony of Russell Square was. I felt most at home in the pubs at night, where workingmen talked politics over pints of beer. The laborer, wherever he was, could be depended on; his prejudices were few and they seldom changed direction. The trouble with the world was simple, and on a mild night with a small drink before an open fire with a roast turning slowly on a spit in the pub near my hotel—it was nothing to worry about. It was, in fact, no more than the ending of an old song:

> It's the same the whole world over,
> It's the poor gets all the blame.
> It's the rich gets all the gravy;
> Ain't it all a bleeding shame?

It wasn't a bleeding shame, of course, and the poor knew it. The rich had none of their content, none of their pleasure in physical usefulness, none of their mental poise in matters of urgency, none of their pleasure in physical usefulness, none of their sense of spiritual security, none of their freedom from goods and station. But the poor in England, so far as I could see, were not snobbish in their superiority. They regarded the well-to-do as if they were equals; if they pitied them they did not show it. One night at dusk I hailed a taxi and asked the driver, a middle-aged man with full moustaches, if he would take me to the hotel at which Cynthia was staying.

"D'you mind if I don't, Gov'nor?" he said. "It's all the the way across town, you see, and the missus is expecting me home in half an hour, and she'll have supper all cooked and ready."

I said I didn't mind at all, and he got down from his seat and said he would get me another cab. While I waited he explained that it wasn't like an ordinary night, a lamb stew night for instance, when the meal could be kept a while without spoiling, but a roast night, when being on time was important. He helped me into the first empty cab that came along and told the driver where I wanted to go and what time I was due there. The warmth of him stayed with me all through the evening, and when I sat at dinner with Cynthia and she squeezed my hand under the table I squeezed back until she whimpered.

Beattie and her sister went with me to the boat train. On the platform they pointed out Liam O'Flaherty, the Irish novelist, and told me to look him up during the voyage. The ship was the *Majestic,* then the largest vessel in the world. It was so long a boat that in the Bay of Biscay two nuns who were circling the deck in the direction opposite to mine were lifted slowly above me as they gravely walked toward me. I went into the bar and found O'Flaherty.

He was reading a book but he put it aside when I introduced myself and we settled down to a drink and some talk. He was lean and silver-haired, with pale blue eyes and a ruddy complexion. He had been to Ireland for the races at Punchestown, and somewhere between Dublin and London had mislaid his lower plate. He was on his way to Hollywood, where one of his novels, *The Informer,* was to be made into a film. I had read the book; it was the same bitter story that runs through all of Ireland's attempts to break the British rule—Irishmen betrayed by an Irishman, sold to the English for a hundred pounds.

I asked him about The Troubles of the nineteen-twenties, and about the Easter Rebellion of 1916, and about the time he kept a red flag flying over the Rotunda in Dublin for a week. We talked through the night, and when the bar closed we ordered thirty beers and set them on our table. They were almost gone when he told me of the day he stood in a Dublin crowd, a price on his head, a pistol in his raincoat pocket, his right hand on its butt, and heard an Irishwoman say, "God blast that dirty black murdering Liam O'Flaherty; I hope they catch him and I hope they hang him!"

The words hit him like a hail of bullets. He turned from the crowd and walked away, and the next day he left Ireland.

We finished the beers and went to bed after that, but in the following days and nights of the voyage we walked the decks and talked some more and ordered flocks of beers when the bar closed, and I heard about the Aran Isles and about Irish horses and writers and women and about young Chester A. Arthur, grandson of the American President, who went to Dublin and worked for the Irish cause until he discovered that it was not a fight for freedom but a struggle to take the Irish from one master and deliver them to another.

"When people are able to rule themselves," O'Flaherty said, "they won't need guns to get their freedom. They'll have it without lifting a hand."

He leaned against the rail and looked at the sea. "Writing's the only game," he said. "You make something out of nothing and it becomes more real than yourself."

From New York, after seeing O'Flaherty off to Hollywood, I sailed for Havana. From Havana I went to Mexico. At Mexico City I got aboard a train for Los Angeles. It was a long ride, consuming four days and four nights. As we ambled up the coast near Mazatlan I sat on the rear platform of the observation car. On both sides of me the mass of jungle green through which we had been passing turned black, covered by night.

Suddenly on my left the glow of a city appeared. I turned to watch it, trying to reason from my memory of the train schedule what place it might be. Then the glow softened and disappeared. I stared at the spot where it had been. There was only darkness. Suddenly the glow reappeared, building until it resembled the sky over Coney Island on the night before the Fourth of July. Then it faded again, and I realized what it was—the simultaneous brightening and dimming of millions of fireflies. They were on my right, too, I found, swarms of them, their light waxing and waning in rhythm, as if a sleeping monster were exhaling phosphorescent steam. For almost an hour we rode through this gleaming, ghostly fairyland. Then there was only night again and the July heat sucking at the little breeze made by the moving train. I put my neck against the top of the chair on which I was sitting and turned back my head until its weight was set against the tension in my neck.

I had been trying with fumbling skill to knit a fabric of secondary consciousness, to improvise from judgments and theories and formulae existing outside of myself a substitute for the integrated, elastic, infinitely adaptable tapestry I had lost. I had not been very successful; such notions as I had strung together made only a thin, rough strip of reference, not wide enough for a hammock, not soft enough for a bed. I clung still to the periphery of my being, meeting the moment without help from reflection, meditation, or any other of the multiple facets of Joseph's intellectual talent. It was slow work; I was like a man born rich, learning now for the first time how hard it is to make a dollar.

From Los Angeles I flew to San Francisco, where I talked to Upton Sinclair, the author, who was running for Governor of California on an EPIC platform—End Poverty In California. Such strength had rallied to his liberal, socialistic cause that in genuine fright the opposition was pouring money into a campaign of propaganda aimed at convincing every man who owned more than the shirt on his back that if EPIC won he would be stripped of his belongings. Sinclair, fighting another skirmish in a battle he had been waging since 1906, when his novel of the Chicago meat trust, *The Jungle,* appeared, knew what he was up against. He had led his party to the attack; he hoped the party had enough strength to resist the opposition's counterpunching until Election Day. It didn't. Sinclair lost. Only a minority of voters possessed so few goods they were willing to share them with others.

From San Francisco I sailed to Honolulu. On Waikiki Beach I took a room at the Halekulani Hotel. There were casters on my bed, and when I woke in the morning I put my hand on the floor and pushed until the bed rolled out to the lanai porch overlooking the lawn, the beach, and the sea. There I had breakfast, while lovebirds watched me from a tree that swept past the edge of my screen. I flew to the island of Hawaii and saw Kilauea, the volcano on the slope of Mauna Kea, in eruption, its fire pit, Halemaumau, a fantastic furnace of red, boiling rock. I saw the yacht races at Pearl Harbor, with star boats sailing through a double rainbow. I visited gardens of orchids and hibiscus and antherium. I danced on the porch of the Mauna Loa Hotel when the moon was full and my throat and the throat of the girl in my arms were wreathed in ginger blossom leis. If ever I find Joseph again, I thought, I shall come back to this place.

I was packed to leave for Japan when I was informed that a staff of experts had informed my employers that readers of *The American Magazine* are not the sort who can afford a trip to the Far East. Since it would not be wise from the magazine's viewpoint to publish descriptions of journeys its readers could not hope to some time take I was asked to return to California and set out on a tour of the country by automobile. I sailed to San Francisco, bought a Ford, and visited Yosemite, Hollywood, Grand Canyon, Texas, New Orleans, Charleston, and Virginia. As I traveled I tried to put together from what I saw and heard a background of America for the secondary consciousness I was stitching in my mind. It made a lopsided pattern. What I saw was spectacularly beautiful; what I heard was dull.

In Yosemite I lived in a cabin and walked through autumn woods where deer did not move when I approached except to step from my path, and where cliffs leaped up two thousand feet to shine and stare in the sun. In Hollywood I stayed with Jimmy Pollak, who after his years at Washington and Lee had taken to the motion picture business. We went to Palm Springs, a resort in a desert, one week end, and spent Saturday night in a combination saloon and gambling house. There were more familiar faces in the bar than I had seen since leaving Naugatuck, yet I knew no one. It was uncomfortable to be with actors whose physical equipage had become public property; it was unnatural not to be able to speak to them. I watched a frail, exquisite blonde whom I had loved when I was young and she was in her stardom. She sat at a table with friends; she was still beautiful, still youthful. She left her friends after a while and came to the bar and stood by me. She pushed her glass shyly toward the bartender.

"Another triple brandy, please," she said.

When we left at two o'clock the doorman was listening intently to Douglas Fairbanks, who was explaining that a Mr. Fred Astaire would arrive soon and would ask for Mr. Fairbanks' party.

"Mr. Esther?" the doorman said.

"No, no!" Fairbanks said. "Mr. Astaire."

The doorman nodded.

"I will let him in," he said.

It was late November when I left Hollywood; it was early spring when I reached Virginia. I had volumes of notes; I was sleeping better; I could sit still for hours, matching colors and textures of thought for the web of reflection and opinion I was weaving to take Joseph's place. I was slow-witted, pedagogical, talkative, a ruinous bore, but I had defenses, I had assets, I had a jerry-built, sod-roofed, dirt-floored security that saved me from shaking to pieces in the mistral that sweeps always over the moment. I would survive.

I visited the Cayces in Virginia Beach, then drove to Lexington and stayed a while with Fitz. Lexington had not changed and I pretended that I was the same, but I was afraid to kiss Marshall Penick for fear she would know what had happened. I drove to Richmond from Lexington and visited Junkin, who was teaching art at the local division of William and Mary. He had married a pianist, a lovely girl named Margot, and the long sky-lighted living room of their apartment was crowded with canvases, easels, music, and a grand piano. Junkin taught and painted; Margot played the grand piano and kept house; sometimes she played for her husband while he sketched.

The painting I had asked Junkin to save for me so that some day I might give it a proper home was still among the stacks along the wall. It was the face of a street-walker; Junkin had passed her on his way home from work one Wednesday and had painted her from memory the next morning after a night in which she stalked, a cigarette hanging from her mouth, through his dreams. It was a small, brilliant, frightening canvas; the girl's face reflected not only Junkin's pity for her gutted existence but his horror at the prostitution of any talent, whether an artfulness at physical union or an ability to paint.

"It's about time you settled down and gave her a home," he said as he lifted her from her place behind a large canvas and propped her against the edge of a window seat. "If, as you contend, she suffers mainly from discrimination and persecution, under your protection she should reverse the story of Dorian Gray and grow slowly into health and virtuousness."

"She will," I said. "She won't reform, but she will become virtuous."

We talked through most of the night. When I climbed into the Ford late the next morning and set our for Washington it was raining.

"So long," Junkin said. "Remember me to Mary."

His words bothered me as I drove over the drenched macadam. I had made no plans to see Mary during my stay in Washington. It was several years since we had corresponded. She might have married; she at least would be engaged. It was not likely that the most beautiful girl in the city would be accessible to a suitor whose desertion from her retinue had been without sound reason and whose return was unannounced. I could, I thought, write her a note; if she were married I would know it from the signature of her reply.

That, I decided, was what I would do. But as I neared Washington and the rain increased another solution occurred to me. I could call Mary's mother. I would inquire for the members of the family, and I would be told about Mary. That, I thought, was the most sensible procedure. I would call when I was settled in a hotel.

But when I reached the city I drove up Fourteenth Street, swung left at Thomas Circle, and raced out Sixteenth Street to the Ganey home. I demanded abruptly of Mrs. Ganey whether Mary was married. The answer was no. Mary was at work in the Interior Department of the government. Her mother called her on the telephone and told her of my arrival. Mary said she would meet me in an hour at the corner of Eighteenth and I Streets.

The rain stopped as I drove down Sixteenth Street. Traffic slowed me on I Street. From the middle of the block between Seventeenth and Eighteenth Streets I saw Mary standing in front of the Columbia Medical Building, a scarf at her throat, a small, snap-brim hat on her head, her face in profile. She was more beautiful than ever, more serene in the lift of her head, more poised in her body. I drove alongside her and she stepped into the car.

"Hello," she said casually. "It's nice to see you."

"Thanks," I said. "Do you mind if I look for a hotel?"

342

TWENTY-ONE

THE PROFESSOR thumbed absently through his notes, muttering phrases to himself—"delayed adolescence," "romantic irresponsibility," "desire to return to the womb," "centripetal ego," "impractical religious attitude," "environmental maladjustment," "social disorientation," "political infantilism."

After a while he said, "Seems to me you have the ideal equipment for a writer. You should be more successful than you are. Too bad the subjects which send you into frenzy are unpopular. If you were a Communist or a parlor liberal your wildest cries would be printed on rough paper in little magazines and you would be called a political mystic, a social visionary, and a prophet of the people."

"Am I no more civilized than that?" I said.

He put away his notes, gave Miss Iceberg's anatomy its half-hourly inspection, and went on with his judgment.

"At the present time," he said, "you are. Until you lost Joseph you were not. Joseph was your racial memory, your heritage of barbarism and superstition, your primitive longing for return to the sleep of unconscious existence. It should have faded as you grew into adolescence, its disappearance should have signaled your maturity.

"There is, in fact, no maturity of the mind until this raiment of magic and myth is shed. For a large number of reasons—some racial, some religious, some personal and idiosyncratic—you retained the vestigal garment for half a dozen years past the normal date of divestment.

"The process of removing it was therefore painful; it was also done suddenly. You were like a man with weak eyes who loses his spectacles, or a lady who favors one leg and mislays her walking stick. You had a bad time of it for a while. You were certain that your mind could not get along without Joseph, just as the man with weak eyes is convinced that he cannot read without spectacles, and the lady who favors one leg insists she cannot walk without a cane.

"You went through a few difficult months. You were nervous and unsure of yourself. But you began, as a matter of self-preservation, to think for yourself. It is not an easy habit to initiate at twenty-seven, but you made the effort, and by the time you reached Washington you were partly successful.

"You still mourned the grandiose daydreams with which Joseph had provided you. Of all the disciplines of maturity the most difficult for the neophyte to accept is that which decrees that he is an ordinary fellow, on even terms with the rest of humanity. The notion of himself he has fostered since infancy is not easy to abandon. You clung to it as stubbornly as the rest.

"Well, that is that. I will go over the remainder of my notes while you finish talking. Who is Mary? She sounds like the most sensible thing that ever happened to you."

"She was," I said, "but to tell you about her I must go back briefly to the Sunday in September, 1926, when I left Naugatuck for Lexington. I arrived in Washington late that afternoon and prepared to spend the night with Barney O'Connor, a Naugatuck boy who was studying dentistry at Georgetown.

"Barney had a girl named Nora and Nora had a young sister named Mary. Mary was asked to give me a date. At first she refused; she wanted to go roller skating with her girl friends. Under family pressure she reconsidered, but to show her resentment she sat in one spot all evening and did not speak to me except in monosyllables.

"I didn't mind. She was so incredibly beautiful that it was sufficient pleasure to look at her. She had a long full mouth, magnificent brown eyes, a high forehead, and masses of naturally wavy hair. Nora was a blue-eyed blonde, infectiously friendly and proud of her stunning sister.

"When young people spend an evening together they normally achieve at least a first-name acquaintance. You may judge how friendly Mary was on that night of our meeting by the salutation of my first letter to her. It began, 'My dear Miss Ganey.'"

"Good for her," the Professor said. "She put you where you belonged. Too bad she didn't keep you there. I suppose you wriggled your way into her affection by writing of your loneliness, sending her poetry, and turning up in Washington whenever she seemed on the edge of forgetting you."

"I did," I said, "but it was two years before I could hold her hand. By that time she was studying at Trinity College and I was writing for *The Southern Collegian*. We argued about religion. Mary was violently orthodox; she had been taught by nuns since kindergarten. By telling her anything of a philosophical nature that popped into my head and seemed reasonable I discovered that no matter what my mind devised by way of speculation on the spiritual life the odds were a hundred to one it was theologically in error, officially condemned, or dangerously heretical. It was an easy way for me to learn Catholic dogma, but a discouraging one."

"It should have enlightened you," the Professor said. "Mary must have been a patient girl; she apparently suffered from the common failing of good women, a weakness for fools."

"I told her that she personified both the virtues and the evils of the church. She was pure in heart, free and un-sullied at the center of the mystery of her soul. She wore the finest raiment the world was able to devise; her exterior was enslaved by riches. She was certain of the righteousness of her spiritual path beyond the righteousness of all other spiritual paths. She studied biased books. She eased the stringency of the Sermon on the Mount. She neither gave her cloak to an enemy at law nor turned the other cheek when he struck her. I asked her if she had ever visited the imprisoned."

"Oh, come now!" the Professor said. "I hope she didn't stand for such nonsense."

"One afternoon she decided to go to Confession. As we rode down Sixteenth Street I suggested several sins she might add to her list—considering herself more favored by God than a Zulu, coveting a mink coat, tolerating poverty. When we reached Park Road and stopped in front of Sacred Heart Church I said, 'Will you confess them?'

" 'No,' she said coldly.

"She got out of the car and walked into the church and I went into the park and looked at the statue of Cardinal Gibbons. I remembered a story about him. When he returned from Rome after his first visit to the Vatican an acquaintance said, 'Did you talk with the Pope?' 'I did,'

345

said the Cardinal. 'Do you believe he is infallible?' asked the acquaintance. 'Well,' he said, 'he called me Jibbons.' "

"Why did you torment the girl?" the Professor said. "Why did you try to destroy her equanimity of mind and heart only because you did not possess its like?"

"Because," I said, "I was in love with her."

"Precisely," the Professor said. "You are the type who tortures what he loves. Suppose you tell me, for the sake of a footnote in abnormal psychology, what you conceive love to be."

"It is a force which no man can define except in terms of his own realization of it," I said. "So far as my understanding extends I perceive love as the activity of God, the creative movement of the spirit which impels and directs the story of life, the labyrinthine drama of divinity lost in the maze of form. It is the force which sent the quiet at the hub of all being, the quiet on which the wheel of existence turns, trickling through the obscured, confused, differentiated substance of form to the hard periphery which turns against the macadam of time, to begin the drama of creation."

"I wish I had a share of A.T. and T. for every simile you've made for time," the Professor said. "What you are going to say, I'm sure, is that in the beginning love spread the quiet at the hub, which is spirit, through the entire area now occupied by the wheel. Love then organized the retreat of spirit to the center; that was involution. Love now guides the progress of awareness from the periphery to the quiet of the hub, aiding it to conquer and to assimilate the area of the wheel as it proceeds; that is ovolution.

"You experienced a memory of the beginning, the quiet-pervaded, conflict-free dream of precreation in Palestine. Shortly afterward you suffered the shock of awakening to an existence engaged in evolution. Slowly, hesitantly, you began the task of spinning from your awareness on the periphery a web of self-consciousness reaching inward toward the retreated quiet at the hub of your being.

"I had to say that for you because you do it yourself so badly, and with such an excess of words. Well, get along now with your dissertation on love, and since its general meaning has been defined go on to the specific instance of love between man and woman."

"I shall," I said, "and I thank you for saving my breath. I have less and less of it as these treatments proceed.

"Let us divide a man into his three principal parts—body, mind, and spirit. Assembled and seemingly a single entity he meets a woman, also composed of body, mind, and spirit. The man and woman fall in love. Where does this falling in love take place, in what areas of being, in what component parts of the man and woman? What does it mean?

"It does not take place in the body, for attraction in that area makes one person of the opposite sex as acceptable as another within a general area of comeliness.

"It does not take place in the spirit, in the quiet of the hub, for spirit is undifferentiated; it is the same in each of us, making every soul, at its center, as all others are at their centers.

"It must, then, take place in the mind, which is the bridge between body and spirit and which somewhat penetrates both."

"Mind is the spoke between the periphery and the hub," the Professor said. "Don't change metaphors. Now get along to the meaning of falling in love."

"How can I keep an abstraction rigid?" I said. "I am trying to avoid explaining that the spokes are preliminary supports for the periphery—they are the subconscious—to be replaced by the inward-spun web of self-consciousness. I did not wish to be wordy. Falling in love means this.

"It is my belief that when a man meets a woman whose mind is so arranged that he is able to see through it to her spirit he falls in love with her; he enters the activity of God and moves toward the quiet he perceives. Every romantic, religious, philosophical, and poetic notion of love fits that theory. Try a few, and you will see that it is so.

"If the woman finds that the man's mind is so constructed that she can see through it to his spirit, she will fall in love with him; she will enter the activity of God and move toward the quiet she perceives.

"Thus she will see clearly in him what she detects but faintly in herself—the spirit; and he will sight within her what he barely observes in his own being—the spirit. They will embrace, seeking to filter through each other's mind to the quiet which they discern. They will move in opposite directions toward the same goal. They will marry."

"It is a trap!" the Professor said.

"Of course it is a trap," I said. "When the webs of their minds meet they do not create a way of passage, they unite to

347

form a solid block. They fit closely, and the natural oscillation of personality begins a process of abrasion.

"This abrasion is the test of marriage. It produces irritability. It shatters the superficial harmony established in courtship, the harmony of mutual and pleasant expectation. If the man can keep his gaze on the woman's spirit he will endure the abrasion and understand its purpose, which is to stimulate his personal evolution by forcing him to disciplines and to intellectual efforts he would not otherwise undertake. If the woman can resist lowering her eyes to the abrasion she will keep in sight the glowing edge of her husband's inner being and she will understand the reason for her union with him. They will both remain in the activity of God. They will stay in love."

"A neat package of cosmic conniving," the Professor said. "The average man is tricked by love into doing for himself what the mystic sets out to accomplish of his own free will. Marriage is a metaphysical trap, God's delicate snare for catching all in His plan. Man takes a bride for his bed only until he finds one in his soul. Then he proceeds celibate to heaven, a divine androgyne, his abrasion lifted above flesh to a higher sphere.

"Man and woman help each other until each is able to go forward alone. In the desperate embraces of their love, as they batter at the webs of flesh and mind which keep them from each other's spirit, they unwittingly thrust themselves apart."

"By love," I said, "they build their souls, they harvest the activity of God, they move toward the spirit."

"Bah!" the Professor said. "There are not a dozen spiritual marriages, in that sense of the phrase, in the entire world. What about our divorce rate? What's wrong with American marriages?"

"People without philosophical training or religious education glimpse mirages of the spirit—romantic illusions—and when the abrasion begins can neither bear the irritability nor discern the spirit."

The Professor nodded.

"I must admit that many marriages which end in divorce are mistakes of union," he said, "but it seems to me that there should be more successful marriages. I know of none. Do you?"

"No," I said, "but I have not known a saint, and I would expect to find saints and successful marriages in the same proportion in society. Both are daring adventures; for both the goal is far and the way is hazardous.

"When a man and his wife are as much at home with each other's thoughts and body as is each with his own flesh and mind, they have achieved a successful marriage. They have accomplished union in the body, which articulates through action and emotion. They have endured and diminished abrasion in the mind, bearing willfully its articulation through speech and thoughtfulness. They have kept in sight each other's spirit, feeding on its articulation through peace and understanding.

"They make love with their hands, with their words, and with their thoughts, and by their love their bodies are kept cleansed, their minds restless, their spirits in sight; for love, if I may repeat the definition once more, is the activity of God."

"By that definition there are no successful marriages anywhere," the Professor said, "and there never have been. Furthermore, on that idealistic basis you could not have fallen in love with Mary."

"I did," I said. "Her spirit was clearly visible through her mind, however orthodox the architecture through which I looked. We were rubbed raw by each other's religious opinions, though basically it was a clash of positive and negative principles. I wanted to shake and awaken and stimulate the church down to its smallest altar boy. Mary wanted to let the church alone.

"We disagreed so persistently that it seemed wise, after a time, to relinquish our love. We did this. But when I arrived in Washington in the spring of 1935—"

"Mary had moved from rigid orthodoxy to a more normal position," the Professor said, "and you were neither so righteous nor so young a rebel. In the maturity which had come to both of you adolescent arguments on religion were an amusing memory. Now you were deeply, surely in love. You proposed to her. Where?"

"Nothing happened as I wished it to," I said. "I wanted to propose on a spot we both loved, at a small place surrounded by a cluster of evergreen, in the middle of Rock Creek Cemetery."

"Rock Creek Cemetery?" The Professor stopped wetting his thumb and looked up from his notes.

"At the grave of Henry Adams' wife," I said. "It is marked by Augustus St. Gaudens' statue expressing the peace of a woman who has won to the quiet of the hub, who has made her way back to the center from which she came forth.

"It has mistakenly been called 'Grief.' Another misnomer is 'Nirvana.' What came to me from the seated, hooded, robed figure—and I went often to look at it—was the sense of a soul returned to its hub of spirit, but containing, remembering, contemplating its adventures on the wheel of existence.

"St. Gaudens called it, I believe, his most satisfying work. There was nothing about it which displeased him except the fold of the robe at the knee; he would have liked to soften it. It is the only statue in Washington except the Lincoln Memorial worth visiting twice."

"I remember the story," the Professor said. "Adams commissioned St. Gaudens to do the statue. Mrs. Adams, an unfortunate woman, was a suicide."

"There is no marker on the grave," I said. "There is only the bronze statue, in a stone setting with a stone bench, and the surrounding evergreens."

"Well, where did you propose?" the Professor said.

"In a night club," I said.

The Professor nodded. "American and contemporary," he said. "Proceed."

"I wanted the marriage to take place at the Franciscan monastery in the Brookland section of Washington," I said, "at dawn."

"With your sword on the altar, no doubt," the Professor said, "and your hair hanging to your shoulders."

"I thought I would watch at the replica of the Holy Sepulcher during the night," I said.

"Precisely. Well, what happened to upset that Arthurian plan?"

"It was first necessary for me to get permission for Mary to be married outside her home parish. This I obtained. It was then necessary for me to get permission for her to be married in the parish which contains the monastery. This I did not obtain. Too many couples were asking to be married at the monastery, I was informed; they were depriving their home parishes of revenue. The monastery was a lovely place; it had replicas of the catacombs, of the Grotto of Lourdes, and of many holy spots of Jerusalem. Getting married there could become a fad.

"There was nothing to do but be married in Mary's parish. The next move was to get permission to be married without publication of banns, so the ceremony could be accomplished in secret. Mary's rector said he knew little of canon law and hadn't time to look it up. He reported that his reason for requesting permission to marry us without publication of banns was, 'Fear of their going before a minister.' Our real reason was fear of going before relatives."

"That reason I applaud," the Professor said. "Was permission granted for marriage without publication of banns?"

"Yes, and the marriage was performed on time, with only an attending couple for witnesses. There was one guest—the friend I chose as best man, who was barred from the ceremony because he was a non-Catholic. Marriage in the Roman Catholic Church is a sacrament; its participants must be Catholics in a state of grace. Another friend took his place."

"How did you manage the state of grace qualification for yourself?" the Professor asked.

"I wasn't sure it could be accomplished," I said, "so I went, before arrangements for the wedding were made, to see a Jesuit.

"It was at night. I sat in the dark on a straight chair in a small office room and talked for an hour and a half, watching a splash of moonlight dribble along the floor on the other side of the Jesuit's desk. When I was finished I waited for the verdict, wondering whether I was in or out, whether I was to be a bridegroom or a heretic.

"The Jesuit said, 'So far as I can see you have always, in your thoughts and studies, sought truth. That is not a sin.'

"In the moonlight I saw that he was smiling wanly. He said, 'We are only sure of this—that two things, love and the desire to know, survive death.'

"Love and the desire to know—spirit and mind, the soul and its intelligence, the awareness on the periphery and the quiet at the hub—survive death. The rest is the plot of the story, the remembrance and realization, the solving of the maze, the spinning of the web, the birth and life and crucifixion and death and resurrection, the journey from unconsciousness through self-consciousness to superconsciousness.

"We walked outside and stood a while in the moonlight. Then I said good night and walked away. I thought suddenly of Father Higgins, and how fine a priest I thought him to be when I was small. He could have saved me so long a walk to hear so simple a truth; he would not have delayed me with dogma and authority."

"It happened to be something you believed so you called it truth," the Professor said. "Well, you were married at last, by a sensible priest, in a sensible manner, after a visit to a sensible Jesuit—that last adjective is redundant.

"The ceremony took place at eight o'clock in the morning on October 26, 1935. You got a girl you didn't deserve and drove with her to Lexington for a honeymoon. You combined as well as you could the two best things in your life, Washington and Lee and Mary."

He put aside the notes he had been studying and stared at a final page of scribble, squinting and widening his eyes, altering the canthus in an effort to read what he had written.

"You concluded your travels for *The American Magazine* in late spring 1935. You spent the summer in Connecticut, joined the editorial staff of the magazine in September, and in October went to Washington to write an article on Chief Justice Hughes and one on Harry Hopkins. It was then that you married."

"The summer," I said, "was spent at Lake Quassapog. The Kid and O'Connor and I shared a cottage. The Connollys, who lived next door and who had two daughters and three sons, referred to us as The Drinker, The Thinker, and The Stinker. We borrowed their daughters, their ice, and their passkey, which fitted the lock on our door also.

"One night the Kid took over our kitchen and prepared a steak dinner. It took him quite a while and he made a lot of noise but eventually the meal was ready. We sat down at table and the Kid, who was warm from his efforts and who apparently had been appeasing his thirst as he worked, fell asleep sitting upright in his chair.

"I shook him awake and pointed to his plate, which was stacked high with his handiwork. He took a fork and tried the steak, the potato, and the vegetables. Then he looked at me. 'Who the hell cooked this lousy meal?' he said. Without waiting for an answer he got up and walked out of the cottage, contemptuous and insulted."

The Professor nodded.

"The Kid died in the spring of 1936," he said. "Your mother died in the spring of 1937, in May."

"She was ill for a long time," I said. "The night before she died I drove my father and my aunts and Mary home from the hospital in Waterbury and decided to return by myself and sit with the night nurse—my mother was in a coma.

"I drove by way of Middlebury. As I neared the New England Arch, a stone railroad overpass at the top of a hill with an opening wide enough for only a single car, I decided to check my watch by the radio. I turned the switch on the built-in set and the car lights went out.

"I was too close to the arch to stop. I held the wheel lightly, letting the wheels follow the hump in the road. When I felt the descending slope on the other side of the arch I looked ahead for a break in the trees which line that part of the road. On my left a hill rose sharply; on my right was a long drop to a brook.

"I saw the road breaking from the trees; it was gray with moonlight. I reached it safely and drove without trouble to the outskirts of Waterbury, where I stopped at a service station and bought a fuse."

Again the Professor nodded.

"Such symbolism is an integral part of fiction," he said. "It relates the characters to the larger patterns of life. Each of us, now and then, feels the need of discovering in himself a relation to the larger patterns of life and makes an effort to convert himself into a character of fiction. You did it often.

"Let me check off these final entries. You and Mary moved from Manhattan to Oceanside, Long Island, last September, in anticipation of what turned out to be Patsy. You had just finished ghostwriting a book and were preparing to write a novel. One Sunday afternoon while working on an article for *Scribner's Magazine* you felt a chill, then a wave of fever. When the doctor came your temperature was 104. He said you had intestinal influenza.

"A week later you apparently were well. You sat in the living room and read a book. When you tried to get up from the chair your body was stiff. It was difficult for you to straighten your back and to walk.

"That was six months ago. You have been to a lot of places and you have been subjected to a lot of treatments since then. Your trouble seems to be a mixed streptococcic infection; the fever you have been enduring is a weapon for killing it. You have had nearly fifty hours of the weapon now; this is your eighth treatment. It is the last one.

"Tomorrow you will return to Oceanside, to Mary and Patsy. You have lost weight, but there is nothing now to precent you from regaining it; the infection which bothered you is dead. Eat red meat, drink beef juice, sit in the sun. In a month you will be digging in the garden. In six weeks you will be back at work."

He thumbed his notes again, then put them aside.

"What is the judgment?" I asked. "What is my psychotherapeutic rating? What complex must I accept as my crest and wear on my sleeve as signature of my estate in medicine's caste system of the mind?"

"That," he said, "is up to you. Together we have examined the outline and a few of the details of your remembered existence, following the sharp line of external events and articulated opinions through the softening haze of emotion and unprocessed thought until it disappeared into the inaccessible dream whose reflection you are and whose bidding you do.

"Insofar as you are responsible for your own thoughts—and no man knows in this matter how little or how large his burden is—you have given me a full and careful account of your opinions and prejudices, your desires and dilemmas. Since each man when he speaks is his own defender, however honest he intends to be, what you have hidden from yourself has been revealed to me. If I were to tell it to you, and if you were to believe it to be so of yourself, your cause in life would be crippled; its plan of procedure, self-deluding and ego-building, would be revealed. You would know yourself for what you really are; it would terrify you.

"You would not, however, believe it to be so of yourself. Furthermore, if I were to point out to you that a curious and oblique spiritual frustration is the actual reason for your ill-being, that streptococci are an epiphenomenon and arthritis an epiphyte, a parasite on the body of your longing for an epiphany, you would not only not believe me, you would deny, on the chance of its being true, the importance of such patterns of cause and effect."

"I do not deny the importance of such patterns of cause and effect," I said. "I abjure only the practice of interpreting them as unnatural states of being. They are natural states of being. The peregrinating ego creates its own environment; it must solve that environment's problems and adjust itself to that environment's discomforts. It cannot interpret what comes upon it as an unearned illness, as a visitation of misery generated by a force outside itself. Whatever happens

354

it must accept as its own doing; it must meet and manage the matter or go down with it and perish."

"That," said the Professor, "is precisely what I meant. I cannot tell you a thing either about yourself or about your problem. You believe that you got yourself into this mess and you intend to bull it through in your own way, whether you win or lose.

"If you want my verdict it is that you are spoiled rotten, stubborn, quixotic, badly informed, ill-disciplined, irascible, impervious to reason, self-deluded, irrationally idealistic, top-heavy with dreams for the human race, a failure at the business of living, and a fool."

He lifted his gaze from me and stared at Miss Iceberg's neck. I closed my eyes and turned my head more rapidly to and fro. I heard Miss Iceberg get up and I felt a cold cloth on my forehead. It moved to my right temple and it seemed to me that it hesitated there a moment.

"This is my last day with you," I said hopefully.

The cloth moved along my cheek and crossed to the other side of my face.

"Would you like some orange juice?" she asked.

I said yes, and she filled a large glass from the thermos jug. Then for the first time, while she fed it to me, she held my head, not in her hand, but in the cradle of her elbow, with the soft flesh of her bicep pressing against my ear.

"I shall miss you," she said as I drank the orange juice. "You have been a good patient."

The Professor watched us. His eyes had the empty, contented look of a mind which has picked it way through an experience and emerged less filled with God, more glutted with ego, and therefore happy.

"Interesting case," he muttered to himself as Miss Iceberg released my head, letting her forearm brush my chin. "Might make a paper for the society . . . disorientation of personality from environment . . . eschatological neurosis . . . anti-Nirvanist . . . ontogenesis fixation . . . teleological obsession . . ."

TWENTY-TWO

THE MAPLES were leafed and eager for long May days when I returned to Oceanside. Patsy slept in the sun in the back yard, face up in her carriage. When she was awake I stared into her hazel eyes and she looked at me, unwinking. We were curious and uncomprehending about each other. Sometimes I was allowed to feed her.

I had entered the hospital walking with the aid of a cane. I left it on crutches. When I had been at home for two weeks I could no longer get up and down stairs; I was confined to the upper part of the house, to the bedrooms, the bathroom, and the nursery. I sat by the window in my bedroom and let the sun shine on my legs. I ate the blood-building, body-strengthening foods that were cooked for me. I grew weaker.

Each day I walked as much as I could, but each day I walked less. The calves of my legs trembled when I lifted my feet to step. I got on my crutches by sliding my back from the headboard of the bed to the wall, wriggling slowly to an upright position. Toward the end of May my legs began to quiver as soon as I put the burden of my body on them. I had to wait, braced against the wall, for the shaking to pass. I was growing thinner.

On Memorial Day, the thirtieth of May, I wriggled upright against the wall, then returned to the bed because the trembling in my legs did not stop. In a few minutes I tried again. I pressed the insistence of my mind down through my body and the quivering slowed and ceased. I walked to the bathroom, sat before the basin on a low stool, and shaved.

When I was finished I took my crutches and stood up quickly, hoping to strike out into a walk before the quivering could begin. I had to sit down again; both legs trembled violently. I tried again and again, hoping to lunge away from the stool and reach the wall, where I could wait out the shaking. Each time I failed.

I decided to again press the insistence of my mind on my body. After a minute of meditation I rose from the stool. I stepped forward with my leg and felt it shiver and give way. My left leg also was trembling. I could not return to the stool; it was too far behind me. As I fell forward I threw aside my crutches and reached with my arms for the steam radiator. When I had clasped it to me I called to Mary.

She came quickly and put a chair under me. I sat down on it and she went to the kitchen and got Sue, the maid. Together they dragged the chair, with me in it, along the hall and into my bedroom. I slid from the chair into the bed.

After that I could not walk at all. Time after time I wriggled to an upright position against the wall but as soon as I put the weight of my body on my legs they shook and I could not stop the shaking. I called the New York doctors who had supervised the artificial fever treatments and told them what had happened. They were sorry but they had no suggestions. Mine were not the usual reactions to artificial fever; nothing specific could be advised. I was sorry for them; it was not their fault.

My legs began to tremble as I lay in bed, the right more so than the left. I put my right knee against my left knee and managed thus to keep both legs still. Both limbs atrophied. When the right was too weak to move by itself I rode it on the left as I moved about the bed. My local doctor came each day and sat and talked with me; he was a charming, gracious man, but he did not suggest a way of treatment or a means of cure. Not only had I fallen among the twenty per cent not helped by artificial fever therapy, I apparently had landed among the unclassified few who are harmed by it.

As the heat of July moved in I had several unexpected visitors, friends I had not seen for a long time, who gave odd reasons for coming. They sat gravely and respectfully by my bed. Downstairs they talked with Mary. I listened curiously to the rhythms of the conversation. I had heard those rhythms before, at wakes and funerals and in churches. Were they talking about my wake? It was not polite to ask, since I wasn't supposed to know I was going to die, but I was interested. Would my surviving consciousness be at the wake? I hoped so. I had enjoyed a great many wakes. I wanted to have a good time at my own.

I wondered into what awareness my consciousness would drop when I died; there seemed to be many spheres of realization. I awakened at night every hour; pain forced me to move and changing my position was a task I no longer could accomplish in my sleep. As I came awake I watched the tail of my dream. In the early hours of the night my sleep played over and rearranged the incidents and anxieties of the day; in the middle of the night I was taken far away in strange adventures which broke up, when I examined them after waking, into orderly arrangements of symbols; in the morning I slept in play dreams, full of dancing figures and laughter. I surmised that I would die in the center of the night, when my mind was already a distance away from what it would be leaving.

It was quiet and deadly hot in August. I waited for thunderstorms; when they came and the wind blew against a maple that grew outside one of my bedroom windows the branches dipped and brushed their leaves against the panes. I waited for that to happen; it was all I saw of the summer.

Mary gave me Patsy's baby pillow to put between my knees; it kept the sore bones apart. My elbows began to stiffen and the flesh on my arms atrophied. One afternoon while Patsy was sitting on my chest—it was the only place I could entertain her in comfort—she slipped through my hands and rolled forward. I could not bend my arms far enough nor quickly enough to save her. Her face fell on mine, with her soft, small mouth full against my mouth.

I bent my right arm until its hand took hold of the back of her dress; then I put my left hand on my right elbow and managed to pull her up. Her eyes had a puzzled, questioning look. She stared at me steadily, her gaze asking me what had happened. I said, "I'm glad I was the first to kiss you."

I do not know on what night in August it happened. I was asleep; when I woke I was raised on my left elbow; I had taken the telephone from its cradle on the night table and fitted it to my head. As self-consciousness secured itself I remembered what had happened, remembered it, apparently, from my sleep. Someone had called to me. A woman had cried out my name, "Tom!"

It was ten minutes after four. The telephone line was dead. I put the instrument back in its cradle and relaxed on the bed. I played the sound of the woman's cry over and over in my mind, comparing it with the ways in which the women I knew called to me. The voice was not Mary's. It was not my mother's. It did not belong to any woman I remembered. It was a soft voice, lined with strong vibrations; its note was low, caressing, and urgent. I forced it to remain in my mind, sounding it over and over, afraid I would not be able to recall it if I let it slip into memory. Listening to it I fell asleep.

When I woke again I was once more raised on my left elbow, and my legs, trembling violently, were attempting to swing themselves over the side of the bed. I was trying to get up. Someone had called to me. A woman had cried out my name, "Tom!"

It was the same voice, the same cry, with the same beauty and the same strong vibrations; its note was a little deeper, more caressing, more urgent. It was a voice I would follow anywhere, forsaking everything, and it therefore could have but one identity; it was the voice of a banshee, the Irish family ghost who comes to guide those of the clan who are dying over the narrow, wind-swept fields that lie between life and death.

Well, I thought, let her come and get me; I will not go to her. It angered me that she had called me awake; the decent thing would have been to come without disturbing me, to kneel on the bed and to lift out my soul with her hands while I slept. Since she had wakened me I would repay her rudeness in kind. I would die with my eyes open.

I pulled the pillow from behind my head and sat up with my back against the headboard; I put my neck against its sharp wooden edge and stretched my arms along its top. The weight of my head pressed the thin blade of the wood into my neck; that, I thought, will keep me from falling asleep. I wondered if a man could be taken dead while awake.

Waves of drowsiness welled up in me. There was nothing to see but the outlines of the room in the glow of the night light; there was nothing to hear but a whisper of wind now and then in the maple. It was not yet five o'clock.

The drowsiness worked its way into my body; I felt it

along my spine, where it dug its fingers into the tension there; it rubbed the cords in my neck; it massaged the base of my brain and made my head warm.

Suddenly I gasped and looked toward the window, as if I expected to see there what I was realizing in myself. There was no drowsiness in my body; there was something else there instead, something that flowed from my mind. It was Joseph. He had came back. I moaned in my joy.

"Where have you been?" I asked.

"Waiting for you," he said, and I knew what he meant, though I could not see its way or tell myself its logic.

Always there had been Joseph and I and the body between us, the body which anchored us in earth, which cut our dimensions to three, and through which we somehow knew we had to go if we were to proceed on our journey. It was a narrow way; there were only three dimensions and five senses; time went through it in single file. Somehow since last I saw him in Egypt Joseph had managed the trick; he had got through, and he had waited to help me, dragging me the last few feet when I seemed unable to finish the run by myself.

Now we were both on the other side. The body lay behind and beneath us, its chance of following after us small. Joseph was ahead of me; his quiet, multiple-dimensioned strength manned the periphery, his sure awareness met the moment; what approached us from the world submitted before reaching me to his environment. I was protected, safe to spin my web inward toward the quiet of the hub, to take what came off the moment and lay it against measures of judgment, to weave the end of myself further into the cosmos that lay between me and my center, between me and the pool of spirit from which I had been flung.

This was the way it should always have been, Joseph with his sureness on the outside, I with my uncertainty and curiosity within. This was why when first we realized we were in the world, lying on the grass in our back yard in Naugatuck, hearing the sound of a woman's step as it ricocheted in the alley, we knew that something was wrong; I was on the outside, bruised by the impact of the moment; Joseph was within, blocked at every exit.

Now the edges of Joseph were soft and still all around me. Looking through him at what lay beyond us I saw a tongue of dawn lick at the window sill and drip its hunger into the room. When this day came it would touch Joseph first; he would cushion it for me; he would treat it and deflect its hurt; he would react objectively to it and none of it would strike me squarely; he would repel a banshee as if she were a scold. I would not die; he would not let me. Instead I would go on more nimbly through creation, with Joseph to break the way. I would have only to make the maps and notch the trail. I was better off than ever I had hoped to be, more content by far than when I sat on a rock by the Jordan.

"Are you disgusted with me?" I asked.

"Yes," he said, "but don't apologize You never knew any better. You compromised, you dissimulated, you hedged, you tolerated, you diluted, you condoned, you bargained, you procrastinated, you postured. You gave away your substance piece by piece; you scattered yourself in foolishness. You should not have swerved a hairsbreadth from what you knew, what you believed, what you hoped. Each sideways step depleted you.

"You only did right when you did not run away, when you left Egypt and Palestine even though you thought I wanted to stay. You stepped aside then, finally, and let me go ahead; you sacrificed what you wanted to do and what you thought I wanted to do. I was only pressing against you, trying to get you to let me by. When you did I went past you to the place where I belonged. It was a simple metaphysical exercise; you retired your desire in favor of your purpose. That act set me free and placed me on the circumference of your ego."

"I've got things into a mess," I said. "There is no job, there is no money, I am unable to work, there is little hope for my legs, and now I am not going to die. The odds are against us."

"The odds are even," he said. "We'll win."

I saw the walls of the room grow real and watched light come over the bottom of the bed and touch my feet. A splash of wind pushed a branch of the maple against the window screen. Outside the chattering of birds and the hum of insects waxed. The odor of the full, burst earth rose on the warmed and drying air. All these things came first to Joseph, who examined them for my purpose, then bathed me in them, sponging my desire, rubbing the sight of the green leaves of the maple into my eyes.

With my neck still pressed against the headboard's edge and my arms stretched out along its top I fell from the morning into sleep.

EPILOGUE

When my father was writing this book, one of his friends, a fellow Catholic, took exception to the proposed title, "Stranger in the Earth." It comes, as did the titles of many of his books, from the King James translation of The Bible, a work prized by my father for the beauty of its language but one not approved by the Roman Catholic Church.

"What's wrong with 'sojourner in the earth,' the way the Douai-Rheims has it?" the friend asked, referring to the Church-authorized translation. "The meaning is different, not nearly so profound," my father answered, "but aside from that, the rhythm is all off."

"Stranger" implied the soul's feeling of separation from its home in God and also signified, to him, a seeker, one constantly and consciously entering new lands of the intellect. A "stranger in the earth" travelled toward a specific goal, reunion with God; a "sojourner" seemed a mere tourist by comparison.

The friend replied a week later, presenting us with a copy of the spurned Douai-Rheims, the first and only one we ever owned. Perhaps he hoped orthodoxy would march out from between the covers and scrub off a few of Thomas Sugrue's heresies. It didn't.

My father never held an opinion simply because the established group in a church, government, town or university approved it. He tried to live by the

363

teachings of Jesus, especially the Sermon on the Mount. "Blessed are the poor in spirit: for theirs is the kingdom of heaven," the sermon begins, and he judged himself and all others by its standard. Those who in humility enlisted his companionship in the mutual search for truth were welcome. Those who sought to restrict his search, he rejected and ignored. The criteria applied most strenuously to the Church which, he believed, ought to be as beautiful as the doctrines entrusted to it.

"Stranger in the Earth" tells of the struggle to reconcile his soul's yearning to penetrate the mysteries of Judeo-Christian revelation with the realities of the institutional Church. At last, through the loss of livelihood and health in the final chapter of the book, he achieves true poverty of the spirit and reunion with Joseph, the voice of that part of the soul which always keeps its eye on heaven.

Immobile and constantly in pain, jobless with a young family to support, he began a new life. Joseph never deserted him again. Discomfort, discouragement, and criticism never erased the glow of inner peace he exuded and which seemed, protectively, to surround him. He could hardly begin to be angry or depressed before his unshakable optimism would bring off-setting good points to mind.

Oddly, the only parts of his body not affected by illness were his arms. They could still be used for writing, although crooked at the elbow. At first the doctors limited him to 500 words daily. It was all he had strength for. All morning he mentally composed, rewrote, then memorized those 500 words, so that not a moment or an ounce of precious physical energy would be wasted. He wrote all of "There Is A River," the biography of his friend Edgar Cayce, the clairvoyant, in this way.

On the advice of a "reading" by Cayce, we moved to Clearwater Beach, Florida, where, using only his arms, my father could swim in the warm, buoyant, salt water of the Gulf of Mexico. This proved excellent physical therapy, and late in 1945 we returned to New York City where he maintained a full schedule: writing books, articles and book reviews, and producing and appearing on a weekly radio program.

Efforts to regain the use of his legs, never successful, continued for the rest of his life. Exercises with crutches, massages, diathermy, and drug therapy pepper my childhood memories. Aspirin with soda mint three times daily and an injection of cobra venom twice a week deadened the constant pain. Later, he was among the first arthritis patients treated with cortisone.

Denied physical autonomy, he strove to minimize its importance in his life. After completing "Stranger in the Earth" in 1948, he revisited Israel, realizing a long-time dream. He left New York accompanied but reached Tel Aviv alone, after his companion suddenly had become ill and returned home. Israel was fighting her first war of survival against the Arabs, yet her people welcomed the stranger in the wheelchair—American, Irish-Catholic—who had arrived, unannounced, in their midst.

For six months he travelled over bombed-out roads, slept in recently-attacked kibbutzes. The Israelis were fighting for their lives, and my father began each day not knowing who would help him to shave, bathe, dress, get around. Thanks to Joseph, he did not worry, and someone—frequently someone he had never seen before—appeared, ready to do all that was required. My father's joy in each day complemented the zest of the Israelis, and they had a wonderful time together.

Back in the United States, with the book "Watch for the Morning," completed, he embarked on lecture tours for the American-Christian Palestine Committee and for the Association for Research and Enlightenment, a group that studies the Cayce materials. Often he boarded an airplane not knowing exactly who would meet him at his destination. Yet, he was never stranded.

He kept faith, as do the lilies of the fields, and found strength in it always. He was the target of fulminations by Francis Cardinal Spellman of New York for a short book, "A Catholic Speaks His Mind," which detailed the shortcomings of the American Church. Although my father knew that each man must find his own way to himself and to God, he wanted to remain a member of the Church into which he had been born. He did not want excommunication and rejoiced when the threat of it was withdrawn by Rome. Then he inscribed my copy of the book with an irreverent note that it was his "noisiest."

The Professor would not have approved. While "Stranger in the Earth" is full of the real people who shaped my father's life, it brims over with The Professor, the voluble champion of conventional society and middle-class values. Good-natured, witty, merciless, he grills the author on scores of topics from Pythagoras and the Trinity to small town manners and the mysterious effect of women upon men.

Their conversations reflect a lifetime of study in mystical literature. Many of the works referred to—from the "I Ching" and the "Upanishads" to Plotinus and St. John of the Cross—are more widely read today than when the book first appeared. Science, the new religion that my father believed would lead 20th century humanity to a deeper knowledge of

God, even as 19th century discoveries had triggered skepticism, forms a counterpoint theme. Lecomte de Nouy's "Human Destiny," published the year my father began work on "Stranger," proved that one scientist had already found God in his work. Had my father known of Teilhard de Chardin, he would have been overjoyed. But the priest's writings were then still being suppressed by the Jesuit Order.

"Stranger in the Earth" is not simply the story of a man's life. It is the record of a search for true identity and for the path of peace on earth. Thomas Sugrue's search ended in 1953, on the sixth of January, the day the Church observes the end of another search, that of the Wise Men for the Christ Child. They too must have argued philosophy on the journey; I like to think they were as well entertained as this reader of "Stranger in the Earth."

Patricia Sugrue Channon
Brooklyn, New York
August, 1970